John R. Burnett-Doering

T4-AQJ-527

John Barrett-Doerry

DIMENSIONS OF ORGANIZATIONS:

Environment, Context, Structure, Process, and Performance

DIMENSIONS OF ORGANIZATIONS:

Environment, Context, Structure, Process, and Performance

Mary Zey–Ferrell

Illinois State University

**Goodyear Publishing Company •
Santa Monica, California**

Library of Congress Cataloging in Publication Data

Zey–Ferrell, Mary.
  Dimensions of organizations.

  1. Organization. I. Title.
HD31.Z49   301.5'5   78-10271
ISBN 0-87620-217-2

Copyright © 1979 by Goodyear Publishing Company, Inc.
Santa Monica, California 90401

All rights reserved. No part of this book may be reproduced in any form or by any means without permission in writing from the publisher.

Current printing (last digit):
10 9 8 7 6 5 4 3 2 1

ISBN: 0-87620-217-2
Y-2172-8

Printed in the United States of America

CONTENTS

LIST OF TABLES

List of Tables

TABLE   **PAGE**

LIST OF FIGURES

PREFACE

There were two overriding motivations for my writing this text: First, organizations influence, either positively or negatively, nearly every aspect of our daily lives. This influence is so pervasive that I believe an understanding of the causes, functioning, and consequences of organizational behavior is a necessity for anyone living in contemporary society. Second, I believe that much of the comparative research recently conducted on organizations evidences similarities in findings. Therefore, I wish to draw parallels between concepts, definitions, and methods of measurement of these research findings. As the similarities are exposed, differences will also become apparent. Thus, this book is designed to give students of organizations an understanding of the definitions and interrelationships of various organizational dimensions. It is also designed to explain how organizations perform in specific environments and contexts, depending on their particular objectives, processes, and structural arrangements.

It is important at the outset that the reader understand that no single text can adequately cover all units of organizational analysis (individual, group, organizational, and institutional). I have chosen to deal specifically with the organization as the unit of analysis because organizations as entities influence our national and international well-being, as well as our group and individual lives. The debate between the federal government and various oil companies over "spillage control" demonstrates the national influence of organizations; the debate between minority groups and corporations over employment opportunities demonstrates the influences on group life; their influence on the individual is pervasive; newspapers, TV programming, schools, and retail products are all produced and controlled by organizations.

Because of my concentration on the organization as the unit of analysis, much of the research on groups and individuals within organizations is excluded from consideration. The social-psychological orientation, which focuses on the individual within the organization and group processes within the organization, is an important approach to the study of organizations; but these units cannot be comprehensively and systematically explored in an approach in which the unit of analysis is the organization. Consequently, much of the research using the human-relations and the decision-making models of organization, in which the individual and group are the units of analysis, has been excluded from this text. This sociological approach to the analysis of organization does not negate or diminish the importance of other approaches; it merely recognizes that the field is extremely broad, and therefore, in an endeavor of this type, a specific perspective or point of view is required.

Although individuals and groups in organizations are not the central concern of this book, some measures of organizational dimensions are developed from aggregated individual and group responses—attitudinal measures—as opposed to global measures (data obtained from documents, charters, key personnel, etc.). Since both levels of measurement (attitudinal and global) have been used to measure organizational dimensions, findings from both types of research are discussed in this text. Athough the investigators who use these different types of measurements purport to measure the same underlying organizational dimension, I assume that due to differences in operationalizations, the variables being measured are in fact different. For example, it is quite different to conclude that an organization is highly complex based on the number of specialists or divisions of labor in that organization than to do so because the people who work in that organization say it is complex.

This text also concentrates on research findings based on the comparative methods of analysis, which, as opposed to the case study method, concentrates on the measurement of characteristics or dimensions of a large number of organizations. The emerging relationships between dimensions are generalizable to the population of organizations from which the sample was drawn, a major advantage of the comparative research method. A case study, although it affords the investigator in-depth knowledge and insight, does not supply generalizable results.

Finally, only research on work organizations is analyzed in this text. Work organizations are those in which most of the members of the organization are paid employees, including both profit-making firms (manufacturing, commercial) and public service (educational, governmental, welfare) organizations. Organizations in which membership is primarily voluntary and nonpaid, such as friendship groups, professional associations, and some consumer organizations, are not analyzed in this text. Analyzing both work and voluntary organizations would introduce a great deal of heterogeneity to the type of organization being analyzed. Concentrating on work organizations, to the exclusion of voluntary organizations, eliminates some sources of variation in organizational dimensions that would otherwise have to be considered; for example, differences in resource allocation for salaries between employees of a work organization and organizations in which workers are not paid. By limiting the analysis to work organizations, it is hoped that the variance between organizations can be attributed to the dimensions being analyzed.

Although I have attempted to eliminate as many sources of variation as possible by eliminating sources of heterogeneity, several important ones remain. In addition to the conceptual and methodological inconsistencies discussed in Chapter 1, there are several contingency problems which create inconsistencies of findings in the existing research. First, organizations vary in functional type from manufacturing and retail outlets to schools and hospitals. Students of organizations should expect differences in research finds when functional type varies. Many times this variance is introduced by the researcher who includes multiple functional types in a single study sample, thus introducing variation within the sample. At other times, the inconsistency is introduced when analysts attempt to compare findings across studies of differing functional types of organizations. A second contingency problem is introduced when studying organizations from different countries. In most of these studies sociocultural differences are not controlled, thus introducing inconsistencies. This cultural level serves as one level of organizational environment while the task environment serves as another—the same types of inconsistencies may be introduced at the task environment level. Similarly, the third contingency problem is introduced when technology is not controlled. This source of heterogeneity often influences the relationship between variables being analyzed. The fourth, and possibly the most important contingency problem, is the result of a lack of control of intraorganizational variables while analyzing the relationships between other variables. For example, when analyzing the relationship between size and the administrative component, a researcher may find a positive relationship when differentiation is not controlled, but when the effects of differentiation are controlled, the relationship will be negative. As long as research- ers continue to ignore these contingency problems, sources of heterogeneity will be introduced by them, and consequently research findings will be inconsistent.

Thus, this text, by and large, deals with organizational theory and research in which the work organization is the unit of analysis; dimensions of organizations are being analyzed; global and attitudi- nal measures are used to explore these dimensions, and the method of analysis is comparative.

Because of the nature of organizations and because compara- tive research on the relationships of organizational dimensions lends itself to the interchange of variables (that is, what is the independent variable in one analysis may be the dependent variable in another analysis), the content of the chapters overlaps slightly. For example, it is necessary to discuss technology in relation to both the structural and the performance dimensions of organizations.

ACKNOWLEDGMENTS

Many people have contributed either directly or indirectly to this text. It is impossible to acknowledge the support of all my friends and colleagues. However, I would like to thank the following people for their helpful reviews: James Kluegel of the University of California, Riverside; Franz Schurmann, University of California, Berkeley; Joseph E. Champoux, University of New Mexico, Albuquerque; and Jon M. Shepard, University of Kentucky. I would also like to thank my editors, Jim Boyd and Chris Jennison—their encouragement and support have been invaluable. The permissions granted by authors and publishers for quoted materials are also greatly appreciated. Finally, a very special debt of gratitude is owed to Debra Wallace, who typed both rough and final drafts of the manuscript, checked quoted materials, and assisted in all stages of the manuscript preparation—her support and excellent assistance have been invaluable. I would also like to gratefully acknowledge the understanding and sacrifices of O.C. and Jim. As always in the final analysis, the responsibility for any errors of omission or commission rests with the author.

part I
INTRODUCTION AND PERSPECTIVES

The major objectives of Part I are first to introduce the conceptual and methodological issues to be considered in an analysis of organizations. It is assumed that students of organizations will realize that studies that examine a given organizational dimension using different perspectives, units of analysis, levels of measurement, and methods of investigation will not yield the same results. Thus, even though the underlying conceptual dimension is held constant, findings will differ. Other objectives are to present the model of organizational analysis used in this text, and to differentiate between organizational theory, perspectives, and models. Finally, this section will explore the characteristics of the most prominent organizational models to facilitate an understanding of their underlying assumptions, strengths, and weaknesses. This information should aid students in selecting and integrating models for their own studies.

1
INTRODUCTION TO THE STUDY OF ORGANIZATIONS

OBJECTIVES

The objectives of chapter one are:

1. To discuss the importance of studying organizations.
2. To discuss some theoretical issues pertinent to the definition of *organizations*.
   a. to differentiate organizations from the broader concept of *social organization*.
   b. to differentiate organizations from *groups*.
   c. to differentiate organizations from *institutions*.
   d. to differentiate and discuss the unidimensional and multidimensional constructs of organizations.
3. To present the basic model of organizations used in this text.
4. To define organizations.
5. To introduce the concept of organizational perspectives.
6. To define organizational theory.
7. To discuss some methodological issues important to an analysis of organizations.
   a. the unit of organizational analysis:
      i. the individual.
      ii. the group.
      iii. the organization.
   b. the levels of organizational analysis:
      i. attitudinal
      ii. global

     c.   the methods of data collection and analysis:
        i. the case study method.
       ii. the comparative method.

WHY STUDY ORGANIZATIONS?

"Why study organizations?" is the first question that comes to the student's mind. The major reason for studying organizations is to gain an understanding of their functions, which in turn can help one predict organizational behavior and, in some instances, control and change organizations. Such questions as how and why organizations function as they do become increasingly pertinent as the networks of organizations in contemporary society become increasingly pervasive and powerful, exerting major influence in our everyday lives. For example, OPEC influences the price of oil in the Middle East, thus influencing the cost of fossil fuels in the U.S. The American Medical Association, through lobbying and other measures, influences the cost and availability of medical care. General Motors provides over one-half of all domestic autos purchased annually in the U.S., and its 1977 profits were greater than the total gross national product of many nations. Planned Parenthood plays an important role in the family planning of some U.S. citizens. In fact, most of the products and services that we use are supplied by some type of organization, whether public or private. These organizations exist not only in the economic sphere, but also in the other major social institutions in the form of schools, political parties, churches, sports leagues, and so on.

    One so-called common sense idea that most people have about such organizations is that they restrict personal freedom, not because of their superior efficiency, as Max Weber predicted,[1] but rather because of their great inefficiency. The typical large, complex organization is often thought of as powerful and centralized and so complex that it ignores the human element and defies human control. As a result, people tend to fear organizations and feel alienated from them. To explore the validity of these perceptions is a major reason that one should study organizations.

    This text can help one understand how and why organizations function as they do. If an individual understands the behavior of an organization, he or she is better equipped to counter its behavior or, on the other hand, to assist it in the attainment of objectives. As one studies organizations, it becomes apparent that most objectives are

4

accomplished and most goal-directed activities are carried out through organizations. It also becomes apparent that there is more than one way to structure an organization, and that the appropriate means are dependent not only on its objectives but also its environment and context (technology and size).

The recent proliferation of comparative organizational research has led to diverse and fragmented theoretical and operational definitions of the organizational dimensions discussed in this text. Although this rapid growth of knowledge tends to leave those of us who analyze organizations in a rather tenuous state with respect to various conceptual and measurement decisions, this stage is also perhaps the most exciting and creative period in the history of organizational analysis. Because of the number of recent books and articles that deal with the various fragmented organizational dimensions, there is a need for a synthesis of these findings. This synthesis effort is impeded by the fact that these findings are by no means consistent; in fact, they are often contradictory. Our understanding of organizations is not yet sufficient to explain these contradictions; only future research will shed light on them. As these contradictions are discussed, in this text, the reader is asked to keep in mind that our knowledge of organizations and their dimensions is incomplete. Where there is substantial evidence that a particular relationship exists between dimensions, a synthesis of the relationship is attempted, but not where the evidence is inadequate or contradictory. These attempts at synthesis, at the end of some chapters, are presented not to stem the search for knowledge but in the spirit of inquiry. It is hoped that these correlational statements will inspire a systematic testing of the relationships between various organizational dimensions. In other words, no attempt is being made to force a consensus on the findings; just the opposite is true. Many times contradictory definitions as well as various methods of analysis are presented to inform the reader of the diversity and fragmentation of the discipline.

SOME THEORETICAL ISSUES

Social Collectives

Before defining the term *organization,* it is necessary to distinguish this concept from other social collectives (groups, institutions, and societies), and from the all-inclusive concept of social organization. The term *social organization* encompasses all social collectives:

5

groups, organizations, institutions, and societies. These collectives are listed in ascending order of size and complexity, and each of them is made up of the preceding ones. Groups consist of individuals in interaction, which is the binding process of all collectives. For each of these social units the ultimate actor is the individual. Their enduring structure (pattern of social interaction or social relationships) is another common characteristic. The analysis of these relationships is the subject matter of sociology; the analysis of the structure and process of organizations is the focus of the organizational sociologist.

The organization is only one level of social structure. Organizations consist of groups and together they make up institutions. But organizations can be distinguished from both institutions and groups. The relationship between institutions and organizations has been thought to be so important by some theorists that they have defined organizations in terms of this relationship. Koya Azumi and Jerald Hage define organizations as ". . . structured bodies designed to achieve specific objectives that are part of some larger institutional process."[2] Organizations are commonly defined as goal- or objective-achieving structures, but they are less frequently defined in terms of the social institution they support. Thus, Azumi and Hage emphasize the institutional environment in which the organization exists and the reciprocal effects of this institutional environment and the organization.

Major social institutions (political, economic, educational, religious, family, and health and welfare) exist in every society and carry on its major functions through the organizations that support them. For example, elementary schools, high schools, and colleges and universities are among the organizations that comprise the educational institution in the U.S. Similarly, the economic institution consists of such organizations as retail and wholesale outlets, manufacturers, transporters, and so on. These organizations are involved in the production and distribution of scarce resources.

It should be kept in mind that although all organizations in an institution serve essentially the same function, they differ in at least three ways. First, they do *not* work for common goals and objectives. In fact, the organizations within an institution often compete for the same market (domain), rewards, resources, and facilities. For example, although Mobil and Gulf Oil are both part of the economic institution of the U.S., they compete for the same drilling rights, markets, and government contracts. Second, institutions are never as effectively structured or goal-oriented as organizations. Third,

6

within a given society, institutions are larger collectives than the organizations within these institutions. Although some large corporations, such as Exxon and General Motors, are larger (in number of employees and economic resources) than the entire economic institution of some smaller nations, these two companies are only a small part of the entire economic institution of the U.S.

Organizations must also be distinguished from groups. The group, specifically the dyad, is the most elemental form of social relationship. A group may be defined as two or more people, with bilaterally reciprocal role relationships, interacting to achieve a common objective. Bilateral role reciprocality is face-to-face primary interaction. For example, the interaction between student and instructor in a classroom is bilateral. Those persons whose roles are not bilaterally reciprocal to every other person in the group or whose roles are not directed toward the group's objectives are not considered to be a part of the group.[3] For example, the secretary who brings a message to the instructor in a classroom is not part of that class (primary group) because she or he does not share objectives with the class members and does not interact with each class member. This characteristic of primary interaction, as opposed to indirect interaction through a third party or group, distinguishes a group from an organization.

Some theorists have attempted to differentiate between groups and organizations on the basis of such characteristics as goal diffuseness and specificity.[4] Families, peer and friendship clusters, certain recreational groups, and neighborhood associations have been designated by them as groups. They have suggested, further, that the primary distinction between groups and organizations is that organizations are designed to achieve specific objectives, while the objectives of groups are diffuse and nonspecific. While this distinction may hold true as a general tendency, there are many exceptions. The most apparent are work groups within organizations (for example, some research and development departments) that are structured to meet very specific, well defined objectives, e.g., a small group of scientists who develop a new chemical treatment to prevent metal deterioration. The characteristic of voluntary association has also been used to distinguish groups from organizations. Again, there may be a general tendency for groups to be more voluntary in nature than organizations, but professional organizations, labor unions, and the Consumer Federation of America are voluntary associations that could hardly be classified as groups.

7

Dimensionality

Theorists tend to view an organization either as a homogeneous unit (a unidimensional phenomenon) or as a heterogeneous unit with multiple dimensions (a multi-dimensional phenomenon). This approach to organizations is rooted in the writings of Weber, who conceptualized the structure of bureaucracies as being unidimensional. As the organization became more rational (i.e., exhibited greater means-ends congruence), it became more structured (bureaucratic), and as a consequence, was able to achieve its goal of efficiency. Thus, when an organization is perceived as unidimensional, all the dimensions (centralization, formalization, complexity, and so on) are seen as varying in the same direction under a given set of conditions. If, on the other hand, an organization is perceived to be multi-dimensional, these dimensions are seen as varying independently. Under a given set of conditions, some dimensions increase while others decrease, and vice versa.

Since the seminal works of Weber, many researchers have analyzed various types of organizations to determine if they are actually unidimensional or multi-dimensional phenomena. Although Richard Hall's research confirms the unidimensional construct of organizations,[5] most contemporary researchers have found that organizations are multi-dimensional. Within the last decade, many pieces of research have verified the multi-dimensionality of organizations. The Aston Group's 1968 investigation of forty-six work organizations in the English Midlands showed organizational structure to be multi-dimensional,[6] as did John Child's 1972 replication of the Aston Group's study using eighty-two British business organizations.[7] Child's findings did suggest that while Weber's unidimensional model might accurately describe the structure of manufacturing organizations, the multi-dimensional model may be more descriptive of service organizations. In his study, Child found that the service organizations (advertising and insurance firms) did not fit the unidimensional model as well as the manufacturing firms, perhaps due to the differing contextual variables (technology and autonomy) of these types of organizations.

Bernard Reimann's 1973 research, which attempted to clarify some definitional confusion in the aforementioned studies, also found that organizations are multi-dimensional.[8] "While a single dimension may be sufficient for a particular kind of organization in a given environment, several dimensions may be needed to describe and compare organizations in a more general sense."[9] Reimann tested this idea on a variety of manufacturing organizations in the U.S. The organizations varied in function, size, production technology, types of markets, and dependency on parent organizations. Like Pugh et al., he concluded that the multi-dimensional model of organizations was superior to the unidimensional model. Further, he concluded that the "dimensionality of the bureaucratic structure space may be a function of the socio-cultural environment" of the organization.[10] This conclusion was dissimilar to that of Inkson et al. in comparing the Aston Group's British manufacturing firms with a sample of twenty-one American firms. They found similar relationships between variables and concluded that structural differences were "due far more to variations in size, technology, and dependence than to national origin."[11] Reimann found that business organizations in the highly industrialized environment of the U.S. operate successfully with varying degrees of structure along several independent dimensions. Thus, he implied that organizational structure may conform to the equifinality principle, in that a variety of structural arrangements appear to be equally successful.[12]

The overwhelming majority of contemporary empirical research validates the multi-dimensional model of organizations, which will be used in this text in studying each organizational component (environment, context, structure, process and performance). This multi-dimensional model is more fully elaborated in the following section.

Some important dimensions of a multi-dimensional organization are its size, complexity, and degree of formalization. In fact, some sociologists have labeled organizations as "large-scale," "complex," or "formal." Since these dimensions do not always vary together, it is a misconception to think that such an adjective labels anything more than one specific characteristic of the organization. Because this text takes a multi-dimensional approach, these adjectives have been dropped and the generic term *organization* is used. Each dimension of an organization is analyzed in its own right and no assumption is made as to that organization's size, complexity, or degree of formalization. Rather, these dimensions are dependent on the other dimensions of the organization.

Basic Model of Organizations

Most models of organizations have been constructed around dimensions that theorists think are determinants (independent variables) of other organizational dimensions. These determinants have been categorized into five organizational components: environmental dimensions, contextual dimensions, structural dimensions, pro-

TABLE 1-1   Organizational Components: Environment, Context, Structure, Process, and Performance

ENVIRONMENTAL DIMENSIONS	CONTEXTUAL DIMENSIONS	STRUCTURAL DIMENSIONS	PROCESS DIMENSIONS	PERFORMANCE DIMENSIONS
Complexity	Technology	Structural Complexity	Differen- tiation: horizontal, vertical, and spatial	Change: program change and innovation
Change	Size	Power: hierarchical and departmental	Decision- making	Effective- ness and goal attainment
		Standardiza- tion and formalization of rules and procedures	Conformity	Conflict
		Communication	Feedback	Efficiency

cess dimensions, and performance dimensions, as summarized in Table 1-1.

At this time, it is necessary to designate the organizational dimensions that make up each component. (These dimensions will be fully elaborated in later chapters.) The environmental dimensions are change and complexity; the contextual dimensions are size and technology. The structural dimensions are: centralization of power (hierarchy of control and department power); complexity (horizontal differentiation, vertical differentiation, and spatial differentiation); formalization and standardization of rules and procedures; and communication. In this text, the processes underlying the structural dimensions are discussed in conjunction with the structural dimensions they support. The process dimensions underlying these structural dimensions are: the decision-making process that underlies the centralization of power, hierarchy of control and departmental power; the differentiation process that underlies structural complexity; the conformity process that underlies formalization and standardization of rules and procedures; and the feedback process that underlies the communication structure. Finally, the performance dimensions include: program change and innovation; conflict; effec-

10

tiveness and goal achievement; and efficiency. At this time, the student is not expected to have a clear definition of these dimensions or an understanding of their interrelationships—these will become apparent as we progress through the text.

Organization Defined

To be consistent with this basic multi-dimensional model, *organizations* are defined as goal-oriented collectives that consist of groups of individuals and in turn comprise social institutions. Organizations have relatively identifiable boundaries that are open to the environment, and they possess technologies, structures, processes, and perform activities with varying degrees of effectiveness and efficiency. Organizations are constantly changing through conflict and innovation. The major components of organizations are environment, context, structure, process, and performance. These components are assumed to consist, at least in part, of the dimensions found in Table 1–1.

It is not assumed that there is one best way to structure an organization. A highly structured arrangement may be preferable for organizations that deal with routine tasks and employ nonprofessionals, whereas a less structured arrangement may be preferable when tasks are non-routine, and complex, and the employee is a highly competent, educated professional. Further, the degree to which an organization is highly centralized (one structural dimension) is not only influenced by other structural dimensions but also by the dimensions of environment, context, and performance.

A single study is necessarily limited in the number of dimensions that can be analyzed (e.g., structure and performance or technology and structure). The choice of components and dimensions most often depends on the perspective from which the theorist approaches an organization.

ORGANIZATIONAL PERSPECTIVES AND APPROACHES

A perspective is the viewpoint or approach from which the theorist asks questions about the organization. These questions form the basis for the organizational analysis. Regardless of the perspective taken, the theorist will utilize a set of dimensions to define the organizational components; the perspective will define which dimensions are seen as independent and which are seen as dependent variables. The perspective from which the theorist works will also determine which unit of analysis is important and what questions will be asked about it. Consequently, the perspective will determine which characteristics or dimensions of the organization are examined. A human relations model may examine characteristics of the individuals within the organization, while an open-systems model may examine characteristics of the environment in relation to the organization. Any given perspective or approach to organizational study will, by necessity, exclude other perspectives and their dimensions from the theory construction process and hence from the analysis. For example, while the open-systems model concentrates on the influences of the environment on the organization and the relationship between the environment and the organization, it does not examine the attitudinal and behavioral characteristics of the individuals within the organization. These variables are more likely to be analyzed in the human relations model. But the human relations model will not analyze the influences of the environment on the structure of the organization. Knowing the characteristics or dimensions that a given perspective is best able to define and examine enables the researcher to choose the perspective that will most exhaustively answer given questions that she or he feels are most important. The research process then becomes more effective and its results more valid.

All theory is constructed from a perspective that limits which questions will be considered and focuses the efforts of the theorist. Thus a perspective, by nature, sensitizes the theorist to some aspects of the organization, while other perspectives sensitize him or her to other aspects of the organization. The inherent disadvantage of perspectives is that any systematic analysis from one perspective excludes aspects of the organization that would be considered from other perspectives. Thus, the researcher who considers an organization from several different perspectives will gain a broad understanding of that organization, but in many cases this is impractical. Therefore, the researcher must know the strengths and weaknesses of all possible perspectives in order to choose the best one for answering the questions under investigation.

After the theorist decides which dimensions are to be analyzed, she or he must construct statements of the relationships between these dimensions. This is the beginning of the theory construction process.

ORGANIZATIONAL THEORY

Organizational theory enables us to understand the complex network of interrelations among the various dimensions of organizations. The components of any theory are *concepts* (variables), *statements* (of existence and relationship), and a *logical format*. The relationships between variables are generally presented as propositional statements. The format consists of a scheme that enables us to structure relationships between propositions and sets of propositions consistently and systematically. A theory aims at making comprehensible the different levels of knowledge about the organization. These levels are: description or categorization, explanation and prediction, and understanding. In general, then, a theory is a set of integrated propositions that are related in a logical fashion in order to explain, predict, and facilitate an understanding of the relationship between variables.

The basis of any theory is a set of assumptions about the nature of the phenomena being investigated. Some assumptions are not testable, while others are based on observable regularities. An example of this first type of assumption is: people filling roles in an organization function as coordinated parts of a machine. Such assumptions about the nature of humans and the nature of the organization are generally inherent in a given perspective. The second type of assumption, that based on observable regularity, is exemplified by the assumption that all organizations possess the following elements to some degree: power, authority, task differentiation, and rules and procedures. This latter type of assumption may or may not be presented in the formal theory as a statement of existence. If these types of statements are presented in the formal theory, it is generally for the purpose of defining conditions that affect the relationships between variables.

The extension and development of knowledge in the form of these statements of relationship are what the investigation of organizations is all about, their reason for being. But these general statements specifying the relationship between two or more variables are not testable until the variables within this relationship are operationalized, thus facilitating the observation and measurement processes. The specific statement of the relationship between two or more such variables is called an *hypothesis*. Hypotheses are statements that can be subjected to empirical testing to evaluate the theory from which they were derived. Deductive theorizing is the process of test-

13

ing an hypothesis to either verify it, thus adding to the body of knowledge, in this case organizational knowledge, or show it to be inconsistent with the evidence.

Theorists generally concentrate on one of three units in developing a theory and testing the corresponding hypothesis: the individual, and his or her attitudes and/or behavior; the group and the interaction within it; the organization as a whole and its dimensions. These units of analysis are discussed in a following section.

SOME METHODOLOGICAL ISSUES

The separation of theoretical issues from the methodological issues is somewhat academic—all of these issues must be considered simultaneously by the researcher investigating an organization.

Types of Organizational Measures

The two types of measures are the *attitudinal* (subjective or analytical) and the *global* (objective or institutional) levels. The first type involves asking an employee his or her attitude about a particular dimension; the latter measures the dimension through characteristics of the organization. This distinction is based on the operationalization (questions asked of the respondent or examination of documents) of the variable. Institutional measures use such direct-measure sources as documents, charters, organizational spokespersons (executives or members of the board), while attitudinal measures rely on the opinions of persons within the organizations (rank-and-file members at various levels within the organization). Here questionnaires and interview schedules are generally used in acquiring the data, and the measure is based on the aggregation of data from these organization members. Many methods of acquiring data exist for both institutional and attitudinal measures of a given organizational dimension. These will be discussed in the chapters to follow.

The institutional approach (see Blau 1972, Pugh et al. 1968, Hinings 1971)[13] has the advantage of providing information that is not biased by the interviewee's perspective in that it is based on objective variables, for example, the ratio of managers to workers or the number of the levels of hierarchy. This type of data is not necessarily more reliable or valid than attitudinal measures because it, too, is subject to human error and reflects the reliability of the source, but it provides a very different kind of information. It should be remembered that, although measures may be equally valid empirically, not all measures furnish equally valid answers to a given question.

Of particular interest is the degree to which institutional and attitudinal measures that purport to measure the same organizational dimension correspond. Johannes Pennings examined the relationship between the structural dimensions of centralization and formalization using both institutional and attitudinal measures to determine if the relationship between those of a single structural dimension was stronger when both dimensions were measured institutionally or attitudinally. Pennings pointed out that:

Agreement on the naming of variables does not necessarily imply conceptual and/or operational agreement, and the inconclusive character of some of the results may be a function of the methodologically limited nature of the conclusions at which different authors arrive. For example, studies using institutional methods (Blau, 1970; Pugh et al., 1968) found a negative correlation between concentration of authority and standardization of organizational activities, while Hage and Aiken (1967) and Hall (1963), using survey aggregation [attitudinal] methods, found a weak positive and a strong positive correlation, respectively, between these two dimensions.[14]

The differing conclusions reached in the studies by Hall and Blau have implications for the uni- versus multi-dimensional question considered earlier. Because Hall found a strong positive correlation between centralization and standardization, he concluded that organizations are unidimensional.[15] Blau argued that centralization and standardization are alternative methods of control; thus he conceptualized organizations as multi-dimensional.[16] Here the institutional level of measurement resulted in findings that supported the multi-dimensional model, while the attitudinal level resulted in findings that supported the unidimensional structural model. Attitudinal measures may be correlated because respondents have formed logically consistent perceptions of organizational dimensions; while global (institutional) measures are not subject to this perceptual effect.

In Pennings' analysis of the relationship between centralization and formalization,[17] measured institutionally and attitudinally, he utilized Inkson, Pugh, and Hickson's institutional measures[18] and

15

Hage and Aiken's and Perrow's attitudinal survey measures.[19] He utilized the multi-trait/multi-method procedure that measures the convergent and discriminant validation of more than one characteristic by more than one measure. The researcher would expect to find that the common variance of different indicators probing a latent trait is higher than the common variance among indicators within one approach measuring different traits. In other words, Pennings expected the two sets of measures to be highly intercorrelated when probing the same underlying dimension. The object was to see to what degree the systematic bias of the common method of measurement effected the relationship between variables. Pennings concluded that the two structural dimensions—formalization and centralization—are not completely independent as measured by the two methods but that each method probed different dimensions. He also concluded that the operational definitions of structural dimensions did not reflect the unidimensional phenomenon of "bureaucracy." Thus there is serious doubt as to the unidimensionality of the structural component. Pennings also concluded that there was insufficient convergence of the institutional and attitudinal indexes to conclude that they probed the same dimensions. "In particular, in indices of centralization derived from the configuration of authority roles, such as, for example, the numbers of direct supervisors, do not bear a significant relationship to questionnaire measures of centralization."[20]

In his analysis of eleven types of occupations in twenty-seven organizations, Hall also found that the institutional and attitudinal aspects of professionalization do not necessarily vary together.[21] He measured the institutional aspects of professionalization using Harold Wilensky's stages of professionalization of an occupation (full-time occupational employment, establishment of training schools, formation of professional associations, and formation of a code of ethics). The attitudinal aspects of professionalization were measured by such variables as reference group orientations, service ideals, dedication, belief in self-regulation, and feelings of autonomy.

The findings of Pennings and Hall substantiate the idea that dimensions of organizations measured institutionally and attitudinally cannot be expected to result in the same findings. Thus, in the ensuing chapters, the research on each organizational dimension will be separated into that which uses institutional measures and that which uses attitudinal measures. Then comparisons of research findings will be made.

Units and Levels of Organizational Analysis

Organizations have been conceptualized and analyzed utilizing different units of analysis. The term *unit* designates the entity or collective from which the data are gathered and to which findings of the research may be generalized. The unit of sociological analysis may be the individual, the group, the organization, the institution, or the society. Only the first four units are applicable to our discussion of organizations.

The Individual   The first unit of analysis is the *individual*. Both the behavior and attitudes of the individual have been analyzed in organizational research. As has been discussed, psychological and social psychological analyses deal with the employee's attitudes and work roles. The researcher may be interested in such characteristics as commitment, job satisfaction, or professional attitudes of the individual.

Organizational theorists analyzing group and organizational variables often use means of observation (operational instruments) in which the individual is the unit of analysis. For example in measuring the centralization of an organization, they would ask the members of the organization their perception of the degree of centralization of decision-making. Thus, the findings are determined by the employees' perceptions of the situation. James Coleman recognized that these methods do not measure group or organizational variables when he wrote:

> Survey research methods have often led to the neglect of social structure and of the relations among individuals. . . . The *individual* remained the unit of analysis. No matter how complex the analysis, how numerous the correlations, the studies focused on individuals as separate and independent units. The very technique mirrored this well: Samples were random, never including (except by accident) two persons who were friends. . . . As a result, the kinds of substantive problems on which such research focused tended to be problems of "aggregate psychology," that is, within-individual problems, and never problems concerned with relations between people.[22]

Typically the researcher will sample survey the workers' attitudes within the organization or work group. The responses are then summated in order to say something about or describe the group or organization. The *focus* of analysis is the group or organization, but the *unit* of analysis is the individual. This information is often acquired through interviews or questionnaires.

Behavior is the second level that can be analyzed using the individual as the unit of analysis. Here the researcher is interested in the individual's behavior while filling his or her specific roles in an organization. This behavior may be observed by such techniques as participant observation, nonparticipant observation and self-report of the respondent (member of the organization). Studies of turnover and individual productivity are records of individual behavior. These studies are not about the dimensions of organizations or the principles that govern their processes; these are treated as givens. They are, rather, studies of the attributes and behavior of people who make up organizations. Research of this type suggests that individuals' attributes affect their performance and, through interaction, their co-workers. Thus, individual attributes influence the functioning of work groups and, ultimately, the organization itself.

The Group   The second unit of analysis is the *group*. When the work group is the unit of analysis, the focus is on the social relations of the individuals in the group, which is part of the larger organizational structure. As in the studies of the individual group members, organizational dimensions are givens when the group is the unit of analysis. The emphasis is on the interaction of individuals in the group and such group attributes as cohesion, leadership, communication, competitiveness, productivity, etc.

In utilizing the group as the unit of analysis, the researcher is concerned with obtaining information from all the members of the group in order to draw conclusions about the processes and structures of the group and the effects of these structures on the interaction of group members. Since group process and structure are central to the analysis, the organizational context in which they occur is secondary, and serves only as a limiting factor.

One example of research utilizing the group as the unit of analysis is Blau's case study of elemental groups in two government bureaus. He investigated the influence of statistical records of performance on the interpersonal relations in the work groups and, consequently, on group performance.[23] This research analyzed the nature of the work groups but not the nature of the organizations.

The Organization   The third unit of analysis is the *organization*. Here the organization as a whole is treated as a discrete entity.

18

When the organization is the unit of analysis, the interrelated contextual, environmental, structural, process, and performance dimensions are analyzed. The researcher may choose to focus on the principles that explain the organization's performance in terms of its structural dimensions (formalization, complexity, communication, centralization, and so on), since the underlying processes that produce a particular dimension are often inferred. Or the researcher may focus on explaining the structure as a consequence of contextual variables, considering the performance dimensions as givens.

The focus of this text is the analysis of organizations (human collectives designed to achieve objectives) as entities in their own right. Although it is recognized that individuals are the core of these organizations and that they interact to form groups, the focus is on the organization as the unit of analysis. This does not imply that individuals or work groups are not important in organizational analysis. Both these units supply valuable information about the organization. When the goal is to explain the organizational system, however, knowledge of these units is meaningful only when combined with an analysis of organizational dimensions. Further, given the vast literature focusing on each of these units, only one could be adequately explored here. Thus, much of the diversity that would be incorporated if all three units of analysis were combined has been eliminated. Because organizational knowledge (research in which the unit of analysis is the organization) is less obvious and common-sense-oriented, a deliberate attempt is made not to confuse matters by bringing the other two units of analysis into our discussion.

In order to measure organizational dimensions, it is necessary to compare a large number of organizations of a particular type in that theoretical explanations of why organizations have certain dimensions depend on comparisons of many organizations of the same type. Information from intense case studies of the social processes of one or two organizations cannot be generalized. The comparative method is required. Through comparative analysis, generalizations and predictions concerning the structure and functioning of organizations can be made. Blau's *The Organization of Academic Work* is an example of comparative analysis using the organization as the basic unit.[24]

METHODS OF ORGANIZATIONAL ANALYSIS

Two major methods are used in organizational analyses: the case study method and the comparative method. The case study method

19

dominated the field until the last twenty years. With the increased knowledge of advanced statistical techniques and the aid of computers, the comparative method has recently gained prominence in organizational analysis. Although there are other methods of organizational analysis (e.g., experimental laboratory studies), the comparative method is most often used to analyze structural dimensions of organizations, while the case study is most often used to analyze organizational processes. Since this text concentrates on both aspects of organizations, both methods of analysis will be discussed here.

The Case Study Method

A case study is an intensive investigation of a single organization. The researcher approaches the investigation with general questions, which are refined and extended as the research progresses. Because case studies are "in the field analyses" of the actual functioning of the organization, the researcher gains a feeling for the situation and an intimate understanding of organizational process. Consequently, the researcher can adjust the techniques of data collection (interviews, questionnaires, participant observation or organizational documents) to cover unanticipated questions and problems and to explore additional sources that can furnish maximum information. Thus, the case study method affords the investigator a great deal of flexibility both in the questions asked and the methods of data collection.

The case study method of organizational analysis has several advantages. First and most important, it affords the investigator a depth of knowledge about actual organizational processes that is unattainable through other methods of investigation. The investigator can not only record what is occurring, but can ascertain why processes are taking place in a particular way. A second advantage of the case study method is that first-hand knowledge of the organization enables the researcher to respond to the realities observed and adjust measurement techniques to gain new insights into the organization. A third major contribution of the case study method is that it calls attention to group structures, encouraging intensive investigation of these structures and the attendant social processes.

In his case study of New York University, J. Victor Baldridge pointed out that the case study method is beneficial "(a) if there is little data assembled on the topic, (b) if the research is basically exploratory, (c) if the objective is in-depth research, and (d) if change and dynamic process are crucial to the investigation."[25] The case study method, then, becomes an ideal method of analysis if the ob-

20

jective of the research is to gain an in-depth understanding of the processes underlying the dimensions of a single organization.

However, this method of investigation also has several major weaknesses. By concentrating on process, the individual and the group within the organization usually become the units of analysis. Comparisons between individuals and groups within a single organization can be made, but in-depth study of more than one organization at a time is necessarily excluded. In this case, the investigator can say little about organizations per se. Secondly, by limiting the investigation to one organization, it is impossible to make use of comparison as a tool of analysis. When there is no comparative base other than that found in the literature on similar organizations, the analysis becomes descriptive. The third major weakness is the specific nature of the results. An objective of science is to find results that can be generalized for similar situations so that relationships can be predicted. The assumption that a sample of organizations is representative of the larger population of organizations allows such generalizations to be made. In the case study method, there is no assurance that the organization chosen for the study is representative of a particular type of organization. Thus, findings cannot be generalized to other organizations.

The Comparative Method

If the aim of organizational analysis is to explain the interrelated dimensions of various kinds of organizations, it is not possible to simultaneously analyze the attitudes and behavior of the members of the organization while also examining group relations within the organization. The comparative method attempts to explore the contextual, environmental, structural, and performance dimensions of organizations. Blau was among the first to define the comparative method of organizational analysis as:

the systematic comparison of a fairly large number of organizations in order to establish relationships between their characteristics. In short, the term is used here to refer to quantitative comparisons that make it possible to determine relationships between attributes of organizations.[26]

Blau specifies that his definition is not meant to imply a preoccupation with mathematical models and advanced statistics, but rather a concern that qualitative and quantitative comparisons be built into the methodology. It is also important that we do not perceive that differences in the case study method and comparative methods of analysis are synonymous with qualitative and quantitative analyses, respectively, for both methods can be either quantitative or qualitative.

The major advantages of the comparative method are innate to the scientific method. The first and most obvious is the ability to make comparisons and therefore to differentiate organizations on the basis of common dimensions. The second advantage is the ability to test statements of relationship between, for example, two structural dimensions or a structural dimension and a performance dimension. A third advantage is the ability to generalize these findings to a larger population from which the organizations were drawn, and to use them for explanation and prediction. Yet another advantage is that comparative research does not necessitate an in-depth study of each member of an organization, since data can be obtained from documents, records of the organization, and interviews with key informants. As was pointed out earlier, this method sacrifices in-depth analysis for a broader data base that permits comparisons.

By definition, the comparative method contributes to our knowledge of the relationship between the dimensions of the organization. But the strength of comparative analysis is that it can focus on organizational dimensions and their interrelationships; however it cannot focus on the processes that support these dimensions. Although comparative analysis can discover the relationship between dimensions of an organization, it must infer the causal link of process because of the absence of detailed information on the internal functioning of the organization. Consequently, comparative analysis, unlike the case study, cannot contribute an in-depth understanding of process.

Social relationships within an organization cannot be deduced from knowledge of its structural dimensions. For example, one cannot predict the style of leadership from knowing the organization's degree of centralization. In order to study these social relationships directly, the case study method of analysis is necessary. Because organization process and structure are closely interrelated (patterned process results in structure), the comparative and case study methods can be used to compensate for each other's shortcomings. Certainly the use of both methods to gain a more complete understanding of process and structure would provide an ideal investigation of organizations. But more often than not, a single piece of research will measure only structure or process using either comparative or case study analysis, respectively. This is because the method of data collection typically follows from the research questions asked. When the structural dimensions of an organization are being analyzed, the method of data collection is the comparative analysis of a large sample of organizations with data obtained from selected informants in each organization and from the organizations' records. On the other hand, when the actual social relationships are analyzed, data is obtained through interviews, questionnaires, and observations of one or a relatively small number of organizations. Multiple types and levels of employees are studied.

One notable exception to the practice of using one method of data collection to the exclusion of the other is found in the research of John Brewer. Brewer argues that case studies and comparative studies can complement one another to explain some of the contradictory findings in analyses using different methods of data collection.[27] Case studies cannot establish the association among organizational dimensions that is required to develop a theory of organizational structure. Organizational theorists who have conducted comparative research and found relationships between structure variables of an organization move to the processes within organizations to explain these structural relationships. Brewer pointed out that:

> The constraint of collecting data from many organizations in comparative research frequently makes it impossible to collect the very data describing actual social relationships that would verify these explanations. So long as they remain unverified, they are subject to continuous *ad hoc* revision to bring them into line with current structural findings, and structural studies are thereby deprived of a firm theoretical base from which to make predictions.[28]

It is a fundamental requirement of any organizational theory that the social processes that underlie relationships among organizational dimensions be established empirically. This can be accomplished through case studies.

Yet the case study alone cannot specify the relationship between the formal structure of the organization and the processes within the organization. Brewer writes:

> Comparative studies of structural variation can provide criteria for classifying individual cases in terms of their formal structural characteristics and, when these comparative studies make explicit their assumptions about intervening internal processes,

23

can also lead to explicit differential predictions about the nature of internal social processes under the different structural conditions.[29]

Thus, this text will concentrate heavily on comparative studies.

SUMMARY

In this chapter, we have differentiated organizations from groups, institutions, and the more inclusive concept of social organization. Organizations were defined as goal-oriented collectives made up of groups of individuals that in turn comprise social institutions. The perspective taken is eclectic in that an attempt is made to synthesize at least a portion of our knowledge from the models that use various environmental, contextual, process, structural, and performance dimensions as explanatory variables. Thus our approach is definitely multi-dimensional. Finally, this text concentrates on the organization as the unit of analysis and deals with those comparative studies in which attitudinal and global institutional indexes are used to measure organizational dimensions. After examining various perspectives and models of organizations, we will progress through the organizational dimensions found in our model and, where possible, define their relationships.

In any examination of organizations, it is important to specify the nature of organizational dimensions and the relationships among these dimensions. The reader should keep in mind that, although there have been many studies of the dimensions of organizations, there have been few attempts to integrate these dimensions in any systematic, comprehensive fashion. An understanding of the nature of each dimension and its relationship to others will place us in a better position to understand the functioning of organizations. Due to the diversity and seemingly unrelated nature of the research of these dimensions, the integration problem is a monumental one. First, it is necessary to organize and review the various studies dealing with each organizational dimension. Such reviews yield widely diverse sets of findings. Next, these findings must somehow be tied together into a logically consistent body of knowledge so that useful generalizations can be made concerning the relationships between dimensions. For this reason, the model of organizations found in this chapter was constructed, based on a review of the research on organizational dimensions.

NOTES

1. Max Weber, *The Theory of Social and Economic Organization*, trans. A. M. Henderson and T. Parsons (New York: Oxford University Press, 1947).
2. Koya Azumi and Jerald Hage, *Organizational Systems* (Lexington, Mass.: D. C. Heath Company, 1972), p. 7.
3. Alvin L. Bertrand, *Social Organizations* (Philadelphia: F. A. Davis Company, 1972), p. 44.
4. Azumi and Hage, *Organizational Systems*, pp. 7–9.
5. Richard H. Hall, "Intra-organizational Structural Variation: Application of the Bureaucratic Model," *Administrative Science Quarterly* 7, no. 3 (December 1962): 295–308.
6. D. S. Pugh, D. J. Hickson, C. R. Hinings, and C. Turner, "Dimensions of Organization Structure," *Administrative Science Quarterly* 13, no. 1 (June 1968): 65–105.
7. John Child, "Organization Structure and Strategies of Control: A Replication of the Aston Studies," *Administrative Science Quarterly* 17, no. 2 (June 1972): 163–177.
8. Bernard C. Reimann, "On the Dimensions of Bureaucratic Structure: An Empirical Reappraisal," *Administrative Science Quarterly* 18, no. 3 (September 1973): 462–476.
9. Ibid., p. 463.
10. Ibid., p. 462.
11. J. H. K. Inkson, J. P. Schwitter, D. C. Pheysey, and D. J. Hickson, "A Comparison of Organization Structure and Managerial Roles: Ohio, U.S.A. and the Midlands, England," *A Journal of Management Studies* 7, no. 3 (October 1970): 347–363.
12. Reimann, "On the Dimensions of Bureaucratic Structure: An Empirical Reappraisal," p. 469.
13. Peter M. Blau, *The Organization of Academic Work* (New York: Wiley Interscience, 1973); Pugh, Hickson, Hinings, and Turner, "Dimensions of Organization Structure," pp. 65–105; C. R. Hinings and G. L. Lee, "Dimensions of Organization Structure and Their Context: A Replication," *Sociology* 5, no. 1 (January 1971): 83–93.
14. Johannes Pennings, "Measures of Organizational Structure: A Methodological Note," *American Journal of Sociology* 79, no. 3 (November 1973): 688.
15. Richard H. Hall, "The Concept of Bureaucracy: An Empirical Assessment," *American Journal of Sociology* 69, no. 1 (July 1963): 32–40.
16. Peter M. Blau, "Decentralization in Bureaucracies," in M. N. Zald, ed., *Power in Organizations* (Nashville, Tenn.: Vanderbilt Press, 1970), pp. 150–174.
17. Pennings, "Measures of Organizational Structure," pp. 688–689.
18. J. H. K. Inkson, D. S. Pugh, and D. J. Hickson, "Organization Context and Structure: An Abbreviated Replication," *Administrative Science Quarterly* 15, no. 3 (September 1970): 318–239.
19. Jerald Hage and Michael Aiken, "Relationship of Centralization to Other Structural Properties," *Administrative Science Quarterly* 12, no. 1 (June 1967): 72–91; Charles Perrow, "Technology and Structure," working paper, mimeographed (Madison, Wis.: University of Wisconsin).
20. Pennings, "Measures of Organizational Structure," p. 702.
21. Richard H. Hall, "Professionalization and Bureaucratization," *American Sociological Review* 33, no. 1 (February 1968): 92–104.

22. James Coleman, "Relational Analysis: The Study of Social Organizations with Survey Methods," in Norman Denzin, ed., *Sociological Methods* (Chicago: Aldine, 1970), pp. 115–116.

23. Peter M. Blau, "Cooperation and Competition in a Bureaucracy," *American Journal of Sociology* 59, no. 6 (May 1954): 530–536.

24. Blau, *The Organization of Academic Work.*

25. J. Victor Baldridge, *Power and Conflict in the University* (New York: John Wiley & Sons, Inc., 1971).

26. Peter M. Blau, "The Comparative Study of Organizations," *Industrial and Labor Relations Review* 18, no. 3 (April 1965): 323.

27. John Brewer, "Flow of Communications, Expert Qualifications and Organizational Authority Structures," *American Sociological Review* 36, no. 3 (June 1971).

28. Ibid., p. 476.

29. Ibid.

26

2
ORGANIZATIONAL PERSPECTIVES

OBJECTIVES

The major objectives of this chapter are:

1. To explain why theoretical perspectives exist.
2. To present the major theoretical perspectives and models of organizations.
   a. To enumerate the assumptions and characteristics of these models.
   b. To enumerate their strengths and weaknesses.

PERSPECTIVES AND MODELS

Why do different theoretical perspectives and models of organizations exist? As suggested in the last chapter, each perspective provides a different way of looking at organizations; each one concentrates on different aspects of the organization and makes different assumptions about it. Some of these assumptions are listed in Table 2–1. Although not exhaustive, Stogdill's list[1] is indicative of the lack of agreement on the basic assumptions about the nature of organizations. At first glance, many of these assumptions appear contradictory. This is because organizational theorists place different emphases on various aspects of the organization. Perspectives are differentiated on the basis of which aspects of organizations they consider to be paramount. For example, some theorists place major emphasis on change through conflict (conflict perspective), while others emphasize stability of the organization (structural-functional perspective).

TABLE 2–1 Some Basic Premises and Orientations in Theories of Organization

1. Organization as a cultural product
2. Organization as an agent of exchange with its environment
3. Organization as an independent agency
4. Organization as a system of structures and functions
5. Organization as a structure in action over time
6. Organization as a system of dynamic functions
7. Organization as a processing system
8. Organization as an input–output system
9. Organization as a structure of subgroups
10. Subgroups in interaction with the organization
11. Subgroups in interaction with each other
12. Groups as biological–social entities
13. Groups as cultural products
14. Groups as independent entities
15. Groups as interaction systems
16. Groups as interaction–expectations systems
17. Groups as collections of individual members
18. Groups as summations of member characteristics

Source: Ralph M. Stogdill, "Dimensions of Organization Theory," in James S. Thompson and Victor Vroom, eds., *Organizational Design and Research* (Pittsburgh: University of Pittsburgh Press, 1971), p. 4.

Within a given perspective, the organizational models differ in both the unit of analysis and the explanatory variable. The concept of unit of analysis was discussed in chapter 1. Explanatory variable means that the theorist views one variable (for example, the environment) as influencing all other dimensions of the organization (objectives of the organization, arrangement of structural variables, the nature of the decision-making processes, and so on). Some theorists construct a model in which technology influences structure (technological model), while others see structure influencing goals and performance (structural model). See Table 2–2 for a typology of models based on these various explanatory variables. Due to the emphasis on given dimensions, each model has unique advantages over other models. Conversely, due to the lack of consideration of other dimensions, each has inherent weaknesses.

TABLE 2-2 Dimensions Emphasized by Organizational Models

MODEL	EXPLANATORY VARIABLES
Structural Models	Structural Dimensions
Bureaucratic	
Nonbureaucratic	
Technological Model	Technological Dimensions
Goals Model	Performance Dimensions
Decision-making Model	Decision-making Process
Human Relations Model	Characteristics of Individuals
General Systems Model	Environmental Dimensions

Before the student of organizations begins to analyze differing theoretical models, one point should be made clear. There is no single perspective or model that synthesizes all knowledge of organizations. Though desirable, this integration is not possible because of the differences in the underlying assumptions on which the perspectives and models are based. If two models are from the same general perspective, the knowledge obtained from both can be synthesized, but if the two models are from different perspectives, the assumptions and therefore the knowledge may be contradictory. For example, we cannot assume both that an organization is a unified system with a consensus of objectives and that it is made up of separate and conflicting interest groups that compete for power. Also, because different types of organizations have different functions and structures, it is imperative that organizational models be selectively applied. Just as there is no "one best" organizational structure or technology for all organizations, there is no "one best" theoretical model of these diverse organizations. For example, an organization with fairly routine tasks, in which employees are nonprofessionals, structure is highly stable and stratified, and decisions are few and highly centralized, lends itself to the bureaucratic structural model or the classical management model. Similarly, when the decisions are programmatic and infrequent, a decision-making framework that attempts to simulate executive behavior would be beneficial. A decision-making model that emphasizes uncertainty would be useful in a situation where nonroutine tasks are involved. Likewise, in organizations where employees are professionals, and where technology is highly sophisticated and nonroutine and deadlines are secondary to effectiveness, a nonbureaucratic structural model would be more useful. Thus, it can be seen that some models are more congruent with given organizations and their dimensions.

The scope and degree of abstractness of models are other factors that limit their applicability. For example, an organizational model may be so specific and narrow that, while it does an excellent job of describing one specific type of organization, it is not applicable to a wide variety of organizations. On the other hand, a model may be so broadly based that it affords only descriptive knowledge and no information about interrelationships among organizational dimensions. Likewise, a model may be so abstract that any organization will fit the basic terminology, while the model itself contributes very little descriptive and analytical information about a specific type of organization, much less about the relationships between the various dimensions of organizations. The general (open) systems model discussed later in this chapter has been accused of being both too broad and too abstract.

This chapter will examine some of the most popular models of organizations, emphasizing that the usefulness of each model depends on (1) how closely it corresponds to the type of organization being analyzed (its external validity), (2) how well it deals with the components of the organization that are being analyzed (its internal consistency), and (3) the degree to which the basic assumptions underlying the model correspond to observed reality. The above discussion is not meant to give the impression that all organizational models are equally adequate in dealing with given organizational components. In fact, just the opposite is true.

FUNCTIONAL AND CONFLICT PERSPECTIVES

Organizational perspectives are of two general types—*functional* and *conflict*, with the overwhelming majority fitting the functional category.[2] Within the functional perspective there are both closed- and open-systems models. This classification scheme is depicted in Table 2–3. Many of these more recently developed models are simply modifications of earlier models, thus, there is great overlap among them (e.g., the bureaucratic model overlaps the classical management model).

The Functional Perspective

Six of the major assumptions that apply to models of the functional perspective are discussed here. The first assumption is that organizations are systems of interrelated parts. Each part is seen as

30

TABLE 2-3   A Classification of Organizational Models

FUNCTIONAL PERSPECTIVE		CONFLICT PERSPECTIVE
Closed-Systems Models	*Open-Systems Models*	
1. Structural Models a. Bureaucratic b. Nonbureau- cratic 2. Technological Model 3. Goals Model 4. Decision-making Model 5. Human Relations Model	1. General Systems Models	1. Conflict Models

affecting every other part and the system as a whole. For example, what occurs in the marketing department affects what happens in production and research, and vice versa. So popular is the "system" assumption of organizations that Dean Champion wrote, ". . . all organizations, regardless of their degree of complexity, formality, or size may be viewed as social systems of interaction."[3] Second, the functional perspective views causation of the organization's functioning as multiple and reciprocal. Causation is multiple in that many dimensions of the structure affect the performance of the organization, as do contextual and process variables. Causation is reciprocal in that process influences structure and vice versa. Third, the functional perspective concentrates on maintaining the order, coordination, and control of the organization. This characteristic is often called integration and is accomplished through the assumption of common objectives and goals, the fourth major assumption of the functional perspective. Although all organizational members are not assumed to have common interests, they are assumed to be guided by common organizational objectives. Activities directed toward the achievement of these objectives holds the organization together. These activities are coordinated and controlled by a dominant administrative coalition. Two of the assumptions of the functional perspective are centered around its view of organizational change: Change is viewed as occurring in a gradual evolutionary manner. An

31

organization changes by adjusting to its environment, i.e., new technology, as well as to new products and services. Change is gradual and evolutionary rather than revolutionary; the nature (structure, goals, processes) of the organization remains relatively constant. This perspective views conflict as dysfunctional. Often conflict is labeled as "stress-strain" or "tension." The functional theorist attempts to eliminate organizational conflict because it is detrimental to order and integration of the system.

In summary, the assumptions of the functional perspective are:

1. The organization is a system of interrelated parts, and each part affects the functioning of every other part and the whole;

2. Causation is multiple and reciprocal;

3. Integration is central to the maintenance of the organization;

4. The major integrating factors are common objectives and goals;

5. Change occurs in a gradual manner, as adjustment;

6. Conflict is dysfunctional.

The Conflict Perspective

The conflict perspective is used rather infrequently in organizational theory and research. Although most functional models present a dimension of change and/or conflict, conflict is not treated as a central and pervasive aspect of organizations and is often depicted as undesirable. For example, Max Weber's bureaucratic model views conflict as an element that should be structured out of an organization. Therefore, when conflict does occur it is most often viewed in this model as a result of human rather than structural weaknesses. This type of conflict is often labeled *personality conflict*. On the other hand, the classical management theorist is more likely to view conflict as a result of inadequate planning and control, reflecting poor administration and management. For the human relations theorist, conflict reflects a failure of leadership, a lack of participative management and employee involvement. Thus, those who deal with conflict *within* organizations as the subject of their analysis often view the organization as a system, that is, they view the organization from a functional perspective.[4] For other functionalists, conflict is primarily an interpersonal problem, although they may occasionally and briefly deal with group conflict.[5] Charles Perrow emphasized that a theory of organizations rather than individual interaction should be able to accommodate group conflict.[6] This theory should see conflict as an inevitable part of organizational life stemming from the characteristics of individuals. Recently, some attempts have been made toward this conceptualization.

The assumption of inherent internal conflict within organizations challenges several functional assumptions: one, that organizations are oriented toward one specific goal or a specific set of goals. The conflict perspective assumes that the goals of organizations are multiple and generally not well integrated; consequently, they are often in conflict. Some structural arrangements and processes of the organization may maximize a given goal while minimizing others. For example, an organization may maximize efficiency while minimizing effectiveness. Richard Cyert and James March pointed out that the goals and objectives of management may not have reached the stage of development where they are clearly defined; rather thay are ambiguous and inoperative.[7] This adds to the possibility of conflict. Similarly, Perrow found that when the stated goal of an organization is translated into operational goals (those for which specific operations can be discovered), several goals involved, and maximizing one will usually be at the expense of another.[8] According to Cyert and March, these conflicting goals can be met. Organizations can pursue goals in a sequence; it is not necessary that they all be pursued at once. At time 1, goal A may take precedence over B; and vice versa at time 2. Consequently, many goals are not in conflict over the short run. In the functional tradition, Cyert and March outline mechanisms that stabilize the goal-attainment process, thus maintaining the system.[9]

Of course, multiple goals and the means of attaining them do exist in organizations. Conflicting groups within these organizations have different interests and support different goals; the group members have different values and do not share equally in the rewards—security, power, and autonomy—of the organization. Groups compete for these rewards, resulting in overt, visible conflict. These assumptions do not negate the fact that groups with higher positions in the organizational structure more often realize their interests and goals than do groups positioned at lower levels.

In an attempt to distinguish the basic assumptions of the conflict perspective from the functional perspective, Ralf Dahrendorf pointed out that the functional perspective views the unit of analysis (here an organization) as a "relatively persistent, well-integrated configuration of elements" (a system), whereas the conflict perspective views the organization as subjected at every moment to change, with every element in the organization contributing to it.[10] While the functional perspective views the organization as resting on a consensus of its members, the conflict perspective views the organization as resting on the constraint of some of its members by others.

Organizational conflict will be discussed more extensively in Chapter 10. The purpose here is not to discuss the issues involved in the analysis of organizational conflict, but to present the assumptions of the conflict perspective of organizations. J. Victor Baldridge, in his recent analysis of New York University, pointed out that a conflict perspective:[11]

1. emphasizes the fragmentation of social systems into interest groups, each with its own goals.

2. analyzes the interaction of these different interest groups and especially the conflict processes by which one group tries to gain advantages over another.

3. views interest groups as clustering around divergent values, and the study of the conflicting interests is a key part of the analysis.

4. views the study of change as the central feature of the conflict approach, for change is to be expected if the social system is fragmented by divergent values and conflicting interest groups.

5. emphasizes the goal setting activities not the goal maintenance activities; emphasis is on decision making, not on efficiency of the organization in carrying out the decisions.

6. views power as central to the analysis; influence (informal power), as opposed to position based authority, is especially important to conflict theory.

7. finally, conflict and influence of internal groups, as well as external groups, are considered.

Thus, the conflict perspective of organizations emphasizes different aspects of organizational process than does the functional perspective—conflict and change as opposed to order. Because it makes different assumptions about the nature of organizations, a conflict analysis concentrates on analyzing different aspects of the organization. Specifically, it concentrates on the differing interests, values and goals of groups within the organization; on the decision-making process; and on the power acquisition processes of the organization. The functional perspective is more likely to concentrate on the common values, interests, and goals of groups within organizations; on the structural arrangement after decisions have been made; and on the power structure in the organization. One perspective is no less valid than another because both order and conflict exist in all organizations. However, the conflict perspective will more adequately depict the functioning of an organization during conflict and decision-making, whereas the functional perspective will more adequately depict routine functioning that follows the decision-making process.

OPEN- AND CLOSED-SYSTEMS MODELS

Although some basic assumptions are central to all models in the functional perspective, these models may be differentiated in two ways: (1) whether the system is depicted as open or closed and (2) whether organizational behavior is depicted as rational or nonrational. The basic distinction between the closed- and open-systems models is that the closed-systems models are concerned with components within the organization as explanatory variables; that is, technology, structure, process, and performance account for organizational functioning or behavior. The open-systems models are concerned with analyzing the relationship between the organization and its environment. The organization is seen as adjusting or adapting to its environment; thus, environmental variables are explanatory.

The Organization as a Closed System

An organizational analyst may assume that an organization is an open system, but may be interested in analyzing only the internal structure of the organization; thus, the theoretical model tested is a closed-systems model. In the history of organizational theory, many closed-systems models have been developed, perhaps because of the comparative ease of investigating such models. If a model analyzes an organization without considering external factors, the researcher is able to deal only with interrelationships of internal components and their dimensions; comparatively, a smaller number of variables are dealt with in a closed-systems model than in an open-systems model. These internal variables are not only fewer in number but are more assessable than external variables, thus facilitating their measurement. Variables such as decision-making and the allocation of resources are specific processes about which the researcher may as-

35

certain information by questioning members of the organization or by examining organizational records. On the other hand, environmental dimensions, such as change and stability, are so broad in scope that they are difficult to operationalize and measure.

Of course, closed systems do not exist in reality. A closed-systems model is only a way of viewing and analyzing organizations. George Rice and Dean Bishoprick pointed out that a closed system is a hypothetical construct:

> There never was, and probably never will be, a completely closed system because components are always influenced by forces not being considered—that is, by forces outside the system itself. But closed system analysis as a way of *thinking about* the interaction of components is extremely useful.[12]

The closed system allows the researcher the luxury of excluding broad, difficult to measure environmental influences. As a result of this exclusion, however, the resulting knowledge is incomplete and often inaccurate.

Closed-systems models can assume either a rational or nonrational organizational behavior. Under the assumption of rationality, organizational goals and performance are expected to result from certain technological, structural, process, or social factors within the organization. It is assumed that if the organization is well structured, it will function as a well-integrated system with high efficiency or productivity. The nonrational assumption holds that even when the organization is structured according to plan, there are unexpected consequences that keep the organization from functioning as a well-integrated system. These consequences are not necessarily dysfunctional, but these are the instances that concern the organizational analyst.

When making assumptions about organizational rationality, it must be made clear to which unit of analysis the assumptions apply. For example, one model may assume that individuals are totally rational; another may assume that individuals are not totally rational, but that organizations make them so. Thus, the nature of humans and of the organization may be considered to be quite different. Perrow pointed out that in Chester Barnard's cooperative management model, humans are viewed as nonrational but the organization as a whole is viewed as rational.[13] Thus, humans achieve rationality through organizations. This view is quite different from that of Herbert Simon, who posited that humans are intended rational, but

36

their organizational involvement does not produce greater rationality.[14] In this text, if a model views the organization in terms of means-ends relationships, i.e., if certain objectives are expected from certain technological, process, or structural factors, it is considered rational.

Although Weber does acknowledge the influence of external environment on the organization, he is often classified as a closed-systems theorist because he defines bureaucratic organization as rational in that it is internally structured to maximize efficiency. As will be elaborated later in this chapter, Weber's ideal bureaucracy represents clear, explicit goals that can be achieved through rational calculation and the applications of procedures. This rational assumption is also at the basis of the classical management model, the non-bureaucratic model, technological model, goals model, and decision-making model, and some human relations models. These models differ as to their explanatory variable, but they all attempt to explain organizational ends or performance using other intraorganizational dimensions.

When the researcher limits the analysis to internal dimensions alone, rationality may be more easily discernable; thus, the closed-systems model aids the researcher's effort to define organizations as rational systems. James Thompson captured the essence of the researcher's attempt at rationality: "The rational model of an organization results in everything being functional—making a positive, indeed an optimum, contribution to the overall result . . . All action is appropriate action, and its outcomes are predictable."[15]

Limitations of the Closed-Systems Models   The major limitation of the closed-systems model is its disregard for the dynamics between the organization and its environment. First, the humans who make up the organization do not always act rationally to achieve organizational goals. Humans are not parts of a machine; therefore, the organization never functions exactly as designed. Even discounting the human factor, no design is perfect for all situations. Further, environmental influences must be considered. Organizations may buffer themselves against the environment, but they seldom control their environment well enough to gain the predictability necessary for complete rationality. This disregard for the external environment leaves no room for the organization to change to meet environmental demands, much less to redistribute its resources to control that environment. Daniel Katz and Robert Kahn underscored this weakness of the closed-systems model:

37

The major misconception is the failure to recognize fully that the organization is continually dependent upon inputs from the environment and that the inflow of materials and human energy is not a constant. The fact that organizations have built-in protective devices to maintain stability and that they are notoriously difficult to change . . . should not obscure the realities of the dynamic interrelationships of any social structure with its social and natural environment. The very efforts of the organization to maintain a constant external environment produce changes in organizational structure. The reaction to changed inputs to mute their possible revolutionary implications also results in changes.[16]

Because environmental factors are not considered, feedback concerning the functioning of the organization in relation to its external environment is also ignored. Katz and Kahn noted that these environmental factors cannot be controlled either in research or practice.

Most organizational theorists quickly come to the conclusion that the closed-systems perspective is both inadequate and inaccurate in its analysis of organizations. A model of organizational behavior must consider both the internal dimensions and external environment of the organization in order to explain its functioning. When the closed-systems model is used, it is with the understandings that it explains only part of the functioning of organizations; that organizational rationality cannot be fully realized (although attempting to achieve rationality brings some order); and that organizational environment must be acknowledged by either adapting to or controlling it. With these understandings, the closed-systems models continue to be useful for defining observed relationships among the internal dimensions of organizations.

The Organization as an Open System

The weakness of the closed-systems models prompted the development of the open-systems approach. The first open-systems theorists recognized that closed systems models consider only those variables *within* the organization, thus ignoring the organization's close relationship with the environment. The organization's continual effort to maintain its relationship with the external environment has consequences for internal process, structure, and performance. The open-systems model sees the organization as working with the environmental demands: anticipating environmental changes, protecting itself from undesirable environmental influences, and attempting to manipulate those elements that can be controlled. Thus, the open-systems model recognizes that organizations are dependent on the external environment (both social and natural), and recognizes the constant interchange between the external systems and the internal system.

Where the closed-systems model concentrates on the principles of internal functioning—integration and coordination, the open-systems model concentrates on the system's flexibility. In meeting the demands of the external environment, this flexibility is a more important requirement than stability and integration. In addition to the flexibility *of* the organization, the open-systems model recognizes the importance of flexibility *within* the organization. The closed-systems model often posits one best method of reaching a goal; the open systems model emphasizes the principle of equifinality (that there is more than one way to achieve an objective). Thus, rigid structuring is not seen as the most effective means of reaching ends—they may be met in many different ways.

Finally, conceptualizing a system as closed results in the failure to develop feedback and communication systems. A nonexistent or underdeveloped feedback system can destroy the organization. Through lack of needed adjustment in its product or service, the organizational output may become unacceptable to its environment. On the other hand, if the organization has well developed research and consumer complaints departments that supply negative feedback from the external environment, it might well correct some of its major problems.

Walter Buckley expected the open-systems model to be a panacea for the weakness of the closed systems model. He posited that it would:

1. supply a common vocabulary unifying the several "behavioral" disciplines;

2. supply a technique for treating large, complex organizations;

3. supply a synthetic approach where piecemeal analysis is not possible due to the intricate interrelationships of parts that cannot be treated out of the context of the whole;

4. be a viewpoint that gets at the heart of sociology because it sees the sociocultural system in terms of information and communication nets;

5. be the study of *relations* rather than "entities," with an emphasis on process and transition probabilities as the basis of a flexible structure with many degrees of freedom;

6. be an operationally definable objective, non-anthropomorphic study of purposiveness, goal seeking system behavior, symbolic cognitive processes, consciousness and self-awareness, and sociocultural emergence and dynamics in general.[17]

Of course, many of these claims were not fulfilled. The open-systems model did not supply a common vocabulary of the social sciences nor did it get at the heart of sociology.

The open-systems model does depict the organization as rational, as do some closed-systems approaches. Consequently, the system is viewed not as goal-seeking but rather as meeting its needs for survival. In meeting these needs, the system is seen as relatively unplanned, responsive, and adaptive to its environment. Katz and Kahn attempted to avoid the debate over whose goals are more important and the fallacies of assuming that the goals of the administration are synonymous with the organizational goals and objectives, which is characteristic of the goals perspective.[18] They recommended starting an organizational analysis, not with identifying the purpose and goals of the leaders (which may conflict with the organization's), but with the theoretical concept of the system, with the energic input-output system. The researcher using an open-systems model thus begins by identifying and mapping the repetitive cycles of events (inputs, outputs, and throughputs).

The characteristics of the open-systems model have been enumerated by both Katz and Kahn[19] and Bertrand.[20] The following points were adapted from Bertrand's list of open systems characteristics:

1. *Inputs* are new supplies of energy brought into the organization from the external environment.

   a. *Maintenance inputs* serve to energize the system and make it ready to function.

   b. *Signal inputs* are accepted by the system for processing.

2. *Throughputs* are the work that is done in the system (organization). The input is altered in some way as materials are processed or people are served.

3. *Outputs* are the products that emerge from the organization to be used or rejected by the environment.

40

4. *Cycles of events* are the total import-export activities of an open system. It is the processes rather than the structure that make up the repetitive chain of events. Each cycle may be composed of subsystems and be part of a larger system.

5. *Negative entropy* is the organization's attempt to import more energy than it exports. Entropy is the process by which all systems move toward less efficiency and eventual death; negative entropy is the process that maintains survival.

6. *Feedback* and *coding* are the receiving of input that tell whether the system is operating consistently within the external environment. Feedback is the informational input, while coding is the process by which information coming into the system is made consistent with the receiving process. The mechanisms which receive feedback are so structured that they receive only that feedback which enters the system at the proper place and that which is properly coded. Through feedback it is possible to make corrections or deviations (new programming) in the system.

7. *Boundary maintenance* is a screening process that accepts certain inputs and rejects others. Not only does the boundary of a system perform coding and decoding functions, it also controls the rate of input-output flow and filters output. The boundary of a system is the "exit" port for the products of the system, and it is here that a determination is made as to whether or not the product will be useful to the suprasystem, that is, whether or not it is marketable. Finally, boundary maintenance is the point at which one system is coupled to another to form a larger system. These smaller systems are coupled through interaction interfaces, where the boundaries of organizations come together.

8. The *steady state (dynamic homeostasis)* is the system in equilibrium. Systems attempt to control threatening external factors. As growth and expansion occur, basic system characteristics tend to remain constant. The boundary maintenance processes function in such a way as to allow an open system to achieve some constancy in input-output exchanges. When a balance is reached, the system is said to be in a steady state. This is not to imply that the system is static—there are continual dynamics in the exchange between a system and its environment, but the relation between the system's parts remains at or near a balance.

9. *Storage* and *memory*—storage is the process of reserving inputs

41

for later utilization; memory refers to a record of inputs that have been processed by the system.

10. *Differentiation* is the tendency toward elaboration of roles and specialization of function. There is an increased tendency to assign functions in terms of highly specialized roles, such as those necessitated by increasing technology. Buckley used the term *morphogenesis* to denote processes that tend to elaborate or change a system's given form, structure, or state.

11. *Adaptation* refers to a system's ability to survive within its environment. Though entropic processes are normal to all systems, open systems have the ability, through responsiveness and adaptation, to prolong existence. Adaptation is accomplished through feedback loops that indicate what strategies might be used to counter disturbances or errors. Buckley refers to adaptation as the process of morphostasis—"those processes in complex system-environment exchanges that tend to preserve or maintain a system's given form, organization, or state."[21]

12. *Equifinality* is the principle which states that "multiple means to the same ends exist within organizations." As knowledge increases, the number of relevant means may be reduced, but there will still be more than one way to accomplish objectives.

13. *Tension* is normal in social organizations because no two actors share the same interpretation of behavioral expectations. All types of systems include some type of stress in their makeup.

Limitations of the Open-Systems Model   As is obvious from the above list of characteristics of the open-systems model, many of these concepts are very abstract. Because of their abstractness and breadth, they are difficult, if not impossible, to operationalize. At the present time, operational definitions are either underdeveloped or nonexistant, largely because of the inclusive nature of environmental variables. Even if researchers did have both the ability to operationalize these variables and the techniques for analyzing the data, the research process would be extremely expensive. Perhaps the data collection stage of the research process would be the most expensive in time and money. Thus, the researcher must evaluate the added costs of the open-systems model against the gains in theoretical and empirical knowledge.

Another limitation of the open-systems model is that there is no way to anticipate, much less measure, the latent effects of the environment. Because the organization is subject to the effects of the environment, a great deal more uncertainty is introduced into the analysis than with the closed-systems models.

Finally, the open-systems model specifies the dimensions of organizations but does not state relationships between these dimensions. Thus, although it offers a relatively comprehensive conceptual framework, it does not present a theory of organizations—the model is merely descriptive and does not contribute to an understanding of organizations. In fact, in order to use the conceptual framework of the open-systems model, the researcher must supply the basic knowledge as to the relationships between dimensions of the organization.

As has been demonstrated, the closed- and open-systems models differ in many respects. The objective of the closed-system model is to predict accurately the state of the system. Through prediction and understanding comes the ability to determine and control the system. Closed-systems analysis concentrates on the components within the organization—specifically, the relationships among contextual, structural, process, and performance dimensions. This approach necessitates knowledge of all variables and of their relationships to one another. If closed-systems models were valid, they would certainly be the most effective models for organizational analysis. But, although people favor closed systems to avoid uncertainties and facilitate logical processes, organizations do not function as closed systems. Obviously, if the researcher does not know all the variables which influence the organization, she or he cannot consider them in the analysis. What is even more certain is that, if the researcher knows the environmental factors that influence the organizational dimensions but intentionally omits them from the analysis, thereby closing the system, the analysis will be less valid.

Because of the difficulty of dealing with a model that includes all the many relationships of organizational dimensions, most researchers analyze only a small portion of any given theoretical model, e.g., the relationship between formalization and centralization. This does not denote a closed-system theoretical model—it merely omits environmental as well as other variables from the analysis. But the researcher cannot explain the effect of the environment using such a model. Many times this approach is taken because of limitations of statistical techniques, economic resources, or the researcher's interest in given organizational dimensions.

The open-systems model analyzes the processes that take place within the system and between the organization and other systems, with a concentration on process as opposed to structure. Further, the open-systems model assumes that the system and its environment contain some variables of which we have no knowledge and cannot predict; thus, uncertainty is assumed. This does not mean that the system is irrational or nondeterminant but merely that our knowledge of the system is incomplete.

Most contemporary organizational theorists have attempted to combine the best attributes of both the open- and closed-systems models. The organization is seen as open and constantly adjusting to its environment. The organization is placed in a position of constantly defining, evaluating, and dealing with these uncertainties; but at the same time, it is subject to the need for rationality, requiring predictability and certainty in order to survive. Thompson, for example, sees organizations as striving for rationality in an uncertain environment.[22] Organizations attempt to be rational, controlling their internal and external environment to the best of their ability. Of course, despite their attempts, organizations never gain complete control because both the external environment and the internal processes of the organization are constantly changing. The degree to which the organization is successful in achieving control is dependent upon the strength of the internal and external pressures and the organization's capacity to handle these pressures.

ORGANIZATIONAL MODELS

As depicted in Table 2-2, organizational models vary in their explanatory variables. For example, structural models, both bureaucratic and nonbureaucratic, use structural variables to explain organizational performance. The technological model uses the nature of raw material, knowledge, and operative technologies to explain both organizational structure and performance, while the goals model concentrates on organizational performance dimensions, such as effectiveness and efficiency. The organizational models that concentrate on the dimensions outlined in our basic organizational model (see Table 1-1) will be elaborated here (excepting the open-systems model, which has been discussed). These include the structural, technological, goals, and decision-making models. The human relations model, in which personal and social psychological characteristics of employees serve as explanatory variables, is an important organizational model; but because this text analyzes only that research in which the organization is the unit of analysis, a discussion of the human relations model is not germane.

44

The importance of each model will become apparent as the student reads the chapter on each dimension which is the explanatory variable of that model. For example, the research conducted by the theorists who see technology as paramount and hence use the technological model is discussed in chapter four. The theory and research analysts using the decision-making model are found in chapter 5 on organizational power and centralization, characteristics determined by the decision-making process. Although theorists have developed models of organizations that aid them in researching a limited number of organizational dimensions, the student should keep in mind that all dimensions are interrelated and be cognizant of the effects of all dimensions on the one being analyzed.

Structural Models

The structural models of organizations are of two general types: bureaucratic (classical management and Weberian) and nonbureaucratic. Both types of models are composed of the same structural dimensions (centralization, formalization, and so on). Their major differences are that the bureaucratic models concentrate on the more structured aspects of each dimension, such as high centralization of power, controlled communication, high formalization of job descriptions; while nonbureaucratic models concentrate on decentralization of power, low formalization of job descriptions, and frequent communications (both horizontally and vertically).

Bureaucratic Models   The two major bureaucratic models are the classical management model and Weber's bureaucratic model. The basic assumptions, characteristics, and limitations of these two models are very similar. It is also interesting to note that the early work of classical management theorists appeared at about the same time as Weber's works on bureaucracy, and they shared the objective of maximizing organizational efficiency through rationality. Both models recommend structuring the organization in ways that will afford the organization the greatest efficiency.

The Classical Management Model.   Most of the classical management theorists were practicing managers of business and industrial organizations who observed what worked in their organizations and used these observations to write about how organizations *should* function and how managers *should* manage. This approach takes the position that all organizations are essentially the same and that there is a best way to structure and manage organizations to achieve maximum efficiency. This optional way is specified in six major principles that state the relationships between the management process and the formal structure of organizations. These principles have been extracted from various works and summarized by Joseph Massie.[23] The first principle is the *scalar* principle, the essence of which is a hierarchical (vertical) arrangement of positions through which the chain of command flows. This principle states that authority and responsibility should flow in a clear, unbroken line from the highest executive to the lowest operative. This conceptualization of the vertical stratification of the organization is illustrated in the formal bureaucratic organizational chart. The second principle is that of *unit of command,* which states that no member of an organization should receive orders from more than one superior. Fayol and other classical theorists viewed unity of command as the most fundamental principle, to be given priority over other management principles. Thus, the major structure of the organization is a formal line authority with roles of line and staff clearly defined to decrease ambiguity. Third is the *exception* principle, which states that frequently-recurring decisions should be reduced to a routine and delegated to subordinates, and only important issues or those that are nonrecurring should be referred to superiors. All decisions then would be made at the lowest level commensurate with the person's ability to make such decisions. The fourth principle is that of *limited span of control.* This principle states that the number of subordinates reporting to a supervisor should be limited. Some writers have specified a small number of subordinates for positions at the apex of the hierarchy and a larger span for lower-level positions. Thus, the span of control helps define the shape of the formal organizational structure. The fifth principle is that of *organizational specification* (the division of labor). This principle assumes that organizational administrators have complete knowledge of all the tasks and activities necessary to accomplish organizational objectives. Thus, they can group homogeneous activities into departments or divisions. The sixth principle is the *profit center* principle, which states that various parts of a large organization should be divided into integrated, self-centered units, each with its own facilities and staff-support. Each division operates on a competitive basis in an effort to maximize profit. This principle rests on the assumption that competition will increase efficiency.

At the basis of these principles are assumptions about the nature of humans, organizations, and humans working in organizations. Humans are assumed to act rationally. Their actions are assumed to be in the direction of organizational goal-attainment, specifically toward increased efficiency or productivity. People are viewed as parts of (or extensions of) machines. There is no consideration of human factors; the employee and activities of the group are viewed in an objective and impersonal manner. Workers are defined as being motivated purely by economic needs; therefore, incentives are solely in the form of monetary rewards. These workers are defined as disliking and avoiding work, making close supervision and accountability necessary. Consequently, management must lead people fairly but firmly in ways antithetical to their nature. Human beings are also defined as preferring the security of a definite task and not valuing the freedom of determining their own activities. Employees must be supervised and instructed in their roles because they are unable to define their work roles and manage the relationships among their positions without detailed guidance and supervision. Unless job limitations are clearly defined and enforced, employees will conflict. Further, it is viewed that simple tasks are easier for workers to master; thus simplification of tasks through a division of labor increases productivity.

The classical management model views the manager as possessing a different type of nature than the employee or worker, as being able to predict and establish patterns of organizational activities and the relationships among activities and workers. The manager can, therefore, map the total sequence of activities. This planning and its coordination is achieved at the top of the organizational hierarchy and delegated downward and are based on the principles enumerated above. These principles can be learned and applied regardless of environment or quality of personnel. If this is done well, the organization will be efficient.

Both the principles and assumptions of the classical management model have been heavily criticized. First, the model views organizations as closed systems that management can control. Therefore, it encompasses the limitations of the closed-systems model enumerated earlier. General cultural and specific environmental influences on employees and their tasks are not considered. Second, the assumptions concerning the machine-like nature of humans and the oversimplification of the knowledge, motives, and abilities of the worker have been attacked by human-relations theorists and generally by the disciplines of sociology and psychology. Also questioned are the assumptions of human rationality in pursuit of organizational interest.

Another major limitation of the classical management model is that the principles enumerated above, which were devised from practical experiences, do not apply to all organizations in all situations. Thus, these principles have not held up under empirical analysis. Furthermore, these principles are stated as laws, as opposed to propositions; they cannot be tested. They are stated as characteristics of the ideal organization, not as descriptions that have been validated by empirical evidence.

Another limitation of this model is that it completely neglects analysis of any informal characteristics of the organization. For example, informal communication and power based on influence and competency, as opposed to formal positional authority, are not considered. It ignores the fact that individuals who hold the same positions do not in fact exercise authority in the same way. The classical management model cannot deal with individual differences in employees because such considerations are outside the scope of the model.

In summary, the classical management model errs in omitting from consideration many major aspects of the organizations. First, it simply does not treat the social psychological reaction of individuals to the organization. Second, it deals only with formal structure of the organization. Third, it deals with the internal structure of the organization to the exclusion of interorganizational relationships or the relationship of the organization to its environment or technology. Fourth, central processes such as feedback and decision-making are not considered. Finally, by viewing efficiency as the overriding goal of all organizations, the performance variables of effectiveness, job satisfaction, and adaptiveness have been overlooked.

Weber's Bureaucratic Model. The bureaucratic model is very closely related, in both principles and assumptions, to the classical management model; consequently, their limitations are similar. The most influential proponent of the bureaucratic model was Max Weber. Weber's work began with an analysis of the heart of bureaucratic structure—the authority structure. He argued for the maximization of organizational efficiency as a consequence of legitimate, rationally-based authority. Weber had little regard for practices of favoritism based on status (especially family connection) and hiring of personal friends and saw bureaucratic organizations as correcting such practices. Weber lists three kinds of legitimate authority:

1. Rational-legal authority—resting on a belief in the "legality" of patterns of normative rules and the right of those elevated to authority under such rules to issue commands.

2. Traditional authority—resting on an established belief in the

sanctity of immemorial traditions and the legitimacy of the status of those exercising authority over them; and finally,

3. Charismatic authority—resting on devotion to the specific and exceptional sanctity, heroism, or exemplary character of an individual person, and of the normative patterns of order revealed or ordained by him.[24]

Under legal authority, obedience is owed to the established impersonal order, the authority of the office; under traditional authority, obedience is owed to the status of tradition; under charismatic authority, obedience is owed the person who exhibits heroism or other valued characteristics. Of these three types of legitimate authority, only rational–legal authority is impersonal; it provided the impetus for Weber's bureaucratic organizational structures.

Much of Weber's writing is concerned with how organizations can be structured to achieve maximum rationality in the pursuit of goals. Weber's preoccupation with structure is apparent from his assumption that if goals are explicitly defined, then organizational rules, procedures, and positions can be structured to achieve those goals; thus maximizing overall organizational efficiency and effectiveness. According to this model, positions are structured in a hierarchical arrangement with each office having authority over those below it. The authority to make decisions is limited to a designated level within the hierarchy. In order to control the authority of a given level, formalized rules and regulations regarding obligations and privileges of each position are explicitly defined. If each person obeys the rules, management will be able to anticipate and control the functioning of the organization to maximize efficiency.

Rules and regulations ensure objectivity and impersonality in the hiring, firing, and promotion processes. The selection process incorporates testing, which ensures proficiency and promotes uniform work quality. Participation in the organization is formalized through contractual agreement, which specifies a financial remuneration. Each employee can predict, within some range, what his or her economic rewards will be from one year to the next. The employee is promoted based on seniority and/or performance. Positions as well as promotions are open to competition and all qualified persons are considered, thus ensuring that the position will be filled by the most competent individual available.

Organizational positions are constant and independent of the persons holding them. A position is not influenced by the incumbent; consequently, the individual's personal characteristics should have no bearing on the position or the quality of work performed. The person filling the position (office) is relevant to the organization only to the degree to which that person competently executes, according to the rules of the organization, the roles assigned to him or her. Personal characteristics are not relevant to filling positions or role execution. Rather, technical competency is the criterion underlying these two processes. Each person has a jurisdiction, permitting complete authority over a sphere of work activities. The sphere is clearly defined to eliminate duplication of function, and the activities encompassed in this sphere are highly specialized.

Weber outlined the following characteristics of rational-legal authority:[25]

1. A continuous organization of official functions bound by rules.

2. A specific sphere of competence:
   a. A sphere of obligations to perform functions which have been marked off as a systematic division of labor.
   b. The provision of the incumbent with necessary authority to carry out these functions.
   c. The means of compulsion are clearly defined and their use is subject to definite conditions.

3. The organization of offices follows the principle of hierarchy, that is, each lower office is under the control and supervision of a higher one. Rights of appeal and statement of grievances run from lower to higher offices.

4. The rules which regulate the conduct of an office must be applied in a fully rational manner which necessitates specialized training.
   a. Only those who have demonstrated an adequate technical training are eligible for appointment to official positions.

5. It is a matter of principle that the members of the administrative staff should be completely separated from ownership of the means of production or administration.
   a. Officials are obligated to render an account of the use of the non-human-means of production.
   b. Spatial separation of home and office is specified.

6. Official positions are appropriated to the incumbent. He or she does not have the authority of this appropriation.

7. Administrative acts, decisions and rules are formulated and re-
    corded in writing even in cases where oral discussion is the rule
    or is mandatory.

Thus, Weber's bureaucratic model has many assumptions and principles in common with classical management theory. Among these
are: the organization as a closed system; rationality; maximization of
efficiency; impersonal social relations; appointment and promotion
on the basis of merit; hierarchy of authority; authority inherent to
the position; abstract rules or laws covering assignment of tasks and
decision-making; and specialization and division of labor.

Many criticisms have been leveled against the bureaucratic
model. Among the most insightful are those of Champion, Philip
Selznick, and Victor Thompson.[26] First, as noted earlier, people do
not behave like parts of an efficient machine, that is, people are not
completely rational. They are at least partially emotional and their
feelings interfere with their rationality. Consequently, there are always differences between what a person should do according to
bureaucratic theory and what he or she actually does.[27] In its ideal
form, a bureaucracy would eliminate all unwanted extra-orga-
nizational influences on the behavior of its members. Thus, the individual would act only in the organization's interest and in doing
so, would serve their own. In reality, individuals do not always act in
the organization's best interest, which is sometimes in conflict with
their own. In addition, they may not have complete knowledge to
define the best interests or goals of the organizations.

The second major criticism of the bureaucratic model is that, in
most organizations, rules cannot be written to govern every situation.
According to Weber, anyone can carry out the supervisor's role effectively to the extent that she or he complies with the rules governing the role. But Selznick notes that events frequently occur that do
not fall clearly within any given department's jurisdictional boundaries.[28] In other situations, there may be clear jurisdiction but no
formal rules and procedures to cover the situation. At every level
within an organization, situations will arise in which there is no substitute for a person who can function independently in the absence
of formalized rules and procedures. Overconformity to rules can be
detrimental as well as beneficial in promoting organizational effectiveness. Formalized rules and conformity to them can obstruct
creativity and flexibility. Particularly during periods of organizational
change, lack of flexibility may result in conflict. The bureaucratic

model of organization, although characterized by high productive efficiency, generates structural arrangements that support low innovative capacity.[29] In a competitive economic environment, organizations must manifest some adaptability of economic resources and new product markets if they are to successfully compete and survive. The perpetuation of the status quo poses certain structural obstacles that can seriously restrict innovation. The bureaucratic model deals with stable, routine tasks; under these conditions, efficiency can be maximized. When an organization is in rapid flux and a change in tasks is necessary, a stable division of labor is not possible. Other processes such as planning, coordination, and production must be adjusted to the given changes whether they be technological, structural, processual, or goal-oriented. When this occurs, the efficiency of the organization is decreased.

Informal groups, which continuously modify existing impersonal social arrangements, exist in formal organizations. The formal hierarchies of authority and communication channels are often in competition with the informal social networks of employees who communicate information. Rule enforcement is also often subject to informal worker approval. Likewise, Selznick noted that every organization creates an informal structure and that even organizational goals are effected through such structures.[30]

The bureaucratic model fails to take into account the relations between the various subsystems within the organization. Because of the overriding concern for structure, the bureaucratic model usually does not deal adequately with the problem of intraorganizational conflict of interest.[31]

The final criticism that we shall consider is that the bureaucratic model cannot deal with structural inconsistencies such as the manager having less technical knowledge than subordinate employees over whom he or she has authority. The discrepancy between expertise of the superior and subordinate has fostered much research on the professional and the professional organization, which will be discussed in more detail later in the chapter.

Nonbureaucratic Model   The bureaucratic model is based on an externalized form of rational control manifest in the centralization of power (hierarchy of authority positions) and formalization. A second type of rational control—professionalization—has emerged from the comparative research of Arthur Stinchcombe, Richard Hall, and Peter Blau, Wolf Heydebrand, and Robert Stauffer.[32] Highly professionalized organizations with large numbers of employees who possess high levels of competency, experience, and education may at the same time exhibit low levels of such bureaucratic characteristics as supervision and control of the work process, formalization of job-related rules and procedures, and centralization of decision-making.

Jerald Hage's axiomatic theory of organization is a contemporary example of a structural model of organization.[33] This model is rational (means-ends oriented). It deals with the same structural variables (centralization, formalization, specialization or complexity, and so on) and performance variable (effectiveness and efficiency) as does the bureaucratic model. However, the objective of Hage's model is to maximize effectiveness, adaptability, and job satisfaction as opposed to efficiency. The model thus emphasizes the opposite end of the continuum of structural and performance variables than does the Weberian Model. From a theory construction perspective, Hage's theory is certainly more sophisticated than earlier structural models. It incorporates seven propositions and twenty-one corollaries (see Table 2-4). This model considers four ends, or performance dimensions, and four means, or structural dimensions. The structural dimensions of (1) complexity, or specialization, (2) centralization of power, or hierarchy of authority, (3) formalization, or standardization, and (4) stratification are seen as means variables that influence the organizational ends of (1) adaptiveness, (2) production or effectiveness, (3) efficiency, and (4) job satisfaction. Organizational ends are operationally defined as follows: adaptiveness is the number of new programs and procedures adopted per year by the organization; production, or effectiveness, is the number of units produced per year and the rate of increase in the number of units produced per year; efficiency, or cost, is the output per year; and job satisfaction, or morale, is the turnover rate of employees per year.[34] Hage's four organizational means are operationally defined as follows: complexity, or specialization, is the number of occupational specialities and the level of training required; centralization and hierarchy of authority are the proportion of employees who participate in decision-making and the number of areas in which they participate; formalization, or standardization, is the number of jobs that are codified and the range of variation allowed within jobs; and finally, stratification is the differences in income and prestige among jobs or status levels.[35]

Thus, the organization is viewed as a system apart from other organizations and the nonsocial environment. There is no consideration in Hage's model of environmental influences or contextual dimensions; thus this axiomatic theory is a closed-system model that

53

TABLE 2–4 Major Propositions and Corollaries of Hage's Axiomatic Theory

Major Propositions:

I. The higher the centralization, the higher the production.

II. The higher the formalization, the higher the efficiency.

III. The higher the centralization, the higher the formalization.

IV. The higher the stratification, the lower the job satisfaction.

V. The higher the stratification, the higher the production.

VI. The higher the stratification, the lower the adaptiveness.

VII. The higher the complexity, the lower the centralization.

Derived Corollaries:

1. The higher the formalization, the higher the production.

2. The higher the centralization, the higher the efficiency.

3. The lower the job satisfaction, the higher the production.

4. The lower the job satisfaction, the lower the adaptiveness.

5. The higher the production, the lower the adaptiveness.

6. The higher the complexity, the lower the production.

7. The higher the complexity, the lower the formalization.

8. The higher the production, the higher the efficiency.

9. The higher the stratification, the higher the formalization.

10. The higher the efficiency, the lower the complexity.

11. The higher the centralization, the lower the job satisfaction.

12. The higher the centralization, the lower the adaptiveness.

13. The higher the stratification, the lower the complexity.

14. The higher the complexity, the higher the job satisfaction.

15. The lower the complexity, the lower the adaptiveness.

16. The higher the stratification, the higher the efficiency.

17. The higher the efficiency, the lower the job satisfaction.

18. The higher the efficiency, the lower the adaptiveness.

19. The higher the centralization, the higher the stratification.

20. The higher the formalization, the lower the job satisfaction.

21. The higher the formalization, the lower the adaptiveness.

Limits Proposition:

VIII. Production imposes limits on complexity, centralization, formalization, stratification, adaptiveness, efficiency, and job satisfaction.

Source: Jerald Hage, "An Axiomatic Theory of Organizations," *Administrative Science Quarterly* 10, no. 3 (December 1965): 300.

allows for the maximization of rational (means-ends) relationships between these internal variables. It is even possible to study the interrelationships of means and of ends, resulting in maximum functional interdependence of organizational dimensions. With rationality comes predictability and with predictability comes control.

Much of Hage's subsequent research views organizations as open systems. This is evidenced by his work on organizations as cybernetic systems[36] and his analysis of interorganizational dependency reflected in joint programs.[37] This research will be discussed in chapters eight and eleven, respectively.

Jerald Hage and Michael Aiken's models have been tested, revised, and extended by Steven K. Paulson.[38] Paulson developed a causal theory of interorganizational relationships by integrating Hage's propositions found in Table 2–4 with Hage and Aiken's propositions found in Table 2–5. He later tested two expressions of this theory. Paulson's asymmetrical causal model of relationships between means and ends variables with interorganizational relations as the ultimate dependent variable is depicted in Table 2–6. His operational definitions of concepts differ somewhat from those in Hage's model. This initial attempt at causal model-building is not meant to be a full-scale theory but rather a partial theory that permits ordering variables in terms of their causal priority. This model is based on the structural (means) and performance (ends) variables enumerated by Hage. Paulson adds the term *linkage variable* to refer to communication within the system. He took the rationale for the ordering of the variables from the works of Hage and Aiken.[39] The explanation set forth by Paulson for the causal ordering of the variables is as follows: Initially, an organization has a certain degree of specializa-

TABLE 2–5   A Set of Propositions Which Represent an Explanation for the Degree of Interorganizational Relations as Measured by the Number of Joint Programs

1. A high degree of complexity varies directly with a high number of joint programs.
2. A high degree of program innovation varies directly with a high number of joint programs.
3. A high rate of internal communication varies directly with a high number of joint programs.
4. A high degree of centralization varies inversely with a high number of joint programs.
5. A high degree of formalization varies inversely with a high number of joint programs.

Source: Michael Aiken and Jerald Hage, "Organizational Interdependence and Intraorganizational Structure," *American Sociological Review* 33, no. 6 (December 1968): 915.

TABLE 2–6   Paulson's Asymmetrical Model

STRUCTURAL (MEANS) VARIABLES			LINKAGE VARIABLE	PERFORMANCE (ENDS) VARIABLES				FOCUS VARIABLE
X_1 COMP	X_3	X_4	X_5	X_6	X_7	X_8	X_9	X_{10}
STRT	CENT	FORM	COMM	EFFC	JOBS	EFFT	INNO	IORS
X_2								

X_1 = Complexity (COMP)—internal specialization in terms of variety of personnel skills and training and number of specific tasks.

X_2 = Stratification (STRT)—individual status mobility.

X_3 = Centralization (CENT)—degree of hierarchical authority with respect to involvement in decision making.

X_4 = Formalization (FORM)—standardization of behavior.

X_5 = Communication (COMM)—degree of transmission of internal information.

X_6 = Efficiency (EFFC)—amount of resources expended relative to goal attainment.

X_7 = Job Satisfaction (JOBS)—morale of organizational members.

X_8 = Effectiveness (EFFT)—degree of goal attainment (production).

X_9 = Innovation (INNO)—flexibility in adapting programs to the environment (adaptiveness).

X_{10} = Interorganizational relationships (IORS)—interdependence among organizations on the basis of resource need (number of joint programs).

Source: Steven K. Paulson, "Causal Analysis of Interorganizational Relations: An Axiomatic Theory Revised," *Administrative Science Quarterly* 19, no. 3 (September 1974): 321, 324.

tion of skills and tasks (complexity) and status mobility (stratification). Changes in these variables are initiated by variables outside the system (these external variables are not discussed). Here the organization is viewed as an open system with the ultimate dependent variable of interorganizational relations. Complexity and stratification are assumed by Paulson to be causally unrelated with complexity increasing and stratification decreasing. According to Paulson, as complexity increases, more persons have the skills and roles that qualify them to participate in decision-making, making it more diffuse and decentralized. As decision-making becomes decentralized, the formal mechanisms of control decrease; thus, formalization decreases.

The increase in specialization, decentralization of decision-making and decrease of formalization and stratification results in a greater need for communication, since information necessary for performance becomes more diverse in content and source. As the organization becomes more diverse and less formalized (a less restrictive environment), efficiency of performance decreases and job morale increases. Paulson posits that effectiveness also decreases because as formal controls lessen and specialization increases, the emphasis will be in terms of qualitative achievement. Finally, Paulson writes:

> As organizational members become increasingly specialized and experience more freedom (more control over decision making, fewer regulations, increased communication), encouragement (lower status differentials, higher inducements either as salaries or resources available for task completion) and an emphasis on quality performance rather than quantity of production they will develop and recommend improvements, modifications, and expansion of products and/or services; that is, innovation will increase. . . . As innovation increases, the organization requires resources to implement the new programs and services which can be obtained by establishing relationships with other organizations.[40]

At this point, it is important to point out that Paulson's model also concentrates on the structural and performance variables of organizations, as does Weber's bureaucratic model. However, unlike the bureaucratic models, which are designed to maximize efficiency, this model is designed to maximize innovative and interorganization relations. Thus, the two models emphasize opposing structural and performance variables, as depicted in Table 2–7.

The bureaucratic structural model may be applicable to a small number of highly structured organizations, but it cannot be applied to a large number of other organizations in which professionals are employed at lower levels within the organization and power is related to both competency and position. To impose a bureaucratic model on such organizations would be dysfunctional for both the organization and its employees. A structural model that assumes variability of raw material inputs, nonroutine knowledge, complexity of employees, task differentiation, decentralization of power, and low formalization of work-related rules and procedures, is a more viable one for this type of organization than the bureaucratic model. However, assuming that all organizations are composed of professionals with high levels of education is equally fallacious as imposing the

TABLE 2-7   Characteristics of the Bureaucratic and Nonbureaucratic Models

DIMENSIONS	BUREAUCRATIC MODEL	NONBUREAUCRATIC MODEL
Complexity	Low	High
Stratification	High	Low
Centralization	High	Low
Formalization	High	Low
Communication	Low	High
Efficiency	High	Low
Job Satisfaction	Low	High
Effectiveness*	High	Low
Innovation	Low	High
Interorganizational Relationships	Low	High

*Weber defines effectiveness in terms of efficiency, while Paulson defines it in terms of degree of goal attainment (production).

bureaucratic model on all organizations. Thus, the assumption of variability in these structural and performance variables from organization to organization is a more viable approach and forms the basis for the model used in this book.

Goals Model

The goals model is derived from the structural models just presented, but it emphasizes the performance dimensions of the organization as opposed to the structural dimensions of the organization. Thus, the goals approach is based on many of the same assumptions and organizational dimensions as the structural models, but emphasis is on the degree to which the organization effectively accomplishes its goals. The performance (ends) variables, outlined in Hage's Axiomatic Theory in the previous section, are organizational goals in the most general sense.[41] More specifically, some researchers equate "effectiveness" with the "goals approach."[42] An extensive review of the literature on organizational goals and effectiveness is found in chapter eleven. The purpose of this discussion is to review the assumptions, characteristics and limitations of the goals model.

A considerable number of organizational theorists define a complex organization as goal-oriented. Peter Blau and Richard Scott stated that formal organizations are social units "established for the explicit purpose of achieving certain goals."[43] Edward Gross wrote that whatever else theorists have to say on the general subject, there seems to be agreement that "it is the dominating presence of a goal that marks off an 'organization' ... from all other kinds of systems."[44] Definition of goals as implicit or explicit,[45] profit or nonprofit,[46] quality or quantity,[47] stated or real, systems- or product-characteristic,[48] operational or nonoperational[49] has consumed a great deal of effort by those who write from the goals perspective.

Three major assumptions underlie this model:

1. The organization exists to achieve goals.

2. The organization develops a rational procedure for the achievement of goals.

3. The organization is assessed in terms of the effectiveness of goal attainment.

There are several problems in attempting to define organizational goals. Two of the most important are (1) deciding whose goals are most relevant to the organization or research and (2) differentiating between "actual goals" and "stated goals." In establishing who is to define the organization's goals there are several viable possibilities, such as: the chief executives of the organization; top management levels in the hierarchy of authority; published accounts such as five-year plans. All these sources have limitations, however. The chief executive will obviously represent the "establishment's" view, while top managers may be more concerned with specific goals of their departments. Published accounts often posit aspirations and therefore reflect what should be achieved as opposed to what is possible.

The discrepancies between the ideal (stated) and the real organizational goals is frequently left undefined and therefore unmeasured. The stated goals are often substituted for actual goals by an interviewee asked to list organizational goals. Selwyn Becker and Duncan Neuhauser suggested a way of measuring organizational efficiency that gauges the discrepancy between stated goals and actual goals:

If, ignoring minor differences in wording, the stated goal structures are in accord with the central function of the organization, then measures of how efficiently the central function is achieved constitute a good gauge of relative organizational efficiency.[50]

59

This definition leaves unanswered the question of how to measure efficiency (goals) if the stated goal structure is not in accord with the organization's central function. The application of the goal model leads to comparison between the ideal and real organizational goals, in that the organization's effectiveness depends on how closely the ideal and real correspond. Therefore, an organization may appear to be more effective than it actually is because the ideal held by those defining the goals is relatively low. Conversely, a truly effective organization may appear to be ineffective because of the unrealistically high expectations held by those defining the goals. Thus, Amitai Etzioni observed, the effectiveness of the organization depends not on its performance but on the expectations of the goal definer.[51]

The most serious criticism of the goals model pertains to goal identification. If the goals of an organization cannot be identified, organizational effectiveness cannot be measured because the goal approach defines effectiveness in terms of the degree of goal achievement. If goals cannot be defined, a model of analysis that rests on measuring their attainment cannot be applied. A related criticism of the goals model is that there is no general way of measuring effectiveness—this depends on the specific type of organization being studied. The goals of a business organization may be centered around the percentage of net worth, while schools, hospitals and welfare organizations may measure effectiveness in terms of the quality of services delivered to or received by the client.[52]

Etzioni argued that most organizations do not attain their goals in any final sense.[53] Organizations are dynamic, ever-changing entities; their structural characteristics are constantly changing along with their goals. Thus, an ultimate state of goal attainment is next to impossible; rather, the organization survives through the processes of goal substitution and supplementation. For example, the March of Dimes substituted a new goal—a campaign against birth defects—after polio was virtually eliminated by the Salk vaccine.

Most organizational theorists and researchers agree that organizational goals are difficult to define and, if desired, equally difficult to measure in terms of degree of attainment. Chapter eleven discusses in detail organizational goals and their attainment.

Technological Model

Three of the major exponents of the technological model are Joan Woodward, James Thompson, and Charles Perrow.[54] Those theorists who see technology as the major determinant (explanatory dimension) of organizations generally show the various structures and performances that result from differences in the technological

60

system of organizations. For example, Woodward found different operations technologies influence the number of levels of the hierarchy, the degree of centralization, and other organizational dimensions.[55]

The technological model makes no assumption that all organizations are either bureaucratically structured or nonbureaucratically structured; rather, it assumes that many types of organizations exist. Structure and goals are not the bases for typing organizations; organizations are classified according to the kinds of operations technology, tasks and expertise of personnel. These technologies are assumed to influence both the structure and the goals of organizations, Perrow describes the two extreme types of technology in relation to structure:

> When the tasks people perform are well understood, predictable, routine, and repetitive, a bureaucratic structure is the most efficient. . . . Where tasks are not well understood, generally because the "raw material" that each person works on is poorly understood and possibly reactive, recalcitrant, or self-activating, the tasks are nonroutine. Such units or organizations are difficult to bureaucratize. More discretion must be given to lower-level personnel; more interaction is required among personnel at the same level; there must be more emphasis upon experience, "feel," or professionalization. If so, it is difficult to have clear lines of authority, a high degree of division of labor, rules and procedures for everything, exact specifications of duties and responsibilities, and so on. . . .[56]

Similarly, Woodward's three types of organizations are based on three basic types of technology: (1) unit and small-batch production processes (for example, engineering prototypes and original fashion designs); (2) large-batch, mass-production and assembly-line processes (for example, autos, unit construction modules, and metal industries); and (3) continuous-process industries (for example, oil, gas, and chemicals).[57] Woodward has found that no one organizational structure is successful at all times. Rather, in order to be successful, the structure of the organization must be adapted to the operations technology of that organization. Thus, one finds different types of organizational structure (from highly bureaucratic to nonbureaucratic) depending on whether the organization's technology is unit, mass-production, or continuous-flow process.

The first limitation of the technological model is the confusion over the theoretical definition of technology. Woodward defined technology in terms of operations, mostly in industrial organizations, while Perrow defined technology in terms of tasks (routine or non-routine) performed on raw materials (uniform and nonuniform). Naturally, the confusion over the theoretical definition leads to disagreement over the operational definition. The disagreement, as documented by Perrow, is over whether technology "should be restricted to the basic work-flow process, allowing us to measure it through fairly pure indices such as the proportion of single-purpose machines, or whether other aspects of the organization should be included—e.g., sales, personnel, accounting, research and development, industrial relations and so on."[58] When technology is operationalized in terms of the work-flow process, it has little relation to structural characteristics of the organization.[59]

The third limitation has to do with the inability of the model to account for changes in structure that do not proceed from changes in technology. Technological change, like other forms of organizational innovation, is seen as producing organizational communication and input into the decision-making process at the middle management level. This should shift the power from the centralized top management level down to the scientist and engineer at the upper-middle management level, an arrangement that functions best during organizational problem-solving. Most organizations resume their routine functioning after the innovative phase. At this time, the organization would have to be flexible to return to the more centralized structure in which scientists and engineers function purely as technologists, not as decision-makers. If they remain as decision makers, others must be assigned their former roles or the organization will experience a reduction in output. To eliminate the necessity for role transition, tasks involving innovative technology are often assigned to a special research and development department, but of course, this arrangement does not redistribute power. In this case, increased technology does not decentralize the power structure, and the technological model has little explanatory value.

In this text, technology is an important dimension of organizations (for fuller discussion, see chapter four) but it is only one of many that influences the processes, structure, and performance of organizations.

Decision-making Model

The works of James March and Herbert Simon are essential to any discussion of the decision-making model.[60] Their model views humans neither as passive instruments capable only of following directions and incapable of initiating action or exerting influence, nor as sentiment-laden individuals who can be manipulated or motivated to induce participation in the organization. This model views the individual as capable of being a decision-maker. The thought processes that underlie the problem-solving process and rational human choice are central to this model.[61] But, humans are viewed as possessing limited "human intellective capacities in comparison with the complexities of the problem that individuals and organizations face. . . ."[62] Humans are "intended rational" but not wholly rational because (1) not all alternatives of choice are known; (2) not all consequences attached to alternatives are known; (3) people do not have a complete ranking of all possible alternatives and consequences.[63] The decision-making model depicts humans as grossly simplifying the problem in order to make a satisfactory, if not optimum, decision.

March and Simon acknowledge broadly the sentiments, attitudes, beliefs, and desires of humans, but individual characteristics are not analyzed. The organization is the unit of analysis and because individuals satisfy their personal needs (income, job satisfaction, etc.) through the organization, their behavior is controlled. Organizational and personal ends are not necessarily the same except possibly in the case of top administrators. Thus, employees are goal-motivated, but they do not accept goals because they believe in them but rather because the organization has reward mechanisms that are valued by the individual, in this way ensuring his or her involvement.

Perrow wrote that one important implication of March and Simon's model is that to change individual behavior one does not have to change the individual, in the sense of altering his or her personality in teaching human relations skills. Instead, what is necessary is to change the premises on which decisions are made. Thus, one shapes employee behavior presumably by making rewards and sanctions coincide with desired premises.[64]

March and Simon's simplified model for decision-making has a number of characteristics:

(1) Optimizing is replaced by satisfying—the requirement that satisfactory levels of the criterion variables be attained. (2) Alternatives of action and consequences of action are discovered sequentially through search processes. (3) Repertories of action programs are developed by organizations and individuals, and these serve as the alternatives of choice in recurrent situations. (4) Each specific action program deals with a restricted range of

situations and a restricted range of consequences. (5) Each action program is capable of being executed in semi-independence of the others—they are only loosely coupled together.[65]

According to the decision-making model, action in organizations is considered to be goal-oriented and adaptive. Organizations are viewed as rational systems consisting of various parts (departments) making decisions that affect relations with other parts and the organization as a whole. Thus, the decision-maker who wishes to achieve an objective chooses from available strategies. The chosen strategy, the state of the organizational givens and the competitive strategies determine the decision-maker's success in achieving organizational goals.[66]

This concentration on goal achievement is not unlike the structural models or the goals model discussed earlier. The important difference is that the decision-making model emphasizes the decision making process and the quality of the resulting decision. The structural models, by contrast, are concerned with the means or structural dimensions that result in varied goal attainment, and the goal model centers on goals and any organizational component or dimension that will result in the attainment of that goal. Similarities in the decision-making and bureaucratic models include the view of authority from the top down, division of labor, specialization, and concentration on stability with limited adaptive processes.

The major weakness of the decision-making model is the lack of emphasis on the organizational components (environment, technology, structure, and so on) that are not central to the decision-making process. This model views all structural and process variables in terms of their effect on the decision-making process, which in turn affects organizational performance. Thus, all structural and process variables are considered to have only indirect effects on goals; their direct effects are ignored.

The decision-making model can also be criticized for not dealing adequately with individual's ideas, attitudes, beliefs, and sentiments. In short, it does not deal with interpersonal relations and the informal organizational structure. Although this criticism can be made of all the other models presented, this limitation is especially critical for the decision-making model because of the part informal power plays in the decision-making process.[67]

The final limitation of the decision-model is that although complete knowledge of all decision-making alternatives and access to all possible strategies is not assumed, this model does assume that the decision-maker will act objectively in relation to the organizational goals, regardless of personal priorities. This assumption is highly unrealistic. Individuals do not always act objectively in the best interest of the organization. In fact, they often act in their own best interest, which is frequently in conflict with that of the organization.

SUMMARY

In this text, the organization is viewed as an open system. Consequently, by accepting organizational outputs and supplying inputs, the environment has a continuous effect on organizational contexts, structure, process, and performance. But the position is taken that no single organizational component or dimension is *the* determinant of all other organizational components and dimensions. Rather, each dimension influences every other dimension and in turn is influenced by them. In order to adequately assess the organization in its entirety, an integration of related assumptions, characteristics, and concerns of the structural, technological, decision-making, and goals models is necessary. It is hoped that the model presented in chapter one, which integrates all the dimensions of the organization, will aid the reader in understanding how each of the models in this chapter contributes to a more complete knowledge of organizations.

The major weakness of this model is the omission of the human relations dimensions, in which the individual is the unit of analysis. This text concentrates on the organization as the unit of analysis, and thus only implicitly includes these dimensions. Of course, the human dimensions are extremely important; but a model can only incorporate a limited number of dimensions and analyze a limited number of relationships between them. It is assumed throughout this text that the individual is the basic interacting unit and that human relations are the basis of all social entities—groups, departments, and organizations.

NOTES

1. Ralph M. Stogdill, "Dimensions of Organization Theory," in James D. Thompson and Victor Vroom, eds., *Organizational Design and Research* (Pittsburgh: University of Pittsburgh Press, 1971), p. 4.
2. The possible exceptions to this statement are the works of J. Victor Baldridge and Charles Perrow. See J. Victor Baldridge, *Power and Conflict in the*

University (New York: John Wiley & Sons, Inc., 1971); and Charles Perrow, *Complex Organizations* (Glenview, Ill.: Scott, Foresman, and Company, 1972).

3. Dean J. Champion, *The Sociology of Organizations* (New York: McGraw Hill, 1974), p. 27.

4. Philip Selznick, *TVA and Grass Roots: A Study in the Sociology of Formal Organizations* (Berkeley: University of California Press, 1960). For a more systematic view, see Philip Selznick, *Leadership in Administration* (Evanston, Ill.: Row Peterson, 1957).

5. Melville Dalton, *Men Who Manage* (New York: John Wiley & Sons, Inc., 1959).

6. Perrow, *Complex Organizations*.

7. Richard M. Cyert and James G. March, *A Behavioral Theory of the Firm* (Englewood Cliffs, N.J.: Prentice Hall, Inc., 1963), chapters 1, 2, 3, and 6.

8. Charles Perrow, "The Analysis of Goals in Complex Organizations," *American Sociological Review* 26, no. 6 (December 1961): 854–866.

9. Cyert and March, *A Behavioral Theory of the Firm*, p. 35.

10. The above discussion was adapted from Ralf Dahrendorf's discussion of the difference in the structural functional and conflict perspectives of society. The term *social organization* was changed to *organization*. Ralf Dahrendorf, "Toward a Theory of Social Conflict," *The Journal of Conflict Resolution* 2, no. 2 (June 1958): 170–183.

11. Baldridge, *Power and Conflict in the University*, p. 14.

12. George H. Rice, Jr., and Dean W. Bishoprick, *Conceptual Models of Organization* (New York: Appleton-Century-Crofts, 1971), p. 165.

13. Perrow, *Complex Organizations*, pp. 148–149. See also Chester Barnard, *The Functions of the Executive* (Cambridge, Mass.: Harvard University Press, 1938).

14. Herbert A. Simon, *Administrative Behavior*, 2nd ed. (New York: The Macmillan Company, 1957), p. 102.

15. James D. Thompson, *Organizations in Action* (New York: McGraw-Hill, 1967), p. 6.

16. Daniel Katz and Robert L. Kahn, *The Social Psychology of Organizations* (New York: John Wiley & Sons, Inc., 1966), p. 26.

17. Walter Buckley, *Sociology and Modern Systems Theory* (Englewood Cliffs, N.J.: Prentice Hall, 1967), p. 39.

18. Daniel Katz and Robert L. Kahn, "Open Systems Theory," in Oscar Grusky and George A. Miller, eds., *The Sociology of Organization* (New York: The Free Press, 1970), p. 150.

19. Ibid., pp. 152–156.

20. Alvin L. Bertrand, *Social Organization: A General Systems and Role Theory Perspective* (Philadelphia: F. A. Davis Company, 1972), pp. 97–103.

21. Buckley, *Sociology and Modern Systems Theory*, p. 58.

22. Thompson, *Organizations in Action*.

23. See Henri Fayol, *General and Industrial Management*, trans. Constance Storrs (London: Pitman, 1949); Oliver Sheldon, *The Philosophy of Management* (London: Pitman, 1923); J. D. Mooney and A. C. Reilley, *The Principles of Organizations* (New York: Harper and Row, 1939); L. H. Gulick and L. Urwick, eds., *Papers on the Science of Administration* (New York: Columbia University, Institute of Public Administration, 1937); Mary Parker Follett, *Dynamic Administration* (New York: Longman, 1941); Frederick W. Taylor, *Scientific Management* (New York: Harper and Row, 1947); Joseph Massie,

"Management Theory," in James G. March, ed., *Handbook of Organizations* (Chicago: Rand McNally and Company, 1965), pp. 394–402.

24. Max Weber, *The Theory of Social and Economic Organization*, trans. A. M. Henderson and T. Parsons (New York: Free Press, 1947), pp. 328–340.

25. Ibid.

26. Champion, *The Sociology of Organizations*, pp. 36–40; Philip Selznick, "An Approach to a Theory of Bureaucracy," *American Sociological Review* 8, no. 1 (February 1943): 47–54; Victor Thompson, "Bureaucracy and Innovation," *Administrative Science Quarterly* 10, no. 1 (June 1965): 1–20.

27. Champion, *The Sociology of Organizations*, p. 36.

28. Selznick, "An Approach to a Theory of Bureaucracy," pp. 47–54; Selznick, *TVA and Grass Roots: A Study in the Sociology of Formal Organizations*.

29. Victor Thompson, "Bureaucracy and Innovation," pp. 1–20.

30. Selznick, "An Approach to a Theory of Bureaucracy," pp. 47–54.

31. James G. March and Herbert A. Simon, *Organizations* (New York: John Wiley & Sons, Inc., 1958).

32. Arthur Stinchcombe, "Bureaucratic and Craft Administration of Production: A Comparative Study," *Administrative Science Quarterly* 4, no. 3 (September 1959): 168–187; Richard H. Hall, "Professionalization and Bureaucratization," *American Sociological Review* 33, no. 1 (February 1968): 92–104; Peter M. Blau, Wolf V. Heydebrand, and Robert E. Stauffer, "The Structure of Small Bureaucracies," *American Sociological Review* 31, no. 2 (April 1966): 176–191.

33. Jerald Hage, "An Axiomatic Theory of Organizations," *Administrative Science Quarterly* 10, no. 3 (December 1965): 289–320.

34. Ibid., p. 393.

35. Ibid., pp. 393–394.

36. Jerald Hage and Michael Aiken, *Communication and Organizational Control: Cybernetics in Health and Welfare Settings* (New York: Wiley-Interscience, 1974).

37. Michael Aiken and Jerald Hage, "Organizational Interdependence and Intraorganizational Structure," *American Sociological Review* 33, no. 6 (December 1968): 912–930.

38. Steven K. Paulson, "Causal Analysis of Interorganizational Relations: An Axiomatic Theory Revised," *Administrative Science Quarterly* 19, no. 3 (September 1974): 319–337.

39. In addition to the studies cited in notes 33 and 37, Paulson mentions the following work as especially relevant to the ordering of these variables: Jerald Hage and Michael Aiken, *Social Change in Complex Organizations* (New York: Random House, 1970), pp. 43–45.

40. Paulson, "Causal Analysis of Interorganizational Relations: An Axiomatic Theory Revised," p. 325.

41. Hage, "An Axiomatic Theory of Organizations," pp. 289–320.

42. James L. Price, *Handbook of Organizational Measurement* (Lexington, Mass.: D. C. Heath and Company, 1972).

43. Peter M. Blau and Richard W. Scott, *Formal Organizations: A Comparative Approach* (San Francisco: Chandler Publishing Company, 1962), p. 1.

44. Edward Gross, "The Definition of Organizational Goals," *British Journal of Sociology* 20, no. 3 (September 1969): 277.

45. James D. Thompson, "Models of Organization and Administrative Sys-

tems," in *The Social Sciences: Problems and Orientations* (The Hague: Mouton/ UNESCO), pp. 395–405.

46. Martin Albrow, "The Study of Organizations—Objectivity or Bias?" in J. Gould, ed., *Penguin Social Science Survey, 1968* (Harmondsworth, England: Penguin, 1968), pp. 146–167.

47. Perrow, "The Analysis of Goals in Complex Organizations," pp. 854–866.

48. Jerald Hage and Michael Aiken, "Routine Technology, Social Structure, and Organizational Goals," *Administrative Science Quarterly* 14, no. 3 (September 1969): 366–377.

49. March and Simon, *Organizations*.

50. Selwyn Becker and Duncan Neuhauser, *The Efficient Organization* (New York: Elsevier, 1975), p. 47.

51. Amitai Etzioni, *Modern Organizations* (Englewood Cliffs, N.J.: Prentice-Hall, 1964).

52. Basil S. Georgopoulos and Floyd C. Mann, *The Community General Hospital* (New York: Macmillan Co., 1962).

53. Etzioni, *Modern Organizations*.

54. Joan Woodward, *Industrial Organizations: Theory and Practice* (Oxford, England: Oxford University Press, 1965); James Thompson, "Models of Organization and Administrative Systems"; Perrow, *Complex Organizations*.

55. Woodward, *Industrial Organizations: Theory and Practice*.

56. Perrow, *Complex Organizations*, p. 166.

57. Woodward, *Industrial Organizations: Theory and Practice*.

58. Perrow, *Complex Organizations*, pp. 168–169.

59. David J. Hickson, D. S. Pugh, and Diana C. Pheysey, "Operations Technology and Organizational Structure: An Empirical Reappraisal," *Administrative Science Quarterly* 14, no. 3 (September 1969): 378–379.

60. This discussion of the decision-making model has drawn heavily from two major works: March and Simon's *Organizations* and Simon's *Administrative Behavior*.

61. March and Simon, *Organizations*, p. 169.

62. Ibid., p. 169.

63. Ibid., pp. 137–150.

64. Perrow, *Complex Organizations*, p. 154.

65. March and Simon, *Organizations*, p. 169.

66. David W. Miller and Martin K. Starr, *The Structure of Human Decisions* (Englewood Cliffs, N.J.: Prentice-Hall, 1967), p. 27.

67. For a more complete discussion of this criticism, see Blau and Scott, *Formal Organizations: A Comparative Approach*, p. 38.

part II
ENVIRONMENTAL AND CONTEXTUAL DIMENSIONS

As open systems, organizations must deal not only with their environments but also with a number of contextual dimensions. Environmental dimensions include the complexity and stability of the cultural and social structures, both macro and micro, that are external to the organization. Contextual dimensions are internal characteristics of the organization, such as size and technology. These contextual and environmental dimensions place constraints on organizational structure and performance. Chapter three deals with the dimensions of environmental change and complexity, while chapter four elaborates the major contextual dimensions of technology and size. Theoretical and operational definitions of each of these dimensions are explored. Through structural-contingency-model research, chapter three explores the interrelationships of environmental dimensions and their effect on the organizational dimensions. Chapter four examines the interrelationships of contextual dimensions and their effect on the structural dimensions of organizations.

3

ENVIRONMENTAL DIMENSIONS

OBJECTIVES

The major objectives of this chapter are:

1. To explore the implications of the open-systems model of organizations.
2. To differentiate between macro and micro environments of organizations.
3. To elaborate the organization's interdependency with its task environment.
4. To discuss approaches to the relationship between the organization and its environment.
    a. the natural-selection model
    b. the structural-contingency model
    c. the resource-dependency model
5. To differentiate between two types of organizational dependency:
    a. functional–economic
    b. political–legal
6. To elaborate the correlates of organizational dependency.
7. To discuss the effect of the organizational decision-maker's uncertainty about the environment.
8. To define and elaborate two major dimensions of organizational environment:
    a. complexity
    b. change
9. To discuss research exploring the structural-contingency model of organization–environment relations.

INTRODUCTION

From the discussion in chapter one of the model that forms the basis of analysis for this book, it should be readily apparent that organizations are viewed as open systems. Thus, the environments of organizations are critical to the functioning of organizations and to our understanding of them. Organizations are not perceived as determined by any one factor but as influenced by many factors—context and goals as well as environment. Consequently, the position taken here is that there is no single organizational structure that is most effective in all types of organizational environments.

DEFINITION OF ORGANIZATIONAL ENVIRONMENT

Although the terms "organizational environment" and "organizational context" are often used interchangeably in the literature, they have been given separate meanings in this text. *Organizational environment* designates all influences on the organization that are *external* to the organization. The environment consists of all elements (persons, groups, and organizations) with which the organization exchanges inputs and outputs. *Organizational context* is used to designate such dimensions as size and technology that are found within the organization but are not structural, process, or performance dimensions (for example, organizational technology is the internal operations and activities that convert the organizational inputs into outputs). This chapter examines the organizational environment; chapter four analyzes the contextual dimensions of organizations.

The environmental elements can be grouped into two levels. The first level is the macro level, which consists of the general cultural conditions in which the organization exists. These include the political–legal, economic, educational, and religious influences on the organization. Organizations in all areas of the world operate within the context of these larger institutional environments. Relatively little research has been conducted on the influence of the cultural environment on the organization because the cultural environment is the most difficult to define theoretically and operationally, making it difficult to analyze. One study of the effects of the political–legal institutional environment on organizations is the research of William Evan, which explored the effects of law on the origin of organizations.[1] Evan found that after the organization emerges it may be functional or dysfunctional for the law that pre-

72

cipitated it. Thus, Evan detected the reciprocal relationship between the cultural environment and the organization that functions in such an environment. Also at the macro level are social structural elements of the environments that affect organizations. Included in this category are communities and societies.

Although research dealing with cultural and macro structural environments is relatively scarce, Koya Azumi has set up propositions defining general environmental elements that are necessary for the proliferation of organizations.[2] Unsupported by research, Azumi hypothesized that organizational proliferation is a consequence of both environmental needs and the abundance of environmental resources (knowledge, power, wealth, and population). From Seymour Lipset's generalization that organizations proliferate in environments that are urban, industrialized, highly populated, and well-educated,[3] Azumi formulated the propositions found in Table 3–1. Thus, as environmental needs and resources increase in a given society, the number of organizations will increase.

TABLE 3–1   The Proliferation of Organizations

PROPOSITION 1
The greater the articulated environmental needs, the larger the number of organizations.

PROPOSITION 2
The greater the environmental resources, the larger the number of organizations.

PROPOSITION 2.1
The greater the knowledge in the environment, the larger the number of organizations found in it.

PROPOSITION 2.2
The greater the power in the environment, the larger the number of organizations found in it.

PROPOSITION 2.3
The greater the wealth in the environment, the larger the number of organizations found in it.

PROPOSITION 2.4
The larger the population in the environment, the larger the number of organizations found in it.

Source: Koya Azumi, "Environmental Needs, Resources, and Agents," in Koya Azumi and Jerald Hage, eds., *Organizational Systems* (Lexington, Mass.: D. C. Heath and Company, 1972), p. 94.

The micro level of environment includes individuals, special-interest groups, professional organizations, and organizations other than the focal one. This micro environment is often called the *task environment* because it is the portion of the total setting relevant for goal setting and goal attainment.[4] On the whole, most analyses of task environments concentrate on organizations with which the system under analysis interacts (interorganizational networks). The elements of the environment are identified in terms of the focal organization's actual or potential interaction or transactions, both inputs and outputs. It is this task environment that has been most often related, through research, to the internal structure and processes of the organization.

Although the task environment of organizations is made up of individuals and groups as well as other organizations, the latter are the most numerous and powerful elements. A set of organizations with which the focal organization interacts can be mapped in much the same way sociograms are constructed. These organizations form an "organizational set" that provides the inputs and receives the outputs of the focal organization.[5] Thus, interorganizational dependency or organizational sets are formed when organizations seek to improve their position and use exchange as a process to accomplish this. This organizational set by no means consists of the same organizations over time, nor do the relationships remain the same. A portion of the environment that may be significant for the organization at one time may not be significant at another time. This is due not only to the fact that elements of the environment vary from being hostile to neutral to supportive, but also because the goals and needs of the focal organization vary over time.

Although the relationships between the organization and its micro environment has been more thoroughly researched than its relationship with the macro environment, knowledge concerning these relationships remains inadequate. For this reason, and because the focus of this text is on the dimensions of organizations and how they vary, emphasis will be placed on the dimensions of the task environment that influence the dimensions of organizations.

ORGANIZATIONAL – ENVIRONMENTAL DEPENDENCY

Organizations function in conjunction with their environment, both receiving inputs from this environment and producing output for the environment to consume. Thus, there is an exchange process between any organization and its environment. As the focal organization interacts with the environment to secure resources, it becomes dependent on the environment. Reciprocity is established as the focal organization reciprocates by supplying resources necessary for the survival of its environment. Because reciprocity is binding, the obligated organization gives up some decision-making autonomy. This process of reciprocity consists of both conflict and cooperation. Environmental dependency is the degree to which a system relies on specific elements in the environment for growth and maintenance.

This conjunctive relationship can be viewed as being controlled by the environment, in which case the environmental dimensions are viewed as predictor variables for various structural and performance dimensions of the organization. Paul Lawrence and Jay Lorsch state that "if an organization's internal states and processes are consistent with external demands, the findings of this study suggest it will be [efficient]."[6] Here the organization is viewed as adjusting to the environment; the environment is the predictor variable. On the other hand, the organization can be viewed as the independent variable influencing other organizations in positive or negative ways. James Thompson also saw the interaction between environment and organizations as paramount; but he viewed the organization as dominant over its environment, pointing out that an organization must "manage" its environment.[7]

Thus, there are two major approaches to the relationship between organizations and their environments. The natural-selection and structural-contingency models are of the first type in which the environment is seen as controlling the organization. The resource-dependency model is of the second type in which the organization is seen as controlling its environment. As Howard Aldrich and Jeffrey Pfeffer pointed out, these two models agree on the importance of the relationship between the organization and its environment but differ on which is the predictor variable.[8] The natural-selection and structural-contingency models posit that environmental dimensions select those organizational dimensions that are most congruent with the environment; the resource-dependency model focuses on the decision-making process within the organization. According to the natural-selection model, only those organizations that are congruent with their environment survive. The process by which an organization becomes congruent is often not analyzed; thus, this model does not consider the decision-making process. Although both the structural-contingency and the natural-selection models posit maximum fit between the organization and its environment, the structural-contingency model emphasizes the role of administrators in changing the organization to fit its environment, whereas the natural-selection model sees this congruency as a natural survival process.

Unlike the selection and contingency models, the resource-dependency model portrays the organization as active. Organizations not only change themselves but also their environments. Pfeffer wrote that administrators manage environments as well as organizations, and the former may be as important as the latter.[9] Paul Hirsch found that pharmaceutical manufacturing firms are more successful than phonograph record manufacturing firms in controlling relevant aspects (pricing and distribution, patents and copyright laws, and opinion leaders) of their environment.[10] There is no doubt that organizations attempt to gain and control relevant aspects of the environment. Environmental causation fails to allow sufficiently for the human ability to choose and control situations. John Child pointed out that decision-makers controlling organizations make choices as to the location in which their organization functions, the clients which will be served, and the type of employees to be hired.[11] Thus, the relationship between an organization and its environment is defined to some extent by the decision-makers in organizations. Both the focal organization and external sectors of the environment make decisions relevant to the organization's operations. In analyzing and discussing this relationship, the influence of the environment is often over-emphasized, while the influence of the focal organization is de-emphasized or not considered.

Perhaps a model recognizing the reciprocal influences of both the environment and the decision-makers within the organization more accurately reflects this interdependency. The ability of the decision-maker to cope with and control the strategic contingencies of the environment should be recognized, along with the influences of the environment on the organization. Simply stated, the relationship between an organization and its environment is as follows: The organization exists in and depends on exchange with external entities (environment). This dependency on the environment imposes a degree of constraint on the organization, just as the focal organization places constraints on the elements within its environment.

Factors That Influence Dependency

It is generally assumed that organizational administrators prefer as much autonomy of decision-making and control of the environment as possible. This autonomy of decision-making is lost when the organization interacts with and becomes dependent on its environment. Those who utilize joint programs as a measure of interdependency, for example, assume that the greater number of joint programs, "the more organizational decision-making is constrained through obligations, commitments, or contracts with other organizations, and the greater the degree of interdependency."[12] At the base of this process is more than a simple exchange of inputs and outputs; rather, processes of cooperation and conflict accompany an organizational exchange in which there is a sharing of clients (customers), funds, and employees.[13]

Through the constraints on decision-making that dependency on task environment places on the focal organization, it can be seen that dependency is the obverse of power. The focal organization has power to the extent that it has control over its decision making and is not dependent on its task environment to satisfy its needs through the supply of scarce resources. Thompson, Azumi, and Evan have enumerated general propositions that define the power relationships an organization maintains with its task environment in attempting to minimize its dependency. One way in which an organization minimizes the influence on the task environment is by maintaining alternative organizations from which to acquire inputs and to which to export output.[14] A large number of alternative sources dilutes the focal organization's dependency by scattering it among many organizations in its task environment, thus reducing its dependency on any one organization. Evan utilized public and private universities to illustrate the differences in concentration of input resources.[15] A public university's sources of revenue are generally limited to one organization in its set, the state legislature, since state revenues account for the largest portion of the operating budget. On the other hand, private universities generally receive revenue from multiple sources, none of which supplies a portion comparable to that supplied to public universities by the state. Consequently, public universities are dependent on the state legislature and in most cases exercise a lower degree of decision-making autonomy than do the private universities, which have other sources of revenue as well as a lower concentration of revenue in a single source.

Azumi pointed out that the lower the integration of suppliers and consumers of an organization, the greater its autonomy.[16] If multiple consumers and suppliers exist but are so integrated that they eliminate alternative markets of resources, the organization loses its autonomy. Autonomy depends on the existence of multiple sources of inputs and receivers of organizational outputs.

Both Evan and Azumi suggested that if the focal organization is placed in the unfortunate position of being functionally similar (producing the same product) to other organizations in its task environment, competition will arise and the focal organization will have a lower degree of autonomy.[17] Just as increasing the alternatives for inputs and outputs makes an organization more autonomous, eliminating alternatives for those environmental collectives gives the focal organization greater control. When the focal organization supplies a scarce commodity or service, it has greater control over the environment. By attempting to control or eliminate competition, the organization creates a more known, stable, and therefore, a more predictable environment in which to function.

Evan posited that size of the organization set or scope of the task environment influences the dependency of the focal organization: "The greater the size of the organization–set, the lower the decision-making autonomy of the focal organization, provided that some elements in the set form an uncooperative coalition that controls resources essential to the functioning of the focal organization, or provided that an uncooperative single member of the set controls such resources."[18] The larger the organization–set, the more opportunity for coalitions to form. When the focal organization is not a part of the coalition in power, it is forced to operate under serious limitations. Evan noted that we would expect organizations that are constrained by near monopolized suppliers to maneuver to achieve power to offset their dependency.

Finally, the greater overlapping membership between the focal organization and organizations in the organization–set, the lower its degree of decision-making autonomy. A case in point is the overlapping membership of industrial organizations and trade unions, which if accompanied by overlapping goals and values, may engender a conflict of loyalties that in turn diminishes the autonomy of the focal organization.[19]

FUNCTIONAL–ECONOMIC VERSUS POLITICAL–LEGAL DEPENDENCY

It is useful to differentiate between two types of dependency based on the nature of the relationship between the focal organization and its environment: The relationship may be a functional–economic dependency or a political–legal dependency. *Functional–economic* dependencies are defined in terms of the focal organization's relative position in the market system of suppliers and customers, or in a service system of clients; while *political–legal* dependency is defined in terms of the focal organization's relationship to an owning or controlling organization. Specific indicators of functional dependency

78

are the relative independence of decision-making within various functional sectors, e.g., independence in critical decisions to expand, diversify, merge, appoint top personnel, allocate resources, or generally commit the organization to certain long-term objectives or courses of action. Specific indicators of political legal dependency, as measured by the Aston Group, include the relative size of the focal organization in relation to the parent organization, the status of the focal organization (i.e., subsidiary, branch, and so on), representation of the focal organization in policy-making bodies of parent organizations, and the number of specializations the focal organization contracted from the parent organization.[20]

An organization may be economically or functionally autonomous and at the same time be legally and politically dependent (owned by another company). The reverse may also be true: an organization may not be legally owned, but it may be economically dependent on other organizations or groups for scarce resources. Dependency between two organizations that are functionally dependent differs from the parent–subsidiary relationship in at least two ways. First, the two organizations, although they must cooperate, are assumed to interact under a conflict of interest; they are each attempting to maximize their goals. Second, though both organizations exert power and must be recognized in the interaction process, the weight of the influence exerted is more equally distributed between the functionally interdependent organizations than in the parent–subsidiary relationship. In the latter relationship, the parent organization generally controls the subsidiary, which in turn is responsible to the parent organization.

Correlates of Political–Legal Dependency

Generally, Pugh and associates found legally dependent organizations to be those that were:

impersonally founded, publicly accountable, vertically integrated, with a large number of specializations contracted out, small in size relative to their parent organization, low in status, and not represented at the policy making level in the parent organization.[21]

Pugh and associates found legal dependency on the environment to be more highly correlated with organizational centralization and less autonomy in decision-making than any other structural variables (structuring of activities, line control of work flow, and relative size

Methodological Notes:

The correlation and regression coefficients in this text are presented to aid the reader in evaluating the strengths of the relationships. The reader will find that these relationships are labeled as weak, moderate, or strong by the researcher and should aid in the interpretations of the findings.

The reader should be cautioned about making comparisons of coefficients across studies. First, many of the early studies of organizational dimensions report only bivariate relationships; consequently, the coefficients are not standardized. Thus, comparisons across studies that did not measure the same variables and did not control for the effects of variables measured are extremely dangerous.

Finally, some of the studies reported standardized beta coefficients. We can have greater faith in the stability of these relationships because other variables in the analysis are controlled.

of supportive component). Measures of the degree of centralization and lack of autonomy were grouped together under concentration of authority. Legal dependency on the environment was strongly correlated with concentration of authority (r = .66); conversely, environmentally independent organizations had more autonomy and the decision-making was decentralized down through the hierarchy. Centralization was measured in terms of the hierarchical level in the organization that had authority to make certain decisions—the higher the level, the greater the centralization. Autonomy was measured by the decisions that could be made within organizations as opposed to those which had to be referred to the next highest level. Environmentally dependent organizations also had a tendency to standardize the procedures of selection and advancement (r = .40).[22] C. R. Hinings and G. L. Lee's data exhibited similar positive and significant relationships of dependency to centralization and lack of autonomy.[23] When ownership was viewed as a link between an organization and a parent organization, and combined with links between a unit and its suppliers and customers into what Pugh and associates, and Hinings and Lee call dependency, it was found that environmentally dependent organizations had less autonomy and more centralized decision-making than did environmentally independent organizations.[24]

In a comparison of work organizations in Canada, Britain, and the U.S., D. J. Hickson and associates found a similar relationship between environmental dependency and autonomy.[25] They found that the degree of autonomy in decision-making rests on the focal organization's position in relation to the parent organization because owners retain ultimate financial and marketing decisions. They found further that large parent or controlling organizations limit organizational autonomy in all three countries regardless of the product produced. The smaller the focal organization in relation to other organizations within the owned groups, the less its autonomy and specialization. That is, the more it relies on the parent organization for these specialities, the more dependent it is.

Correlates of Functional–Economic Dependency

Interorganizational dependency on organizations other than the parent or controlling unit has been measured in several ways. One of the most often-used indicators is the kind and amount of resource investment between two organizations.[26] The major disadvantage of this measure is that it is an indication of only one type of functional dependency. David Rogers developed an alternative to this type of measure in his multiple item sequential scale, which includes the following items: director acquaintance, director interaction, information exchange, resource exchange, overlapping boards, and written agreements. Rogers wrote that "when a single item is used to measure interaction . . . all units . . . are aggregated into a single homogeneous group. Other types of interaction may still occur . . . and this information would be lost through the use of a single indicator."[27] Roger's measure of interdependence has not yet been fully tested but it has the advantage not only of multiple indicators of interdependency but also of sequential ordering, which should facilitate a description of the development of the interdependency process.

In their research on sixteen welfare organizations, Michael Aiken and Jerald Hage examined the relationship between interorganizational dependence and multiple intraorganizational dimensions of the organization.[28] They operationalized interdependency as a single measure—the number of joint programs, which not only encompasses the exchange of clients and funds, but also signifies an enduring relationship indicating a high degree of organizational

TABLE 3–2 Assumptions and Hypotheses about Organizational Interdependence

ASSUMPTIONS:

I. Internal organizational diversity stimulates organizational innovation.

II. Organizational innovation increases the need for resources.

III. As the need for resources intensifies, organizations are more likely to develop greater interdependencies with other organizations, joint programs, in order to gain resources.

IV. Organizations attempt to maximize gains and minimize losses in attempting to obtain resources.

V. Heightened interdependence increases problems of internal control and coordination.

VI. Heightened interdependence increases the internal diversity of the organization.

HYPOTHESES:

1. A high degree of complexity varies directly with a high number of joint programs.

2. A high degree of program innovation varies directly with a high number of joint programs.

3. A high rate of internal communication varies directly with a high number of joint programs.

4. A high degree of centralization varies inversely with a high number of joint programs.

5. A high degree of formalization varies inversely with a high number of joint programs.

Source: Michael Aiken and Jerald Hage, "Organizational Interdependence and Organizational Structure," *American Sociological Review* 33, no. 6 (December 1968): 915.

commitment of resources (personnel, finances, space) by all participating organizations.[29]

Aiken and Hage's assumptions and hypotheses concerning the relation of the environment to the internal dimensions of the organization are found in Table 3–2. Aiken and Hage analyzed both size and technology (contextual variables) in relation to organizational interdependence. They found that size had a moderately positive relationship to the number of joint programs; thus the larger the organization, the more joint programs in which it was involved.[30] Technology—measured by the degree of uniformity of work activities—was also related to the number of joint programs in the expected direction, but the relationship was weak ($r = -.24$). The less routine or uniform the work activities, the larger the number of joint programs. Thus, large size and nonuniform technology support the existence of interorganizational dependence in the form of joint programs.[31]

Aiken and Hage defined complexity as the diversity of occupational activities in the organization and the degree to which these diverse occupations are anchored in professional societies.[32] They found a strong relationship (r = .87) between the number of different types of occupations in an organization and the number of joint programs. They posited that organizations that are able to support a large number of joint programs must be complex. Two other measures of complexity, both relating to the professionalization of the individual, were utilized by Aiken and Hage. The first, the degree to which the employees received professional training, had little relationship to the number of joint programs. The second, the degree to which employees were active in professional activities (that is, attended meetings, gave papers, and held office) was strongly related to the number of joint programs (r = .60). See Table 3–3 for a summary of these findings.

Aiken and Hage measured centralization of decision-making in terms of how often the individual participated in such specific decisions as hiring of personnel, adoption of policies, and adaptation of new programs and services. A weak positive relationship was found between degree of participation in decision-making and the number of joint programs (r = .30). Despite a slight decentralization of decisions concerning organizational resources, a centralization of work decisions was exhibited. The decision-making with regard to work was measured with a scale of "hierarchy of authority," which was found to be positively related to the number of joint programs (r = .33). When the number of new program innovations was controlled, the relationship between the hierarchy of authority and the number of joint programs was reversed; i.e., the members of organizations with many joint programs had more control over their individual work tasks. Thus, Aiken and Hage found that a large number of new programs caused a decentralization of controls over individual work decisions in organizations involved in joint programs.[33]

Aiken and Hage measured internal communications as the number of committees in the organization and the number of committee meetings per month. They found a moderate relationship (r = .47) between the number of organizational committees and the number of joint programs, and a strong relationship (r = .83) between the number of committee meetings per month and the number of joint programs.[34] Thus, an increase in the number of

TABLE 3–3 Relationships Between the Number of Joint Programs and Organizational Characteristics

ORGANIZATIONAL CHARACTERISTICS	PEARSONIAN PRODUCT–MOMENT CORRELATION COEFFICIENTS BETWEEN EACH ORGANIZATIONAL CHARACTERISTIC AND THE NUMBER OF JOINT PROGRAMS
1. Degree of Complexity	
Index of Professional Training	.15
Index of Professional Activity	.60**
Number of Occupations: 1967	.87****
2. Degree of Organizational Innovation: 1959–1966	
Number of New Programs (including new programs that are joint programs)	.71***
Number of New Programs (excluding new programs that are joint programs)	.74****
3. Internal Communication	
Number of Committees	.47*
Number of Committee Meetings per Month	.83****
4. Degree of Centralization	
Index of Participation in Decision Making	.30
Index of Hierarchy of Authority	.33
5. Degree of Formalization	
Index of Job Codification	.13
Index of Rule Observation	−.06
Index of Specificity of Job	−.06

*P < .10.
**P < .05.
***P < .01.
****P < .001.

Source: Michael Aiken and Jerald Hage, "Organizational Interdependence and Intraorganizational Structure," *American Sociological Review* 33, no. 6 (December 1968): 921.

joint programs initiated greater internal communication or vice versa. One explanation is that with the expansion of tasks and joint decision-making comes a need for greater control and coordination, which in turn necessitates communication.

Thus, Aiken and Hage found that those organizations that were environmentally linked to other organizations through joint programs were structurally more complex, somewhat more decentralized, and more active in external communication than those not linked by joint programs. They found no relationship between interdependency and formalization.[35]

Aiken and Hage analyzed the relationship of one performance variable—organizational innovation—to interorganizational dependence. The degree of organizational innovation was measured by the number of new programs successfully implemented over an eight-year period. The relationship between number of joint programs and the number of new programs was high ($r = .74$).[36] Thus, it may be concluded that organizational interdependency supports organizational innovation.

More recently, Steven Paulson developed a model of interorganizational relationships by integrating Hage's axiomatic theory[37] with Aiken and Hage's work on interorganizational relationships (joint programs)[38] and testing the relationships on data collected in health and welfare organizations.[39] The organizations studied by Paulson were similar to Aiken and Hage's population of social welfare and health organizations and included 64 units at the state and multi-county level and 74 at the county level. However, the operationalizations of nearly every variable differed from those of Aiken and Hage. Paulson's variable symbols and definitions are found in Table 2–6. In testing Hage and Aiken's model of two-variable relations, Paulson reported not only the zero order but also partial correlations. Of the five structural variables thought to be related to interorganizational relations, three were associated: complexity was positively related with a zero order correlation and partial correlation of .31; centralization was inversely related with a zero order correlation of $-.37$ and a partial correlation of $-.20$; internal communications was positively related to interorganizational relations with a zero order correlation and a partial correlation of .20.[40] Each of these relationships were in the direction hypothesized by Aiken and Hage but were all rather weak. Stratification and formalization were not significantly related to interorganizational relations. The direction of the relationships was positive for both variables, whereas, Aiken and Hage had hypothesized negative relationships. Thus, complexity and internal communication increase and centralization decreases with expansion of interorganizational relations.

The performance variables that Paulson correlated with interorganizational relations were efficiency (with a correlation of $-.32$ and a partial correlation of $-.29$) and innovation (with a correlation of .25 and a partial correlation of .23).[41] Both efficiency and innovation were related to interdependency of organizations in the directions hypothesized by Aiken and Hage. Effectiveness and satisfaction were not related to interorganizational relations (interdependency). Thus, organizations that are dependent on other organizations are more innovative and do not emphasize low costs (efficiency) as much as independent organizations.

DIMENSIONS OF THE ENVIRONMENT

Another method of analyzing the organization–environment relationship, other than specifying the elements (consumers, competitors, suppliers, and so on) of the task environment, is to specify the major dimensions of the task environment—complexity and change. Like those of organizational structure, these dimensions are conceptualized on a continuum from static to dynamic and from simple to complex. They are not only related to each other, but also to the degree of certainty with which organizational decision-makers can predict the environment and to the structural dimensions of organizations.

Knowing the dimensions of the environment of a particular organization is advantageous for several reasons. First, there are a large number of elements in the environment that can influence the organization, making it difficult to operationalize and measure their influence. Further, it is impossible to control those factors not known to the researcher. A complete description of the elements in the focal organization's environment is prohibitive. William Dill suggested that a more manageable approach is to use dimensions that describe the essence of the environmental effects on the organization.[42] Although the past decade has seen an increasing amount of research on dimensions of the organizational environment, there is not, at this time, a widely accepted set of such dimensions, without which a discussion of the environment and its relationships to the focal organization remains vague. The following discussion is directed toward the clarification of these dimensions.

Several points of controversy exist of which the student of organizations should be conscious in analyzing the dimensions of the organizational environment and their effect on the focal organization. First, although theorists agree that organizations are dependent on other organizations, there is disagreement concerning the nature and impact of this relationship for the focal organization. As was demonstrated in the sections on correlates of organizational dependency, dependency leads to greater organizational complexity. Similarly, Talcott Parsons and Edgar Schein have viewed this dependency among organizations as a facilitator in the specialization of tasks and goals.[43] Eugene Litwak and Lydia Hylton contend that high dependency levels lead to extensive cooperation and coordination among related organizations for the benefit of all.[44] Lawrence and Lorsch also found that higher levels of dependency lead to more extensive integration and differentiation among efficient organizations.[45] Although these theorists have a positive view of environmental dependency of organizations, several theorists have found dependency of one organization on others to have a negative effect on one or all of the organizations.[46] Thompson proposed that dependency can be viewed in terms of constraints; an increase in dependency makes the management of the environment more difficult. Thus, dependency is particularly negative for the subordinate organization.[47] Shirley Terreberry posited that if interorganizational dependency is considered alone, it has a positive effect on the focal organization. But when it is considered in conjunction with an unstable (or risk-prone) environment, the effects will be negative.[48] Thus, organizational dependency coupled with an unstable environment has a negative effect on the organization's performance.

A second point of controversy is the lack of conceptual clarity, which becomes obvious when discussing environmental dimensions. Different terms have often been used to designate the same environmental dimension. For example, the terms *stability* and *change* have both been used to denote rate of environmental change. In an attempt to make generalizations more universal, the researcher may unwittingly obscure the precise object of measurement, with the result that the student of organizations may interpret the conclusions as meaning that a highly unstable (volatile) environment is related to organizational dependency, when in fact the researcher found that a fairly stable environment with a high rate of change was related to organizational dependency. This is a hypothetical case, but it does demonstrate the confusion over definitions of concepts.

Another conceptual drawback is that a single term has been used to designate conceptually different environmental measurements. For example, some organizational analysts may operationalize objective measures of environmental complexity as the *number* of groups and organizations in the focal organization's environment, while another may operationalize complexity as the different *types* of groups and organizations in the focal organization's environment.

87

Some of the conceptual confusion rests in the relative youth of using environmental dimensions as predictor variables for organizational structure and performance. The environmental dimensions have not been clearly established, and the discipline is in great need of a typology of these dimensions with corresponding conceptual and operational definitions.

Another source of much conceptual confusion is the use of the subjective measures of organizational uncertainty to determine to what extent decision-makers in the organization feel the environment is complex and change-oriented. Indicators of subjective uncertainty have been used to encompass measures of both environmental change and complexity. In actuality, these three measures are distinct. For example, the environment may be highly complex and subject to change, but the decision-makers may still feel relatively certain about it. Theoretically, one would expect both change (rate, variability, and stability) and complexity of environmental conditions to increase the uncertainty of decision-makers about the environment, but these measures are not the same conceptually nor are they necessarily correlated. While change and complexity are characteristics of the organization's environment, uncertainty is a subjective characteristic reflecting the decision-maker's knowledge and perception of that environment.

There are also several methodological problems facing those who analyze the organizational environment. One of these is that a single environmental dimension may be operationalized at both the objective and subjective levels. These two levels of measurement, more often than not, are not highly correlated, thus indicating that two different concepts are being measured.[49] Because the two types of operationalizations are not measuring the same dimension nor the same aspects of a dimension, the research findings are not comparable and in some cases yield contradictory results. For example, studies relying on subjective data (attitude responses to questionnaires and interviews) provide support for the structural-contingency model. The research of Lawrence and Lorsch, and Robert Duncan attests to this.[50] On the other hand, studies using objective measures (institutional records), such as that by Pennings,[51] do not evidence relationships between environmental, structural, and performance variables. When research utilizing subjective measures is repeated utilizing objective measures, the results are not consistent. For example, Henry Tosi, Ramon Aldag, and Ronald Storey used records to repeat Lawrence and Lorsch's questionnaire study of the relationship of environmental and structural variables and obtained contradictory findings.[52] Similarly, H. Kirk Downey, Don Hellriegel, and John Slocum's research verified that when subjective and objective measures of environmental variables are compared, they are found to be unrelated.[53] Assuming that the measures of variables at both levels are appropriate, it can be concluded that the subjective and objective measures of a given variable do not measure the same underlying conceptual construct.

Even if an organizational analyst operationalizes all the dimensions using the same type of measure, she or he could still conceivably employ any of a large number of indicators of that dimension. Thus, the results could be inconsistent because of the use of different indicators. The measurement instruments vary so greatly that most of the studies, unless they are replications, are not comparable.

Finally, the comparative research on the relationship between environment and organizational structure is a relatively new model. Consequently, only one or two pieces of research now exist on a single environmental dimension's relationship to a given organizational structure or performance dimension. In fact, there is no quantitative comparative research on the relationship of environmental change and complexity to some organizational structural and performance dimensions. For the most part, those relationships that have been analyzed have not been replicated in the same or even different types of work organizations. Therefore, there is no common body of research findings from which to draw empirical generalizations. The existing research is summarized in the following sections.

Environmental Complexity

John Child was among the first organizational theorists to define environmental complexity to include both *diversity* and *range* of activities.[54] *Range* is the number of elements in the task environment; *diversity* is the degree of heterogeneity of these elements. The simple adding together of like elements in the organization's environment is not a measure of diversity; rather, it is a measure of environmental scope or size. Thus, environmental complexity refers to the heterogeneity and range of environmental elements that are relevant to the focal organization's operations. A simple, or placid, environment is one in which the external factors with which an organization must deal are few in number and relatively homogeneous. Organizations that deal with relatively simple environments exert smaller amounts of effort to process inputs because the types of information from the various environmental elements are more likely to be homogeneous and, hence, relatively consistent. Since the task environment is made up largely of relatively homogeneous organiza-

89

tions, the focal organization can more easily anticipate the other organizations' goals, demands for inputs, outputs, communications processes, and so on, and can thereby more accurately gauge its own reactions. The more homogeneous this environment, the fewer types of inputs that will have to be assimilated and the less complex the decision-making process for the focal organization. On the other hand, the greater the complexity of the environment, the greater the number of inputs relevant to organizational decision-makers. It is here posited that the greater the number of inputs entering an organization, the greater the role specialization of those who deal with the environment. The problems of communication, coordination and control become more complex, necessitating greater specialization within the organization.

Environmental complexity is difficult to operationalize because it assumes access to all environmental elements and a knowledge of their diversity. One way to measure environmental complexity without having to deal with the indefinite and unlimited environment is to indirectly ask the decision-makers of the focal organization if they perceive the environment to be complex or noncomplex. Here environmental complexity does not depend on any universal operational definition that could be applied to all organizations, but rather relies on the perception of the respondent. This process would give the researcher a definition of organizational complexity congruent with William Starbuck's statement that "the same environment one organization perceives as unpredictable, complex, and evanescent, another organization might see as static and easily understood."[55]

Robert B. Duncan defined complexity as the degree to which the elements in the focal organization environment were both (1) great in number (range) and (2) are dissimilar to one another (heterogeneity).[56] Duncan computed a simple–complex environmental index by multiplying the number of decision factors with which the decision makers must deal (F) by the number of environmental elements (components) $(C)^2$. He thus obtained an indication of the number of environmental factors to be considered in decision-making and the degree to which they are similar (found in one component) or dissimilar (found in several components). This measure, of course, is an indicator of the complexity of the decision-making process in relating the organization to its environment.

Environmental Change

We must consider the degree of change in the organization's environment. This change dimension is multifaceted, consisting of at least three different aspects: (1) the frequency of change in relevant environmental activities (rate), (2) the degree of difference involved in each change (variability), and (3) the degree of irregularity in the overall pattern of change (instability). Thus, change in the organizational environment may be due to an increased rate of change, variability, or instability with which the activities in the environment change relative to the focal organization.

In differentiating between the rate of environmental change and environmental stability, Ray Jurkovich pointed out four types of environmental movement: low stable change, high stable change, low unstable change, and high unstable change.[57] From the perspective of the organization, an environment with low stable change would be one in which the organization has considerable control over its functioning because of the ability to anticipate long- and short-range change and plan accordingly. When the change rate of the environment is low but unstable, the ability to control the environment becomes more problematic; although the change can be anticipated, timing is questionable. High change rates and stable environments give the organization the ability to predict the rate of change, but rapid change increases the speed of structuring, processing, and goals formation. Change that is too rapid may not allow for routinization of activities, and thus may obstruct goal attainment by diverting energies into continual restructuring. Finally, the most chaotic environment in which an organization might exist is that in which the rate of change is rapid and the nature of change is unstable. This environment is both unpredictable and unstructured, increasing the potential for conflict. Organizations in this situation design internal strategies and tactics to cope with the environment. This adjustment process may include such measures as: decentralizing the power so each subunit has more flexibility to adjust to the environment; increasing the number of administrators to communicate change and anticipated changes to other parts of the organization; increasing the research and planning units to gain greater information and predictability of the environment; and constructing buffers against the environment.

To add greater complexity to an already complex problem, some aspects of an organization's environment may remain static, while others are dynamic. For example, an industry's raw materials and supplies may remain stable even though customer demands are extremely volatile. The customer may be influenced by government regulations of energy necessary to operate a particular product (e.g., automobiles or home heating). For example, in the mid-1970's the consumer demand for large automobiles shifted to small automobiles due to the energy crisis, but by 1977 had shifted back to

91

large automobiles with the resulting prospect of federal taxation on these purchases. The knowledge and raw-materials technology necessary to produce such automobiles remained relatively stable but consumer demands changed rapidly.

DECISION-MAKERS' CERTAINTY OF ORGANIZATION-ENVIRONMENT RELATIONS

The dimensions of complexity and change affect the focal organization either alone or through interaction with each other. These two dimensions are important to our understanding of the degree of certainty with which organizations can make decisions concerning future courses of action. Environmental uncertainty is a result of three conditions: (1) a lack of information concerning the environmental factors associated with a particular organizational decision-making situation; (2) an inability to accurately assign probabilities with regard to how environmental factors will affect the success or failure of a decision-making unit; and (3) a lack of information regarding the costs associated with an incorrect decision or action.[58] Environmental uncertainty has been used to denote the nature, amount, and reliability of information that decision-makers have about the environment. Thus, certainty–uncertainty is not a dimension of the environment; rather, it is a characteristic of the decision-makers' view of their information about the environment.

Decision-makers respond to what they perceive, and such perceptions may or may not correspond to objective reality. If decision-makers accurately perceive the degrees of complexity and stability in the environment, the probability of appropriate organizational response and adaptation would appear to be enhanced. If, on the other hand, an organization "enacts" an unrealistic environment (through, for example, inaccurate information, lack of expertise, or insufficient time), the negative effects on organizational success could be substantial.

The certainty with which the environment may be approached by the focal organization depends on the amount of information and the degree of certainty about that information. If there is little information about the environmental elements and little or no access to that information, the environment becomes highly uncertain. Jurkovich outlined three conditions under which the environment becomes nonroutine: when "people complain that (a) they cannot gain access to critical information, (b) they cannot trust a significant portion of the information, or (c) the set of information categories they need for decision making is uncertain."[59] The higher the percentage of organizational members with information problems and the more severe the problems, the more uncertain the decision and the more nonroutine the problem-solving in relation to the environment.

In research to be discussed later in this chapter, Lawrence and Lorsch measured uncertainty with a nine-item questionnaire assessing three subenvironments of the organization—marketing, manufacturing, and research—using three questions about each one. These questions were designed to reveal to what extent each of the respondents perceived: (1) a lack of clarity of information, (2) general uncertainty of cause-and-effect relationships, and (3) lack of definitive time span of feedback about results related to each functional subenvironment.[60] Responses to the three questions from each subenvironment yielded an uncertainty score for each of the respondents. Duncan later concluded that Lawrence and Lorsch's uncertainty concept was too "broad" and "vague" and that this inhibited the development of specific operational measures of uncertainty. But he utilized Lawrence and Lorsch's broad concept to develop the first two components of his operational definition of uncertainty: (1) the lack of information regarding the environmental factors associated with a given decision-making situation, and (2) lack of knowledge about how much the organization would lose if a specific decision is incorrect.[61] He then developed a third component; the inability to assign probability with any degree of confidence to how environmental factors will affect the success or failure of the decision unit in performing its function. Duncan's third component measured the certainty of assigning probability to the outcome of organizational events, not their probability. Noting that Duncan added scores from subscales to produce total uncertainty scores, Downey, Hellriegel, and Slocum suggested that because these subscales were highly dissimilar, this summation, without standardization, may have led him to erroneous results.[62]

In an effort to integrate the change and complexity dimensions with the issue of uncertainty in organizational decision-making, Duncan has proposed a model that attempts to describe the environmental conditions resulting from such interrelationships.[63] See Table 3-4. This model suggests that the "static–simple" environments contain the least amount of uncertainty for organizational planners and decision makers, and the "dynamic–complex" environments contain the greatest amount of uncertainty. Duncan's empirical investigation provided general support for the model. Not

Environmental and Contextual Dimensions

TABLE 3–4   Environmental State Dimensions and Predicted Perceived
Uncertainty Experienced by Individuals in Decision Units

	Simple	Complex
	Cell 1: low perceived uncertainty	Cell 2: moderately low perceived uncertainty
Static	(1) Small number of factors and components in the environment (2) Factors and components are somewhat similar to one another (3) Factors and components remain basically the same and are not changing	(1) Large number of factors and components in the environment (2) Factors and components are not similar to one another (3) Factors and components remain basically the same
	Cell 3: moderately high perceived uncertainty	Cell 4: high perceived uncertainty
Dynamic	(1) Small number of factors and components in the environment (2) Factors and components are somewhat similar to one another (3) Factors and components of the environment are in continual process of change	(1) Large number of factors and components in the environment (2) Factors and components are not similar to one another (3) Factors and components of environment are in a continual process of change

Source: R. B. Duncan, "The Characteristics of Organizational Environments and Perceived Environmental Uncertainty," *Administrative Science Quarterly* 17, no. 3 (September 1972): 320.

only was the dynamic–complex environment found to be associated with the largest amount of perceived environmental uncertainty, but it was seen to be a more important contributor to perceived uncertainty than the simple–complex dimension. Duncan concluded:

Decision units with dynamic environments always experience significantly more uncertainty in decision making regardless of whether their environment is simple or complex. The difference in perceived uncertainty between decision units with simple and complex environments is not significant, unless the decision unit's environment is also dynamic.[64]

When we discuss the degree of complexity and change in the environment, we are in effect raising questions about the degree of uncertainty in organization–environment relations. The greater the uncertainty, the less the predictability. The capacity of an organization to successfully adapt to its environment is facilitated to a large extent by the decision-makers' ability to predict what the external environment will be like in the future. The more certain these decision-makers are about future environmental states, the more opportunity they have to respond.

RESEARCH ON ORGANIZATION–ENVIRONMENT RELATIONS

Environment is often studied in relation to the structural dimensions of organizations in an attempt to define those relationships that produce the most effective (successful and efficient) organization. The findings of such structural contingency-model research has been mixed. Because of variation in the types of organizations, measurement instruments, and variables utilized, several major pieces of research will be reviewed.

In an early study of organization–environment relations, Tom Burns and G. M. Stalker examined twenty British electronics firms.[65] The dimension of the environment on which these researchers focused was the *rate of change* in both the relevant technology and market. Burns and Stalker then developed a dichotomous typology of organizations. These two types of organizations were called *mechanistic* and *organic* and were dependent to a large extent on the relationship between the organization and its environment, with major emphasis on the environment as determinant of the internal structure of the organization. See Table 3–5. Mechanistic organizations are characterized by centralization of control and authority, a high degree of task specialization, and primarily downward vertical communication. Organic organizations, on the other hand, generally exhibit a higher degree of task interdependence, greater decentralization of control and authority, and more horizontal (interdepartmental) communication. Mechanistic systems are seen as relatively fixed and inflexible entities, while organic systems are viewed as flexible and adaptive.

TABLE 3—5 Comparison of Mechanistic and Organic Systems of Organization

MECHANISTIC	ORGANIC
1. Tasks are highly fractionated and specialized; little regard paid to clarifying relationship between tasks and organizational objectives.	1. Tasks are more interdependent; emphasis on relevance of tasks and organizational objectives.
2. Tasks tend to remain rigidly defined unless altered formally by top management.	2. Tasks are continually adjusted and redefined through interaction of organizational members.
3. Specific role definition (rights, obligations, and technical methods prescribed for each member).	3. Generalized role definition (members accept general responsibility for task accomplishment beyond individual role definition).
4. Hierarchic structure of control, authority, and communication. Sanctions derive from employment contract between employee and organization.	4. Network structure of control, authority, and communication. Sanctions derive more from community of interest than from contractual relationship.
5. Information relevant to situation and operations of the organization formally assumed to rest with chief executive.	5. Leader not assumed to be omniscient; knowledge centers identified where located throughout the organization.
6. Communication is primarily vertical between superior and subordinate.	6. Communication is both vertical and horizontal, depending upon where needed information resides.
7. Communications primarily take form of instructions and decisions issued by superiors, of information and requests for decisions supplied by inferiors.	7. Communications primarily take form of information and advice.
8. Insistence on loyalty to organization and obedience to superiors.	8. Commitment to organization's tasks and goals more highly valued than loyalty or obedience.
9. Importance and prestige attached to identification with organization and its members.	9. Importance and prestige attached to affiliations and expertise in external environment.

Adapted from T. Burns and G. M. Stalker, *The Management of Innovations* (London: Tavistock, 1961), pp. 119–122.

Burns and Stalker did not argue that one type of system was more effective than the other, but that each was more effective in a given environment. In highly stable and predictable environments, where market and technological conditions remain largely unchanged over time, the mechanistic system is the more appropriate organizational design. Because the environment is highly predictable under such conditions, it is possible to routinize tasks and centralize decisions (a bureaucratic structure) in order to maximize efficiency and effectiveness. On the other hand, where the environment is in a constant state of flux and where an organization has to change direction constantly to adapt to its environment, an organic system is more appropriate because of added flexibility and adaptability. Here change in environmental conditions produces uncertainty in the decision-maker's ability to predict the organization–environment relationship, resulting in a nonburcaucratic structure (decentralization and de-emphasis on rules and procedures) to maximize efficiency and effectiveness. The role of organizational decision-makers then becomes one of understanding environmental conditions and adapting organizational structure to meet and exploit such conditions.

In an attempt to understand which structural dimensions correspond to given environmental dimensions in effective organizations, Lawrence and Lorsch explored six organizations in the plastic industry, which were selected for their varying degrees of success.[66] The performance measures used to rank the organization include change in profits in the past five years and new products introduced in the past five years as a percent of the current sales. In addition to these objective measures, the researchers acquired the appraisal of performance from the chief executive of each organization. This subjective appraisal correlated closely with the total performance index. Lawrence and Lorsch categorized their six organizations: two high-performing, two medium-performing, and two low-performing. They found that two structural characteristics (differentiation and integration) in effective organizations depend on the demands of the environment. To measure the effects of the environment, an uncertainty score was constructed consisting of: (1) clarity of information, (2) uncertainty of cause-and-effect relations, and (3) time span of definitive feedback. They found that scientific knowledge was the most uncertain, followed by market knowledge, and that techno-economic knowledge was most certain. In order to facilitate comparisons, Lawrence and Lorsch explored two other industries that were found to have less dynamic and diverse environments (i.e., more predictable ones) than the plastic industry—the container industry and the food industry.

97

They studied effects of the environment on two structural characteristics of organizations—differentiation and integration. It should be noted that structural differentiation as defined by Lawrence and Lorsch refers to "the difference in cognitive and emotional orientations among managers in different functional departments."[67] Thus, it referred not only to the degree of specialization of labor or departmentalization, but also to what might be termed the "psychological" departmentalization, that is, the extent to which managers in different departments differ in attitudes and behavioral orientation. The greater the psychological distance between managers in different departments, the greater the differentiation. Integration referred to the "quality of the state of collaboration that exists among departments that are required to achieve unity of effort by the demands of the environment."[68] Thus, integration referred to the nature and quality of interdepartmental relations as well as the processes by which such relations were achieved. Such integration can be brought about in several ways, including the creation of rules and standard operating procedures that govern behavior, plans, and objectives.

Lawrence and Lorsch found organizations operating in more dynamic and complex environments such as the plastic industries tended to exhibit a greater degree of differentiation between functional departments than did those firms operating in less turbulent environments such as the container industries. The packaged-foods firms, which operated in a moderately dynamic environment, exhibited a moderate degree of differentiation. In other words, the greater the instability in the external environment, the more psychological distance was created between departments in effective organizations.

Generally, successful firms within each industry had higher scores than did unsuccessful firms for both differentiation and integration. Thus, it would appear that one component of organizational effectiveness, as defined and measured here, is the capacity of an organization to achieve an optimal balance of differentiation and integration that is consistent with environmental demands. On the other hand, one hallmark of less effective organizations is an inability to grant various departments sufficient latitude to increase their contribution to organizational goals through functional specialization; another is an inability to devise sufficient means to integrate and coordinate these diverse departments in order to achieve success.

Different environments call for different methods of integration. In the dynamic environment, the effective plastic firms employed a formal integrating department, whose task was to ensure that the various functional areas worked together. In the moderately dynamic environment the effective packaging firms used individual integrators whose primary responsibility was to ensure mutuality of purpose. Finally, in the more stable environment, the effective container firms used direct managerial contact through the chain of command to maintain integration. Thus, effective organizations are characterized by an ability to establish a vehicle for integration that is commensurate with the environment. The more complex the environment, the more elaborate the integrative mechanisms.

In conclusion, Lawrence and Lorsch found that the internal structure (differentiation and integration) of effective organizations will differ depending on the dimensions of the environment. In a diverse, dynamic environment, the effective organization must be highly differentiated and integrated, whereas in a more stable, less diverse environment, the effective organization must be less differentiated but retain a high degree of integration. Thus, these authors emphasize the need for organizational decision-makers to understand the environment and structure the organization accordingly. Although the nature and scope of these findings are more comprehensive than those reported by Burns and Stalker, the basic conclusions are similar: environment does play an important role in the relation between structuring activities and organizational effectiveness.

Richard N. Osborn and James G. Hunt investigated the effects of environmental complexity on organizational effectiveness in twenty-six small, rigidly structured social service organizations in a midwestern state.[69] Environmental complexity was defined in terms of three interrelated variables: (1) the amount of risk involved in organization–environment relations: (2) environmental dependency, or the degree to which an organization relies on elements in the environment for growth and survival; and (3) the nature (the degree of favorableness) of interorganizational relationships. The results of this study indicated that the degree of risk present in the external environment is unrelated to effectiveness. However, both environmental dependency and interorganizational interaction were found to have a positive, significant relationship to measures of effectiveness. Of the three environmental variables, interorganizational interaction (the ability of an organization to develop favorable exchange relations with its environment) was found to be most closely associated with effectiveness.

Thus, this recent research of Osborn and Hunt did not generally support the structural-contingency-model findings of Lawrence and Lorsch and Burns and Stalker. Instead, it found the ability of an organization to develop favorable environmental relations and, to a lesser degree, environmental dependency to be positively related to effectiveness. Osborn and Hunt did point out that the degree of heterogeneity among the task environments under study may not have been sufficient to secure an adequate measure of environmental risk.

The structural-contingency model has been more rigorously investigated by the recent research of Johannes Pennings.[70] In a study of forty widely dispersed branch offices of a large U.S. brokerage organization, Pennings used both subjective and objective measures to explore the degree of association between organizational structure and environmental dimensions. The goodness of fit between the structural and environmental variables were then analyzed as to their ability to explain organizational effectiveness. Pennings found that the structural-contingency model was not generally supported by his analysis of the relationship between the environmental variables (knowledge of competition, specificity of feedback, number of competitors, quality of organizational intelligence, uncertainty, instability, and demand) and the structural variables (power, lateral communication, vertical communication, participativeness, frequency of meetings). Only resourcefulness and complexity were generally related to the structural variables. Further, the contingency model was not supported because of the lack of variance in the effectiveness variables (morale, anxiety, total production, decline in production) explained by the goodness of fit between the environmental and structural variables.[71] Thus, Pennings, like Osborn and Hunt did *not* find support for the structural-contingency model.

It may be observed that the two earlier studies of organization–environment relations supported the structural-contingency model, while the two more recent studies did not. With the recent intense interest in the questions of organization–environment relations, the question will undoubtedly receive continued attention. Only with the findings of future research will the apparent inconsistencies of this research be explained.

SUMMARY

Accepting the evidence that organizations and environments are interdependent, we have concentrated on the micro-level task environment of the organization. Neither the natural-selection model, in

100

which the environment determines the organization, nor the resource-dependency model, in which the organization controls its environment, is a satisfactory model of organization–environmental dependency. Rather, a model in which both the environment and the organization have some power is more accurate. Thus, both the focal organization and the social entities in its task environment are affected by this interdependency. Functionally dependent organizations (i.e., those which form joint programs) tend to be larger in size and more innovative; have greater knowledge technology; and to be structurally more complex, communicative, and decentralized.

Environmental complexity and change tend to make the focal organization more dependent on its environment. Dynamic–complex environments foster uncertainty of decision within the focal organization. The greater the uncertainty, the less the predictability. The capacity of an organization to successfully adapt to its environment is facilitated to a large extent by the decision-maker's ability to know what the environment will be like in the future.

Finally, research on organization–environmental relations is in its formative stages. At this point in our research endeavors, more support exists for, than against, the contingency model of this relationship. Briefly, this model sees the effectiveness of an organization as dependent on the fit between its environmental and its structural dimensions. That is, the internal structure of an effective organization will differ depending on the dimensions of the environment. Thus, to obtain an effective organization, there is no one best set of environmental and structural dimensions; rather, effectiveness is determined by the fit between these dimensions. This generalization will become more apparent as we examine the various contextual, structural, and performance dimensions.

NOTES

1. William M. Evan and Mildred A. Schwartz, "Law and the Emergence of Formal Organization," *Sociology and Social Research* 48, no. 3 (April 1964): 270–280.
2. Koya Azumi, "Environmental Needs, Resources and Agents," in Koya Azumi and Jerald Hage, eds., *Organizational Systems* (Lexington, Mass.: D. C. Heath and Company, 1972), p. 94.
3. Seymour M. Lipset, *Political Man* (Garden City, N.Y.: Doubleday, 1960), pp. 45–76.
4. This task environment has been defined by William R. Dill in "Environment as an Influence on Managerial Autonomy," *Administrative Science Quarterly* 2, no. 4 (March 1958): 409–443; and by Richard N. Osborn and James G. Hunt, "Environment and Organizational Effectiveness," *Administrative Science Quarterly* 19, no. 2 (June 1974): 231–246.

5. William M. Evan, "The Organization–Set: Toward A Theory of Interorganizational Relations," in John G. Maurer, ed., *Readings in Organization Theory: Open Systems Approaches* (New York: Random House, 1971), pp. 33–45. This article was reprinted from James D. Thompson, ed., *Approaches to Organizational Design* (Pittsburgh: University of Pittsburgh Press, 1966).

6. Paul R. Lawrence and Jay W. Lorsch, *Organization and Environment* (Boston: Harvard University, Graduate School of Business Administration, Division of Research, 1967), pp. 156–157.

7. James D. Thompson, *Organizations in Action* (New York: McGraw-Hill, 1967).

8. Howard E. Aldrich and Jeffrey Pfeffer, "Environments of Organizations," in Alex Inkeles, James Coleman, and Neil Smelser, eds., *Annual Review of Sociology*, Vol. 2 (Palo Alto, Calif.: Annual Review, Inc., 1976), pp. 79–105.

9. Jeffrey Pfeffer, "Beyond Management and the Worker: The Institutional Function of Management," *The Academy of Management Review* 1, no. 2 (April 1976), 36–46.

10. Paul M. Hirsch, "Organizational Effectiveness and the Institutional Environment," *Administrative Science Quarterly* 20, no. 3 (September 1975): 327–344.

11. John Child, "Organizational Structure, Environment and Performance: The Role of Strategic Choice," *Sociology* 6, no. 1 (January 1972): 2–22.

12. Michael Aiken and Jerald Hage, "Organizational Interdependence and Intraorganizational Structure," *American Sociological Review* 33, no. 6 (December 1968): 913.

13. For a more complete discussion of this process, see Sol Levine, Paul E. White, and Benjamine D. Paul, "Community Interorganizational Problems in Providing Medical Care and Social Service," *American Journal of Public Health* 53 (August 1963): 1183–1195.

14. Thompson, *Organizations in Action,* p. 33.

15. Evan, "The Organization–Set: Toward A Theory of Interorganizational Relations," p. 36.

16. Azumi, "Environmental Needs, Resources, and Agents," p. 98.

17. Evan, "The Organization–Set: Toward A Theory of Interorganizational Relations," p. 38; Azumi, "Environmental Needs, Resources, and Agents," p. 98.

18. Evan, "The Organization–Set: Toward A Theory of Interorganizational Relations," p. 38.

19. Ibid.

20. D. S. Pugh, D. J. Hickson, C. R. Hinings, and C. Turner, "The Context of Organization Structure," *Administrative Science Quarterly* 14, no. 1 (March 1969): 91–114.

21. Ibid., p. 108.

22. Ibid.

23. C. R. Hinings and G. L. Lee, "Dimensions of Organization Structure and Their Context: A Replication," *Sociology* 5, no. 1 (January 1971): 90.

24. Pugh, Hickson, Hinings, and Turner, "The Context of Organization Structure"; Hinings and Lee, "Dimensions of Organization Structure and Their Context: A Replication"; C. J. McMillan, D. J. Hickson, and C. R. Hinings, "The Structure of Work Organizations Across Societies," *Academy of Management Journal* 17, no. 4 (December 1973): 555–569.

25. D. J. Hickson, C. R. Hinings, C. J. McMillan, and J. P. Schwitter, "The Culture-Free Context of Organization Structure: A Tri-National Comparison," *Sociology* 8, no. 1 (January 1974): 72–73.

26. Those using resource investment as an indicator of interorganizational dependency include: Sol Levine and Paul E. White, "Exchange as a Conceptual Framework for the Study of Interorganizational Relationships," *Administrative Science Quarterly* 5, no. 4 (March 1961): 583–601; and Cora B. Marrett, "On the Specifications of Interorganizational Dimensions," *Sociology and Social Research* 56, no. 1 (October 1971): 83–97.

27. David L. Rogers, "Towards a Scale of Interorganizational Relations Among Public Agencies," *Sociology and Social Research* 59, no. 1 (October 1974): 61.

28. Aiken and Hage, "Organizational Interdependence and Intraorganizational Structure," pp. 912–930.

29. Ibid., p. 919.

30. Ibid., p. 926.

31. Ibid., p. 927.

32. Ibid., p. 920.

33. Ibid., pp. 924–925.

34. Ibid., p. 923.

35. Ibid., p. 912.

36. Ibid., p. 922. The number of new joint programs were excluded from the correlation.

37. Jerald Hage, "An Axiomatic Theory of Organizations," *Administrative Science Quarterly* 10, no. 3 (December 1965): 289–320.

38. Aiken and Hage, "Organizational Interdependence and Intraorganizational Structure," pp. 912–930.

39. Steven K. Paulson, "Causal Analysis of Interorganizational Relations: An Axiomatic Theory Revised," *Administrative Science Quarterly* 19, no. 3 (September 1974): 319–337.

40. Ibid., p. 323.

41. Ibid.

42. William R. Dill, "The Impact of Environment on Organizational Development," in Sidney Mailick and Edward H. Van Ness, eds., *Concepts and Issues in Administrative Behavior* (Englewood Cliffs, N.J.: Prentice-Hall, 1962), pp. 94–109.

43. Talcott Parsons, *Structure and Processes in Modern Societies* (New York: The Free Press, 1960), and Edgar H. Schein, *Organizational Psychology* (Englewood Cliffs, N.J.: Prentice-Hall, 1965).

44. Eugene Litwak and Lydia Hylton, "Interorganizational Analyses: A Hypothesis on Coordinating Agencies," *Administrative Science Quarterly* 6, no. 4 (March 1962): 395–421.

45. Lawrence and Lorsch, *Organization and Environment*.

46. Among those who discuss the negative effects of dependency are Fred E. Emery and Eric L. Trist, "The Causal Texture of Organizational Environments," *Human Relations* 18, no. 1 (February 1965): 21–31; and Shirley Terreberry, "The Evolution of Organizational Environments," *Administrative Science Quarterly* 13, no. 4 (March 1968): 590–613.

47. Thompson, *Organizations in Action*.

48. Terreberry, "The Evolution of Organizational Environments."

49. For an example of research that did not evidence an adequate correlation between objective and subjective measures of the same concept, see the discussion of the environmental variables in Johannes Pennings, "The Relevance of the Structural-Contingency Model of Organizational Effectiveness," *Administrative Science Quarterly* 20, no. 3 (September 1975): 399. Of course,

one would not expect all of these variables to be highly correlated because they are measuring conceptually different dimensions.

50. Lawrence and Lorsch, *Organization and Environment;* and Robert B. Duncan, "Characteristics of Organizational Environments and Perceived Environmental Uncertainty," *Administrative Science Quarterly* 17, no. 3 (September 1972): 313–327.

51. Pennings, "The Relevance of the Structural-Contingency Model for Organizational Effectiveness," pp. 393–409.

52. Henry Tosi, Ramon Aldag, and Ronald Storey, "On the Measurement of the Environment: An Assessment of the Lawrence and Lorsch Environmental Subscales," *Administrative Science Quarterly* 18, no. 1 (March 1973): 27–36.

53. H. Kirk Downey, Don Hellriegel, and John W. Slocum, Jr., "Environmental Uncertainty: The Construct and Its Application," *Administrative Science Quarterly* 20, no. 4 (December 1975): 613–629.

54. Child, Organizational Structure, Environment and Performance: The Role of Strategic Choice," pp. 2–22.

55. William Starbuck, *Organizations and Their Environment* (Berlin: International Institute of Management, 1973), p. 24.

56. Duncan, "Characteristics of Organizational Environments and Perceived Environmental Uncertainty," p. 325.

57. Ray Jurkovich, "A Core Typology of Organizational Environment," *Administrative Science Quarterly* 19, no. 3 (September 1974): 380–394.

58. Duncan, "Characteristics of Organizational Environments and Perceived Environmental Uncertainty."

59. Jurkovich, "A Core Typology of Organizational Environment," p. 383.

60. Lawrence and Lorsch, *Organization and Environment,* p. 28.

61. Duncan, "Characteristics of Organizational Environment and Perceived Uncertainty," p. 318.

62. Downey, Hellriegel, and Slocum, "Environmental Uncertainty: The Construct and Its Application," p. 615.

63. Duncan, "Characteristics of Organizational Environment and Perceived Uncertainty."

64. Ibid., p. 325.

65. Thomas Burns and G. M. Stalker, *The Management of Innovation* (London: Tavistock Publications, Ltd., 1961).

66. Lawrence and Lorsch, *Organization and Environment,* p. 39.

67. Ibid.

68. Ibid.

69. Osborn and Hunt, "Environment and Organizational Effectiveness."

70. Pennings, "The Relevance of the Structural-Contingency Model of Organizational Effectiveness."

71. Ibid.

4

CONTEXTUAL DIMENSIONS

OBJECTIVES

The major objectives of this chapter are:

1. To discuss the various ways in which organization technology has been conceptualized and operationalized.
2. To analyze the relationship of various types of technology to organizational structure:
   a. operations technology
   b. raw materials technology
   c. knowledge technology
3. To discuss the various ways organizational size has been conceptualized and operationalized.
4. To analyze the relationship of organizational size to organizational structure.

INTRODUCTION

Since the mid '60s, organizational theorists have been concerned with the context within which organizations function. The term *contextual dimension* is here used to denote the internal environment (size and technology) in which structure develops. In this chapter, we will be looking at the effects of technology and size on organizational structure and, to some extent, on organizational performance. Those who analyze these relationships assume that structure is a product of the context within which it functions, and therefore, that variation in organizational structure can be explained by contextual factors. For example, Peter Blau has attempted to show that size is the major determinant of structure;[1] while Joan Woodward has argued that operations technology and Charles Perrow that task routineness are the most important determinants.[2]

Before considering the specific effects of size and technology on the various structural dimensions of organizations, we should examine the effects of combined contextual dimensions in explaining structural dimensions. To this end, the Aston Group (Pugh and associates) conducted two studies in which seven primary dimensions of organizational context—origin and history, ownership and control, size, charter, technology, location and dependence on other organizations—were related to three structural variables: 1) structuring of activities, that is, the degree to which the intended behavior of employees is overtly defined by task specialization, standardized routines, and formal paper work; 2) concentration of authority, that is, the degree to which authority for decisions rests in controlling units outside the organization and is centralized at the higher hierarchical levels within; 3) line control of workflow, that is, the degree to which control is exercised by line personnel rather than through impersonal procedures.[3] The contextual and structural variables of the Aston conceptual scheme are found in Table 4–1. In 1969, Pugh and associates analyzed forty-six English Midland organizations. Two contextual variables (size and technology) predicted the structuring of activities (r = .75). Two other contextual variables—dependence (discussed in chapter three) and location—predicted concentration of authority (r = .75).[4] These findings were supported in the 1970 replication study using the abbreviated measures on a sample of forty organizations in the English Midlands. Structuring of activities was found to be primarily related to organization size and, to a lesser extent, technology.[5] Thus, size and technology are two major contextual predictors of structuring of activities.

TECHNOLOGY

As may be recalled from chapter two, the technological model of organizations depicts organizational structure and performance resulting from organizational technology. A researcher may conceptualize an organization as a highly interdependent, complex system, and simply designate one variable as independent for research purposes—this is simply an analytical strategy. But for many theorists, the technological variable is considered to be a true determinant of the type of structure that develops. The interest in

106

TABLE 4–1   Conceptual Scheme for Empirical Study of Work Organizations

CONTEXTUAL VARIABLES	STRUCTURAL VARIABLES†
Origin and history	*Structuring of Activities*
Ownership and control	Functional specialization
Size	Role specialization
Charter	Standardization (overall)
Technology	Formalization (overall)
Location	
Resources	*Concentration of Authority*
Dependence	Centralization of decision making
ACTIVITY VARIABLES*	Autonomy of the organization
Identification	Standardization of procedures for
(charter, image)	selection and advancement
Perpetuation	*Line control of workflow*
(thoughtways, finance,	Subordinate ratio
personnel services)	Formalization of role performance
Workflow	recording
(production, distribution)	Percentage of workflow superordinates
Control	*Relative size of supportive component*
(direction, motivation,	Percentage of clerks
evaluation, communication)	Percentage of nonworkflow personnel
Homeostasis	Vertical span (height)
(fusion, leadership, problem	
solving, legitimization)	PERFORMANCE VARIABLES
	Efficiency (profitability, productivity,
	market standing)
	Adaptability
	Morale

*Bakke (1959)
†Pugh, et al. (1968)

Source: D. S. Pugh, D. J. Hickson, C. R. Hinings, and C. Turner, "The Context of Organization Structure," *Administrative Science Quarterly* 14, no. 1 (March 1969): 92.

technology as an independent variable stems from the recognition that the work processes of an organization provide the foundation upon which social structure is built. Thus, it is posited that technology does influence the structure of organizations and that technology and organizational structure operate together to set limits on the organizational performance. This is a contingency model in which technology is the determinant.

Technology Defined

A cursory examination of the research and writings on the technological dimension reveals that this concept has been used in many different ways. For example, in recent investigations, the concept of technology has been operationalized in terms of the extent of task interdependence,[6] automation of equipment,[7] uniformity or complexity of materials used,[8] and the degree of routineness of work.[9] Regardless of these diverse operational definitions of technology, there seems to be general agreement that organizational technology involves either the mechanical or intellectual processes by which an organization transforms inputs, or raw materials, into outputs.

In defining technology, the first distinction that must be made is whether technology is conceptualized as a characteristic of the entire system, which includes work done by machine, or as a task completed by an individual. For example, Woodward considered technology to be a characteristic of the entire system and analyzed the complexity of the system of production and the predictability and control of operations technology.[10] Continuous flow production is considered more complex from the perspective of the entire operation than unit or mass production. Thus, technology ranges from unit to batch to continuous flow production in progressive degrees of complexity. It is assumed here that the nature of the manufacturing processes in each firm affects both structure and performance of the entire organization.

On the other hand, several other studies (for example, those of Jerald Hage and Michael Aiken and Perrow[11]) used such variables as noise level, task interdependence, and routineness of task at the individual level as measures of technology. This approach assumes that technologies may vary from department to department. Thus, there may be a different relationship between technology and structure or effectiveness for research and development than for accounting or production. When tasks are ordered on the basis of the routineness of transforming raw materials, the continuous process production and unit production are routine, unlike mass or batch production. That is, as one moves from unit production to continuous flow production, the task routineness takes on a curvilinear shape—from less to greater and back to less routine. Perrow here defines technology in terms of the raw material on which the operation is performed—as "the action that an individual performs upon an object . . . in order to make some change in that object."[12] Thus, Perrow concentrates on the nature of the raw material or *material*

108

technology. Also using the individual as the unit of analysis, Perrow developed the concept of *knowledge technology,* which he regards as the ability to understand the raw material or the extent of knowledge about it.[13]

If we compare the definitions of technology with the level of analysis of the various studies, it appears that these definitions are at least in part a function of the level of analysis employed. Systemwide studies focus on the general type of production technology used throughout an organization, a more global measure. On the other hand, individual-level studies are typically concerned with task or job technology. The organizational analyst should be cautioned against drawing general conclusions concerning the effects of technology without specifying in advance the particular aspect—as well as the level—of technology that is measured.

It is necessary to differentiate between these three broadly defined types of organizational technology. Hickson, Pugh, and Pheysey et al. have listed them as: operations technology, materials technology, and knowledge technology.[14] *Operations technology* is defined as *"the equipping and sequencing of activities in the workflow."*[15] These activities may range from hand piece work to continuous flow production. Workflow here means the producing and distributing of output. *Material technology* is defined as *"the characteristics of the materials used in the workflow."*[16] These materials, for example, steel, gas, people, are called "raw materials" by Perrow. He separates them into two categories: uniform and nonuniform.[17] *Knowledge technology* is defined as *"the characteristic of the knowledge used in the workflow."*[18] They specify that this knowledge about the raw material and its processing can be developed and standardized or left to chance and variability. The amount, quality, and sophistication of knowledge about the raw material and its processing may vary. It is important to note that all three of these types of technology exist in a single organization. For example, in the production of custom-built automobiles, the operations technology may be unit construction by hand. The material technology may be of a relatively simple, routine raw material, but the process may require highly skilled, trained employees with a great deal of knowledge technology.

Operations Technology   One of the earliest and most widely quoted typologies of operations technology was developed by Woodward.[19] Focusing on industrial firms, Woodward constructed three categories of technology based largely on the level of technical complexity of the production process. The first category is *small batch* or *unit production.* Here the product is "custom-made" on a small scale, sometimes to consumer specifications (for example, airplanes, locomotives, and printing). Operations performed on each unit are typically nonrepetitive, and the unit is distinctive. The second category is *mass production.* Here the product is manufactured on an assembly line (for example, automobiles, radios, televisions). The operations performed are repetitive, routine, and predictable. The third category is *continuous process production.* Here the product is transformed from raw material to finished good using a series of machine or process transformations (for example, chemical and oil refining). Woodward argued that the technical complexity of an organization increases as it moves from unit to continuous process production. Later, the Aston Group refined Woodward's scale of "technical complexity" and called it "production continuity." Hickson and associates defined technology in terms of a general factor called "work-flow integration" based on the degree of task interdependence, rigidity of work-flow sequence, automation of equipment, and the degree to which measurement was used in the evaluation of operations output.[20] The greater the automation, task specificity, etc., the greater the work-flow integration index score.

Structural Correlates of Operations Technology. Woodward's book entitled *Industrial Organizations: Theory and Practice* was written to assess how accurately the principle of classical management theory corresponds to organizational practice and to assess the relationship between technology, structural dimensions, and performance dimensions. Although we are interested in both of these endeavors, we will concentrate on the latter. On preliminary examination of her data, Woodward found that, in terms of structural dimensions, successful industrial organizations seemed to have little in common. But when she analyzed the successful organizations controlling for type of operations technology, she found that all unit production organizations possessed common structural characteristics, as did the large batch or mass production firms and the continuous process production organizations. This relationship between organizational success, technology, and structural characteristics suggested to Woodward that the system of production is an important variable in the determination of organizational structure. Woodward found that successful unit production organizations had short, broadly based pyramids. Successful continuous process production organizations were characterized by taller pyramid structure with narrow bases, small ratios of direct to indirect labor, large spans of control, and a large number of levels of management. The successful mass production and large batch organizations had the most clearly and precisely defined codified duties and responsibilities of managerial and supervisory staff, a close adherence to the principles of unity of command, and a separation of advisory and executive responsibilities. Thus, these successful large batch or mass production organizations seem to adhere most to the principles of classical management theory discussed in chapter two.[21]

Similarly, in her analysis of organizational change, Woodward observed that as the type of technology changed so did the organizational structure. As large batch production firms were converted to continuous flow production, the command hierarchy lengthened, the span of control of the chief executive widened, and the ratio of managers and supervisors to total personnel increased. On the other hand, the firms that had reverted to unit production, thereby abandoning the standardized production of parts, saw a reduction of levels of authority from eight to four.[22]

Woodward concluded that while there is no single way to structure all organizations, there are particular organizational structures appropriate to given operations technologies if an organization is to be successful. Implementing this structural-contingency model of organizations with technology as the determinant variable, a more highly structured, formalized, bureaucratized structure is appropriate in mass production organizations. On the other hand, at both ends of the technological continuum (unit or batch and continuous process), successful firms are less structured, formalized, and bureaucratic.

It should be noted that not all subsequent analyses have supported Woodward's early findings. For example, Hickson and associates, in their study of thirty-one manufacturing and fifteen social service organizations, tested her hypothesis that technology and structure are strongly related; they did not find the linear relationships between structural variables (specialization and standardization) and technology evidenced in Woodward's research.[23] But they did find a relationship between size and the structural variables, unlike Woodward. These relationships between operations technology and structural variables are noted in Table 4–2. The differences in specific indicators may account for these differences in findings, or the findings may simply be a result of examining different types of organizations.

TABLE 4-2 Comparison with Woodward's Findings (1958, 1965)

SOUTH-EAST ESSEX FINDINGS		EQUIVALENT BIRMINGHAM RESULTS (N = 31)	
Structural Variable	Relationship*	Structural Variable	Relationship†
"Length of line of command" (N = 80)	Positive linear	Vertical span	0.26‡§
"Span of control of chief executive" (N = 80)	Positive linear	Span of control of chief executive	0.08
"Ratio of direct to indirect labour" (N = 75)	Positive linear	Not available (total hourly paid indirect labour not separated from total nonworkflow personnel)	—
"Ratio of managers to total personnel" (N = 45)	Positive linear	Percentage of workflow superordinates to total employees	0.13
"Ratio of clerical and administrative staff to manual workers" (N = 75)	Positive linear	Percentage of nonworkflow personnel to total employees	0.04‡
"Span of control of first-line supervisors in production departments" (N = 78)	∩-shaped curvilinear	Subordinate-supervisor ratio	−0.09 (0.36#)

*Relationship with "technological complexity" over three production groups; unit, batch-mass, process.
†Product-moment (linear) correlation with production continuity scale.
‡Partial correlation coefficient holding (log) size constant.
§Not significant.
#Correlation-ratio coefficient of nonlinear correlation (η).

Source: D. J. Hickson, D. S. Pugh, and D. C. Pheysey, "Operations Technology and Organization Structure: An Empirical Reappraisal," *Administrative Science Quarterly* 14, no. 3 (September 1969): 392.

Hickson and associates' study produced evidence of a convex curvilinear relationship between the subordinate–superordinate ratio, the percentage employed in inspection and maintenance, and the degree of role specialization in workflow control on the one hand and technology on the other.[24] Likewise, John Child and Roger Mansfield found that several configurational variables displayed convex curvilinear functions in relation to workflow integration: subordinate–superordinate ratio and percentage direct work. Chief executive span displayed a concave curvilinear function in relation to workflow integration. Child also found that certain role specialist areas tended to be curvilinearly related to workflow integration. The percentages in sales and after-sales activities and percentage in market research exhibited convex curvilinear relationships to workflow integration.[25]

Hickson and associates summarized that although their research did not support a sweeping "technological imperative" hypothesis, seven structural variables were found to be associated with technology. Subordinate–supervisor ratio, proportion in inspection, and proportion in maintenance were curvilinearly related to the production continuity variable (operations technology); proportion in workflow (production) control had a negatively linear relationship to production continuity; proportion in transport and dispatch had a positive linear relationship to both production continuity and workflow integration; both proportions in employment (personnel) and specialization had a negative linear relationship to workflow integration.[26] The Aston Group findings concerning the relationship of technology to structure are summarized in two of their conclusions. First, as demonstrated above, ". . . only those [structural dimensions] directly centered on the production workflow itself show any connection with technology. . . ."[27] Thus, technology appears to effect organizational structure only in departments implementing that technology. Second, in large organizations, variables of operations that are centered in the workflow process (supervisor–subordinate ratios, etc.) are affected. By the function of size, the workflow process (technology) will be separated from the administrative components of these organizations. Thus, one would not expect the relationship between workflow and administrative hierarchy or decision-making to be as great a factor in large organizations as in small ones. In small organizations, the workflow technology strongly influences the administrative component because everyone is close to the production process, whereas in large organizations, managers and administrators are at a greater social and geographic distance from the operations technology; here the department heads and specialists (greater complexity and formalization) often impinge on the influence of technology on administrators. Although the Aston Group did not discount technology as an influence on structure, they did conclude that technology is not its major cause. Rather, size predominates as a predictor of structure. Hickson and associates concluded by constructing the following hypothesis of the relationship between structure and technology:

> Structural variables will be associated with operations technology only where they are centered on the workflow. The smaller the organization the more its structure will be pervaded by such technological effects: the larger the organization, the more these effects will be confined to variables such as job-counts of employees on activities linked with the workflow itself, and will not be detectable in variables of the more remote administrative and hierarchical structure.[28]

Thus, Pugh, Hickson, and associates constructed a contingency model in which technology affects structure through the intervening variables of size and departmental function. In conclusion, technological determinism does not seem to be a viable model for explaining organizational structure and performance. Rather, the relationship between operations technology and structure and performance is mediated by organizational size and departmental function.

Materials and Knowledge Technology   Perrow defined technology as "the actions that an individual performs upon an object . . . in order to make some change in that object."[29] According to Perrow, the object or raw material may be "a living thing (human or otherwise), a symbol, or an inanimate object"—for example, people are raw material in universities and service organizations; symbols are raw material in advertising agencies and research organizations.[30] James Thompson[31] contends along with Perrow that the nature of raw materials influences how organizations are structured and function.[32] One important aspect of this technology is the number of "exceptional cases" for which there are no specific rules to guide its processing. Few exceptional cases exist when objects are stable and uniform. When the raw material is a human being or human interaction, it is expected to be nonuniform and to manifest many exceptional cases, whereas when the raw material is natural gas, it is much more uniform. The search process (method of proceeding) must vary when exceptional cases are found in the raw material.

Raw materials have two major characteristics: (1) the extent to which their nature can be understood; and (2) their stability or variability. These two characteristics deal with the state of knowledge that exists about the material and the extent to which the material can be handled in a standardized fashion. Increased knowledge of the nature of the material leads to a greater understanding of its varieties. Thus, the level of knowledge technology is directly related to the type of raw material.[33]

Thompson's typology of technology is based on two dimensions that were made explicit in the previous discussion of Perrow's work: (1) the degree to which operating procedures are established and (2) the degree to which raw materials are standardized. In Thompson's typology of organizations, consisting of long-linked, mediating, and intensive), long-linked technology is based on repetitive application of a single technology to a standardized product. This is Woodward's continuous flow operations technology. In Perrow's scheme, long-linked technology involves low variability or standardized raw materials and analyzable search procedures (a well-established process). The mediating type of technology operates in a standardized manner with unstandardized raw materials, such as clients. Thompson argued that bureaucratic rules are beneficial with this type of technology, in that they help reduce the variability during the unanalyzable search procedure. Although exceptions continue to exist, one way in which the variability of the raw materials (clients) is reduced is by the categorization of certain dimensions (e.g., type of service needed). That is, customers of a bank may be classified as depositors and borrowers and subsequently be dealt with according to standardized procedures. Intensive technologies (for example, hospitals) involve the application of a variety of techniques, skills, and services in the transformation of an object (in this case, the patient). Through feedback, the object determines the nature of transformation. The application of a variety of techniques usually requires the use of unanalyzable search procedures, which in turn require the completion of nonroutine tasks.[34]

Both Thompson's and Perrow's typologies of technology are based on the nature of knowledge applied within the organization. A comparison reveals that Thompson's and Perrow's typologies are capable of including a wider variety of organizations than Woodward's. Woodward addressed herself specifically to industrial organizations, while Thompson and Perrow sought to include almost every type of work organization.

In keeping with the Woodward research model, Perrow and Thompson treated technology as an independent variable and structure and performance as the dependent variables. Perrow distinguished between structure and technology by pointing out that technology involves *changing* the raw material, while structure involves the *form* that interaction takes in changing the raw materials (the arrangement of the relationships). Perrow agreed that the distinction between technology and structure has its gray areas, but basically this is the difference between an individual acting directly upon a material that is to be changed and an individual interacting with other individuals in the course of trying to change that material.[35]

Organizational goals are also perceived as a dependent variable in Perrow's analysis. Perrow typed organizations on the basis of the routineness of their technology as opposed to their societal function. He wrote that types of organization—in terms of their function in society—will vary as much within each type as between types. Thus, some schools, hospitals, banks, and steel companies may have more in common, because of their routine character, than routine and nonroutine schools, routine and nonroutine hospitals, and so forth. Perrow further asserted that to assume that one is holding constant the major variable comparing several schools or several steel mills is unwarranted until one looks at the technologies employed by these organizations.[36] His models suggest several implications for comparative studies of organization. First, he posited that it would not make sense to expect a particular relationship found in one organization to be found in another unless we know these organizations are similar in their technology. Finally, Perrow's model has implications for those perspectives of organizations that call for decentralization, representative bureaucracy, collegial authority, or employee-centered, innovative, or organic organization. This type of structure can be realized only with certain types of technology. The organization will necessarily have to sacrifice rate of output to perpetuate this form of structure. Perrow, like Weber, posited that the bureaucratic structure is the optimum one for increased efficiency when the technology is routine.[37]

Structural Correlates of Material and Knowledge Technology.
Hage and Aiken analyzed the relationship between organizational technology, specifically the degree of routineness of work and the

116

structure and performance goals of sixteen health and welfare organizations, where the raw material is people.[38] They adopted Perrow's definition of routineness of task as their measure of technology because, unlike the types of operation technology enumerated by Woodward, it is applicable to people-processing organizations. Because Perrow's definition includes both the relative stability or variability of the raw material as well as how much is known about that material and process, it could be applied to the degree to which the clients were stable and uniform and to the extent to which knowledge existed about their processing. These health and welfare organizations tend to be on the nonroutine end of the continuum. If some of the organizations had been toward the other end of the continuum, as are some industrial organizations, the differences exhibited in the findings would have been even greater.

In this research, aggregated employee attitudes were used to measure technological, structural, and goal variables. Hage and Aiken found that organizations with more routine work are more centralized and formalized and have less professionally trained personnel. Stratification was found to be unrelated to routineness of work. Routine organizations were found to emphasize goals of efficiency and the quantity of clients served rather than innovation, staff morale, or quality of client service.[39]

Richard Hall also utilized Perrow's definition of technology. In his attempt to operationalize Perrow's definition, he ranked organizations according to the degree to which they manipulated "objects" as opposed to "ideas" and the extent to which they worked with "people" as opposed to "inanimate objects." When raw materials were objects, rather than ideas, the organizations were more bureaucratized (structured). Similarly, people-oriented organizations were somewhat less structured than non-people organizations. Like Woodward and unlike the Aston Group, Hall found little association between size and bureaucratization. He concluded that the nature of an organization's technology influences its structure.[40] The more amenable the application of knowledge is to routinized practices, the more likely rules and procedures will guide the processes within the organization. Hall found that long-linked technologies exhibited high levels of impersonality, extensive hierarchies of authority and divisions of labor, and formalized rules and procedures, while organizations based on intensive technologies exhibited low levels of these characteristics.[41]

In a secondary analysis of Hall's 1968 data, Elizabeth Morrissey and David Gillespie examined the relationship between professionalism and rationality within organizations with different types of technology. They hypothesized that in professions where components of the professional task were more amenable to routinization, a higher compatibility would exist between the dimensions of professionalism (self-regulation and individual autonomy) and organizational rationality (formalization of rules and procedures and technical competency). They found that organizations that were based on intensive technologies, and employed professionals whose tasks were also intensive, resulted in fewer organizational rules and procedures and more reliance on technical competency, self-regulation, and autonomy. In organizations based on long-linked technologies with professionals involved in mediating tasks, emphasis was placed on rules and procedures with less reliance on self-regulation, technical competency, and autonomy. They concluded that the relationship between professionalization of the labor force and the bureaucratization of organizational characteristics is dependent on organizational technology and the nature of professional tasks.[42]

ORGANIZATIONAL SIZE

Definition

When one refers to a "large organization" what is meant by the term "large"? Does it refer to the organization's net assets? To the number of employees? The number of clients? Of course, assets, employees, and clients are all indicators of organizational size. But what is the relationship of these indicators to each other and to the structural dimensions of organizations?

The most frequently utilized definition of size is the number of employees or personnel holding positions in the organization. However, there are several complicated issues to be considered in computing the number of employees. In order to avoid the complication of voluntary vs. paid involvement, the term "position" is used to denote either type of personnel—in most measures of organizational size, the paid and nonpaid workers are considered to be equivalent. Similar considerations are involved when both full-time and part-time personnel are employed. For example, the number of university faculty may far exceed the number of full-time faculty positions. Thus, when relating the number of faculty to other measures of size, such as assets, or to other organizational dimensions, the findings may be misleading unless the measure is standardized by using the number of full-time equivalent positions (FTEs). This practice en-

118

ables the researcher to compare labor force size across organizations. Another advantage of this measure is that, all other variables being equal, computing the number of full-time equivalent positions gives a better indicator of the amount of work accomplished.

Utilizing the number of clients as a measure of organizational size is a common practice in studying service organizations; number of clients reflects the number of personnel needed to service them. On the other hand, an industry such as an automobile manufacturer may speak of the number of cars produced or number of customers purchasing the commodity in a given time period. This is an indication of output and indirectly of personnel and assets of the manufacturer. When the type of technology is controlled, the number of customers may well be a good predictor of personnel. But number of customers may be an inaccurate indicator of personnel when used across organizations with differing degrees of automation.

Furthermore, there is often confusion over whether a person is an employee or a client of an organization. For example, a student in a university is a client, and if the researcher is defining size in terms of full-time equivalent positions, that person should not be computed in the size of the organization. At the same time, that same student may hold a maintenance, clerical, or teaching position in the university while being enrolled. In this instance the person holds a position that would be computed as organizational size if the researcher is defining size as the number of full-time equivalent employee positions. If a person holds both employee and client positions and the researcher is defining organizational size to include both employees and clients, the person should be counted as both. Thus, when positions rather than persons are being used as the measurement, much of the confusion over whether a person is a client or an employee is eliminated. This definition has the extra advantage of being based on the roles in which the person is involved. In some instances, the individual may be involved in employee roles and at other times in client roles. This approach avoids the limitations of defining the person as client *or* employee based on a psychological measure of where his or her major interests lie and on an arbitrary assignment to a single role—employee or client—when in fact the person is involved in both.

Interrelationships of Size Indicators

Organizational assets are often used as indicators of size by those who study industrial and business organizations, while those who study universities, welfare organizations, hospitals, and so on

119

often utilize the number of clients served. Service organizations use the number of customers served to justify the need for more state and federal funds; industrial organizations use net assets to measure their success and justify the need for more support from their controlling or parent companies. How do each of these indicators compare with the number of employees? This question may be answered by examining studies that have made such comparisons. For example, Pugh and associates measured the size of forty-six English industrial organizations as the number of employees and as the assets of the organizations. They found the correlation between number of employees and net assets was strong (r = .78).[43] One might correctly conclude that the number of employees is closely related to the financial assets of an organization. It stands to reason that, under most conditions, more prosperous industries are better able to support large numbers of employees. Of course, there are exceptions. In continuous flow or highly automated technological industries, one would expect much higher net assets with a lower number of employees than in either the unit production or mass production type of technology. This is so simply because machines are accomplishing the work that would otherwise be accomplished by employees. One would expect a much higher correlation between net assets and number of employees in business or industrial organizations than in public service organizations. This idea was documented by Child, who found a relatively low correlation between number of employees and net assets because twenty-seven of the organizations he studied were in two service industries—advertising and insurance.[44] The role of financial assets in service organizations was not comparable to their role in industrial organizations. When the remaining subsample of manufacturing organizations was taken separately, the correlation between the numbers of employees and net assets rose (r = .86). Thus, a strong relationship exists between net assets and number of employees in industrial and manufacturing organizations. However, this relationship does not seem to hold for service organizations.

In their study of hospitals (a type of service organization), Theodore Anderson and Seymour Warkov analyzed the relationship between the number of employees and the number of clients. They found a correlation of .97 and .98 between average daily patient load and the total number of employees.[45] Similarly, in another type of service organization—colleges and universities—Amos Hawley, Walter Boland, and Margaret Boland found correlations of .94 between the number of students and faculty.[46] Thus, research has shown that the size indicators of both number of clients (in service organizations) and net assets of organizations (in industrial organizations) are highly correlated with the number of employees (full-time equivalents) of the organization. But it is unknown whether net assets and number of employees are highly related in service organizations. Consequently, most organizational researchers have taken the number of full-time equivalents as their operational definition of size, especially when relating size to structure. Since people are organized, one would expect their numbers to have a closer relationship to structure than other aspects of size.

Structural Correlates of Size

Size is the contextual variable most frequently conceptualized as influencing organizational structure. There is a long standing, intense debate concerning direction, shape, and magnitude of the relation between size and structural variables. In other words, just how critical is size as a predictor of organizational structure? Its importance has been argued theoretically and empirically by Woodward and Thompson, who found that the tasks and technology of organizations are better than size as predictors of structure;[47] by Pugh and his associates, who found that size influences structure through the intervening effects of frequency of decision-making and social control;[48] by Hall, who found that size is no more important than other factors in understanding structure;[49] and finally, by Child, who found that size exerts a dominant influence on the level of organizational complexity, but that organizational control, formalization, and decision-making are not determined specifically by size.[50] Perhaps the most conclusive evidence of the importance of size as both an independent and causal variable is Marshall Meyer's longitudinal path analysis of data from 194 city, county, and state departments of finance in 1966 and 1971.[51] Meyer found that size affects both horizontal (number of subunits) and vertical (levels of hierarchy) differentiation as well as number of supervisors; that size causes changes in these variables but the reverse is not true (a unidirectional relationship was specified); and that the relationships between other structural variables vanishes when size is controlled.[52]

Child analyzed the structural correlates of organizational size used in his own National Sample of eighty-two varied work organizations; the Aston Group's study of forty-six varied work organizations;[53] in C. R. Hinings and G. L. Lee's analysis of nine engineering firms;[54] and in Malcolm Warner and Lex Donaldson's study of seven

121

TABLE 4-3 Product–Moment Correlations of Selected Structural Variables with Size of Organization (Log. Number Employees)

Structural variables (Blau & Schoenherr in parentheses)	NATIONAL STUDY		ASTON STUDY				
	Total Sample (N = 82)	Manufacturing orgs. (N = 40)	Total Sample (N = 46)	Manufacturing orgs. (N = 31)	Manufacturing orgs.° (N = 9)	Labor unions† (N = 7)	U.S. employment security agencies‡ (N = 53)
Functional specialization (Number of divisions)	.61	.65	.67	.75	.84	.73	.55
Overall role specialization (Division of labor)	.72	.90	.74	.83	.87	not available	.82
Overall standardization (Extent of regulations)	.63	.76	.56	.65	.84	.82	.41
Overall documentation (No equivalent measure)	.58	.69	.55	.67	.83	.70	—
Overall centralization (1. Delegation personnel 2. Delegation budget 3. Decentralization: influence)	-.58	-.74	-.39	-.47	-.64	-.62	1. -.27 φ 2. -.21 φ 3. -.33 φ
Vertical span (Number of hierarchical levels)	.65	.63	.67	.77	.82	.74	.73

°Hinings and Lee (1971)
†Warner and Donaldson, unpublished data
‡Blau and Schoenherr (1971)
φSign reversed.

Source: John Child. "Predicting and Understanding Organization Structure," *Administrative Science Quarterly* 18, no. 2 (June 1973): 170.

labor unions.[55] All four studies were of British organizations and utilized the Aston study's measure of organizational structure.[56] Some comparisons from Peter Blau and Richard Schoenherr's research were also included.[57] The structural variables were operationalized as in the multi-item measurement developed by Pugh and associates: (1) functional specialization, (2) role specialization, (3) standardization of rules and procedures, (4) overall documentation (formalization), (5) vertical span, and (6) centralization–decentralization. Through cross study comparison, Child found that not only were correlations between size and each structural variable consistent as to direction, but in most cases the level of correlation, as an indicator of strength of association, remained stable. Child felt this degree of stability was noteworthy in view of the fact that the five samples of organizations differed in geographic location and types of activity. The strength of the correlation in the Blau–Schoenherr findings departed from the studies using the Aston measures with respect to extent of regulations and delegation. Child felt this departure may have been due to these measures being less comparable to the Aston equivalents.[58] These findings are summarized in Table 4–3. Child concluded that with a few exceptions, the proportion of variance in the major dimensions of organizational structure were predictable from knowing the organization's size. Furthermore, large organizations were found to be more bureaucratic and specialized; to have more rules, documentation, extensive hierarchies, and greater decentralization of decision-making within the hierarchies. It can also be seen from Table 4–3 that the strength of the relationship between size and structure was greater in the manufacturing organizations. Child noted that it is not now clear whether this variance pointed to a real difference between service and manufacturing organizations, or whether it was partly a product of the Pugh and associates' schedule of measures, which was slightly oriented toward manufacturing operations.[59]

In order to explore the above question, Child concentrated in his own research on the predictability of structure from a knowledge of size across multiple types of organizations. Holding size constant, he found that in the manufacturing industries of electronics, pharmaceuticals, and confectionaries, there was more diversity of structure in small than in large organizations, whereas organizations in the service industries (advertising and insurance) tended to have relatively unbureaucratic structures at all size levels. In the newspaper industry, smaller organizations were moderately bureaucratic for their size, while larger organizations were relatively unbureaucratic for their size. Thus, although increasing size indicates increasing structure, given a certain number of employees the structural arrangement within different industries varies. These differences could be explained by the nature of the industry.[60]

When structure is considered a unidimensional construct and termed bureaucratic if rigid and detailed, some important findings are masked because not all the structural dimensions of organizations are related to size, and the remaining ones are certainly not related in the same directions. For example, formalization is positively related to size, while centralization is negatively related. In this text, organizational structure is assumed to be multi-dimensional. Therefore, the remainder of this section is devoted to an analysis of the relationship of size to the major structural dimensions of organizations.

Complexity Correlates

Before clarifying the relationship between size and organizational complexity, it is necessary to point out that not all theorists define structural complexity in the same manner. There are many indicators of organizational complexity, and they deal with essentially different, though related, aspects of organizations. Complexity can be based on (1) differentiation of roles, (2) differentiation of function, and (3) an application of high levels of expertise in the completion of roles. Most researchers measure complexity in only one of the above ways, but Child operationalized complexity utilizing all three indicators: overall role specialization, functional specialization, and level of specialist qualification.[61] Child postulated that viewed in conjunction with other contextual variables, size would be a major predictor of complexity, but that complexity would have a more direct, and therefore stronger, influence than size on the extent to which a bureaucratic strategy of control was present. Formalization and centralization of decision-making were taken to represent the bureaucratic control strategy. In analyzing the relationship between size and complexity, Child found that the size of the organization exerted a dominant influence on the level of organizational complexity. Similarly, in his analysis of the relationship of organizational size (number of full-time employees) to horizontal and vertical differentiation of finance departments, Meyer found that size had a causal effect on both number of subunits (.21) and number of levels of hierarchy (.36).[62] Yet neither horizontal nor vertical differentiation influenced size nor were horizontal and vertical differentiation related when the effects of size were controlled. Thus, both Child and Meyer found positive relationships between size and various aspects of organizational complexity.

Much of the current research on the relationship of size, complexity, and control was initiated by Blau. Blau and his associates found relatively strong relationships between size and structural differentiation.[63] From his research on government bureaucracies, Blau constructed a formal theory of differentiation in which size was the major causal variable. According to his theory, expanded size increases the subdivision of responsibilities, facilitates supervision, widens the span of control of supervision, and at the same time creates structural differentiation and problems of coordination that require supervisory attention. Blau's theory consists of two basic generalizations: (1) increasing organizational size generates differentiation along various lines at decelerating rates and (2) differentiation enlarges the administrative component in organizations to effect coordination.[64] From these generalizations, nine propositions were deduced. These generalizations and propositions are found in Table 4-4. Blau used the number of employees as his operational measure of size; for his operational definition of differentiation, he used the number of branches, occupational positions (division of labor), hierarchical levels, divisions, and sections within the branches or divisions.

In addition to analyzing the relationships of size to differentiation, Blau analyzed the consequences of structural differentiation. These relationships will be discussed more thoroughly in chapter six. They are important to this discussion of size because increased size influences the control and coordination in organizations (both formalization and centralization of decision-making) through complexity or increased differentiation. In delineating the influence of size on differentiation and on control and coordination, Blau utilized an economy of scale theory. As is demonstrated by the above proposition, Blau's theory states that larger organizations and their subunits are more differentiated than small organizations with respect to organizational responsibilities and tasks. Thus, large organizations not only have more structural subunits to handle the tasks, but these components are larger than in smaller organizations. Thus, in large organizations, the mean number of units of structure and the size of the individual subunits is greater than in small ones. The work carried on *within* each structural unit is very much the same, thus simplifying supervision and widening the span of control of supervi-

TABLE 4–4 Generalizations and Propositions of Blau's Formal Theory of Differentiation in Organizations

GENERALIZATION 1: Increasing size generates structural differentiation in organizations along various dimensions at decelerating rates.

1A. Large size promotes structural differentiation.

1B. Large size promotes differentiation along several different lines.

1C. The rate of differentiation declines with expanding size.

1D. The subunits into which an organization is differentiated become internally differentiated in parallel manner.

Propositions:

1.1 As the size of organizations increases, its marginal influence on differentiation decreases.

1.2. The larger an organization is, the larger the average size of its structural components of all kinds.

1.3. The proportionate size of the average structural component, as distinguished from its absolute size, decreases with increases in organizational size.

1.4. The larger the organization is, the wider the supervisory span of control.

1.5. If the proportion of managerial personnel declines with size and their span of control expands with size, this means that large scale operations reduce the proportionate size of the administrative overhead, specifically, of the complement of managers and supervisors.

1.6. The economy of scale in administrative overhead itself declines with increasing organizational size.

GENERALIZATION 2: Structural differentiation in organizations enlarges the administrative component because the intensified problems of coordination and communication in differentiated structures demand administrative attention.

Propositions:

2.1. The large size of an organization indirectly raises the ratio of administrative personnel through the structural differentiation it generates.

2.2. The direct effects of large organizational size lowering the administrative ratio exceeds its indirect effects, raising it owing to the structural differentiation it generates.

2.3. The differentiation of large organizations into subunits stems the decline in the economy of scale in management with increasing size, that is, the decline in the decrease in the proportion of marginal personnel with increasing size.

Source: Peter M. Blau, "A Formal Theory of Differentiation in Organization," *American Sociological Review* 35, no. 2 (April 1970): 204, 206–214.

sion. Thus, there is a lower administrative ratio in these larger organizations than in smaller ones, a manifestation of the economy of scale. At the same time, the work carried on among the structural units produced by differentiation creates problems of coordination, control, and communication, which are met by increasing the number of administrative personnel. If the work carried on by the differentiated units is not the same, that is, if functional differentiation occurs, the coordination problems become more intense. Blau did not deal with other methods of handling the problems of coordination and control; he postulates that the large size raises administrative overhead, and that this increase is countered by effects of economy of scale and cost of administrative overhead. The increased size has a "diminishing marginal influence on expanding differentiation."[65] Thus, size promotes differentiation at a declining rate.

Blau deduced his theory from his research on employment security agencies and later tested it on 416 major finance departments of large cities, large counties, and states in the U.S. This independent test confirmed the propositions suggested by the theory. Blau did not generalize his findings to all types of organizations but did note that whether the theoretical generalizations were also valid for private and other public organizations must be determined by further research.

Administrative Ratio Correlates

The administrative component of an organization coordinates, facilitates, supports, supervises, and communicates the organization's activities. These tasks carried on by the administrator help control the organization and may lead to greater formalization and centralization. The administrative component is usually measured in terms of the "supervisory ratio" or "administrative ratio"—the ratio of number of supervisors and administrators to the total number of all other employees within the organization.

Most of the research on the ratio of administrators has dealt with its relationship to organizational size in an attempt to determine economy of scale. More recently, this ratio has been related to organizational size through the complexity variable. Proponents of this hypothesis emphasize that the significant factor in the disproportionate growth of administrative personnel is not necessarily related to the total number of personnel because increases in the number of employees do not increase problems of coordination and control unless the employees differ in function, specialty, or some other dimension. Thus, the total number of employees and the administrative ratio are directly related only where the increase in employees is positively related to complexity. When complexity increases, there is greater need for coordination and control and a need for larger numbers of administrators. Thus, an organization could conceivably remain constant in size and due to increased complexity, require a larger number of administrators.

The relationship between size and the proportion of administrators has been a concern to organizational researchers since the formulation of Parkinson's Law (work expands proportionally with the time available for its completion).[66] This law has been supported by the 1955 research of Frederic Terrien and Donald Mills, who hypothesized that "the relationship between the size of an administrative component and the total size of its containing organization is such that the larger the size of the containing organization, the greater will be the proportion given over to its administrative component."[67] They found support for this hypothesis in data from 428 California school districts during the 1951–1952 school year. The findings of Terrien and Mills may be explained by the fact that the units being studied were not organizations but rather multi-organizational structures found in multiple locations, and the larger proportion of administrators in larger units may have been due to the need to coordinate, supervise, and communicate between multiple locations.

Contrary to the findings of Terrien and Mills, the more recent research of Anderson and Warkov demonstrated a negative relationship between organizational size and the proportion of administrators. Their data was obtained from forty-nine Veterans' Administration tuberculosis centers and general hospitals. They categorized the manager's office employees, the registrar's office employees, the fiscal office employees, and personnel and supply office workers as administrators; organization size was measured as annual average daily patient loads. They added the variable of functional complexity (defined as number of objectives and extent of internal differentiation) to their analysis and found a positive relationship between it and relative size of the administrative component. They considered the general hospitals to be more complex than the TB hospitals because not only were all tasks performed in the TB hospital also carried out in the general hospitals, but many other services regularly rendered in the general hospitals were not provided in the TB hospitals.[68] Of course, "type of hospital" included many variables other than complexity; it encompassed multiple dimensions that could be influencing the relationship of complexity to the administrative ratio. Anderson and Warkov found that there was a significant relationship between type of hospital and organizational size. The data indicated that the general hospitals were significantly and substantially larger than the TB hospitals, that is, the larger hospitals were also more complex. The fact that about 12.5 percent of the employees were in administration in both types of hospitals was clearly inconsistent with the research findings of Terrien and Mills and the dictum of Parkinson's Law. The administrative ratio did not increase with increasing size.

The samples for both Terrien and Mills and Anderson and Warkov were drawn from service organizations. William Rushing's sample was drawn from forty-one industries, but he also found that the relative size of the administrative component was inversely related to organizational size and positively related to complexity.[69] Rushing used more refined measures of the administrative component—he separated the managerial and clerical personnel into different aspects of the administrative component. He operationalized complexity as the division of labor. Rushing found:

1. The relative number of administrative personnel is directly related to the division of labor among production personnel, but inversely related to the total number of production personnel. This is true for all administrative groups.
2. Controlling for the effects of size and division of labor does not usually cause the relationship between the other variable and the relative size of the administrative groups to disappear. In fact, control for the division of labor increases the relationship between industry size and administration. To this extent, the effects of the two variables are independent.
3. At the same time, however, the variables interact. The effects of the division of labor are greater in smaller industries, while the effects of industry size are greater in industries where the division of labor is high. This finding, however, is not true for the relative number of professional personnel.
4. Finally, the ratio of clerical and professional personnel to managerial personnel increases as the division of labor increases.[70]

129

These data were generally consistent with the theory that coordinative difficulties increase with the division of labor and that the major function of administrative personnel is to resolve these difficulties.[71]

One of the limitations of these earlier studies has been corrected in the research of Blau and associates and others by the use of multivariate analysis rather than simple correlations.[72] The effects of size on the administrative component cannot be assessed without controlling for differentiation. Certainly other variables should also be controlled, but differentiation or complexity has been shown to have an intervening effect on the relationship between size and the administrative component. The empirical facts demonstrate that size independently gives rise to increased structural differentiation and that differentiation independently generates the need for more managerial, administrative, and supervisory personnel. But increasing size alone produces economies of scale in the administrative component because a larger body of employees or members requires a relatively smaller proportion of administrators.

A final note about the new trend toward longitudinal studies is necessary. Longitudinal research on size and administrative ratio demonstrated somewhat different findings from the cross-sectional research. In their analysis of forty-one urban school systems in Canada over a five-year period (1964–1969), Edward Holdaway and Thomas Blowers found support in their cross-sectional data for the thesis that larger organizations tend to have smaller administrative ratios. However, their longitudinal data did not supply similar verification. The proportion of administrators did not rise or fall as the organizations grew over the five year period.[73] Thus, a researcher should be careful not to report cross-sectional data with large and small organizations and infer that patterns of administrative ratio to organizational size reflect growth curves. Inferences have been incorrectly drawn that cross-sectional curves, obtained by plotting administrative ratios against size, represent the way in which the ratio changes as a system grows larger. In order to predict growth, both size *and* time variables should be considered.

Formalization Correlates

When increased organizational size results in increased complexity, thus generating administrative problems of coordination, one response is to increase bureaucratic control through formalization, that is, to expand the standard rules, procedures, and documentations. Thus, size indirectly determines formalization, while complexity directly determines it. With increased complexity

130

comes a larger number of administrators, and in organizations where the employees have high levels of expertise and decision-making is distributed downward in the hierarchy (decentralized), the method of organizational control is likely to be standardization of procedures and documentation or increased formalization.

Pugh and his associates found that large organizations tend not only to be more specialized, but also more standardized and formalized than small organizations.[74] Child later tested the relationships between organizational size (number of employees), complexity (role and task specialization), and formalization.[75] He found that role specialization was the major predictor of overall standardization and documentation and a better one than functional specialization, but both measures of specialization or complexity were better predictors of formalization than was organization's size. Child concluded that with regard to formalization it is neither theoretically convincing nor statistically demonstrable that size is the major determinant of bureaucratic control. The specialization and expertise of employees as measured by role and functional specialization was found to be an important intervening variable between size and formalization.[76] In light of these findings, it should be noted that increased formalization as a means of control is more likely to occur in industrial and manufacturing organizations, in which the raw materials are uniform and technology routine, than in service organizations, in which the raw materials are nonuniform and tasks nonroutine.

Centralization Correlates

Another method of bureaucratic control is through the centralization of decision-making. Pugh and his associates measured two aspects of the concentration of authority, that is, autonomy and centralization of decision-making. Although there was no relationship between autonomy and size (r = .09), there was a negative relationship (r = −.39) between size and centralization. Therefore, the larger the organization, the more specialized, standardized, and formalized it is, but also the more decentralized.[77] Child's 1973 research led him to a more definitive conclusion regarding the relationship between size and decentralization of organizational power: He found size to be the major predictor of decentralization. The relationship between size and decentralization was considered stronger than that between level of role specialization and decentralization, although a high level of role specialization was related to decentralization.[78] One might be tempted to conclude that as size increases and roles become more specialized there would result a

131

greater decentralization down through the organizational hierarchy. But Child found that the relationship between size and decentralization was direct, unlike that between size and formalization; when role specialization was controlled, decentralization resulted from increased size.[79]

Boland's study of 115 colleges and universities (a type of service organization) also focused on the relationship between size and the decentralization of decision-making power down through the hierarchical structure—in this case, to the faculty senate and academic departmental chairpersons. Boland found that large universities had more powerful faculty governments and chairpersons than did smaller colleges. Boland concluded that the professional staff was more powerful than the administrative staff in large universities. This finding was quite different from that of Pugh and associates regarding industrial organizations because of the relatively higher level of expertise of the lowest rank of employees in universities (faculty) over that in most industries (blue collar workers). Most analysts of industrial organizations will not find greater power among the lower levels than the administrative levels. (See the nonbureaucratic model of organizations in chapter two.) As Amitai Etzioni has pointed out, the staff–line relationship in professional organizations such as universities tends to be reversed compared to industrial organizations.[80]

SUMMARY

The two major contextual dimensions of organizations are technology and size. The studies of Woodward and Zwerman found operations technology to be a major correlate of organizational structure when structure was defined in terms of configurational indicators (span of control, levels of hierarchies, numbers in certain specialties).[81] In general, it may be said that technology defined in terms of workflow is related to configurational measures of structure. The research of Pugh, Hickson, and associates found technology to be a major correlate of those structural variables directly related to the workflow process; furthermore, in small organizations the workflow technology strongly influences the administrative component and the decision-making process because of the close proximity of the administrators to the production process.[82]

By studying aggregated individual responses, Hage and Aiken found organizations with nonroutine technologies to be more decentralized, less formalized, and more complex. These organizations

132

deemphasized efficiency, while emphasizing innovation, staff morale, and quality of service.[83]

The research of Blau and Schoenherr, Pugh and associates, and Child and Mansfield found size to be a major determinant of structure.[84] Large organizations were generally more complex, horizontally and vertically. When the work carried on in the various organizational units was homogeneous, there was a lower administrative ratio in large organizations, but heterogeneous work required coordination, communication, and control. Therefore, the administrative ratio was high. Furthermore, large organizations were found to be generally more decentralized than small organizations, but there was little evidence that size was related to formalization.

Child and Mansfield pointed out that the findings of various researchers demonstrate that both technology and size predict various structural dimensions of organizations and these findings are not necessarily contradictory when one realizes that the structural variables being analyzed by the "technological" and "size" theorists are not for the most part the same indices of structure, nor do they use the same indices of technology.[85] Yet, it should be noted that the overwhelming majority of those who do operationalize size, technology, and structural variables in the same manner found size to be the major correlate of structure.[86]

NOTES

1. Peter M. Blau, "A Formal Theory of Differentiation in Organizations," *American Sociological Review* 35, no. 2 (April 1970): 201–218.

2. Joan Woodward, *Industrial Organizations: Theory and Practice* (London: Oxford University Press, 1965); Charles Perrow, "A Framework for the Comparative Analysis of Organizations," *American Sociological Review* 32, no. 3 (April 1967): 194–208.

3. D. S. Pugh, D. J. Hickson, C. R. Hinings, and C. Turner, "The Context of Organization Structure," *Administrative Science Quarterly* 14, no. 1 (March 1969): 91–114; and J. H. K. Inkson, D. S. Pugh, and D. J. Hickson, "Organization Context and Structure: An Abbreviated Replication," *Administrative Science Quarterly* 15, no. 3 (September 1970): 318–329.

4. Pugh, Hickson, Hinings, and Turner, "The Context of Organization Structure."

5. Inkson, Pugh, and Hickson, "Organization Context and Structure: An Abbreviated Replication."

6. D. J. Hickson, D. S. Pugh, and D. C. Pheysey, "Operations Technology and Organization Structure: An Empirical Reappraisal," *Administrative Science Quarterly* 14, no. 3 (September 1969): 378–397.

7. Peter M. Blau and Richard A. Schoenherr, *The Structure of Organization* (New York: Basic Books, Inc., 1971).

133

8. Lawrence B. Mohr, "Organizational Technology and Organizational Structure," *Administrative Science Quarterly* 16, no. 4 (December 1971): 444–459.

9. Jerald Hage and Michael Aiken, "Routine Technology, Social Structure and Organizational Goals," *Administrative Science Quarterly* 14, no. 3 (September 1969): 366–377; and Charles Perrow, *Organizational Analysis: A Sociological View* (Belmont, Calif.: Wadsworth, 1970).

10. Woodward, *Industrial Organizations: Theory and Practice.*

11. Hage and Aiken, "Routine Technology, Social Structure and Organizational Goals"; Perrow, "A Framework for the Comparative Analysis of Organizations."

12. Perrow, "A Framework for the Comparative Analysis of Organizations," p. 195.

13. Ibid., p. 195.

14. Hickson, Pugh, and Pheysey, "Operations Technology and Organization Structure: An Empirical Reappraisal."

15. Ibid., p. 380.

16. Ibid.

17. Perrow, "A Framework for the Comparative Analysis of Organizations."

18. Hickson, Pugh, and Pheysey, "Operations Technology and Organization Structure: An Empirical Reappraisal," p. 380.

19. Woodward, *Industrial Organizations: Theory and Practice,* pp. 68–80.

20. Hickson, Pugh, and Pheysey, "Operations Technology and Organization Structure: An Empirical Reappraisal."

21. Woodward, *Industrial Organizations: Theory and Practice,* p. 51.

22. Ibid., p. 45.

23. Hickson, Pugh, and Pheysey, "Operations Technology and Organization Structure: An Empirical Reappraisal," pp. 378–397.

24. Ibid.

25. John Child and Roger Mansfield, "Technology, Size, and Organization Structure," *Sociology* 6, no. 3 (September 1972): 381.

26. Hickson, Pugh, and Pheysey, "Operation Technology and Organization Structure: An Empirical Reappraisal," p. 395.

27. Ibid., p. 295.

28. Hickson, Pugh, and Pheysey, "Operation Technology and Organization Structure: An Empirical Reappraisal," pp. 394–395.

29. Perrow, "A Framework for the Comparative Analysis of Organizations," p. 195.

30. Ibid.

31. James D. Thompson, *Organizations in Action* (New York: McGraw Hill, 1967).

32. Perrow, "A Framework for the Comparative Analysis of Organizations," pp. 195–196.

33. Ibid., pp. 195–197.

34. Thompson, *Organizations in Action,* p. 16.

35. Perrow, "A Framework for the Comparative Analysis of Organizations," pp. 194–195.

36. Ibid.

37. Ibid., pp. 194–208.

38. Hage and Aiken, "Routine Technology, Social Structure and Organizational Goals," pp. 366–376.

39. Ibid.

40. Richard H. Hall and Charles Tittle, "Bureaucracy and Its Correlates," *American Journal of Sociology* 72, no. 3 (November 1973): 267–272.

41. Richard H. Hall, "Professionalization and Bureaucratization," *American Sociological Review* 33, no. 1 (February 1968): 92–104.

42. Elizabeth Morrissey and David F. Gillespie, "Technology and the Conflict of Professionals in Bureaucratic Organizations," *The Sociological Quarterly* 16, no. 3 (Summer 1975): 319–332.

43. Pugh, Hickson, Hinings, and Turner, "The Context of Organization Structure," p. 98.

44. John Child, "Predicting and Understanding Organization Structure," *Administrative Science Quarterly* 18, no. 2 (June 1973): 169.

45. Theodore Anderson and Seymour Warkov, "Organizational Size and Functional Complexity: A Study of Administration in Hospitals," *American Sociological Review* 26, no. 1 (February 1961): 25.

46. Amos Hawley, Walter Boland, and Margaret Boland, "Population, Size, and Administration in Institutions of Higher Education," *American Sociological Review* 30, no. 2 (April 1965): 253.

47. Woodward, *Industrial Organization: Theory and Practice;* Thompson, *Organizations in Action.*

48. Pugh, Hickson, Hinings, and Turner, "The Context of Organization Structure," pp. 91–114.

49. Richard Hall, "Bureaucracy and Small Organizations," *Sociology and Social Research* 48, no. 1 (October 1963): 38–46.

50. Child, "Predicting and Understanding Organization Structure," pp. 168–185.

51. Marshall W. Meyer, "Size and the Structure of Organizations: A Causal Analysis," *American Sociological Review* 37, no. 4 (August 1972): 434–441.

52. Ibid., p. 434.

53. D. S. Pugh, D. J. Hickson, C. R. Hinings, and C. Turner, "Dimensions of Organization Structure," *Administrative Science Quarterly* 13, no. 1 (June 1968): 65–105; and Pugh, Hickson, Hinings, and Turner, "The Context of Organization Structure."

54. C. R. Hinings and G. L. Lee, "Dimensions of Organization Structure and Their Context: A Replication," *Sociology* 5, no. 1 (January 1971): 83–93.

55. Malcolm Warner and Lex Donaldson, "Dimensions of Organization in Occupational Interest Associations: Some Preliminary Findings." (Paper presented at the Third Joint Conference on the Behavioral Sciences and Operational Research, London.)

56. Pugh, Hickson, Hinings, and Turner, "Dimensions of Organization Structure."

57. Blau and Schoenherr, *The Structure of Organization.*

58. Child, "Predicting and Understanding Organization Structures," p. 171.

59. Ibid.

60. Ibid., pp. 168–185.

61. Ibid., p. 168.

62. Meyer, "Size and the Structure of Organizations: A Causal Analysis," p. 437.

63. Peter M. Blau, Wolf V. Heydebrand, and Robert E. Stauffer, "The Structure of Small Bureaucracies," *American Sociological Review* 31, no. 2 (April 1966): 179–191.

64. Blau, "A Formal Theory of Differentiation in Organizations," p. 201.

65. Ibid., pp. 216–217.

66. C. Northcote Parkinson, *Parkinson's Law* (New York: Ballantine Books, 1964), pp. 15–27.

67. Frederic W. Terrien and Donald L. Mills, "The Effect of Changing Size upon the Internal Structure of Organizations," *American Sociological Review* 20, no. 1 (February 1955): 11–13.

68. Anderson and Warkov, "Organizational Size and Functional Complexity: A Study of Administration in Hospitals," pp. 23–28.

69. William A. Rushing, "The Effects of Industry Size and Division of Labor on Administration," *Administrative Science Quarterly* 12, no. 2 (September 1967): 267–295.

70. Ibid., pp. 293–294.

71. The following researchers reported such finds: Rushing, "The Effects of Industry Size and Division of Labor on Administration"; Louis R. Pondy, "Effects of Size, Complexity, and Ownership on Administrative Intensity," *Administrative Science Quarterly* 14, no. 1 (March 1969): 47–61; Bernard P. Indik, "The Relationship Between Organization Size and Supervision Ratio," *Administrative Science Quarterly* 9, no. 3 (December 1963): 301–312; Seymour Melman, "The Rise of Administrative Overhead in the Manufacturing Industries of the United States 1899–1947," *Oxford Economic Papers* 3, (February 1951): 61–112; Reinhard Bendix, *Work and Authority in Industry* (New York: Harper and Row, 1956), pp. 221–222; Anderson and Warkov, "Organizational Size and Functional Complexity: A Study of Administration in Hospitals," pp. 23–28; Eugene Haas, Richard H. Hall, and Norman J. Johnson, "The Size of the Supportive Component in Organizations: A Multi-organizational Analysis," *Social Forces* 43, no. 1 (October 1963): 9–17; Frederic W. Terrien, "The Effect of Changing Size upon Organizations" (San Francisco: Institute of Social Science Research, San Francisco State College, March 1963), pp. 2–4; Hawley, Boland and Boland, "Population Size and Administration in Institutions of Higher Education," pp. 252–255.

72. Blau and Schoenherr, *The Structure of Organizations;* Peter M. Blau, Cecilia McHugh Falbe, William McKinley, and Phelps K. Tracy, "Technology and Organization in Manufacturing," *Administrative Science Quarterly* 21, no. 1 (March 1976): 20–40; Pugh, Hickson, Hinings, and Turner, "The Context of Organization Structure"; Child and Mansfield, "Technology, Size and Organization Structure"; Dennis S. Mileti, David F. Gillepie and Eugene Haas, "Size and Structure in Complex Organizations," *Social Forces* 56, no. 1 (1977): 208–217.

73. Edward A. Holdaway and Thomas A. Blowers, "Administrative Ratios and Organization Size: A Longitudinal Examination," *American Sociological Review* 36, no. 2 (April 1971): 278–286.

74. Pugh, Hickson, Hinings, and Turner, "The Context of Organization Structure," p. 98.

75. Child, "Predicting and Understanding Organization Structure," p. 181.

76. Ibid., p. 183.

77. Pugh, Hickson, Hinings, and Turner, "The Context of Organization Structure," p. 98.

78. Child, "Predicting and Understanding Organization Structure," p. 181.

79. Ibid., p. 183.
80. Amitai Etzioni, "Authority Structure and Organizational Effectiveness," *Administrative Science Quarterly* 4, no. 1 (June 1959): 43–67.
81. Woodward, *Industrial Organization: Theory and Practice;* W. L. Zwerman, *New Perspectives on Organization Theory* (Westport, Conn.: Greenwood Publishing Company, 1970).
82. Pugh, Hickson, Hinings, and Turner, "The Context of Organization Structure"; and Hickson, Pugh and Pheysey, "Operations Technology and Organization Structure: An Empirical Reappraisal."
83. Hage and Aiken, "Routine Technology, Social Structure and Organizational Goals."
84. Blau and Schoenherr, *The Structure of Organization;* Pugh, Hickson, Hinings, and Turner, "The Context of Organization Structure"; Child and Mansfield, "Technology, Size, and Organization Structure," pp. 369–393.
85. Child and Mansfield, "Technology, Size, and Organizational Structure," p. 370.
86. Pugh, Hickson, Hinings, and Turner, "The Context of Organization Structure"; Hickson, Pugh, and Pheysey, "Operations Technology and Organizational Structure: An Empirical Reappraisal"; and Child and Mansfield, "Technology, Size, and Organization Structure."

part III
INTRAORGANIZATIONAL DIMENSIONS

The third part of this text deals with the intraorganizational structural components of organizations, which can be summarized in the following four dimensions: (1) power and centralization, (2) complexity, (3) formalization, and (4) communication. These dimensions are the focuses of chapters five, six, seven, and eight, respectively. Taken together, they determine to what degree an organization is controlled and coordinated. Stated differently, these dimensions, in various combinations, define the coordination and control structures and functions that all organizations exercise. This control may be achieved through decision-making (power and centralization); differentiation (hierarchical ordering of organizational positions, division of labor, and span of control); fixed rules and procedures (formalization and standardization; and regulation of horizontal and vertical communication.

The following four chapters discuss research analyzing the interrelationships of these structural dimensions. Where possible, the findings are synthesized; where synthesis is not possible, the contradictions are examined. In addition to defining and elaborating the relationships between the structural dimensions, each chapter examines the process underlying the structural dimension being discussed.

5
POWER AND CENTRALIZATION

OBJECTIVES

The objectives of this chapter are:

1. To define the concept of power.
2. To define and describe the sources of power.
   a. position
   b. knowledge
   c. personal attributes
   d. tradition and values
3. To discuss the direction of power.
   a. horizontal
   b. vertical
4. To discuss the distribution of power.
   a. centralized
   b. decentralized
5. To relate the distribution of power (centralization) to the structural dimensions of organizations.
   a. complexity and differentiation
   b. formalization and standardization
   c. communication

ORGANIZATIONAL POWER DEFINED

Theoretical Definition

The generic concept of power is defined as a relationship between two or more actors (individuals or collectives) in which the action of one is determined by that of another or others. This definition is adapted from Robert Dahl's definition of power. "A has power over B to the extent that he can get B to do something B would not otherwise do."[1] Power can only exist within social relationships; it is not an inherent attribute of an individual or group. Thus, power is generated through the processes of interaction (or social organization). An actor possesses power relative to other actors. Some social scientists agree with Amos Hawley's somewhat extreme position that ". . . every social relationship is a power equation, and every social group or system is an organization of power."[2] Certainly all social relationships possess the potential for power. Not only is power generated through the processes of the organization, but it is also a causal factor in creating organizations. Subsidiaries or new organizations may be formed through the power of one or more organizations. Thus, power and the process of organizing are reciprocal relationships.

Power is exerted by organizational members making decisions; thus the decision-making process is the basis of any power structure. The unit of analysis may be an individual, group, department, or the organization. Although theoretical distinctions may be made between interpersonal (individual) and organizational power, it is difficult to operationally separate the two phenomena. Of course, this problem originates because power exists in relationships in which individuals act as representatives of the organization.

Several aspects of our definition of power as a relationship should be clarified. First, power is an aspect of all interaction and is asymmetrical in that "the power holder exercises greater control over the behavior of the power subject than the reverse, but reciprocity of influence—the defining criterion of the social relation itself—is never entirely destroyed except in those forms of physical violence. . . ."[3] Asymmetry exists in a relationship where A has power over B with respect to a given decision-making issue and B has power over A on another issue. Thus, over the duration of a relationship a pattern may emerge where both A and B have power over each other with respect to certain organizational issues. For example, personnel decisions are typically the domain of university faculty, whereas financial decisions are typically the province of administrators. Although each interaction between the two groups is characterized by the power of one over the other, the question of who holds the power on a given occasion is dependent on whether the issue is a personnel or fiscal one. This reciprocity of power becomes more apparent when the lateral power of functional areas within organizations is discussed. The amount of power a functional area (such as marketing, production, and research) has depends on the issue under consideration. This point is important because power is often defined as a unilateral hierarchical relationship excluding the possibility of horizontal power related to different issues. See the section on lateral power.

Although participation in the decision-making processes of an organization is the mark of an actor's power, the types of issues being decided determine the extent of that power. For example, many times decisions about work operations and procedures are delegated downward in the organizational hierarchy, while fiscal and personnel decisions are retained at the top levels of the organization. Those actors making the more important policy decisions are naturally more powerful. Their importance is in part determined by the pervasiveness of their effects. For example, a system-wide decision such as the distribution of profits is often more important, and consequently controlled by those with greater power than is evident for issues such as group leadership that have limited scope (i.e., are of concern to only the members of one group or department).

Operational Definitions

Since the time of Max Weber's classical works, power has been defined in terms of the powerholder's *chance, capacity,* and *possibility* of exercising power. Weber defined power as ". . . the chance of a man or a number of men to realize their own will in a communal action even against the resistance of others who are participating in the action."[4] Similarly, Dennis Wrong and Arnold Rose defined both potential and actual power and elaborated potential power in terms of chance.[5] The issue underlying the definition of power as potential rather than actual is that the two do not necessarily coexist. All those who exercise power must have the potential, possibility, and chance, but the converse is not necessarily true (i.e., not all those who have potential, possibility, and chance do in fact exercise power). This distinction between *having* power and *exercising* power is pertinent to the method of measuring power. In order for B's power over A to be real when it is not exercised by B, A must *perceive* that B has power (the capacity to control) and behave accordingly; then B *actually* has power. In order to measure potential power there must be not only an assessment of the accumulation of organizational resources to show potential, but also an assessment of the power subject's perception of the holder's power and subsequent modification of behavior.

143

Of course, there are other methods of measuring organizational power, such as observing the decision-making processes of groups and departments to define who actually makes the decisions on major issues. It is important to note that regardless of who makes the decision, if the decision can be changed at a higher level, the committee or department of origin is only advisory and *does not* have decision-making power in actuality. The ultimate power rests with the actor who has the last say on a given issue.

Organizational power is frequently measured by asking organizational members about their participation in the decision-making processes of the organization. For example, Arnold Tannenbaum and associates identified two types of participation in decision-making—formal and informal. Formal participation is a system in which rulers explicitly and legally establish decision-making structures through which all members contribute to decisions. Members may participate directly, entering personally into the deliberations that lead to binding decisions, or they may participate indirectly through representation.[6] One might measure participation in the formal decision-making process by asking an organizational member such questions as: "Do workers participate in making important decisions related to their work?" and "Do workers participate in making important decisions related to general organizational problems and issues?"

On the other hand, informal participation is defined in terms of style of management, the degree to which supervisors share their authority with subordinates. Informal participation, according to Tannenbaum and associates, refers to the receptiveness and responsiveness of managers and supervisors to ideas and suggestions of subordinates, and managerial sensitivity to employee needs. In a bureaucratic organization, if lower-ranking persons have influence in a system, it is through their immediate superior, and this influence is usually limited to operational tasks of the group.[7] One might measure informal participation through such questions as: "Does your immediate superior ask your opinion when a problem comes up that involves your work?" and "Is your immediate supervisor inclined to take into account your opinions and suggestions?"

Finally, power may be defined by assessing the actor's (person's, group's, or organization's) rank in a hierarchy. Hierarchical rank in a work organization implies differential authority and influence for different positions. In addition, hierarchically ranked positions accrue differential rewards (intrinsic and extrinsic) and responsibilities.

144

SOURCES OF POWER

We will proceed with the awareness that authors have used the concepts of power and authority interchangeably. Weber, Robert Peabody, Amitai Etzioni, John French and Bertram Raven, and Donald Warren are but a few of the many sociologists and social psychologists who have analyzed the sources of power or authority.[8] Those who have developed conceptualizations of organizational power and authority have often taken one of two approaches: power has been defined broadly and the concept of authority has been limited to positional power only, or authority has been defined broadly and the concept of power limited to coercion only. The term that is chosen for broad definition is then ascribed to relevant sources or bases. For example, Weber differentiated power from the broader concept of authority—power involved force or coercion and therefore did not hold great relevance to his discussion of organizational authority. On the other hand, authority was found to be based on four types of social action: (1) purposive–rational, (2) value–rational, (3) traditional, and (4) affectual. Weber eliminated the value–rational social action bases when defining types of authority and concentrated on the three types of legitimate authority: legal, based on rational legal action; traditional, based on traditional action; and charismatic, based on affectual action.[9] Legal authority— the most routine type—is based on the position the individual holds in the organization. It is this type of power that is labeled "authority" by those who define power as a broad concept. Charismatic authority is based on the personal characteristics of the powerholder that are valued by those subject to its influence. This type of power is possessed by initiators and leaders of movements and is sometimes evident in bureaucratic organizational leadership. The third type of authority enumerated by Weber was traditional authority, which is based on a belief in the sanctity of tradition. Here positions are inherited. This type of power is, of course, found in the monarchies of Europe, crime syndicates in the U.S., and family-owned businesses.

French and Raven, Etzioni, and Warren categorized power based on the perception or involvement of those in organizational relationships. French and Raven enumerated five types of interpersonal power,[10] which Warren utilized in his research.[11] Etzioni enumerated three types along with three types of congruent involvement on the part of lower participants in organizations.[12] The question remains, what are the sources of power? That is, what gives

TABLE 5–1 Sources of Power

SOURCES	POSITION	KNOWLEDGE	PERSONAL ATTRIBUTES	TRADITIONAL
French & Raven	Punishment Reward	Expertise Power	Referent	Legitimate
Warren	Punishment Reward	Expertise	Referent	Legitimate
Etzioni	Punishment Remunerative	—	—	Normative
Peabody	Position	Competence	Personal Attributes	Legitimate
Weber	Position	—	Charismatic	Traditional

power to some individuals and collectives and not to others? A summary of the sources of power discussed by various researchers is found in Table 5–1. The four major sources of power are: *position, knowledge, personal attributes,* and *traditional values.*

Positional Power

In positionally-based power, defined as rational–legal authority by Weber, obedience is owed to the person who fills a given position. Those who hold higher-ranked positions in the organization are called administrators or executive managers and possess greater power than those below them in the hierarchy. The rules and procedures of the organization are structured in such a way as to ensure the gradual increment of power as one moves up the hierarchy. Along with this position the administrator is allocated resources (rewards and facilities), assigned roles, and granted the right to sanction those in lesser positions under his or her jurisdiction. If one conforms to the directives, one is rewarded. Some authorities distinguish the power to *reward* from that to *punish.* One may act in accordance with directives to prohibit punishment and be rewarded. Many times the lack of reward, salary increments, and other benefits are considered to be punishment in and of themselves.

Knowledge Power

Knowledge-based power is often called professional power, and persons possessing it are called professionals. This type of power is based on knowledge and competency acquired through the formal avenues of extensive training and education or through the experience, the informal avenue. This knowledge enables the professional to guide and direct the client of the service organization or perform highly complex processes within an industrial organization. Whereas the administrator has positional power over the professional, the professional has control over an area of knowledge and client relationships. Thus, in relation to the hierarchy of authority within an organization, the professional holds the lower position and is constantly having to persuade the administrator that his or her knowledge is superior and, therefore, his or her directives should be followed.

Naturally, some overlap of jurisdiction between bureaucrats (those who possess positional power) and professionals (those who possess knowledge power) exists in all organizations; the more struc-

147

tured the organization, the less the overlap. In many social service organizations, such as universities and hospitals, the domains of professionals and bureaucrats are constantly negotiated. In his work *The Organization of Academic Work* (chapter seven), Peter Blau analyzed the extent to which power is focused, in the bureaucratic sense, in the hands of administrators and trustees of universities or is decentralized to the lower authority of faculty positions in accordance with the professional model of organizations. He examined the power of the faculty and administration in the two decision areas of educational policies and faculty appointments. These areas were chosen because they were not obviously the domain of either administrators or professionals. Blau's research showed general consensus and little negotiation between faculty and administration over financial policies, the jurisdiction of administrators, and over course content and research, the jurisdiction of the faculty. In the areas of educational policy and faculty appointment, however, there were great differences as to whose jurisdiction these decisions came under.[13] Although some persons who hold upper administrative positions in an organization have superior knowledge, this is not generally what gives them power. Their power rests on their ability to sanction those below them in the hierarchy. The scope of this power is defined by the rules and procedures of the organization. Although positional and knowledge power may occur together, they are not generally complementary; they are rather alternative methods of organizational control.

As was further demonstrated by other research of Blau, where there were large numbers of experts in the organization, the power was decentralized.[14] Hiring professionals was not compatible with centralized power and close supervision. When a large ratio of managers to workers was employed in an organization with a larger number of professionals, they were hired for communication and coordination purposes, not for supervisory purposes, one reason being that they often knew less about the specialized skills needed to carry on organizational activities than did their now expert subordinates. Professionals further promoted decentralization because administrators were more apt to delegate decision-making to lower levels of the organization if they consisted of competent professionals.[15] Though their measures of centralization were qualitatively different, both Blau and Jerald Hage and Michael Aiken found a negative relationship between the competency of workers and organizational centralization.[16] Thus, it appears that knowledge-based power and centralization of positional power are alternative methods of control.

Personal Attribute Power

Personal attribute power was described by Weber as charismatic power. When people value a particular attribute, the individual possessing it gains power. The powerholder becomes a referent for others—a role model or reference group; people wish to be associated with or similar to those who possess these valued personal attributes. This type of power and traditional power are less relevant to our discussion of organization power than are position and knowledge based power.

Traditional Power

Traditional power derives from inheritance rather than merit or personal characteristics and rests on the power subject's acknowledgment of the powerholder as possessing the *right* to a given position. For example, the positions of kings and queens are valued by their subjects, and this granting of legitimacy, not personal characteristics, knowledge, or performance of those who hold these positions, creates this type of power.

Empirical Research on the Sources of Power

Using French and Raven's bases of power, Tannenbaum and others explored six reasons that persons are able to exercise control:[17] An individual (1) has superior knowledge relevant to the task; (2) can disperse rewards, (3) can disperse punishment; (4) is attractive as a person; (5) has the right to exercise control. The sixth base of power was the employee's sense of commitment to a larger purpose served by the organization. In their multi-plant, five-country analysis, they found the same pattern in all plants, large and small. "Legitimacy" (the right to exercise control) and "commitment to a larger purpose served by the organization" were rated as the most important sources of power in all countries, followed by expertise, referent, reward, and coercion. It should be noted that a similar pattern was also reported in Jerald Bachman and associates' analyses of utilities, colleges, clerical workers, and factories.[18] Thus, legitimacy and commitment to larger purposes served by the organization are more often perceived by employees as reasons for their continued acceptance of organizational power, while reward and coercion are least frequently given as reasons.

DIRECTION OF POWER

Of course, all organizations have both hierarchically and vertically arranged units, and power relationships exist between these units. Vertical links connect superior with subordinate units in the organization; horizontal links connect similarly-ranked units, which are differentiated by function as opposed to rank.

Vertical Power (Hierarchy of Authority)

The division of labor is the basis of the hierarchy of authority. Labor is differentiated into units where tasks are more similar within than between units. As a result, the units and the groups within the units are assigned different values, which leads to inequality or a ranking on some subjective or objective basis: prestige, salary, facilities. This ranking carries with it differential power. Thus, power is stratified along a continuum called the hierarchy of authority. An organization has a system of rules and procedures to ensure that the directives and decisions of those in higher positions are carried out. Thus, positional power can be said to be a correlate of organizational hierarchy. The differential between the highest- and lowest-ranking position within the hierarchy is a measure of organizational stratification, and movement between ranks is a measure of organizational mobility. This hierarchy of authority is related to three of the structural dimensions of organizations: (1) complexity, because it is based on the division of labor into hierarchical ranks; (2) power and authority, because positions with higher ranks have greater authority and hence more rational-legal power within the organization; and (3) stratification, because the differential between the highest and lowest ranks of the hierarchy creates inequality. This section will deal with the relationship of hierarchy of authority to power and its centralization.

The average person would probably characterize a large complex organization, with multiple levels of hierarchy, as being highly centralized in its decision-making. This is partially because a large number of hierarchically arranged levels makes communication cumbersome, and the inability to communicate blocks knowledge of decisions. But this common sense knowledge does not stand up to close analysis. It is much more likely that if one wished to centralize the power structure, for example in a university, he or she would eliminate several levels of the multi-level hierarchical structure. Eliminating the college deans would require the department heads to communicate directly to a central administration. Here communication from the department heads and faculty of each department would go directly to the top level; conversely, information would flow down the hierarchy more efficiently. This would facilitate control and centralization. Increasing the number of levels in the hierarchical structure, assuring that each level has decision-making responsibilities, decentralizes power. For example, Marshall Meyer analyzed 254 city, county, and state departments of finance to determine the relationship between centralization of decision-making and two types of differentiated authority structures, the hierarchical and the vertical. Meyer's findings may be summarized as follows:[19]

1. Hierarchical differentiation—the proliferation of supervisory levels in an organization was found to be positively associated with decentralization of decision-making and the existence of formal rules which partly determine decisions in advance.
2. Functional differentiation—the proliferation of organizational subunits of more or less equal status is positively associated with centralization of decision-making and a lack of rules and practices that allow much discretion to top managers in making decisions.

Although common sense knowledge concerning hierarchies of control generally supports the idea that greater proliferation of levels of hierarchy leads to greater centralization, hierarchical differentiation was shown to increase the delegation of decisions to lower levels, at the same time increasing the importance of rules that remove decisions from top levels of the hierarchy.[20]

If we accept that power originates from different sources and that professionals have knowledge power, while administrators have position-based power, then an organization is merely substituting one type of control for another when it increases the number of professionals. Because professionals are not found at the top of the organization, the control merely becomes positioned at different levels of the structure and originates from a different source. Walter Boland's research on universities demonstrated that the type and source of power depends on the particular issue that is the focus of decision-making: internal technical affairs are more frequently the domain of professionals, while external relations tend to be dealt with at the top levels of the hierarchy.[21] Boland also incidentally demonstrated that a university may simultaneously experience centralization of power in the hands of the administration and decentralization of power to the faculty. Boland found that with increasing size, the external decision-making issues were centralized at the highest organizational level, the administration. These issues were the most critical to the maintenance and development of the organization, lending it legitimacy and ensuring material support. Power over educational policy and matters of particular interest to each functional area, the departments, were decentralized to the faculty senate and department heads. Thus, the power of faculty in large universities was considerably more than that in small universities. They participated in a larger number of decision-making areas, but they did not make critical decisions related to external relations. The decisions most critical to the maintenance of the organization were still centralized in the hands of a small group of individuals at the top of the hierarchy. Here the distinction between functions of administrators and professionals is quite clear: The functions of the top administrators are to maintain the organization; the functions of the professionals (faculty) are to deal with those aspects of the organization related to the client (personnel and educational matters). The activities of the top administrators are more involved with the organizational input, while the activities of the faculty are more involved with the organizational output. The decisions retained (not delegated to lower levels) by the top levels of the hierarchy are generally defined by administrators to be the most critical organizational decisions.

Lateral Power (Departmental Power)

Most research on the direction of power has focused on the vertical superior–subordinate relationships. The study of horizontal power differs from vertical power in that organizations are perceived as interdepartmental systems based on the division of labor, a functional as opposed to a status division. Functional units are linked to or dependent on other functional units because the total labor process is divided among them. When analyzing power, the question then becomes, which subunit is the most powerful? Beyond this question is the one that D. J. Hickson et al. and Gerald Salancik and Jeffrey Pfeffer attempted to answer: what factors function to vary dependency and to vary power?[22]

Charles Perrow's research on industrial firms sought to answer the first question (Which department has the most power?). He delineated four functional units: (1) sales (marketing), (2) production (engineering), (3) research and development, and (4) finance and accounting.[23] Perrow simply asked respondents to rank each of the four departments from one (most powerful) to four (least powerful).

152

He found that the sales department was ranked as the most powerful unit in eleven of the twelve industrial firms he studied. Production was the next most powerful, followed by finance and accounting; considered to be the least powerful was research and development. Perrow reasoned that this occurred because, in a market economy, customers determine the cost, quality, and type of goods that will be produced and distributed. Sales provided the link between the organizations and their customers (the environment). He argued that marketing performed the function of "uncertainty absorption" (the reduction and editing of information for policy decisions). Because this was a key function of the organization, it gave the marketing department more power. Marketing's greater power can also be explained by its lack of dependence on the other three departments while maintaining their dependence on it. Finally because of the lower sunken costs (capital investment) of the marketing department and the greater sunken costs of the other departments, a change in the market and, consequently, the product affected the other departments more severely.[24] Similarly, Paul Lawrence and Jay Lorsch also found that marketing (sales) had more influence than production in both container-manufacturing and food-processing firms, presumably, for reasons similar to those enumerated by Perrow—contact with the external environment (customers) and the opportunity and ability to deal with uncertainty.[25]

C. R. Hinings, D. J. Hickson, J. M. Pennings, and R. E. Schneck studied the power of the same four organizational subunits (sales, production, accounting, and engineering research) analyzed by Perrow.[26] Seven organizations were analyzed: three branch breweries in western Canada with less than one hundred employees; two breweries in the midwestern U.S., one with three hundred and the other with sixty employees; and two semi-autonomous divisions of a container company in Canada employing three hundred people. The sample was purposive in that organizations with varying degrees of uncertainty faced by the departments (in particular the marketing department) were chosen. Hinings and associates were testing the thesis that the power of a subunit results from critical contingent dependencies among subunits created by unspecified combinations of coping with uncertainty, work flow centrality, and nonsubstitutability. Thus, this research did not attempt to delineate which department was more powerful but to answer our second question about lateral power: which variables are most influential in determining power? The basic hypotheses are presented in Table 5–2. They found that uncertainty itself does not give a unit power; rather,

TABLE 5-2 Hypotheses of the Strategic Contingencies' Theory of Departmental Power Generated by Hickson et al.

H1: The more a subunit copes with uncertainty, the greater its power within the organization.
H2: The lower the substitutability of the activities of a subunit, the greater its power within the organization.
H3a: The higher the pervasiveness of the workflow of a subunit, the greater its power within the organization.
H3b: The higher the immediacy of the workflows of a subunit, the greater its power within the organization.
H4: The more contingencies are controlled by a subunit, the greater its power within the organization.

Source: D. J. Hickson, C. R. Hinings, C. A. Lee, R. E. Schneck, and J. M. Pennings, "A Strategic Contingencies' Theory of Intraorganizational Power," *Administrative Science Quarterly* 16, no. 2 (June 1971): 220–222.

power is achieved by coping with uncertainty. Since organizations allocate task areas that vary in uncertainty to their various subunits, those subunits that cope most effectively with the uncertainty have the most power within the organization.[27] Those subunits that were linked directly to organizational output and had pervasive links to other subunits were more powerful, as were those that supplied functions or activities for which there was no substitute. Thus, coping alone did not determine power; rather, the combination of uncertainty, coping, centrality, and nonsubstitutability in a contingent relationship afforded some departments greater power than others.[28]

Salancik and Pfeffer tested the hypothesis that organizational subunits (departments) acquire power to the extent that they provide resources critical to the organization.[29] Building on other researchers' theses of coping with critical uncertainty,[30] these authors assumed that one persistent and critical uncertainty in universities is the provision of resources. Just as power is centered in the marketing department, which links a business firm to the customer, who supplies economic resources, so too, power will accrue to the departments in social service organizations that supply links to discretionary funds. Salancik and Pfeffer studied seventeen departments at the University of Illinois. They used a multi-method measure of power; the department head's perception of power (interview measure), the subunit's representation on important committees (institutional measure), and the subunit's membership on the university research board. For all three indicators of subunit power, the best indicator of power was the proportion of faculty supported by restricted funds. The next best, the relative proportion of graduate students, was followed closely by the department's national rank. Of less importance was the relative proportion of undergraduates taught by the department.[31]

From the research of Perrow, Hinings et al., and Salancik and Pfeffer on a wide variety of business, industrial, and social service organizations, it can be seen that the most powerful subunits are those that control the critical contingencies for other subunits within the organization. The critical contingencies may be resources or access to customers, but the subunit possessing the greatest lateral power generally forms some interstitial link with the external environment. Likewise, in the previous section on vertical power, Boland found that the relationship of the organization (university) to the external environment was controlled by those at higher ranks in the organization, while less critical decisions were often delegated downward in the organization. Thus, those horizontal and vertical units that form effective connective links with the environment, when it harbors critical resources, are the most powerful organizational units.

Line–Staff Relationships

In addition to the two power relationships just discussed—those between vertically ranked professionals and administrators and between functional subunits—there is one other power relationship that has been the focus of a great deal of research. This is the line–staff relationship of industrial organizations. Line–staff relationships are not unlike the professional–administrator relationship discussed earlier. First, those who work on the line possess technical competency and are involved in producing the product that enables the organization to reach its goals. This is similar to the function of the professional. The power of the staff members is based in their positions, and they serve the function of organizational maintenance similar to administrators in professional organizations. Of course staff members hold higher ranked positions than line employees. Thus, both horizontal and vertical power relationships link the line and staff.

One of the best analyses of the interpersonal relationship between line and staff of industrial organizations was written by Melville Dalton.[32] Dalton found that line and staff are in constant conflict similar to that of professionals and administrators. Due to its subordinate position in the hierarchy of authority, the line workers had to play a subservient role when attempting to get their ideas accepted by the staff. Similar to professionals, they could only advise and hope for cooperation from the staff; many times the staff felt insecure and feared that the ideas of the line might make them appear incompetent. This led Dalton to characterize the relationship between line and staff as conflict-ridden.

DISTRIBUTION OF POWER

When actor A controls actor B on one or more issues, a pattern begins to form. This pattern is called a *power structure*. A structure of any kind is "a relatively fixed relationship between elements, parts, or entities."[33] Organizations exhibit several kinds of structures—power, procedural, position, and communication. As decisions are made within an organization, this process becomes a structure, of which there are two major types, with variations on each one. An organization in which all the decisions are made by one or a small number of organizational members is labeled a *centralized power structure*. On the other extreme is the *decentralized power structure* in which the decisions on various organizational issues are made by members distributed laterally and vertically throughout the organization. The more centralized power structures are called dominated structures. Here the power relationship is more vertical in direction and is concentrated in the hands of a few individuals or a small group at the highest levels of the organization. This group makes the decisions on all important issues, thus controlling the functioning of the organization. There may be a difference, of course, in the involvement of those in the lower organizational positions. When the low-level participants do not wish to make decisions or control the functioning of the organization, the structure is called an *inert power structure*. When they cannot gain power, even though they desire to do so, the structure is called an *elitist power structure*. Regardless of the desire of these participants to be involved, the structure is centralized in both the inert and elitist structures.

The second type of power structure is the decentralized structure in which the decision-making and organizational control are distributed downward within the organization. In the decentralized types, power is horizontally and vertically distributed, providing for potential conflict between relatively equal groups or departments. These power groups may coalesce around control over certain issues. A coalescing faction votes as a bloc against the other factions regardless of each member's individual interest. When the organization is regularly divided on issues and control, and the conflicting groups are relatively stable as to these allegiances, the structure is called a *factional power structure*. But the more common type of decentralized power structure is the *pluralistic structure* in which power is dispersed vertically and laterally across the functional areas within the organization. The departments or subunits are more or less equal and vote independently on the basis of the decision making issue. Each vote is of equal weight. Thus, units A, B, C, and D may vote on one side of the issue against W, X, Y, and Z at one time, and the next time, A, D, W, and Z may vote against B, C, X, and Y on another issue; blocs are not formed. In the pluralistic structure, the issue is more important in determining the outcome of the voting than in the factional structure, where the bloc votes together regardless of the issue and the largest bloc makes the decision.

STRUCTURAL CORRELATES OF CENTRALIZATION

Two types of decisions are analyzed in the literature on the centralization of decision-making. The first is an indicator of the decisions about the regular activities that facilitate the organization's output. When work decisions are referred to the next hierarchical level, the decision-making is centralized. This is a measure of the control of the hierarchy of authority. The second is an indicator of centralization of organizational decisions regarding policy and the allocation of resources, which Hage and Aiken call "participation in decision making."[34] The consequences of these decisions are both immediate and pervasive. These two indicators of centralization of power are themselves correlated ($r = -.55$).[35] Thus, those individuals in an organization who participate in major organizational decisions do not rely on work decisions to be made at the next highest level.

Three other studies have dealt with variables similar to those explored by Hage and Aiken. This research was initiated by D. S. Pugh and associates (the Aston Group), who along with C. R. Hinings and G. L. Lee, and Jonn Child, each analyzed the relationship of centralization to specialization, standardization, and formalization.[36] The variables were defined in the following manner:

Centralization: The extent to which the locus of authority to make decisions affecting the organization is confined to the higher levels of the hierarchy.

157

Specialization: (1) Functional specialization—the extent to which official duties are divided between discrete, identifiable functional areas, and (2) role specialization—the extent to which official duties are divided within functional areas between discrete, identifiable positions.

Standardization: The extent to which activities are subject to standard procedures and rules.

Formalization: The extent to which procedures, rules, instructions, and communications are written down.[37]

The Aston Group's measure of centralization dealt with decisions that were pervasive in their effect on the organization as opposed to decisions related directly to work activities. Thus, their measure was similar to Hage and Aiken's measure of "participation in decision making." These two measures differed in that Hage and Aiken measured "participation" while the Aston Group measured "authority to make decisions."

Hage and Aiken studied the relationship of two measures of formalization—job codification and rule observation—and three measures of complexity—number of occupational specialties, degree of professional training, and amount of professional activities—to centralization (hierarchy of authority and participation in decision-making).[38] Their measures were of the aggregated perceptions of the employees within the organizations. The data gathered in the Aston sample, its replication by Hinings and Lee, and the National sample (Child's research) employed an interview schedule designed to elicit information from executives and heads of organizations and departmental managers; information was not obtained from lower-level organizational members. Thus, the information obtained by the Aston Group and the follow-ups contained global institutional measures of information about the organization as opposed to employees' perceptions.[39]

A brief description of the Aston sample and the National sample will demonstrate that although both studies sampled work organizations, in many ways they differed greatly from the welfare and health agencies sampled by Hage and Aiken. Hage and Aiken's sample came from the midwestern U.S., the Aston sample came from the English Midlands, and the National sample came from one region of Britain. The Aston sample included departments as well as autonomous organizations and subsidiaries; the National sample contained whole autonomous organizational units; Hage and Aiken's sample was of government controlled organizational units. Hage and

Aiken sampled social service organizations, while the Aston sample was of multiple types of heterogeneous organizations, and the National sample was of business organizations. Based on these differences one might venture that similar findings would be impossible.

Formalization Correlates

One would expect that in organizations where employees perform relatively routine tasks, formalization of the rules and procedures, in particular work related ones, might be relatively high. As was discussed in chapter four, this type of organization is also relatively centralized. Thus, in a nonprofessional organization one might expect to find a positive relationship between formalization and centralization. In such an organization, those involved in production or customer (client) relationships are assumed to be unable to make organizational or client related decisions; therefore, rules and procedures are highly formalized to exclude such possibilities. On the other hand, in professional organizations where decisions are delegated downward and throughout the organization (that is, decision-making is decentralized), rules and procedures related to work activities are not formalized but left to the discretion of the professional. Hage and Aiken found a positive correlation between decentralization and low formalization of work related activities in professional organizations.[40] But the rules and procedures related to the internal functioning of the organization may be formalized to protect the highly trained professional from arbitrary decisions of administrators. This was evidenced in Blau's analysis of public personnel agencies.[41] When authority was decentralized, the personnel procedures (non-work-flow activities) were formalized. Professionals desire the predictability of formalized personnel selection procedures, salary policies, and other organizational procedures. For example, formalization of stringent criterion in employment ensures highly educated and trained persons will continue to be employed by the organization. Thus, the professional's colleagues will continue to be of high quality. The professional would support this form of formalization, whereas he or she would not support formalization of the work activity itself.

Similarly, the Aston Group found that formalization and standardization of procedures were both negatively correlated to centralization: Overall centralization was correlated with standardization and with formalization. These relationships were further substantiated in the Hinings and Lee and Child findings. See Table 5–3. The Aston Group, and those who replicated the Aston research,

TABLE 5-3 Product–Moment Correlations of Overall Centralization With Structuring Variables

	ASTON N = 46	NATIONAL N = 82	HININGS–LEE N = 9	ASTON MANUFACTURING ONLY N = 31	NATIONAL MANUFACTURING ONLY N = 40*
Functional specialization	-64	-28	-81	-66	-59
Role specialization	-53	-43	-69	-48	-77
Standardization	-27	-46	-82	-25	-76
Formalization	-20	-53	-53	-26	-72
Standardization, selection, etc.	30	-38	-24	21	-50

Decimal points omitted.
*Newspaper organizations excluded.

Source: John Child, "Organization Structure and Strategies of Control: A Replication of the Aston Study," *Administrative Science Quarterly* 17, no. 2 (June 1972): 170.

found that as organizations become more centralized, they become less formalized, and as they become decentralized, formalization increased. The Aston Group explained that centralization and formalization are alternative methods of control. When an organization becomes decentralized, the greater formalization and standardization of work flow serves to control the organization's functioning.[42] A more extensive elaboration of the differences in the operational definitions of these variables and their interrelationships is found in chapter seven. Much depends on the types of rules and procedures that are being analyzed and the types of decisions being related to these rules and procedures.

Complexity Correlates

The number of occupational specialities is a measure of the division of labor in an organization. Thompson suggested that an increase in the number of occupational specialties leads to decentralization.[43] Hage and Aiken empirically validated this relationship by finding a positive relationship between participation in decision-making and the number of occupational specialties (r = .30).[44] See Table 5–4. The more extensive the employees' professional activities, the greater their competency and expertise and the more likely they are to share in the decision-making of the organization. Blau found that on issues of educational policy and faculty appointments, the

TABLE 5-4 Relationship Between Indicators of Low Centralization and of High Complexity and Low Formalization

	INDICATORS OF LOW CENTRALIZATION		
	High partici-pation	Low Hierarchy*	Support for Hypotheses
INDICATOR OF HIGH COMPLEXITY			
Larger number of occupational specialties	.30	−.03	moderate
High professional training	.68	.29	strong
High professional activity	.74	.42	strong
INDICATOR OF LOW FORMALIZATION			
High job codification	−.12	−.14	weak
High rule observation	−.26	−.43	moderate

*The sign has been reversed in this column from that reported in Table 3 to facilitate comparisons between the two indicators of centralization.

Source: Jerald Hage and Michael Aiken, "Relationship of Centralization to Other Structural Properties," *Administrative Science Quarterly*, 12, 1 (June 1967): 89.

higher the qualifications of the faculty, the more decentralized the decision-making about these two issues was perceived to be. Thus, in universities with better qualified faculty, the faculty possessed greater organizational power (decision-making responsibilities) relative to the administration on these two issues.[45] Hage and Aiken also found the relationship between involvement in professional activities and participation in decision-making to be relatively strong (r = .74). Thus, both measures of complexity—occupational specialties and professional activities—were found to be positively related to decentralization of decision-making.[46] See Table 5-4 for a summary of these relationships.

The third measure of complexity utilized by Hage and Aiken was professional training. They found that organizations with highly trained staff were more likely to participate in the decision-making (r = .68). See Table 5-4. Again, centralization was negatively related to complexity. The hierarchy of authority was also negatively related to two of the measures of complexity, professional training (r = − .29) and professional activity (r = − .42). Thus, the greater the centralization of decisions about work, the less the professional training and activities of organizational members.[47]

Several studies independently found relatively strong negative relationships between their measures of complexity—functional specialization and role specialization—and centralization.[48] See Table 5-3 for these correlations. Thus, research findings that strongly support the generalization that the higher the complexity of an organization, the lower the centralization, are consistent across different types of organizations.

Communication Correlates

The process of communication is especially important to the process of decentralization. A centralized organization has a small number of hierarchical levels, which ensures direct communication between the top level of management and each functional area. Thus, at the top levels, the communication system is heavily overloaded. Every question of policy or procedure must move from the bottom to the top of the organization, where a decision is made; then the directive must move from the top down to the bottom levels of the hierarchy, where work is performed. On the other hand, when an organization is decentralized and there is a proliferation of hierarchical levels, some decisions are made by each level. A question of policy moves only to the level that has authority to make a decision—no higher. Likewise, as Meyer pointed out, there is a clear separation between those who define the organizational goals and those who translate them into action and possibly even those who carry out the action.[49] Communications between levels is increased by decentralization, but fewer messages move the entire length of the system. The more formalized rules and procedures in the decentralized organization eliminate the need to have the upper level management make decisions on every issue. Thus, the need to communicate with top level management on every issue is eliminated.

SUMMARY

Assuming that the structural dimensions of an organization are influenced by both the environmental dimensions and contextual dimensions defined and elaborated in chapters three and four, and assuming that the structural dimensions of organizations are interrelated, a model of centralization's effects on other structural dimensions of organizations may be constructed (See Table 5–5):

(1) Contextual dimensions: With unstable and nonuniform raw materials and nonroutine technology, the organization de-

TABLE 5–5 Organizational Centralization Correlates of Contextual and Structural Dimensions

Contextual Dimensions:
1. Interorganizational dependency is negatively related to centralization.
2. Unstable raw materials and nonroutine technology are negatively related to centralization.
3. Organizational size is negatively related to centralization.

Structural Dimensions:
1. Organizational complexity is negatively related to centralization.
2. In organizations where professionals are employed at the lower levels, decentralization is positively related to the formalization of regulative rules and procedures of the organization.
3. In organizations where professionals are employed at the lower levels, decentralization is negatively related to formalization of operative (task related) rules and procedures.
4. In nonprofessional organizations, centralization is positively related to formalization.
5. Centralization is negatively related to the rate of communication.

creases in centralization. And as organizational size increases, so does it complexity, and it becomes more decentralized. Also, as the organization becomes more dependent on a complex external environment, its decentralization increases.

(2) Structural dimensions: As an organization becomes more complex, its decision-making is decentralized down through the organizational hierarchy. With increased complexity and decentralization, organizational procedures become more formalized and standardized but work roles become less formalized. Increased decentralization and complexity lead to increased communications.

It is fairly safe to assume that the top management of any organization is responsible for the effective and efficient functioning of that organization. With the burden of decision-making responsibility on the top executive, when the size and complexity of the organization increases, all other things being equal, the top management delegates to lower levels those decisions which are less important. Here we have the elements of critical decision-making issues and the capabilities of lower level employees influencing the decentralization process. If the employees are well educated, there is pressure to delegate decisions downward. This is especially true when professionals are better qualified (more knowledgable) than the executive level. These pressures may be reinforced by the existence of highly developed technologies that management cannot be expected to master. Thus, pressures to decentralize decisions to the lower level may come with expanded size of the organization and a concomitant increase in differentiation and specialization. Because top executives cannot make all decisions for a large organization, the decision making responsibility is distributed downward and laterally. Large organizations have a larger number of hierarchical levels, which places their administrators in a position of being pressured to delegate authority. As the administration begins to delegate authority, procedures become standardized and rules and policies become formalized, thus ensuring that lower levels of management operate within clearly defined limits and reducing the potential risk of making errors in decisions for which top administrators are ultimately held responsible. Finally, this decentralization process increases communication between tangential hierarchical levels and laterally within levels.

NOTES

1. Robert Dahl, "The Concept of Power," *Behavioral Science* 2 (July 1956): 202–203.

2. Amos H. Hawley, "Community Power and Urban Renewal Success," *The American Journal of Sociology* 68, no. 4 (January 1963): 422.

3. Dennis H. Wrong, "Some Problems of Defining Social Power," *The American Journal of Sociology* 73, no. 6 (May 1968): 673.

4. Max Weber, *From Max Weber: Essays in Sociology,* ed, H. H. Gerth and C. W. Mills (New York: Oxford University Press, 1946), p. 180.

5. Wrong, "Some Problems in Defining Social Power," pp. 677–681; and Arnold Rose, *The Power Structure: Political Process in American Society* (New York: Oxford University Press, 1967), pp. 45–46.

6. Arnold Tannenbaum, Bogdan Kavcic, Menachen Rosner, Mino Vianello, and Georg Weiser, *Hierarchy in Organization* (San Francisco: Jossey–Bass Publishers, 1974), pp. 50–51.

7. Ibid., p. 52.

8. Max Weber, *The Theory of Social and Economic Organizations*, trans. A. H. Henderson and Talcott Parsons, ed. Talcott Parsons (New York: Free Press, 1947), pp. 328–339; Robert L. Peabody, "Perceptions of Organizational Authority: A Comparative Analysis," *Administrative Science Quarterly* 6, no. 4 (March 1962): 463–482; Amitai Etzioni, *A Comparative Analysis of Complex Organizations* (New York: Free Press, 1975); John R. P. French and Bertram Raven, "The Bases of Social Power," in Dorwin Cartwright and Alvin Zander, eds., *Group Dynamics*, 3rd ed. (New York: Harper and Row, 1968), pp. 259–269; Donald I. Warren, "Power, Visibility, and Conformity in Formal Organizations," *American Sociological Review* 33, no. 6 (December 1968): 951–970.

9. Weber, *The Theory of Social and Economic Organization,* p. 328.

10. French and Raven, "The Bases of Social Power."

11. Warren, "Power, Visibility, and Conformity in Formal Organizations."

12. Etzioni, *A Comparative Analysis of Complex Organizations.*

13. Peter M. Blau, *The Organization of Academic Work* (New York: John Wiley and Sons, Inc., 1973), p. 160.

14. Peter M. Blau, "Hierarchy of Authority in Organizations," *The American Journal of Sociology* 73, no. 4 (January 1968): 453–467.

15. Ibid., p. 461–462.

16. Jerald Hage and Michael Aiken, "Relationship of Centralization to Other Structural Properties," *Administrative Science Quarterly* 12, no. 1 (June 1967): 72–91.

17. Tannenbaum, Kavcic, Rosner, Vianello, and Weiser, *Hierarchy in Organizations,* pp. 74–75.

18. Jerald G. Bachman, Clagett G. Smith, and J. A. Slesinger, "Control, Performance, and Satisfaction: An Analysis of Structural and Individual Effects," *Journal of Personality and Social Psychology* 4, no. 2 (1966): 127–136.

19. Marshall Meyer, "The Two Authority Structures of Bureaucratic Organizations," *Administrative Science Quarterly* 13, no. 2 (June 1968): 211–228.

20. Ibid., p. 226.

21. Walter Boland, "Size, External Relations, and the Distribution of Power:

165

A Study of Colleges and Universities," in Wolf V. Heydebrand, ed., *Comparative Organizations* (Englewood Cliffs, N.J.: Prentice–Hall, 1973), pp. 428–441.

22. D. J. Hickson, C. R. Hinings, G. L. Lee, R. E. Schneck, and J. M. Pennings, "A Strategic Contingencies' Theory of Intraorganizational Power, *Administrative Science Quarterly* 16, no. 2 (June 1971): 216–229; Gerald R. Salancik and Jeffrey Pfeffer, "The Bases and Use of Power in Organizational Decision Making: The Case of a University," *Administrative Science Quarterly* 19, no. 4 (December 1974): 453–473.

23. Charles Perrow, "Departmental Power and Perspectives in Industrial Firms," in Mayer N. Zald, ed., *Power in Organizations* (Nashville, Tenn.: Vanderbilt University Press, 1970), pp. 59–89.

24. Ibid., p. 65.

25. Paul R. Lawrence and Jay W. Lorsch, *Organization and Environment* (Boston: Harvard University Press, 1967), p. 111.

26. C. R. Hinings, D. J. Hickson, J. M. Pennings, and R. E. Schneck, "Structural Conditions of Intraorganizational Power," *Administrative Science Quarterly* 19, no. 1 (March 1974): 22.

27. Hickson, Hinings, Lee, Schneck, and Pennings, "A Strategic Contingencies' Theory of Intraorganizational Power," p. 219.

28. Hinings, Hickson, Pennings, and Schneck, "Structural Conditions of Intraorganizational Power," p. 22.

29. Salancik and Pfeffer, "The Bases and Use of Power in Organizational Decision Making: The Case of a University," pp. 453–473.

30. James D. Thompson, *Organizations in Action* (New York: McGraw–Hill, 1967); Perrow, "Departmental Power and Perspective in Industrial Firms," pp. 59–89; and Hinings, Hickson, Pennings, and Schneck, "Structural Conditions of Intraorganizational Power," pp. 22–44.

31. Salancik and Pfeffer, "The Bases and Use of Power in Organizational Decision Making: The Case of a University," p. 460.

32. Melville Dalton, *Men Who Manage* (New York: John Wiley and Sons, 1959).

33. Robin M. Williams, *American Society* (New York: Alfred A. Knopf, 1967), p. 20.

34. Hage and Aiken, "Relationship of Centralization to Other Structural Properties."

35. Ibid., p. 81.

36. D. S. Pugh, D. J. Hickson, C. R. Hinings, and C. Turner, "Dimensions of Organization Structure," *Administrative Science Quarterly* 13, no. 1 (June 1968): 65–105; C. R. Hinings and Gloria L. Lee, "Dimensions of Organization Structure and Their Context: A Replication," *Sociology* 5, no. 1 (January 1971): 83–93; John Child, "Organization Structure and Strategies of Control," *Administrative Science Quarterly* 17, no. 2 (June 1972): 163–177.

37. Child, "Organization Structure and Strategies of Control," p. 164.

38. Hage and Aiken, "Relationship of Centralization to Other Structural Properties," p. 74.

39. Child, "Organization Structure and Strategies of Control."

40. Hage and Aiken, "Relationship of Centralization to Other Structural Properties," p. 89.

41. Blau, "Centralization in Bureaucracies," in Mayer N. Zald, ed., *Power in Organizations,* p. 160.

42. Child, "Organization Structure and Strategies of Control."
43. Victor A. Thompson, "Hierarchy, Specialization, and Organizational Conflict," *Administrative Science Quarterly* 5, no. 4 (March 1961): 485–521.
44. Hage and Aiken, "Relationship of Centralization to Other Structural Properties," p. 89.
45. Blau, *The Organization of Academic Work*, pp. 161–178.
46. Hage and Aiken, "Relationship of Centralization to Other Structural Properties," p. 89.
47. Ibid.
48. Hage and Aiken, "Relationship of Centralization to Other Structural Properties"; Pugh, Hickson, Hinings, and Turner, "Dimensions of Organization Structure"; Hinings and Lee, "Dimensions of Organization Structure and Their Context: A Replication"; and Child, "Organization Structure and Strategies of Control."
49. Meyer, "The Two Authority Structures of Bureaucratic Organization," pp. 226–227.
50. Peter M. Blau and Richard A. Schoenherr, *The Structure of Organizations* (New York: Basic Books, 1971); Pugh, Hickson, Hinings, and Turner, "Dimensions of Organization Structure"; Child, "Organization Structure and Strategies of Control"; Hinings and Lee, "Dimensions of Organizational Structure and Their Context: A Replication," pp. 83–93; Roger Mansfield, "Bureaucracy and Centralization: An Examination of Organizational Structure," *Administrative Science Quarterly* 18, no. 4 (December 1973): 477–488.

6
COMPLEXITY

OBJECTIVES

The major objectives of this chapter are:

1. To define the concept of organizational complexity and the differentiation process that underlies this structural dimension.
2. To distinguish between horizontal, vertical, and spatial differentiation:
   a. horizontal differentiation:
      i. division of knowledge—professionals and specialists
      ii. division of labor—positions and occupations
      iii. division of function—departments and divisions
   b. vertical differentiation:
      i. division of rank—hierarchical levels
      ii. division of function—administrative component
3. To discuss the relationship of horizontal and vertical differentiation to the contextual dimensions of organizations.
4. To discuss the relationships between various types of vertical and horizontal differentiation.
5. To discuss the relationships of both horizontal and vertical differentiation to:
   a. centralization
   b. formalization
   c. communication

COMPLEXITY DEFINED

The term *complexity* is used to refer specifically to structural units into which employees may be categorized. These units can be based on roles, positions, knowledge, functions, rank, and so on. For example, employees can be divided into units based on function, or they can be ranked into hierarchical levels. Function can be divided into horizontally arranged departments or vertically arranged administrative and nonadministrative units. The process by which these units are formed is called *differentiation*. Differentiation takes place either through the segmentation of the existing structure or by the addition of new units to the structure. Regardless of how the process takes place, the consequence is an increased complexity of the structure of the organization. Thus, organizational complexity is the structural result of the process of differentiation. As an organization becomes more differentiated, its coordination, communication, and control become more problematic. Consequently, differentiation has an impact on the other structural and performance dimensions of an organization.

The units into which employees can be divided vary in direction: horizontally, vertically, and spatially. These two aspects of complexity—the units and the direction of their arrangement—occur simultaneously, that is, both functions and positions can be either horizontally or vertically arranged. Furthermore, it should be made clear that all aspects of an organization are not differentiated to the same extent. For example, the positions within an organization may be extensively differentiated, while the departments may evidence a low level of differentiation. Likewise, an organization may be extensively vertically differentiated but experience little horizontal differentiation. As a result of varied intensities of horizontal and vertical differentiation, an organization's structure, visually conceptualized, may be tall and narrow, short and flat, or any variation between these two extreme structural configurations. Not even all departments within a single organization are horizontally and vertically differentiated to the same extent. Evidence is provided by the various departments of General Motors Corporation depicted in Figure 6–1. Several types of horizontal differentiation will be discussed; then our focus will turn to vertical differentiation.

HORIZONTAL DIFFERENTIATION

Division of Functions (Departments)

Departments are the functional subunits of an organization. The functions carried on by any given department are not interchangable with those of other departments. In industry they exist as the marketing, production, accounting, research and development, and maintenance departments, while in universities, they exist as the

169

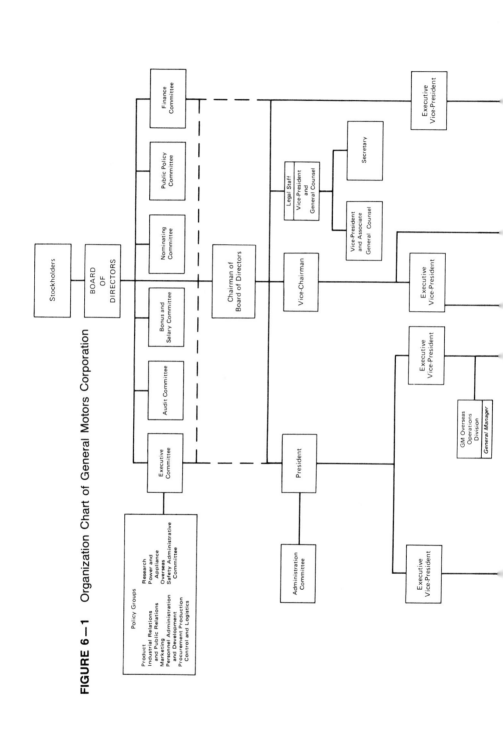

FIGURE 6–1 Organization Chart of General Motors Corporation

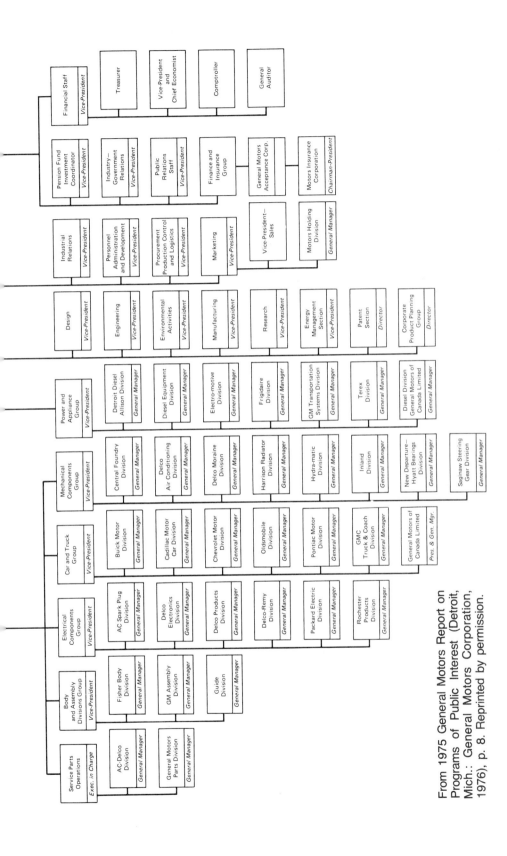

From 1975 General Motors Report on Programs of Public Interest (Detroit, Mich.: General Motors Corporation, 1976), p. 8. Reprinted by permission.

FIGURE 6-2   Horizontal (Functional) Differentiation

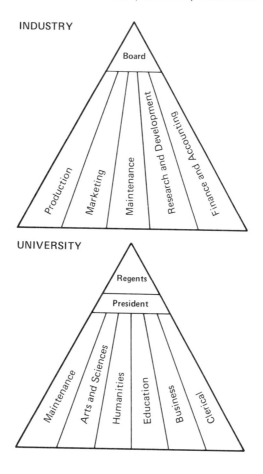

college divisions of arts and sciences (letters), education, and so on, which are in turn divided into departments, for example, music, biology, chemistry, psychology, and so on. Figure 6–2 illustrates this departmentalization. Peter Blau and Richard Schoenherr utilized the number of different subunits in an organization as one aspects of their measure of horizontal differentiation.[1]

Division of Labor

Within given departments, labor must be divided among the employees. The horizontal division of labor can occur in two ways: it can be divided into relatively specialized units either with or without the professionalization of the labor force. A medical doctor is an example of the first type of division of labor, while an assembly line worker is an example of the second type. An advanced division of labor in combination with a professionalized labor force, which exhibits great depth and breadth of knowledge, is generally called *specialized* differentiation. The type of raw material technology that underlies this division of labor is generally nonuniform; therefore, the knowledge of those working with this raw material is nonroutine. Because these highly trained specialists or professionals possess expert knowledge, they are generally responsible for a broad range of activities related to the raw material. This specialized differentiation is exemplified by the division of labor in a public service organization in which the client represents a complex, nonuniform raw material that must be processed in a nonroutine manner. The consequences of specialization are that these professionals assume much of the burden of control (communication and coordination) rather than relying on the administrative component. On the other hand, an organization may have an advanced division of labor in the absence of this professionalization and high level of knowledge. Underlying this more routine division of labor are relatively simple activities or tasks that are performed on relatively uniform raw materials. Here the task is extremely specialized, but the advanced level of knowledge and professionalization of labor force are absent.

Regardless of whether labor is specialized or routinized, the number of different positions and occupational specialties are measures of the complexity of the organization. The number of specialties may be utilized exclusively as a measure of horizontal differentiation, or it may be used in combination with such indicators as the number of years of training (education and experience) of employees. The number of occupational specialties is a formal characteristic of the organizational structure, while the education and experience of the employees are characteristics of individuals employed by the organization.

Division of Knowledge

James Price based his definition of complexity on the differentiation of knowledge—he defined it as ". . . the degree of knowledge required to produce the output of a system. The degree of complexity of an organization can be measured by the degree of education of its members. The higher the education, the higher the complexity."[2] Here the knowledge of the individual, who is highly educated, is concentrated in a given subject matter. Two employees may have nearly equal amounts of knowledge but in different specialized areas. Thus, education in preparation for a given occupational involvement tends to differentiate individuals on the basis of their knowledge. Jerald Hage and Michael Aiken also utilized the term *complexity* to refer to the level of knowledge and expertise of employees in an organization. They defined the length of training acquired by each employee as one indicator of complexity.[3] The longer the period of training for the occupation, the more complex the personnel, and therefore, the more complex the organization. Generally, the label "professional" refers to those who have attained this high level of education and training. The two concepts of "profession" and "professionalism" must be differentiated from that of "professional." Following the distinctions made by Howard Vollmer and Donald Mills,[4] the term *profession* will be used to denote an ideal type of "occupational organization." Each characteristic of a profession may be delineated on a continuum. Thus, one may speak of how professionalized an occupation is with regard to a given characteristic. At the individual level, the term *professional* refers to the individual who has successfully entered an occupation that has completed the structural process and, therefore, is a profession. *Professionalism* is a term used to denote ideal characteristics of individuals who fill such occupational positions. A professional may possess these characteristics in various degrees.

Approaches to the Study of the Professional　　There are three approaches to the study of professionals, professions, and professionalization that are of interest at this point. The first is to define a professional based on a set of attitudinal characteristics of the individual, such as commitment, service orientation, and feelings of personal autonomy, that the researcher uses to measure the individual's professionalism. In the second approach, the researcher assesses the occupation based on a set of characteristics that have been generalized for all professions. In the third approach, the researcher defines professionalization as a process that is analyzed based on a series of stages through which occupations must pass to become professions. The attitudes of individuals, and the structure and process of professionalization, are interdependent phenomena. Because they tend to occur together, some researchers make little methodological distinction as to what is being measured. Other researchers generalize from professional attitudes to the structure of professions; that is, a researcher may measure the professionalism of individuals within the organization and generalize the findings to an occupation as a whole. Thus, it is important to distinguish what is being measured.

Among the characteristics that professionals possess is a more extensive educational and training (socialization) process than persons learning other occupations.[5] The major consequence of this extensive training is a body of more or less consistent knowledge, norms, attitudes, and values that makes the professional more similar to those in that profession than to those in other professions. This bond of knowledge and values is called *professionalism*. Here characteristics of the person as opposed to the profession are being analyzed. In his analysis, Goode does not ignore the structural consequences of these personal characteristics. For example, he points out that professionalism produces a more stringent set of expectations of the persons in the profession than those outside it.[6] A second characteristic of professionals is personal autonomy. Just as the profession strives for autonomy from competing organizations and society, individual professionals strive for autonomy in their work setting and organization. Personal autonomy is the one characteristic that sociologists most often analyze when they find bureaucrats and professionals in conflict within an organization. Such conflicts often occur over the issue of who will evaluate the professional; the professional believes that only peers are qualified to make such evaluations. Another point of conflict arises over whether bureaucratic or professional rules and procedures will be followed by the professional; professionals maintain that they should be free to exercise their judgment without restraint from the organization, their clients, and others external to the profession. A third characteristic of professionals is a client orientation; that is, the client's needs are paramount to the professional. They take priority over the needs of the organization and frequently lead to a resistance to organizational rules that seem to interfere with service to the client. A final characteristic of professionals is knowledge power over the client and, therefore, at least some portion of society.[7] This characteristic was elaborated in chapter five.

There are also several distinguishing characteristics of an occupation as a profession. First, it is organized around a body of knowledge. Both scientists (e.g., biochemists) and practitioners (e.g., dentists) can be defined as professionals. Thus, a major characteristic of a profession is that it is based on systematic knowledge.[8] A second important characteristic is the power of a profession to make judgments and recommendations for services to the client; a third is the power the profession obtains through legitimization by society. This power is manifest in the ability of the profession to obtain accreditation and licenses, determine education and training requirements, set standards, and evaluate those within the profession. A fourth characteristic is a code of ethics that regulates the professional's behavior toward the client and other professionals. A final characteristic is the development of a professional culture, which includes norms for membership, language, and symbols.[9]

Several authors have enumerated sequential steps in the professionalization of an occupation. Harold L. Wilensky empirically identified the following four stages of professionalization:

1. The creation of full-time occupational involvement. Individuals, involved in the occupation, work full-time at that occupation.
2. The development of training schools and their affiliation with established universities. This training legitimized the knowledge, method of obtaining the knowledge, and skills needed in the profession.
3. The development of a professional association. Those who do not receive their training from accredited programs and/or incompetents are restricted from work or practice. Power to deal with society as well as competing organizations is gained through these associations.
4. The formalization of a code of ethics. The code of ethics is a formal statement of the relationship between professional colleagues and between professionals and their clients.[10]

Richard Hall investigated the professional attitudes of individuals in occupations that were in various stages of the process of professionalization. Not surprisingly, he found that the professional characteristics of the occupation did not correlate perfectly with the professional attitudes held by the individuals in that occupation. Some individuals in professions exhibited rather weakly developed professional attitudes, while some in the less professionalized occupations showed strong professional attitudes.[11] For example, nurses, social workers, and teachers held strong professional attitudes ("client orientations and service orientations"), while lawyers, who are in a more professionalized occupation, held lower professional attitudes.

176

VERTICAL DIFFERENTIATION

Knowledge, positions, and functions are usually differentiated not only horizontally but also vertically. In order to be ranked vertically, each characteristic must be differentially evaluated in terms of some characteristic such as power or prestige.

Division of Labor

The positions in a department may be differentiated not only on the basis of involvement in different functions but also on the rank of those functions. Thus, a department head has more authority and prestige than those employees within his or her department. This position is different not only because of supervisory and communication roles (functions), but also because its power and prestige is higher. The vertical differentiation of labor in universities and industries is depicted in Figure 6–3.

Marshall Meyer measured the "proliferation of supervisory levels" as an indicator of hierarchy (vertical differentiation) of authority.[12] This is a measurement not only of power (authority) but also of function in that administrators perform supervisory, coordination and communication functions, while the workers and professionals deal with the workflow and clients of the organization. Similarly, D. S. Pugh and associates suggested that vertical differentiation be measured by a "count of the number of job positions between the chief executive and the employees working on the output."[13] This measure assumes that positions can be vertically ranked on some dimension such as authority, prestige, rewards, and so on. At the same time, an organization may have positions that cannot be hierarchically ranked but are functionally different from other positions. Positions are not hierarchically ranked unless they are differentially valued on a given dimension. Job titles do not always indicate a differentiation in tasks or activities within an organization. For example, the job titles of associate and full professor carry indication of a hierarchical rank of prestige. This prestige in itself may be rewarding and generally carries differential financial remuneration. But, in some universities, the activities, tasks and responsibilities of associate and full professors may be essentially the same; only the job title differs. Again, a hierarchy of positions within an organization may, but does not necessarily, denote differential tasks or activities.

177

FIGURE 6–3   Vertical (Functional) Differentiation

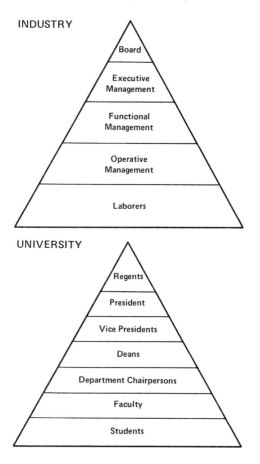

INDUSTRY

- Board
- Executive Management
- Functional Management
- Operative Management
- Laborers

UNIVERSITY

- Regents
- President
- Vice Presidents
- Deans
- Department Chairpersons
- Faculty
- Students

The disparity of rewards (salary, prestige, etc.) between upper and lower positions is a measure of stratification, and the ability of an employee to move from one hierarchical level to another denotes vertical mobility. Hage and Aiken measured stratification as the disparity of rewards between the highest and lowest positions' ranks and by the degree of mobility between ranks.[14] If an employee changes occupations or positions on the same level, horizontal or lateral mobility is evidenced.

Administrative Component   The concept of administrative component refers to the part of the organization charged with coordinat-

178

ing, facilitating, supporting, and supervising the activities of the organization, those who coordinate, facilitate, support and supervise can be differentiated vertically and horizontally from those who do not perform these activities because their function and rank are different.

The concept of the administrative component has been used as an indicator of two aspects of organizations: the closeness of supervision and the closeness of communication and coordination. These two approaches to the administrative component are both measures of the closeness of contact between the superordinate and the subordinate, although they represent different forms of contact. Supervision assumes the superior regulates and has control over the persons within his or her jurisdiction, a vertical power relationship. However, when the ability to communicate is being measured, the assumption of the researchers is that the individuals who work with the administrator have some knowledge or skills that require constant communication between the administration and those within its span of control. This interpretation of the administrative component is most often used in organizations that employ experts or professionals at the lower levels, whereas the supervision interpretation is used in organizations that employ semi-skilled and unskilled laborers in lower levels.

The two most researched measures of the administrative component are the *administrative ratio* and the *span of control*. These two measures are subject to the same types of theoretical and methodological limitations, but they deal with different levels of organizational analysis. The administrative ratio deals with the organization as the unit of analysis, while the span of control utilizes a subunit of the organization—a department or a group—as the unit of analysis. When the unit of analysis is the entire organization, the measure of the administrative component is in terms of the ratio of administrative to nonadministrative personnel. Operationally, the problem is complex. For example, the administrative component can be measured by classifying all personnel as either direct or nondirect. Direct personnel are all those involved in the workflow of the organization. Nondirect personnel are all those not involved in the workflow (the administrative component). This measure incorporates many who are not truly administrators (i.e., clerical and support staff) in the administrative component. Some researchers, such as S. R. Klatzky, have used the concept "staff," which excludes those managers of direct work areas (departments) from the administrative component;[15] other researchers have chosen to omit from the administra-

179

tive component those who provide professional services. In keeping with this definition, if a secondary school were the organization being analyzed, counselors, psychologists, and so on would not be considered administrators. Such measures are more precise than those labeling all nondirect personnel as administrators.

It can be seen that the administrative component consists of several different types of positions that perform differing functional roles. This point is best demonstrated by William Rushing's 1967 research of U.S. Census data from 279 industry occupations.[16] Rushing established categories of administrators: (1) an overall measure of the total number of administrators; (2) managerial personnel, a category that included those who carried on the coordination and supervision functions and were represented by a breakdown of the hierarchy of authority; (3) professional personnel, advisors to managers having technical- and knowledge-based power but not position-based; and (4) clerical personnel. Similarly, Blau and Schoenherr examined fifty-three state offices of the employment security agency in the U.S. and categorized the administrative component into three parts: (1) supervisory ratio, the proportion of participants holding line authority; (2) staff ratio, the proportion of total personnel time devoted to staff and technical services; (3) clerical ratio, the percentage of clerks in the agency.[17]

When the unit of analysis is the department, the ratio of managers to workers is reported as the span of control. The span of control is the relationship of a single manager or administrator to those that he or she controls or supervises. The closeness of control and supervision are not always clearly defined. Regardless of whether span of control is interpreted as a measure of upward communication or downward supervision, a smaller number of workers within the span of control facilitates closer contact (supervision or communication). Of course, a superordinate may spend 80 percent of his or her time in supervision and 20 percent in other activities such as communication, or, conversely, 80 percent communication and only 20 percent in supervision. A measure of span of control giving only the ratio of administrators to subordinates does not specify the percentage of time the administrator spends in supervision, communication, paper work, and other activities. Suppose a manager in department Y of the home office of an insurance agency has a span of control of thirty, while a manager in department Z has a span of control of thirty-five. It would be incorrect to assume that department Y has closer supervision. In order to obtain an adequate measure of the amount of time a manager spends in communication and supervision and derive some measure of each

180

activity, the researcher must ascertain this essential information, not simply assume there is more supervision with a small number of employees per supervisor.

SPATIAL DIFFERENTIATION

Spatial differentiation is the location of the organization and its subsidiary or branch offices in different geographic areas. For example, state welfare offices are dispersed in local communities; branches of retail outlets exist in many trade centers; and sales and distribution offices for major manufacturing industries are located throughout the country. The spatial differentiation may be for one function, that is, for sales alone (a retail outlet) or for production alone (a plant). Or a subsidiary may be a replication of the parent organization in a different area of the country because the parent organization is too small to encompass the additional activity or to provide accessibility to a remote geographic region. This spatial dispersion increases the complexity of organizational functioning.

Spatial differentiation is generally measured in terms of the number of geographic locations of the organization—the number of plants, retail outlets, welfare offices, attendance units, or franchises. Spatial dispersion is complicated by the fact that large corporations have a number of facilities dispersed throughout a geographic area and employees may rotate or move between these facilities. A measure of geographic differentiation should account for the spatial differentiation (number of different units) and the dispersion (distance from the headquarters) of the units as well as the dispersion of personnel.

A RECAPITULATION OF THE CONTEXTUAL CORRELATES OF COMPLEXITY

Although the relationship of contextual variables to organizational complexity was discussed in chapter four, it should be reiterated that both contextual dimensions (technology and size) are related to organizational complexity (horizontal and vertical differentiation of knowledge, positions and functions). This relationship deserves a brief reiteration.

It will be remembered that the Aston Group, unlike other researchers, analyzed the relative importance of both size *and* technology in explaining the dimensions of forty-six work organizations.

181

Size was found to exhibit strong, positive correlations with "the structuring of activities," a factor encompassing differentiation, standardization, and formalization. By contrast, their measure of technology—"workflow integration"—exhibited only modest correlations with all these factors. Thus, the technology variable was not as closely related to the "structuring of activities," including differentiation, as was the size variable.[18] Similarly, Blau and his associates have consistently found strong positive associations between organizational size and various types of differentiation—horizontal (occupational positions), vertical (management levels), and spatial divisions (local offices). These positive relationships were found in Blau and Schoenherr's 1971 analysis of fifty-three state employment security agencies, in Meyer's analysis of 194 finance departments of state and local governments, and in Blau's 1973 analysis of 115 colleges and universities.[19]

Blau also found vertical differentiation in finance departments to be associated with an increase in organizational automation in the form of computer technology.[20] Automation is one method by which the top management of an organization may continue to control the organization when it is highly differentiated vertically. Vertical differentiation separates top management from operations technology; this makes controlling operations difficult for top management. Blau found automation of accounting to be just such a method of indirect, impersonal control in finance departments.[21] Thus, although loss of control is a major disadvantage of vertical differentiation, this factor is balanced in some organizations by automation.

Several researchers have analyzed the relationship between organizational size, technology (defined as complexity of work or tasks), and various measures of complexity such as the size of the administrative component. For example, T. R. Anderson and S. Warkov found that the relationship between organizational size and the size of the administrative component was complicated by task complexity (technology). They regarded general hospitals, which handle more types of illness, as having greater task complexity than specialized hospitals, such as TB hospitals. Anderson and Warkov found that more complex hospitals were characterized by a higher ratio of administrative to nonadministrative personnel. Thus, at the basis of the relationship between these three variables is the fact that an increase in the number of employees does not increase the size of the administrative component unless the tasks (technology) being performed are varied. Thus, the relative size of the administrative component should decrease when individuals performing the same

182

tasks are hired because of what Blau has called economies of scale. When an increase in the number of employees is accompanied by an increase in complexity of tasks, the relative size of the administrative component should increase. In keeping with the logic of Anderson and Warkov, and later Rushing, as the differentiation of tasks or work roles increases, there is a need for integration and coordination; as Rushing pointed out, it is administrative personnel who are concerned with the problems of coordination.[22]

Similarly, in thirty-three small departments in a community hospital, Gerald Bell studied the relationship between the span of control and three factors: (1) the complexity of the tasks performed by subordinates (technology), (2) the extent to which administrators closely supervise their charges, and (3) the complexity of supervisors' jobs (technology). Span of control was an unadjusted raw measure; job complexity was measured by the qualitative difficulty of the job as assessed by the workers; and closeness of supervision was measured by the subordinates' perception of the degree to which their activities were observed and regulated. Respondents were asked two questions: "How often does your supervisor keep a close check on what you are doing and closely observe your work?" and "To what extent does your immediate supervisor influence what you do in a typical work week?" The respondents' scores on the two questions were added and the workers were ranked into nine categories. Complexity of subordinates' and supervisors' jobs were composed of four factors: (1) degree of predictability of work demands, (2) amount of discretion they exercise, (3) extent of their responsibility, and (4) number of different tasks they perform.[23]

Bell found that the complexity of the superordinate's job was positively associated with the complexity of the subordinate's job. Since these conditions are likely to occur together, they have a joint effect of reducing the administrator's span of control. Bell also found as the job complexity of both supervisors and subordinates increased, the span of control decreased. When the superordinate's or supervisor's task is highly complex, the span of control is narrower. However, the worker's perception of the closeness of supervision was not found to be associated with the supervisor's span of control.[24]

Bell's research demonstrated that even though superordinates may have relatively few subordinates, the subordinates may not perceive that they are closely supervised. This may be due to the style of supervision of the administrators, to the control that has been institutionalized through professional norms, and to the formalized

183

rules and standardized processes within an organization. It should be remembered that Bell did not measure the proportion of time the administrator spent in supervision, communication, or other administrative activities. These aspects were presumably innate to the complexity of the supervisor's job. Because time spent in supervision was not separated from other aspects of the administrator's work, it was difficult to assess how much actual supervision took place. William Ouchi and John Dowling posited that:

> If Bell had regarded the span of control as a measure of the closeness of contact, he would still have correctly concluded that as the subordinate's task becomes more complex, he requires more contact and thus causes his superior's span [of control] to narrow. As the superior's job becomes more complex, however, the superior is able to devote less and less time to supervision but more to his other, nonsupervisory duties. Thus, the quantity of organizational manpower that is devoted to supervision is affected by complexity of the subordinate's job, but it is not affected by the complexity of the superior's job.[25]

INTERRELATIONSHIPS OF VARIOUS TYPES OF HORIZONTAL AND VERTICAL DIFFERENTIATION

Peter Blau and his associates have found indicators of vertical and horizontal differentiation to be related. For example, in constructing his formal theory of differentiation, Blau analyzed finance agencies and found that the horizontal differentiation indicator of expertness (the proportion of staff required to have a bachelor's degree) was positively associated with: (1) the overall supervision ratio, (2) number of levels of hierarchy, and (3) the average span of control of middle management. On the other hand, Blau found that his measure of vertical differentiation—the number of hierarchical levels—was negatively related to the number of subunits (horizontal differentiation) and positively related to the span of control of middle management.[26]

Similarly, in their study of public personnel agencies, Blau, Heydebrand, and Stauffer found that division of labor (number of occupational titles) promoted both expertness and fewer hierarchical levels, but in different instances. Because expertness mitigates against a decrease in hierarchical levels, the two forms of control did not exist together. Thus, these researchers suggested that the chances of the hierarchy having fewer levels increases as the division of labor increases only if the employees are nonexperts. When the personnel are experts (college graduates),[27] occupational differentiation promotes a proliferation of hierarchical levels.

Routinized differentiation, which minimizes the need for professional experts, maximizes the need for managerial coordination. Centralized planning and direction are effective means for coordinating fragmented duties performed by a relatively untrained staff. Routinized differentiation accordingly enhances the likelihood of the development of centralized authority structure. Specialized differentiation does not pose the same problem of coordination for management as routinized differentiation does, because tasks are not fragmented, because professionals are qualified to assume wider responsibilities, and because management gains advantages from eliciting their contributions to coordination instead of imposing directives from a central headquarters on them. A centralized management has great disadvantages in a professionalized organization, as has been noted. Hence, specialized differentiation does not enhance the likelihood of the development of a centralized hierarchy.[28]

Blau, Heydebrand, and Stauffer also found that expert qualifications (knowledge differentiation) of these 156 public personnel agencies were associated with a high ratio of managers to total personnel (managerial ratio—a measure of the administrative component).[29] In discussing the ratio of managers to personnel with expert training, years of education was used as the measure of knowledge differentiation. Common sense knowledge would lead one to anticipate that expert personnel would require fewer supervisory or managerial personnel than nonexpert personnel. This was not found to be the case; rather, Blau and associates found that experts:

> make greater contributions to the improvement of operating procedures than men without specialized training. . . . To take full advantage of the contribution experts can make to operations, management must facilitate the flow of upward communication. . . . A high ratio of managers increases opportunities for communication between officials responsible for administrative and those responsible for operating decisions.[30]

Similarly, in his later study of 254 financial agencies, Blau defined the professional as possessing "expert skills" and "a body of knowledge," "professional standards of workmanship and ethical

185

conduct," and "an orientation toward service"; he described the collective of professionals as "a self-governing association of peers.[31] Here again, Blau operationalized expert skills and an abstract knowledge as a college degree with a specialized job-related major. In this investigation, the employment of experts again did not reduce the proportionate size of management staff. He again found that agencies that employ experts are likely to have a high ratio of managers, who are again assumed to function, not as supervisors, but as decision-makers and communicators supplying a link between operations personnel and organizational administrators. Blau's research on finance agencies verified his earlier findings. A higher ratio of managerial personnel was found in agencies with a large proportion of college-trained experts than in those agencies with fewer experts. Because of the managers' greater responsibility, their span of control was narrower where the employees had expert qualifications, creating an inverse association between span of control and the scope of responsibilities. These managers were not involved in supervision but had been delegated responsibilities for budgeting and accounting decisions.[32]

Finally, Blau's *The Organization of Academic Work* indicated that both horizontal differentiation into schools and colleges and vertical differentiation into hierarchical levels were associated with a higher ratio of administrators to faculty.[33] Thus, vertical differentiation in the form of increased size of the administrative component seemed to be positively related to both vertical (number of hierarchical levels) and horizontal (number of divisions and number of sections per division) differentiation.

Similarly, Meyer analyzed the relationship of knowledge complexity to the span of control of first-line supervisors in 254 city, county, and state finance departments, the same sample used by Blau in his analysis of the hierarchy of authority in organizations. Meyer also found that as the level of expertness in an organization's subunits increases, the span of control becomes narrower.[34] Like Blau, Heydebrand, and Stauffer,[35] Meyer interpreted this finding to imply that the span of control in organizations reflects the need for consultation and two-way communication between hierarchical levels rather than the extent of closeness of supervision. Thus, complexity of the task performed within a given department as well as the complexity of employees' knowledge are associated with the span of control. High complexity of subordinates' knowledge and tasks of subordinates both decrease the span of control of the organization. More often than not, experts are responsible for more complex tasks than nonexperts, presumably because of their greater competency. Thus, complex knowledge and tasks of the subordinate occur jointly to reduce the span of control of the supervisors.

STRUCTURAL CORRELATES OF DIFFERENTIATION

Centralization Correlates

Knowledge and the Division of Labor Differentiation (Horizontal) To theoretically support his proposition that higher complexity (more specialists and educated personnel) is associated with lower centralization, Hage cited Thompson's argument that the proliferation of occupational specialties, especially those with long training periods, would result in undermining centralization of control.[36] Rather than assuming that a large number of hierarchical levels was an indication of decentralization, Hage and Aiken measured the proportion of occupations that participated in decision-making and the number of decision-making areas in which they participated. Complexity was measured in terms of occupational specialties and training of personnel. They found a high degree of complexity (occupational specialties and training) was associated with a low degree of centralization. Specifically, the relation between involvement in professional activities and participation in decision-making was relatively strong (r = .74).[37] Hage and Aiken also measured complexity utilizing indicators of professional training. They found that highly trained personnel were more likely to participate in decision-making (r = .68). Again, centralization was negatively related to complexity. Similarly, in his study of academic organizations, Blau found that on issues of educational policies and faculty appointments, the higher the qualifications of the faculty, the more decentralized the decision-making about these two issues was perceived to be. Thus, in universities with better qualified faculty, the faculty possessed greater organizational power than the administration with regard to these two issues.[38] Hage and Aiken also measured participation in work-related decision-making; this indicator, termed hierarchy of authority, was found to be negatively related to the two measures of complexity, professional training (r = − .29) and professional activity (r = − .42). Thus, professionalization was negatively related to centralization of work decisions, supporting the positive relationship between both positional and knowledge differentiation and decentralization. Similarly, the research findings of Pugh et al., Hinings and Lee, and

Child independently found relatively strong negative relationships in industrial organizations between complexity—functional and role specialization (horizontal differentiation)—and centralization.[39]

Thus, in an organization with larger amounts of specialized knowledge and a large number of differentiated positions, the decision-making is likely to be distributed throughout the organization. Because professional employees wish to have both personal autonomy over their work and at least some decision-making power in the organization, it is not surprising that these horizontally differentiated organizations are decentralized. Because organizations that are horizontally differentiated due to large numbers of experts and professionals are found to be decentralized is no reason to assume that organizations that are horizontally differentiated based on a routinized division of labor will also be decentralized. In fact, quite the opposite is true: Organizations such as department stores horizontally differentiated through a routine division of labor are often highly centralized. Thus, various aspects of horizontal differentiation exhibit dissimilar relationships to centralization of decision-making. If knowledge, expertise, and professionalism are widely distributed, power is more likely to be decentralized; if the division of labor is routinized, it is more likely to be centralized.

Functional Differentiation (Horizontal and Vertical)   In his study of 254 city, county, and state departments of finance, Meyer found that the two types of differentiation, vertical and horizontal, had differing effects on the decentralization of decision-making in organizations.[40] Whereas vertical differentiation increased the delegation of decision-making power to the lower levels of the organization, thus decentralizing the organization, horizontal differentiation (functional differentiation) concentrated the authority at the top of the organization, thus centralizing the decision-making process. In the functionally differentiated finance agencies, Meyer found that top executives not only made policy, which is considered to be their function, but specifically defined the manner in which the general policy should be implemented. These methods of implementation had to be communicated downward through the levels of the organization, and questions concerning them had to be communicated back up to the top levels of the organization, thus involving the executives and giving them control over the entire processes of the organization. This type of centralized operation is often stymied because the chief executive cannot be involved in all aspects of the organization at the same time.

188

These findings are similar to those of Blau and associates in their 1966 study. They found the greater the horizontal (functional) differentiation, the more authority was centralized in the top executives of the organization. The work supports the proposition that horizontal differentiation is positively related to centralization of authority. When the span of control is wide and employees are nonprofessionals or not experts, decisions are made at the top of the organization.[41]

Meyer found that where finance agencies were vertically differentiated, the lower levels were involved in decision-making. Here a clear division could be seen in which the executives made the policy decisions but lower level management translated these policies into action.[42] A vertically differentiated organization relies on competent managers at each level to translate policy into methods of achieving goals; thus, vertical differentiation distributes decision-making down the hierarchy and, according to Meyer, decentralizes it. Here the organization is less likely to be stymied. Relieved of devising methods of implementation, the administrator can concentrate on establishing policy. One could make an argument for this organization being highly centralized because those at the lower levels do not have input into major policy decisions of the organization. This is certainly the case in some vertically differentiated organizations. Although lower level employees make decisions, these decisions are of minor consequence to the organization's overall functioning.

Formalization Correlates

Knowledge and Division of Labor Differentiation (Horizontal) Corollary seven of Hage's axiomatic theory states, "The higher the complexity [of the organization], the lower the formalization."[43] Formalization was defined as the proportion of codified jobs and the range of variation that is tolerated within the rules; the less the variation allowed, the more formalized the organization. Aiken and Hage defined formalization in terms of rules that governed the job of the specialist and the degree of tolerance of those rules. Thus, the measure of formalization was not defined in terms of overall organizational rules and procedures, but only those directly related to the employee's job autonomy (operative rules and procedures). They found that highly trained specialists desired minimization of the number and rigidity of rules and procedures; thus, Hage and Aiken's subsequent research supported this seventh corollary.

189

Hage and Aiken's findings may appear to be contradictory to those of the Aston Group and John Child, who found formalization and standardization to be highly positively related to role specialization. However, they are not. The differences result from examining different aspects of the organization with respect to formalization. The Aston Group concluded that organizations with many functional specialists and high role differentiation tend to have more standard routines, more documentation, and a larger support hierarchy. Formalization and standardization are not a result of the specialists' need for more restraint or control, but of these same experts introducing regulative procedures to lend predictability to the organization's resources and personnel.[44] Similarly, Child explored the relationship of functional and overall role specialization to formalization through data, primarily from a British sample of eighty-two business organizations (the National Sample), but also from British labor unions, engineering firms, and the Aston sample of firms.[45] Using the operationalizations of D. S. Pugh, D. J. Hickson, C. R. Hinings, and C. Turner,[46] Child measured differentiation as functional specialization and overall role specialization; formalization was measured as overall standardization of rules and procedures and overall documentation; power as the vertical span, which is a measure of hierarchical differentiation of control and centralization.[47] Child found that both measures of specialization were more highly correlated with standardization and documentation than was organizational size, technology, location, or environmental variables.[48] In this case, the structural variable of complexity was a better indicator of the structural variable of formalization than any of the contextual or environmental variables. These variables of size, technology, environment, and location predict complexity, which in turn predicts formalizations.[49] See Table 6–1. Thus, when differentiation is measured in terms of professionalization and a specialized division of labor, the formalization of job-related tasks is negatively related to this type of complexity; while the formalization of the overall organization is positively related.

Functional Differentiation (Horizontal and Vertical)   Like Child, Meyer found that vertical differentiation supports formalization that enforces the decentralization of the organization. Functional differentiation also supports formalization, but here the attendant rules place authority in the hands of the top management of finance agencies, whereas vertical differentiation increases the accessibility of rules to all its members. Meyer argued that the accessibility of rules

190

Complexity

TABLE 6–1 Summary of Main Predictors of Variables Representing Bureaucratic Control

VARIABLES	BETA COEFFICIENT	LEVEL OF CONFIDENCE	ZERO-ORDER CORRELATION
(1) Prediction of overall standardization (rules and procedures) $N = 79$, $R^2 = .78$, $F = 86.982$, df = (3,75), $p < .001$			
Overall role specialization	.449	$<.001$	.83
Level of qualifications	.312	$<.001$	.76
Size of owning group	.246	$<.001$	.67
(2) Prediction of overall documentation $N = 79$, $R^2 = .67$, $F = 37.023$, df = (4,74), $p < .001$			
Overall role specialization	.412	$<.001$	.72
Level of qualifications	.294	$<.01$	.66
Size of owning group	.295	$<.001$	.65
Workflow integration	–.237	$<.01$	.06
(3) Prediction of overall decentralization $N = 80$, $R^2 = .45$, $F = 20.901$, df = (3,76), $p < .001$			
Size of organization	.480	$<.001$	.58
Workflow integration	–.258	$<.01$	–.13
Overall documentation	.268	$<.025$	.53

Source: John Child, "Predicting and Understanding Organization Structure," *Administrative Science Quarterly* 18, no. 2 (June 1973): 182.

limits the dependency of those at lower levels on those at upper levels. When overall organizational rules and procedures are written, the subordinate has fewer issues that require a decision from the superordinate. Thus, when there are many hierarchical levels in the organization, rules that define the criteria for promotion and merit are more likely to be written, whereas in a functionally differentiated organization, these decisions are made by a superordinate and are not as likely to be formalized. Written rules are more accessible to employees because of uniform application and familiarity. In these organizations, authority rests in the regulation, not in the hands of the executive.[50] Similarly, Blau found written promotions to be positively associated with hierarchical differentiation—with an increase in vertical differentiation, he observed a decrease in the weight given to seniority and supervisory evaluations for promotion decisions.[51] Thus, evaluation for promotion and rank was taken out of the hands of the superordinate and formalized on the basis of merit.

191

Communication Correlates of Vertical Differentiation

Both Blau and Meyer assumed that in organizations with narrower spans of control, larger administrative components, and the proliferation of hierarchical levels, vertical communication would be facilitated. Here managers would be more involved in planning, communicating, and coordinating roles than in supervisory activities, presumably because specialists do not need or desire supervision. The relationship of the communication dimension with other structural dimensions will be discussed more thoroughly in chapter eight.

SUMMARY

Regularities of findings are beginning to emerge in the literature on the relationships between various organizational dimensions. With increases in size, organizations exhibit a proliferation of both horizontal and vertical differentiation. If an organization's technology is nonroutine, the product is nonuniform, and employees at the lower organizational levels are experts, it will be not only highly vertically differentiated but also decentralized with the overall organizational rules and procedures formalized and standardized. The rules and procedures relating directly to the professional's job activities will be less formalized to allow the professional greater personal autonomy. The large organization that employs highly trained experts will also exhibit a larger administrative component with a narrow span of control to facilitate coordination and communication. On the other hand, if the organizational tasks can be subdivided into small, specific, routine tasks performed on uniform raw materials, nonprofessional, relatively unskilled labor will be employed. This organization will be centralized with a small number of hierarchical levels of authority. Job-related activities will be formalized and the members of the relatively small administrative component will have relatively wide spans of control with little upward communication.

In organizations where employees are experts or professionals and knowledge is complex, the proliferation of hierarchical levels works to decentralize power and facilitate the decision-making of lower management and the professionals. The professional who has contact with a client needs this decision-making autonomy. Low formalization of rules and procedures related to the roles of the professional further facilitates this decentralization process, while overall standardization and formalization of rules and procedures related to the organization's functioning protects the professional from arbitrary administrative and management decisions. Top administrators cannot make arbitrary decisions regarding client relationships, rewards, promotions, rank, and so on. This overall formalization removes control from the hands of top management and places it in an objective, uniform context. The span of control is narrow to facilitate communication up and down the hierarchy. See Table 6–2 for a summary of these relationships.

TABLE 6–2 Differentiation Correlates of Contextual and Structural Dimensions

I. CONTEXTUAL DIMENSIONS

  A. *Size*

    1. Size is positively related to the horizontal differentiation of departments or functional subunits in an organization.

    2. Size is positively related to the horizontal differentiation of occupations and positions in an organization.

    3. Size is positively related to the horizontal differentiation of knowledge in an organization.

    4. Size is positively related to the vertical differentiation of the number of hierarchical levels in an organization.

    5. In organizations where the lower levels of personnel are experts or professionals, size is positively related to the proportionate size of the administrative component.

  B. *Technology*

    1. Technological complexity* is positively related to the horizontal differentiation of departments or functional subunits of an organization.

    2. Technological complexity is positively related to the horizontal differentiation of occupations and positions in an organization.

    3. Technological complexity is positively related to the horizontal differentiation of knowledge in an organization.

    4. Technological complexity is positively related to the vertical differentiation of number of hierarchical levels in an organization.

    5. In organizations where the lower levels of personnel are experts or professionals, technological complexity is positively related to the proportionate size of the administrative component.

II. STRUCTURAL DIMENSIONS

  A. *Centralization*

    1. Horizontal differentiation of the departments and functional sub-

units is positively related to centralization of the decision-making in an organization.

2. Horizontal differentiation of occupations and positions (specialized division of labor) is positively related to decentralization of decision-making in an organization.

3. Horizontal differentiation in the form of routinization of the division of labor is negatively related to decentralization of decision-making in an organization.

4. Horizontal differentiation of knowledge is positively related to decentralization of decision-making in that organization.

5. Vertical differentiation of the hierarchical levels of an organization is positively related to decentralization of decision-making in that organization.

6. In organizations where the lower levels of personnel are experts or professionals, the proportionate size of the administrative component is positively related to decentralization of decision-making.

B. *Formalization*

1. Horizontal differentiation of departments and functional subunits is positively related to the formalization of rules and standardization of the overall organization, thus placing power in the hands of the top administration.

2. Horizontal differentiation of the occupations and professions in an organization is positively related to the formalization of overall organizational rules and standardization of procedures.

3. When professionals are employed at the lower levels of the organization, horizontal differentiation of knowledge is negatively related to the formalization of rules and procedures related to the professional's work, but positively related to the formalization of overall organizational rules and procedures. This takes power out of the hands of the top administrators.

4. When professionals are employed at the lower levels of the organization, vertical differentiation of the number of hierarchical levels in an organization is positively related to the overall organizational formalization of rules and procedures. This takes power out of the hands of the top executives.

5. When professionals are employed at the lower levels of the organization, the proportionate size of the administrative component is positively related to the overall organizational formalization of rules and negatively related to formalization of operative rules and procedures.

C. *Communication*

1. Horizontal differentiation of departments or subunits of an organi-

zation is negatively related to the rate of upward organizational communication and positively related to the rate of downward organizational communication.

2. Horizontal differentiation of occupations and positions in an organization is positively related to the rate of organizational communication.

3. Horizontal differentiation of knowledge is positively related to the rate of upward communication.

4. When professionals are employed at the lower levels of the organization, vertical differentiation of the hierarchical levels is positively related to the rate of upward organizational communication.

5. When professionals are employed at the lower levels of the organization, the proportionate size of the administrative component is positively related to the rate of upward organizational communication.

---

* Technological complexity is here defined in terms of the complexity of knowledge and raw materials as opposed to operations technology.

NOTES

1. Peter M. Blau and Richard A. Schoenherr, *The Structure of Organizations* (New York: Basic Books, 1971), p. 16.
2. James L. Price, *Organizational Effectiveness: An Inventory of Propositions* (Homewood, Ill.: Richard D. Irwin, Inc., 1968), p. 26.
3. Jerald Hage and Michael Aiken, *Social Change in Complex Organizations* (New York: Random House, 1970), p. 33.
4. Howard W. Vollmer and Donald L. Mills, eds., *Professionalization* (Englewood Cliffs, N.J.: Prentice–Hall, 1966), pp. v.–viii.
5. William J. Goode, "Encroachment, Charlatanism and the Emerging Profession: Psychology, Sociology, and Medicine," *American Sociological Review* 25, no. 6 (December 1970): 903.
6. Ibid.
7. Many of the above characteristics of the professional are discussed by Edward Gross in *Work and Society* (New York: Thomas Y. Crowell, 1958), pp. 78–82.
8. Ernest Greenwood, "Attributes of a Profession," *Social Work* 2, no. 3 (July 1957): 45–55.
9. Ibid., pp. 47–54.
10. Harold L. Wilensky, "The Professionalization of Everyone," *The American Journal of Sociology* 70, no. 2 (September 1964): 137–158.
11. Richard H. Hall, "Professionalization and Bureaucratization," *American Sociological Review* 33, no. 1 (February 1968): 103.
12. Marshall W. Meyer, "Two Authority Structures of Bureaucratic Organizations," *Administrative Science Quarterly* 13, no. 2 (September 1968): 216.

13. D. S. Pugh, D. J. Hickson, C. R. Hinings, and C. Turner, "Dimensions of Organization Structure," *Administrative Science Quarterly* 13, no. 1 (June 1968): 78.

14. Hage and Aiken, *Social Change in Complex Organizations*, pp. 23-25.

15. S. R. Klatzky, "Relationship of Organization Size to Complexity and Coordination," *Administrative Science Quarterly* 15, no. 4 (December 1970): 428-438.

16. William A. Rushing, "The Effects of Industry Size and the Division of Labor on Administration," *Administrative Science Quarterly* 12, no. 2 (September 1967): 267-295.

17. Blau and Schoenherr, *The Structure of Organizations*.

18. D. S. Pugh, D. J. Hickson, C. R. Hinings, and C. Turner, "The Context of Organization Structure," *Administrative Science Quarterly* 14, no. 1 (March 1969): 91-114.

19. Blau and Schoenherr, *The Structure of Organizations;* Marshall W. Meyer, "Size and Structure of Organizations: A Causal Analysis," *American Sociological Review* 37, no. 4 (August 1972): 434-441; Peter M. Blau, *The Organization of Academic Work* (New York: John Wiley and Sons, Inc., 1973).

20. Peter M. Blau, "The Hierarchy of Authority in Organizations," *American Journal of Sociology* 73, no. 4 (January 1968): 462, 464.

21. Ibid., p. 464.

22. T. R. Anderson and S. Warkov, "Organizational Size and Functional Complexity: A Study of Administration in Hospitals," *American Sociological Review* 26, no. 1 (February 1961): 27; Rushing, "The Effects of Industry Size and Division of Labor on Administration."

23. Gerald D. Bell, "Determinants of Span of Control," *The American Journal of Sociology* 73, no. 1 (July 1967): 100-109.

24. Ibid.

25. William G. Ouchi and John B. Dowling, "Defining the Span of Control," *Administrative Science Quarterly* 19, no. 3 (September 1974): 358-359.

26. Peter M. Blau, "A Formal Theory of Differentiation in Organizations," *American Sociological Review* 35, no. 2 (April 1970): 201-218.

27. "Experts" were defined as those persons possessing "at least a college degree in a particular specialty." This definition does not coincide with the one for a professional.

28. Peter M. Blau, Wolf V. Heydebrand, and Robert E. Stauffer, "The Structure of Small Bureaucracies," *American Sociological Review* 31, no. 2 (April 1966): 187.

29. Ibid., pp. 179-191.

30. Blau, "The Hierarchy of Authority in Organizations," p. 458.

31. Ibid., 455.

32. Ibid., pp. 460-462.

33. Blau, *The Organization of Academic Work*.

34. Marshall W. Meyer, "Expertness and Span of Control," *American Sociological Review* 33, no. 6 (December 1968): 944-951.

35. Blau, Heydebrand, and Stauffer, "The Structure of Small Bureaucracies," pp. 179-191.

36. Jerald Hage, "An Axiomatic Theory of Organizations," *Administrative Science Quarterly* 10, no. 3 (December 1965): 294; Victor A. Thompson, "Hierarchy, Specialization, and Organizational Conflict," *Administrative Science Quarterly* 5, no. 4 (March 1961): 485-521.

37. Jerald Hage and Michael Aiken, "Relationship of Centralization to Other Structural Properties," *Administrative Science Quarterly* 12, no. 1 (June 1967): 74–75.

38. Blau, *The Organization of Academic Work*, pp. 161–178.

39. Pugh, Hickson, Hinings, and Turner, "Dimensions of Organization Structure"; C. R. Hinings and G. L. Lee, "Dimensions of Organization Structure and Their Context: A Replication," *Sociology* 5, no. 1 (January 1971): 83–93; John Child, "Organization Structure and Strategies of Control: A Replication of the Aston Studies," *Administrative Science Quarterly* 17, no. 2 (June 1972): 163–177.

40. Meyer, "The Two Authority Structures of Bureaucratic Organizations," pp. 217, 218.

41. Blau, Heydebrand, and Stauffer, "The Structure of Small Bureaucracies," pp. 179–191.

42. Meyer, "The Two Authority Structures of Bureaucratic Organizations."

43. Hage, "An Axiomatic Theory of Organizations," p. 303.

44. Pugh, Hickson, Hinings, and Turner, "Dimensions of Organization Structure," p. 82.

45. John Child, "Predicting and Understanding Organization Structure," *Administrative Science Quarterly* 18, no. 2 (June 1973).

46. Pugh, Hickson, Hinings, and Turner, "Dimensions of Organization Structure," pp. 165–195.

47. Child, "Predicting and Understanding Organization Structure," p. 170.

48. Ibid., p. 181.

49. Ibid., p. 168.

50. Meyer, "The Two Authority Structures of Bureaucratic Organizations."

51. These relationships were found in Blau's analysis of finance departments in "The Hierarchy of Authority in Organizations" (p. 462).

7

FORMALIZATION

OBJECTIVES

The objectives of this chapter are:

1. To theoretically and operationally define formalization:
   a. To differentiate between standardization and formalization.
   b. to explore the questions of existence and enforcement of rules and procedures.
   c. to differentiate between operative and regulative rules and procedures.
   d. to differentiate between attitudinal and global-institutional measures of formalization.
2. To differentiate between externalized and internalized rules and procedures.
3. To analyze the structural correlates of formalization:
   a. centralization
   b. complexity
   c. communication

INTRODUCTION

The degree of formalization of an organization depends not only on the environment and contextual variables in which that organization exists, but also on the amount of control that the organization experiences as a result of its other structural variables (centralization of power, specialization of the division of labor, and rate of communication). Max Weber is generally credited with being the first to emphasize the importance of formalized rules and procedures within organizations.[1] Weber related formalization to such structural characteristics as centralization of power and the expertise of those working in the organization. These relationships will be discussed later in this chapter. Such modes of organizational control as formalization, standardization, and centralization have contributed some degree of impersonality and efficiency to organizations. Some contemporary writers have viewed these more mechanistic operations negatively because of their detrimental socio-psychological effects on employees' morale. Thus, the degree to which formalization can successfully be used as a method of control also depends on which performance variables (efficiency, effectiveness, morale, and so on) are being maximized by the organization. These relationships will be discussed in Part IV of this text.

FORMALIZATION DEFINED

Scope

The definitions of formalization vary in scope, from considerations of job descriptions alone to those all-inclusive definitions that encompass the formalization of power and communication processes. Pugh, Hickson, and associates noted that formalization or standardization ". . . include[s] statements of procedures, rules, roles . . . and operation of procedures, which deal with (a) decision seeking (applications for capital, employment, and so on), (b) conveying of decisions and instructions (plans, minutes, requisitions, and so on), and (c) conveying of information, including feedback."[2] While the definitions presented here vary in scope, that of Richard Hall, Eugene Haas, and Normal Johnson is the broadest. It includes:

(1) Roles: (a) the degree to which the positions in the organization are concretely defined, and (b) the presence or absence of written job descriptions; (2) Authority Relations: (a) the degree to which the authority structure is formalized (clear definition of the hierarchy of authority), (b) the extent to which the authority structure is formalized in writing; (3) Communications: (a) the degree of emphasis on written communications, and (b) the degree of emphasis on going through established channels in the communication process; (4) Norms and Sanctions: (a) the number of written rules and policies; (b) the degree to which

penalties for rule violation are clearly stipulated; and (c) the extent to which penalties for rules violation are codified in writing; and (5) Procedures: (a) the degree of formalization of orientation programs for new members (systematic socialization for all new entrants), and (b) the degree of formalization of in-service training programs for new members (systematic and continuing socialization of new members).[3]

Standardization Versus Formalization

As has been indicated above, many aspects of the organization can be standardized and formalized. Generally the term *standardization* refers to regularly patterned rules and procedures, while *formalization* refers to the recording of the standardized rules and procedures in written form. Rules and procedures may exist exclusively in the minds of the employees, or they may exist only on paper. That they exist only in the minds of the employees and not in written form does not make them any less real or imperative for the employees. But when the reverse is true and rules and procedures exist only in written form, they do not direct behavior and therefore are of little consequence. Thus, the most important rules to the functioning of the organization are generally not only salient in the minds of the employees, due to standardization, but are formalized as a reference for the employees. Thus, formalization has a legitimizing effect that standardization alone does not have. The term *formalization* is often used to designate both the standardization and formalization of rules and procedures, and will be used here to denote both concepts.

Existence and Enforcement

Definitions of formalization also vary as to whether the mere existence of rules and procedures is considered or whether both existence and enforcement of rules must be present in order for an organization to be considered highly formalized. For example, Jerald Hage's definition included both the existence and enforcement of rules and procedures. He suggested that formalization be ". . . measured by the proportion of codified jobs and the range of variation that is tolerated within the rules defining the jobs. The higher the proportion of codified jobs and the less the range of variation allowed, the more formalized the organization."[4] Rules are constructed to ensure conformity of behavior; when rules are not enforced, the predictability of employee behavior and hence of organizational functioning is lessened and organizational performance may be jeopardized. Of course, it is also possible that the organization may be too rigidly formalized, and the employees may choose not to conform to rules and regulations in an attempt to initiate some new program or procedure. Generally, organizations that maximize the number of rules and enforce them are too rigid to allow the employees latitude to disregard a given rule, thus minimizing innovations and changes initiated by individual employees.

Operative and Regulative Rules and Procedures

Rules govern the activities of both the worker and management on the job. They define which administrators will be evaluated and rewarded, and when and where. Likewise, procedures define not only how the workflow of the organization will function, but also how evaluation and compensation of workers will take place. Thus, rules and procedures deal not only with the workflow and output of the organization, but also with its internal functioning.

The rules and procedures dealing with the tasks of the organization or with operations technology are called *operative* rules and procedures. In industrial organizations in particular, these rules and procedures may be a part of the job description or job manual because they are imperative to the production process. They control the work on the product and the output. *Regulative* rules and procedures, by contrast, control the internal functioning of the organization, for example, how information will be processed and how evaluations will be conducted. A university has operative rules and procedures governing how a professor will interact with students with regard to instruction, evaluation, interpersonal behavior, and so on. At the same time, the university has regulative rules and procedures that cover methods of communication, procedures for hiring and evaluation of personnel, and obtaining access to facilities. Operative rules and procedures controlling the work of lower hierarchical levels are most often a source of frustration for faculty, on whose activities they impinge. Professionals in general may abhor and negate the operative rules and procedures that control and coordinate their interaction with other employees and clients. On the other hand, they may wish to strengthen the regulative rules and procedures related to personnel decisions and allocation of rewards, thus removing power from the hands of arbitrary or highly political administrators. At the same time, professionals at the lower levels of the organization may accept and support self-imposed operative rules and procedures that result from their professional training;

201

but when operative rules and procedures are imposed by the administration, professionals may refuse to follow them because they restrict professional autonomy.

This distinction between operative and regulative rules and procedures is particularly important in the analysis of professional organizations because it can explain why Researcher A may find a negative relationship between the existence of highly trained and educated employees and formalization *when this formalization is measured in terms of operative rules and procedures;* and Researcher B find a positive relationship *when formalization is measured in terms of regulative rules and procedures.* In the first instance, the professionals have internalized professional norms that work against their interaction with the client or their work relationship being formalized and standardized by administrators in the organization. The professional desires the autonomy to regulate this relationship. In the latter case, the professional works to have the regulative rules and procedures in the organization formalized to reduce the occurrence of arbitrary decisions by middle management and centralization of power in the hands of top executives and administrators. Thus, professionals desire personal autonomy in their own work and predictability of the regulative structure or administration of the organization in which they work.

Hage and Aiken's definition of formalization as "job codification" and "rule observation" conceptualizes operative formalization:

> Formalization represents the use of rules in an organization. Job codification is a measure of how many rules define what the occupants of positions are to do, while rule observation is a measure of whether or not the rules are employed. In other words, the variable of job codification represents the degree to which the job descriptions are specified, and the variable [of] rule observation refers to the degree to which job occupants are supervised in conforming to the standards established by job codification. Job codification represents the degree of work standardization while rule observation is a measure of the latitude of behavior that is tolerated from standards.[5]

Attitudinal and Global-Institutional Measures

Hage and Aiken's variables of operative formalization were measured through the use of attitudinal data (the employee's perception of the degree of formalization and standardization); that is, selected members of the organizations were asked to respond to questionnaires and interviews designed to measure formalization. An average (median) score was derived for a set of attitude items administered to employees within the organization or the organizational subunit.[6] Pugh and his associates used a broader definition of formalization, which included ". . . the extent to which rules, procedures, instructions, and communications are written."[7] To this definition they added the variable of standardization, which was defined as the extent to which "rules or definitions . . . purport to cover all circumstances and apply invariably."[8] Like Hage and Aiken, they concentrated on operative as opposed to regulative formalization in that they measured rules and procedures related to jobs and tasks. Unlike Hage and Aiken, they operationalized their variables through the use of global–institutional measures (the organization's official records, documents and key informants). Thus, although the type of formalization being measured was the same—operative, the two studies utilized different levels of measurement (global–institutional and attitudinal), which did not yield the same results. This difference was verified by Johannes Pennings' research on the relationship between formalization and centralization.[9] Pennings compared two different sets of measures designed to assess the degree of centralization and formalization of manufacturing organizations. Pennings's institutional measures encompassed two aspects of Pugh's measure of structuring activities: (1) *formalization of role definition,* which measured the degree to which rules and procedures were written,[10] and (2) *specialization,* which measured the extent to which one or more individuals occupied a non-workflow function on a full-time basis, regardless of the number of specialists.[11] The attitudinal measures utilized by Pennings were: (1) *job codification,* which measured the degree of work standardizations, how the rules defined the activities of organizational members;[12] (2) *job specificity,* which measured the degree to which procedures defining a job were spelled out;[13] (3) *strictness,* which measured a dimension related to rule observation—the degree to which existing rules were enforced;[14] (4) *rule observation,* which measured whether rules were employed and enforced;[15] (5) *written communication,* Pennings's own scale that measured the frequency of written communication as reported by individuals (personal communication).[16]

In studying the relationships of institutional to attitudinal variables, Pennings found that these measures of formalization were not strongly related. See Table 7–1. Furthermore, Pennings's data did not show a sufficient convergence between the two global–institutional measures (r = .24 N.S.), Pugh and associates' indicators of

TABLE 7–1 Multimethod-Multitrait Matrix of Measures of Organizational Structure: Product–Moment Correlations Between Institutional and Questionnaire Measures of Centralization and Formalization (N = 10)

	INSTITUTIONAL APPROACH						QUESTIONNAIRE APPROACH							
	A_{11}	A_{12}	A_{13}	A_{14}	B_{11}	B_{12}	A_{21}	A_{22}	A_{23}	B_{21}	B_{22}	B_{23}	B_{24}	B_{25}
Institutional approach:														
Centralization:														
Autonomy (A_{11})	—	—	—	—	—	—	—	—	—	—	—	—	—	—
Chief executive's span of control (A_{12})	.58	—	—	—	—	—	—	—	—	—	—	—	—	—
Worker/supervisory ratio (A_{13})	.16	.25	—	—	—	—	—	—	—	—	—	—	—	—
Number of direct supervisors (A_{14})	-.40	-.52	-.57	—	—	—	—	—	—	—	—	—	—	—
Formalization:														
Specialization (B_{11})	.30	-.17	.16	.24	—	—	—	—	—	—	—	—	—	—
Role definition (B_{12})	-.59	-.67	.10	.26	.24	—	—	—	—	—	—	—	—	—
Questionnaire approach:														
Centralization:														
Personal participation in decision making (A_{21})	-.73	-.53	-.25	-.10	-.53	.45	.96	—	—	—	—	—	—	—
Hierarchy of authority (A_{22})	-.39	-.41	.05	.21	-.24	.50	.59	.72	—	—	—	—	—	—
Departmental participation in decision making (A_{23})	-.41	-.52	.09	.14	-.15	.55	.71	.93	.83	—	—	—	—	—

	INSTITUTIONAL APPROACH						QUESTIONNAIRE APPROACH							
	A_{11}	A_{12}	A_{13}	A_{14}	B_{11}	B_{12}	A_{21}	A_{22}	A_{23}	B_{21}	B_{22}	B_{23}	B_{24}	B_{25}
Formalization:														
Job codification (B_{21})	−.05	−.09	.49	−.40	−.43	−.05	.45	.50	.61	.78	—	—	—	—
Job specificity (B_{22})	−.02	−.15	−.29	−.16	−.71	−.05	.53	.43	.40	.47	.75	—	—	—
Strictness (B_{23})	−.04	.26	−.09	−.63	−.60	−.25	.29	.09	.04	.25	.50	.64	—	—
Rule observation (B_{24})	−.02	.21	.14	−.44	−.82	−.48	.30	.11	.10	.72	.59	.56	.61	—
Written communication (B_{25})	−.57	−.42	.18	.39	.07	.25	.41	.43	.52	.38	.32	.29	.04	.89

NOTE: A coefficient of .57 is significant on the 5% level. A coefficient of .70 is significant on the 1% level. The values in the diagonal are Spearman–Brown reliability coefficients.

Source: Johannes Pennings, "Measures of Organizational Structure: A Methodological Note," *American Journal of Sociology* 79, no. 3 (November 1973): 693.

structuring of activities.[17] Thus, the method of operationalizing the formalization—attitudinal or global–institutional—variable was found to strongly influence findings. Attitudinal and global–institutional measures of formalization did not measure the same construct.

In addition to differing in scope, the operational definitions of formalization differ in terms of whether: (1) both the existence and enforcement of rules and procedures are measured, (2) attitudinal or global–institutional indicators are utilized, (3) operative or regulative formalization is being measured, (4) only nonwritten or written rules and procedures are enumerated. Formalization is most often operationalized by counting the number of rules in an organization. This method of measurement not only assumes that all rules are of equal weight but that they are all enforced with the same vigor, also that written and nonwritten rules are enforced on an equal basis. A more comprehenisve measure of formalization is to measure both the existence and enforcement of written and nonwritten rules and procedures, both operative and regulative.

EXTERNALIZED AND INTERNALIZED RULES AND PROCEDURES

Many occupations, such as physician, teacher, research analyst, exist for which written job descriptions or exact procedures for workflow are difficult, if not impossible, to establish. During their educational process, most highly trained employees (professionals or experts) have *internalized* their job descriptions and the procedures for dealing with clients. Due to the nature of the raw material and operations technology as well as unpredictable situations, the enforcement of job-related rules and procedures would be virtually impossible. To a great extent, the discretion and the abilities of the individual employee, as opposed to formalized rules and procedures, determine the performance of the organization. Consequently, attempts to formalize operative rules and procedures result in conflicts between professionals and administrators. At the other end of the job continuum is the type for which there are explicitly defined and enforced rules and procedures. A rules manual and extensive job description for each position are generally available. This is considered to be a high degree of formalization of operative rules and procedures. The rules are formalized as to the time the employee punches in, the time taken for breaks and lunch, the interaction he or she has

206

with others, and so on. The procedures are standardized in that *the same material is processed in the same way and the output is the same each day.* These explicitly defined rules and procedures are the same for all those holding a given position; they are written and are generally enforced not by the employee but by a supervisor. The difference between these explicitly defined rules and the internalized rules of the professional is not that one is more real, intense, and restricting than the other, but that, for the professional, control originates from *within,* while for the assembly line worker, it originates from the *outside.*

In differentiating between internalized and externalized rules and procedures, we have again uncovered the nonbureaucratic and bureaucratic methods of coordination and control elaborated in chapter five as professional and positional power, respectively, and in chapter six as knowledge and hierarchical differentiation, respectively. The assumption at the basis of bureaucratic control and coordination is that when the employee is not highly trained and educated (the nonprofessional), the rules and procedures governing the work activities will be *externalized,* that is, specifically defined, codified, and enforced through supervision. At the basis of nonbureaucratic control is the employee who is highly trained and educated (the professional), who has internalized the operative rules and procedures through the socialization process. Here, the behavior of the employee does not need to be controlled from external sources such as supervisors. Close supervision and coercive enforcement from an administrator with greater positional power is ineffective and often dysfunctional.

RECAPITULATION OF CONTEXTUAL CORRELATES OF FORMALIZATION

Before relating these types of bureaucratic and nonbureaucratic control to formalization, the relationship between formalization and the contextual dimensions of size and technology will be reiterated. It will be remembered that Aiken and Hage used the following indexes of formalization: (1) job codification, the number of regulations specifying who is to do what, when, where, and why; (2) rule observation, the diligency with which such rules are enforced; (3) existence of rules manuals; (4) presence of job descriptions; and (5) specificity of job, the procedures defining a job. The sixteen agencies they studied were divided into those which possessed routine and non-routine technology using a method similar to the one advocated by Charles Perrow. That is, technology was defined to include both the relative stability of the raw materials as well as how much was understood about them. Thus, both raw-material and knowledge technology were encompassed in this definition. If the clients were stable and uniform and much was known about the particular treatment process, then the organization possessed a routine workflow.[18]

Hage and Aiken hypothesized that "organizations with routine work are more likely to have greater formalization of organizational roles."[19] They found the relationship to be in the direction expected; therefore, they rationalized that routine work facilitates the process of formalization by promoting lack of variety in clients, which makes possible regulations. As indicated in Table 7-2, five indexes of formalization were found to be related to routinization of technology. Routine work led to the formalization of regulations in the form of rules manuals ($r = .51$), job descriptions ($r = .53$), and the degree of job specificity ($r = .61$); but routinization had little impact on job codification ($r = .21$) and rule observation ($r = .20$).[20] Hage and Aiken posited that "job codification and rule observation refer more to work regulations while the rules manuals, job descriptions, and job specificity reflect basic work guidelines and policies of the organization. These last three are more likely to be manifestations of the programming for the organization's coordination than the other two measures."[21] Thus, Hage and Aiken's research supported the positive relationship between routinization of technology and formalization for three out of five indexes of formalization; but as they pointed out, the significant evidence was that this relationship existed even though health and welfare agencies were on the non-routine end of the continuum. Had some of Hage and Aiken's organizations been industrial or manufacturing organizations, the difference would have probably been greater and more of the formalization indexes would have evidenced significant differences when correlated with routineness of technology.

Hall, Haas, and Johnson investigated the relationship between size, measured as the total number of paid employees, and the formalization of a wide variety of organizations—educational, commercial, military, governmental, manufacturing, religious, and penal.[22] Organizational size ranged from six to 9,000 members. Their five categories of variables and the eleven indexes of formalization were defined earlier in this chapter. It may be remembered that the general areas into which formalization variables were categorized included: (a) roles, (b) authority relations, (c) communications, (d)

TABLE 7 − 2   The Relationship Between Routine Work and Social Structure

STRUCTURAL VARIABLES	PEARSONIAN PRODUCT– MOMENT COR- RELATION COEFFICIENTS	P
DEGREE OF CENTRALIZATION		
Degree of participation in organizational decision	−.72	<.001
Degree of hierarchy of authority in work decisions	−.02	N.S.
DEGREE OF FORMALIZATION		
Degree of job codification	.21	N.S.
Degree of rule observation	.20	N.S.
Presence of a rules manual	.51	<.05
Presence of job descriptions	.53	<.05
Degree of specificity of job descriptions	.61	<.01
DEGREE OF STRATIFICATION		
Effect between supervisors and staff	−.09	N.S.
Distance between supervisors and staff	.19	N.S.
DEGREE OF COMPLEXITY		
Amount of professional training	−.55	<.05
Amount of professional activity	−.12	N.S.
Number of occupational specialties	−.19	N.S.

For a discussion of the construction of all the measures of the variables included here with the exception of the presence of a rules manual and job descriptions and the two measures of stratification, see Michael Aiken and Jerald Hage, "Organizational Interdependence and Intraorganizational Structure," *American Sociological Review* 33, no. 6 (December 1968): 912–930.

Source: Jerald Hage and Michael Aiken, "Routine Technology, Social Structure, and Organizational Goals," *Administrative Science Quarterly* 14, no. 3 (September 1969): 371.

norms and sanctions, and (e) procedures. As depicted in Table 7–3, only four of eleven relationships were strong, those between size and the authority structure (B–1), the stipulation of penalties for rule violation in writing (D–3), and orientation and in–service training procedures (E–1 and E–2). Hall noted that a general association did exist in that larger organizations tended to be more formalized on the other indexes, even though the relationships were weak. A cursory analysis of Table 7–3 suggests some correlation between size and formalization.

TABLE 7—3 Formalization Indicators by Organizational Size

	SIZE		
	Less than 100 (N = 20)	100–999 (N = 35)	More than 1,000 (N = 20)
A. Roles			
1. Concreteness of Positional Descriptions			
Low	45%	17%	20%
Medium	35%	46%	55%
High	20%	37%	25%
Kendall's Tau C = .12			
2. Presence of Written Job Descriptions			
None	35%	26%	20%
Present only at some levels	40%	23%	50%
Present throughout organization	25%	51%	30%
Kendall's Tau C = .01			
B. Authority Relations			
1. Degree of Formalization of Authority Structure			
Low or medium	58%	32%	26%
High	42%	68%	74%
Kendall's Tau C = .25			
2. Codification of Authority Structure in Writing			
Not codified	58%	26%	47%
Codified	42%	74%	53%
Kendall's Tau C = .08			
C. Communications			
1. Degree of Emphasis on Written Communications			
Low	35%	17%	30%
Medium	55%	57%	55%
High	10%	26%	15%
Kendall's Tau C = .05			
2. Emphasis on Using Established Communications Channels			
Low	35%	23%	15%
Medium	25%	37%	30%
High	40%	40%	55%
Kendall's Tau C = .13			

		SIZE	
	Less than 100 (N = 20)	100–999 (N = 35)	More than 1,000 (N = 20)

D. Norms and Sanctions
  1. Number of Written Rules and
    Policies

Less than 12	32%	17%	21%
More than 12	68%	83%	79%

    Kendall's Tau C = .08
  2. Penalties for Rule Violation
    Clearly Stipulated

No	65%	44%	47%
Yes (for at least some members)	35%	56%	53%

    Kendall's Tau C = .14
  3. Stipulation of Penalties for
    Rule Violation in Writing

No	70%	50%	42%
Yes (for at least some members)	30%	50%	58%

    Kendall's Tau C = .22

E. Procedures
  1. Formalization of Orientation
    Program for New Members
    (Only Programs for All New
    Members Included; N = 57)

No Program or Low Formalization	83%	63%	50%
High Formalization	17%	37%	50%

    Kendall's Tau C = .26
  2. Formalization of In-service
    Training Program for New
    Members (Only Programs for
    All New Members Included;
    N = 36)

No Program or Low Formalization	77%	47%	50%
High Formalization	23%	53%	50%

    Kendall's Tau C = .26

Source: Richard H. Hall, J. Eugene Haas, and Norman J. Johnson, "Organizational Size, Complexity, and Formalization," *American Sociological Review* 32, no. 6 (December 1967): 910–911.

Likewise, John Child concluded from his analysis of data from the National Sample, the Aston studies, and Blau's study that "it is neither theoretically convincing nor statistically demonstrable that size in itself is the major determinant of formalization."[23] Yet, although size may not be the major determinant, the correlations between size and overall standardization and documentation were moderate to high for all seven samples. (See Table 4–3 for these relationships.)

STRUCTURAL CORRELATES OF FORMALIZATION

As has been demonstrated throughout this text, several methods of control are available to an organization. Centralization of decision-making, specialization of roles and tasks, standardization and formalization of rules and procedures, internalization of norms and standards by professionals, and the formalization of the communication network are those methods most often considered by organizational theorists. The formalization of rules and procedures allows those at the top of the organization to retain control while delegating the decision-making to positions at lower levels. Thus, with increased levels of hierarchy, organizations become more formalized. Just as decentralized organizations are more likely to be composed of professionals or specialists and have highly complex technologies, they are also more likely to be formalized. Delegation of decision-making, without control, is a high-risk situation for organizational administrators because: (1) subordinates may place personal goals over organizational goals and (2) subordinates do not have complete information or knowledge of the consequences of their decisions. Thus, when decision-making is delegated (decentralization), some other form of control is generally instituted. This often takes the form of employing trained and educated personnel and formalizing rules and procedures. Because the knowledge and skills of the employees as well as the standardized policies and procedures of the organization control its functioning, the manager can concentrate on coordination and communication rather than learning the skills of the employees and supervising their execution of those skills. Rules and regulations take the place of surveillance. Standardization of all organizational elements—inputs, tasks, policies, procedures, rewards, etc.—make the organization more predictable and therefore serve as controls. Standardization eliminates not only alternative behavior but

212

also consideration of alternatives. Thus, standardization maximizes predictability at the expense of innovation.

Formalization and standardization are thus means of control that permit the delegation of decision-making. We would therefore expect standardization and formalization to be negatively related to the centralization of decision-making in that they are alternative methods of control. When all decisions are made by a few people at the top of the hierarchy, there is less need for formalization; control is being maintained through centralization of decision making.

Centralization Correlates

As was documented in chapter six, researchers using different indicators of centralization and formalization have evidenced different findings. More specifically, on testing this relationship, Hage and Aiken found that the two measures of participation in decision-making were only weakly related to the degree of formalization in the predicted direction. Formalization was measured by two indexes (1) job codification and (2) rule observation. However, rule observation and hierarchy of authority (reliance on the chain of command for work decisions) were found to be strongly related. Reliance on others to make work decisions dealt specifically with work operations. One way in which control of the work situation was maintained was to enforce the rules that related specifically to the employees' work (operative rules and procedures). In this way, reliance on the hierarchy for decision-making was complementary to enforcement of rules, or "rule observation."

The two indexes of centralization measured different aspects of power. The degree of participation in decision-making was measured by obtaining "an average of participation by staff members in organization-wide decisions such as hiring of personnel, the promotion of personnel, the adoption of new policies, and the institution of new services. These areas of decision making are common to most organizations, and represent decisions about the allocation of organizational resources such as personnel and money, which are among the most basic kinds of decisions made in an organization."[24] These decision-making areas dealt more with the overall functioning of the organizations; therefore, if the rules and procedures related to these decisions were to be formalized, they would be considered to be *regulative* rules and procedures. But Hage and Aiken were not measuring formalization of regulative rules and procedures. The second measure of power (hierarchy of authority) ". . . refers to decisions involving the work associated with each position. If the occupants are allowed to make their own work decisions, then there is little reliance upon the superordinates and thus a low reliance on hierarchy of authority for social control."[25] When rules and procedures related to work decisions are formalized, they are considered to be *operative* rules and procedures. Hage and Aiken's measures of formalization—job codification and rule observation—both dealt with *operative* rules. Job codification was a measure of how many rules defined what occupants of positions were to do; rule observation measured whether or not rules were employed ("supervision of conformity to standards established by job codifications").[26] Thus, since both variables were related to work roles, a strong relationship could be expected between hierarchy of authority, where employees were not allowed to make their own decisions, and rule observation enforced by surveillance to be sure the employees followed rules. Consequently, hierarchy of authority was a better correlate of formalization than participation in the overall decisions of the organization. This is not surprising due to the similarity of variables measuring the work decisions (hierarchy of authority) and formalization of work rules and procedures (job codification) and the surveillance of their enforcement (rule observation).

Although Hage and Aiken's findings that formalization is positively related to centralization *seem* to contradict those of Pugh and associates and Blau, *they do not.* Hage and Aiken's positive relationship between centralization of work decision and rule observation was found in conjunction with less professional activities.[27] In these nonprofessional organizations, employees perceived that decisions were made on higher levels; they also perceived enforcement and surveillance to be more stringent. Although Blau and Pugh and associates used institutional–global indexes rather than the attitudinal measures used by Hage and Aiken, they also found that where professionals were employed, they did not experience close supervision and they did have input into their work decisions. Thus, the employment of professionals influences the relationship between centralization and formalization of work-related activities. When professionals are employed, the work-related decisions will be decentralized and rules and procedures related to the professional's work will not be formalized. In organizations where nonprofessionals are employed, decisions related to their work will be formalized. Keep in mind that both of these situations deal with *operative* formalization. The question still remains, what will happen to *regulative* rules and procedures when professionals and nonprofessionals are hired?

214

Although professionals desire neither to have their work decisions made for them nor their work tasks regulated by rules and procedures, they do desire formalization of rules and procedures at the *regulative* level (methods of hiring, evaluation, etc.). At this level, when rules and procedures are established, the professional employee as well as the top-level administrators can be relatively certain that decisions are *not* left in the arbitrary hands of middle management. Thus, formalization of regulative rules and procedures ensures decentralization at two levels: The professional employee at the lower level has work autonomy with the certainty that his or her supervisor cannot arbitrarily change the rules and procedures, and the top executives or administrators can rely on a predictable functioning of the organization and therefore do not have to control every decision. Thus, both levels of decentralization are positively related to formalization of regulative policies and procedures. Here, formalization is an alternative to centralization as a method of control. For example, in his analysis of public personnel agencies, Peter Blau found those organizations with highly formalized personnel procedures and rigid conformity to these procedures to be decentralized. Personnel at the local middle management level were entrusted with making personnel decisions (decentralization), but the decisions had to be made according to the formalized rules and procedures (formalization).[28] The formalized personnel procedures ensured the presence of qualified personnel at the lower, local levels of the organization. These qualified personnel, in turn, could be given greater decision-making power, which further decentralized the organizational structures.

In his study of employment security agencies, Blau did not analyze the delegation of decision-making to the lowest level of the organization, but rather defined decentralization as the delegation of decision-making to middle management, either at the headquarters or local office level. Four components of decentralization were analyzed: (1) delegation of personnel authority within the headquarters, (2) delegation of budget responsibilities within the headquarters, (3) influence exercised by heads of divisions at the headquarters over major structural changes in their divisions, and (4) delegation of responsibility to managers of local offices.[29] Blau found that:

Strict conformity with personnel standards in making appointments does not promote centralization of authority in the hands of top management in employment security agencies; neither does the elaboration of these standards into an exten-

215

sive system of formalized personnel regulations; nor does the standardization of the procedure governing the supervisory ratings of the subordinates. On the contrary, all three manifestations of bureaucratized procedures foster decentralization.[30]

Thus, formalized rules and procedures related to decentralization of personnel decisions implement control at several levels: (1) they take these decisions out of the hands of top executives and move them down the hierarchy to middle management (decentralization); (2) they guarantee that employees meet a minimum standard (standardization), thus lowering the risk of the top executive ending up with unqualified personnel; (3) because control is in the rules and procedures, middle management has less latitude for error; and finally, (4) the minimal standards embodied in the rules and procedures ensure qualifications of the operating employee at the lower level who deals with the organizational input. Thus, relatively consistent and reliable performance of the organization is maintained.

Of course, if the formalized policies and procedures did not function to recruit highly qualified personnel, the decision-making in the organization would probably remain centralized because top executives and administrators would hesitate to allocate decisions to lower level employees. Thus, where nonprofessionals and nonexperts are employed at the lower level of the organization, one would expect to find high regulative formalization to be positively related to high centralization of overall decision-making.

The question arises as to whether the negative relationship between centralization and formalization is unique to public service organizations or if this same relationship exists in private enterprises as well. The empirical evidence from both the Aston Group and the National Sample confirm this negative relationship between centralization and formalization, the latter to a greater extent because of differences in the nature of the samples. Although the measures of formalization utilized by the Aston Group and Child were the same, they differed extensively from those utilized by Blau. While Blau dealt with the formalization of personnel decisions, the two British researchers dealt with the formalization of a broader range of operative standards and procedures. As depicted in Table 7–4, overall centralization was negatively related to both overall standardization (Aston Sample, $r = -.27$; National Sample, $r = -.46$) and overall formalization (Aston Sample, $r = -.20$; National Sample, $r = -.53$).[31]

216

Complexity Correlates

The relationship between complexity and formalization has been explored by Hage and Aiken, Pugh and associates, and Child. As has been noted, Pugh and Child utilized the same operationalizations of variables, and their research differs drastically from that of Hage and Aiken as to: (1) the level of the indicators—global–institutional as opposed to attitudinal; (2) the scope—overall measure of formalization and standardization as opposed to formalization of operative rules and processes; (3) sample of organizations—private firms as opposed to public service. Their measures of complexity are even more dissimilar. Hage and Aiken defined complexity as the number of occupational specialties and the level of professional training required for each specialty and professional activity.[32] This is ultimately a measure of differentiation of positions or specialization and the education necessary for this specialization. Pugh and associates and Child defined *functional specialization* as the extent to which official duties are divided within functional areas between identifiable positions.[33] Their concept of role specialization was similar to Hage and Aiken's concept of occupational specialty.

In his *Axiomatic Theory of Organizations,* Hage hypothesized a negative relationship between formalization and complexity. Corollary 7 reads, "The higher the complexity, the lower the formalization."[34] Although not as the major purpose of their analysis, Hage and Aiken later tested the relationship between complexity and formalization. The relationships between job codification and each of the three measures of complexity were weak and mixed: −.12 with number of occupations, +.17 with professional training, and −.03 with professional activities; while rule observation was negatively related to each index of complexity: −.06 with number of occupations, −.43 with professional training, and −.19 with professional activities. Although the relationship between rule observation and professional training was moderate, the relationships were generally weak, which lent little support of the general hypothesis of a negative relationship between formalization and complexity.

Keeping in mind that the British researchers utilized a more general, less work-related measure of formalization, they found a strong positive relationship between their measures of role specialization and overall documentation and standardization. It is important to reiterate that Child found complexity to be a better predictor of formalization than any of the environmental or contextual variables analyzed.[35] The relationship between formalization and vertical

TABLE 7—4 Product–Moment Correlations Between Selected Structural Variables, Aston (A) and National (N) Samples

		1	2	3	4	5	6	7	8	9	10	11	12	13	14	15	16
1. Functional specialization	A	—															
	N	—															
2. Legal specialization	A	32	—														
	N	27	—														
3. Overall role specialization	A	87	34	—													
	N	87	23	—													
4. Overall standardization	A	76	27	80	—												
	N	78	18	83	—												
5. Standardization—selection, etc.	A	−15	47	09	23	—											
	N	34	09	31	44	—											
6. Overall formalization	A	57	26	68	83	38	—										
	N	69	20	73	87	47	—										
7. Recording of role performance	A	66	11	54	72	−12	75	—									
	N	70	02	68	79	26	77	—									
8. Overall centralization	A	−64	−04	−53	−27	30	−20	−27	—								
	N	−28	−33	−43	−46	−38	−53	−22	—								
9. Autonomy of organization	A	50	−15	40	06	−52	−02	10	−79	—							
	N	05	19	11	14	02	18	10	−42	—							
10. Chief executive's span	A	22	15	34	28	04	32	32	10	02	—						
	N	10	−11	14	12	15	16	−01	−06	03	—						
11. Subordinate ratio	A	25	−14	05	13	−46	04	39	−14	−14	−16	—					
	N	07	−20	05	−10	−27	−19	03	41	−12	−10	—					

		1	2	3	4	5	6	7	8	9	10	11	12	13	14	15	16
12. Vertical span (height)	A	57	48	66	57	23	48	33	-28	-06	24	-05	—				
	N	51	41	55	51	24	48	39	-41	10	-06	-28	—				
13. Work-flow superordinates (%)	A	-53	21	-38	-37	39	-24	-52	52	47	12	-50	-01	—			
	N	-31	08	-23	-05	08	05	-01	-16	-14	-08	-45	05	—			
14. Nonwork-flow personnel (%)	A	58	11	56	51	-02	46	43	-40	-32	10	01	21	-43	—		
	N	07	03	-04	03	09	14	-00	-04	15	14	-20	-13	-27	—		
15. Clerks (%)	A	17	12	29	31	31	29	08	-04	-05	12	-24	-01	-05	46	—	
	N	-29	06	-26	-23	09	-07	-22	05	-03	23	-28	-10	08	44	—	
16. Traditionalism	A	-36	-13	-26	-24	06	-47	-54	39	30	-22	-17	-14	19	-26	-08	—
	N	-22	04	-14	-12	-16	-31	-29	14	04	-03	17	-21	-01	-10	05	—

Aston N = 46. National N = 82. Decimal points omitted. With N = 46 all correlations 0.29 and above are at or beyond the 95% level of confidence; with N = 82 this level of confidence falls between correlations of 0.21 and 0.22.

Source: John Child, "Organization Structure and Strategies of Control: A Republication of the Aston Study," Administrative Science Quarterly 17, no. 2 (June 1972): 169.

complexity was also discussed in chapter six, but it should be emphasized that Blau, Meyer, and Child found vertical differentiation (hierarchical levels), with accompanying increase in decentralization, to be positively associated with increased formalization.

Communication Correlates

A few brief distinctions regarding communication are necessary at this point. (These are more fully elaborated in chapter eight.) The directions of communication are the same as those of power and differentiation; that is, communication can be either horizontal or vertical. Two forms of horizontal communication are communication between individuals of the same rank in the organizational structure and between functional units within the organization. Vertical communication links hierarchically ranked individuals in a unit and hierarchically arranged units in the organizational structure.

Another useful distinction is that between formal and informal communication. The formal communication structure is not the same as the organizational chart, which represents hierarchical ranks and departmentalized organizational units. But the formal communication networks are more likely to follow these structural lines than are informal networks, which are apt to be more spontaneous, less developed, and less structured than the formal structure. Informal communication is more likely to occur in a horizontal than a vertical direction. The formal communication network derives its stability and predictability from the formal structure of the organization, that is, from its horizontally and vertically differentiated structures. The informal communication network derives its stability and predictability from the pattern of interpersonal communication flow. The content of the messages communicated through the informal structure are less likely to be work-related information, whereas the content of the messages in the formal structure are more likely to be work-related.

When the rules and procedures at the operative level are standardized and formalized by mandate, less informal and horizontal communication exists between employees and subunits. Here the majority of the communication is vertical and the content is work-related. On the other hand, when the regulative rules and procedures are standardized and formalized, there is less need to communicate vertically. However, many times these regulative rules and procedures serve to encourage horizontal communication within units and between units.

The organization with standardized and formalization regulative rules and procedures is more likely to be decentralized, to be highly vertically complex, and to employ professionals and experts who work with nonroutine raw materials. The lack of a need to communicate with upper levels of the organization, due to standardized rules and procedures, allows the professional to make more decisions without direct contact with his or her immediate supervisor. At the same time, the reduced vertical communication may serve as a communication block for those at lower organizational levels.

SUMMARY

As an organization increases in size and becomes more vertically complex, it becomes decentralized. If at the same time its raw materials are nonuniform and its procedures nonroutine, it may be impossible to formalize and standardize its work-related rules and procedures. Thus, controls are more likely to be in the form of learned norms and values and professional attitudes and an increased rate of communication. Regulative rules and procedures are likely to be formalized to give greater predictability to the organization's function and greater autonomy to the professional. See Table 7–5 for a summary of these relationships.

On the other hand, when the organization increases in size and becomes more horizontally complex, it may become centralized. If at the same time, the raw materials are uniform and the production process routine, it will be possible to formalize operative procedures, making the output of the organization more uniform and predictable.

TABLE 7–5 Formalization and Standardization Correlates of Contextual and Structural Dimensions

I. CONTEXTUAL DIMENSIONS

   A. Size

      1. Size is positively related to the overall formalization and standardization of an organization.

   B. Technology

      1. When experts and professionals are employed at the lower levels of the organization, nonroutinized technology is negatively related to the formalization and standardization of operative rules and procedures.

      2. When experts and professionals are employed at the lower levels of the organization, nonroutinized technology is positively related

221

TABLE 7–5   Formalization and Standardization Correlates of Contextual and Structural Dimensions (continued)

to the formalization and standardization of regulative rules and procedures.

II. STRUCTURAL DIMENSIONS

  A. Centralization

    1. When experts and professionals are employed at the lower levels of the organization, decentralization of decision-making is negatively related to the formalization and standardization of operative rules and procedures.

    2. When experts and professionals are employed at the lower levels of the organization, decentralization of decision making is positively related to the formalization and standardization of regulative rules and procedures.

  B. Complexity

    1. The horizontal differentiation of occupations and roles is positively related to the overall formalization and standardization of an organization.

    2. The horizontal differentiation of departments and functional units is positively related to the overall formalization and standardization of an organization.

    3. The horizontal differentiation of knowledge (employment of experts and professionals) is positively related to the formalization and standardization of regulative rules and procedures.

    4. The horizontal differentiation of knowledge (employment of experts and professionals) is negatively related to the formalization and standardization of operative rules and procedures.

    5. When experts and professionals are employed at the lower levels of an organization, vertical differentiation in the form of number of hierarchical levels is positively related to the formalization and standardization of regulative rules and procedures.

    6. When experts and professionals are employed at the lower levels of an organization, vertical differentiation in the form of hierarchical levels is negatively related to the formalization and standardization of operative rules and procedures.

    7. When experts and professionals are employed at the lower levels of an organization, vertical differentiation in the form of the size of the administrative component is positively related to the formalization and standardization of regulative rules and procedures.

    8. When experts and professionals are employed at the lower levels of an organization, vertical differentiation in the form of the size of

TABLE 7-5 Formalization and Standardization Correlates of Contextual and Structural Dimensions (continued)

the administrative component is negatively related to the formalization and standardization of operative rules and procedures.

C. Communication

1. The formalization and standardization of operative rules and procedures is negatively related to the rate of task communication in an organization.
2. Formalization and standardization of operative rules and procedures is positively related to vertical communication.
3. Formalization and standardization of regulative rules and procedures is negatively related to the rate of overall organizational communication.
4. When regulative rules and procedures are formalized and standardized, communication is likely to be horizontal in direction.

NOTES

1. Max Weber, *The Theory of Social and Economic Organization* (New York: Oxford University Press, 1947).

2. D. S. Pugh, D. J. Hickson, C. R. Hinings, K. M. Macdonald, C. Turner, and T. Lupton, "A Scheme for Organizational Analysis," *Administrative Science Quarterly* 8, no. 3 (December 1963): 303–304.

3. Richard H. Hall, Eugene J. Haas, and Norman J. Johnson, "Organizational Size, Complexity, and Formalization," *American Sociological Review* 32, no. 6 (December 1967): 907.

4. Jerald Hage, "An Axiomatic Theory of Organizations," *Administrative Science Quarterly* 10, no. 3 (December 1965): 295.

5. Jerald Hage and Michael Aiken, "Relationship of Centralization to Other Structural Properties," *Administrative Science Quarterly* 12, no. 1 (June 1967): 79.

6. Ibid.

7. D. S. Pugh, D. J. Hickson, C. R. Hinings, and C. Turner, "Dimensions of Organization Structure," *Administrative Science Quarterly* 13, no. 1 (June 1968): 75.

8. Ibid., p. 74.

9. Johannes Pennings, "Measures of Organizational Structure: A Methodological Note," *American Journal of Sociology* 79, no. 3 (November 1973): 686–704.

10. Pugh, Hickson, Hinings, and Turner, "Dimensions of Organization Structure," pp. 100–101.

11. Ibid., p. 92.

12. Hage and Aiken, "Relationship of Centralization to Other Structural Properties," p. 79.

13. Michael Aiken and Jerald Hage, "Organizational Interdependence and Intra-organizational Structure," *American Sociological Review* 33, no. 6 (December 1968): 926.

14. Charles Perrow, "Technology and Structure" (Working paper, mimeographed, University of Wisconsin).

15. Hage and Aiken, "Relationship of Centralization to Other Structural Properties," p. 79.

16. Pennings, "Measures of Organizational Structure: A Methodological Note," p. 688.

17. Pugh, Hickson, Hinings, and Turner, "Dimensions of Organization Structure."

18. Aiken and Hage, "Organizational Interdependence and Intra-organizational Structure," pp. 912–930.

19. Ibid., p. 921.

20. Ibid.

21. Ibid., p. 372.

22. Hall, Haas, and Johnson, "Organizational Size, Complexity, and Formalization," pp. 903–912.

23. John Child, "Predicting and Understanding Organization Structure," *Administrative Science Quarterly* 18, no. 2 (June 1973): 168.

24. Hage and Aiken, "Relationship of Centralization to Other Structural Properties," pp. 77–78.

25. Ibid., p. 78.

26. Ibid., p. 79.

27. Ibid., p. 86.

28. Peter M. Blau, "Decentralization in Bureaucracies," in Mayer N. Zald, ed., *Power in Organizations* (Nashville, Tenn.: Vanderbilt University Press, 1970), p. 160.

29. Peter M. Blau and Richard A. Schoenherr, *The Structure of Organizations* (New York: Basic Books, Inc., 1971), pp. 112–113.

30. Ibid., p. 116.

31. John Child, "Organization Structure and Strategies of Control: A Replication of the Aston Study," *Administrative Science Quarterly* 17, no. 2 (June 1972): 169.

32. Hage and Aiken, "Relationship of Centralization to Other Structural Properties," p. 72.

33. Child, "Organization Structure and Strategies of Control: A Replication of the Aston Study," p. 164.

34. Hage, "An Axiomatic Theory of Organizations," pp. 229, 300.

35. Child, "Predicting and Understanding Organizational Structure," p. 168.

8
COMMUNICATION

OBJECTIVES

The objectives of this chapter are:

1. To theoretically and operationally define communication.
2. To differentiate between communication that originates outside and inside the organization.
3. To differentiate between formal and informal communication.
4. To differentiate between horizontal and vertical communication networks.
   a. horizontal networks between persons on the same level in a given department and between different departments
   b. vertical networks between persons at different ranks in the same hierarchical level and between different hierarchical levels:
      i. upward communication
      ii. downward communication
5. To explain how communication serves as a form of coordination.
6. To relate organizational communication to the other structural dimensions of organizations:
   a. complexity
   b. centralization
   c. formalization

INTRODUCTION

With the continued emphasis on viewing the organization as an open system has come a recent proliferation of writing and research that places communication at the center of organizational focus and views the communication dimension as an all-encompassing explanation of organizational functioning. The centrality of communication has been exhibited in the writings of many theorists. For example, Chester Barnard, one of the early organizational theorists, stated that "In an exhaustive theory of organization, communication would occupy a central place, because the structure, extensiveness, and scope of organization are almost entirely determined by communication technique,"[1] Daniel Katz and Robert Kahn affirmed this approach by noting that "communication is . . . a social process of broadest relevance in the functioning of any group, organization, or society" and is "the very essence of a social system or an organization."[2] One of the foremost general systems theorists who viewed communication as an all-encompassing process was Walter Buckley.[3] Similarly, Keith Davis and William Scott demonstrated the centrality and pervasiveness of communication when they stated that "without communication, there can be no organization. . . . Communication is the bridge over which all technical knowledge and human relationships must travel."[4] Certainly communication networks and the communication processes are as central to organizational functioning as power and the decision-making process. Because communication is pervasive, the open-system perspective views an organization as an extensive mass of interconnected communication channels that carry information to and from the organization's environment and throughout its internal structure. The vital messages communicated involve organizational decisions and policy, feedback to all levels concerning performance, and information about established goals, objectives, and procedures. Communicated messages connect the various units and subunits of the organization. Thus, communication serves as the lifeline to each organizational unit.

An emphasis on communication often implies that if everyone in the organization communicates, coordination will be enhanced; that communication alone is the answer. This rather naive position disregards the fact that the individuals in an organization have vested interests that affect how they relate to others. The communication networks of an organization often carry highly emotional and value laden messages that lead to conflict. Furthermore, too much communication may create excess work for certain individuals. The point is, communication does not solve all organizational problems. Many organizational problems are oversimplified by attributing them to causes such as "failures to communicate" or "communication breakdowns."

Content, nature, direction, origin, method, and rate are important aspects of organizational communication. Because organizational communication does occur in a more or less structured context, these aspects plus the relationships of communication to the other structural dimensions of organizations will be discussed in this chapter.

COMMUNICATION DEFINED

Communication, like power, is relational—it exists only as a result of the interaction of two or more actors (individuals, organizations, etc.). Communication is the process by which one or more ideas are transferred from a sender to a receiver with the intention of changing the receiver's behavior. But the communication process is not static or one way; rather, it is a dynamic, on-going, ever-changing, transactional process. The use of the prefix *trans* (in transactional) emphasizes that communication is a reciprocal process in which both parties—senders and receivers—mutually affect each other as they send and receive messages. Each actor is engaged in sending and receiving messages *simultaneously;* thus, each actor is affected by the others.

Everett Rogers and Rekha Agarwala–Rogers identified seven major elements of the communication process:[5]

1. Source or sender: The originator of the message (individual, group, organization, etc.).
2. Message: The stimulus (idea) that the source transmits to the receiver. The message may consist of verbal and/or non-verbal symbols.
3. Meanings: The sender's and receiver's interpretations of the message. Based on prior socialization or meanings. Messages have no innate meanings, only those imparted by the sender and receiver.
4. Channel: The network by which a message travels from source to receiver. This is the path through which the message is transmitted.

5. Receiver: The actor to which the communication is transmitted. Without the receiver there would be no communication.
6. Effects: The changes in the receiver's behavior that occur as a result of the transmission of a message. Rogers and Agarwala–Rogers noted that effective communication results in changes in the receiver's behavior that were intended by the source. They enumerate three main types of communication effects:
   a. changes in receiver's *knowledge*.
   b. changes in receiver's *attitudes*.
   c. changes in receiver's *overt behavior*.
7. Feedback: A response by the receiver to the source's message.

Communication feedback is perhaps the most important aspect of the communication process; it makes the process transactional. Feedback can be horizontal or vertical, and vertical feedback may be transmitted upward or downward. Feedback not only has direction but also a qualitative aspect of being viewed either positively or negatively by the receiver. Rogers and Agarwala–Rogers wrote, "Feedback may be thought of as messages to the source conveying knowledge of the effectiveness of a previous communication. *Positive feedback* informs the source that the intended effect of a message was achieved; *negative feedback* informs the source that the intended effect of a message was not achieved."[6] At the organizational level, the consequences of negative feedback may be a disruption of sender–receiver relationships. At the emotional level, the consequences may be hostility between sender and receiver. Although negative feedback is more likely to be viewed negatively by the receiver and thus receive negative sanctions in the form of withdrawal of rewards or punishment, negative feedback is generally more important in the long run to the survival of the organization than is positive feedback.

EXTERNAL AND INTERNAL ORIGINS
OF COMMUNICATIONS

Communication, of course, is vital to the organization's information exchange with its environment. Harold Guetzkow wrote, "The communication system serves as the vehicle by which organizations are embedded in their environments."[7] As was noted in chapter five, those subunits and individuals that link the organization with other organizations are more powerful because of their control over information and knowledge of the organizational environment. For example, in business firms, the marketing department communicates with customers and clients and therefore defines and evaluates this environment for the organization. It is here assumed that organizational communication with the external environment is of utmost importance. Any system that does not communicate with the external environment, thus acquiring information and energy inputs and exporting energy and information outputs, will not survive. But the internal communication networks of the organization is the major thrust of this chapter. The following discussions of formal and informal communication networks, vertical (upward and downward) and horizontal communication apply to internal communication.

METHODS OF INFORMATION DIFFUSION

The term *diffusion* implies that messages are disseminated throughout the organization, both horizontally and vertically. But by what means do these messages travel? Most methods of disseminating information in an organization can be divided into two general categories: *software* and *hardware.* The former depends on the individual's abilities and skills in writing, speaking, and listening. This method is characterized by face-to-face interaction (verbal and non-verbal) and written activities. The types of face-to-face communication include conversation, meetings, interviews, and discussion; written communication includes memos, letters, bulletins, reports, proposals, policies, manuals, and so on. The hardware method of dissemination depends on electrical power to make it function: telephones, teletypes, microfilms, radios, C.B.s, videotapes, computers, and so on. The use of both software and hardware methods are essential in large, complex organizations.

CONTENT OF COMMUNICATION

Based on its content, communication can be divided into two categories: work-related and non-work-related. Work-related communication is sometimes labeled *formal communication,* while non-work-related communication is labeled *informal communication.* Of course, work-related information has a wide variety of contents: information concerning tasks, decision-making, personnel, and so on.

229

Two types of work-related messages are task and maintenance messages. Task messages deal with products and services (improving sales, markets, quality of service, quality of products, etc.). Maintenance messages deal with policy, personnel, and regulations that help to perpetuate the organization. Non-work-related messages deal with personal information, nonwork-related news, and so on.

Because people are human, personal relationships exist in all organizations. Some interpersonal communication takes place in nearly all transactions. Barnard recognized this when he wrote:

> . . . informal organization is so much a part of our matter-of-course intimate experience of everyday association, either in connection with formal organization or not, that we are unaware of it. . . . Yet it is evident that association of persons in connection with a formal or specific activity inevitably involves interactions that are incidental to it.[8]

Furthermore, Andre Delbecq has noted that informal communication occurs between persons who are in close proximity, have similar work activities, interests, and values, and complementary personalities and social characteristics.[9]

FORMAL AND INFORMAL COMMUNICATION NETWORKS

Communication within an organization varies as to the degree of structure. Some communication occurs infrequently and randomly and therefore is not part of the predictable structure. Other communication is routine and regular and therefore can be predicted. These messages are part of the communication "networks," "systems," or "structure" of the organization. These networks may be either formal or informal. It is important to keep in mind that the informal communication network may be as structured and systematic as work-related networks.

Formal Networks

Work organizations usually have planned networks of communication and feedback designed to transmit work-related information to and from all positions and subunits within the organization. These planned, structured networks, which deal largely with

230

work-related content, are the formal networks of the organization. In short, the formal communication networks are patterns defining which actor(s) in which position(s) are supposed to send and receive what kinds of information or messages. For example, a person in a secretarial position must communicate with the boss, other secretaries, and support staff in and outside a given department.

It is possible for a communication network to exist that includes only two people, or that includes nearly the entire organization, but the scope of most networks falls somewhere between these two extremes. Some networks correspond somewhat to the formal organizational chart, while others resemble the chart very little. Often formal communication networks are elaborated and described as though they are intended to replicate the formal line chart of the organization. For example, during the widely televised Watergate investigations, the organizational charts of the federal government were used to trace who had authority to make certain decisions related to illegal buggings. At other times, these same organizational charts were used to determine who communicated to whom concerning these activities. The assumption was that the organizational chart, in addition to depicting the authority structure, also replicated the communication networks of the organization. This assumption was false, and consequently, such questions and their answers rarely shed any light on the subject. One bit of information was apparent—the line chart did not correspond to the communication network. There is no contention here that formal communication is expected to exactly follow a chart of the hierarchical and horizontal arrangement of positions in an organization. As empirically evidenced in the research of Jerald Hage, Michael Aiken and Cora Bagley Marrett, the communication flow is quite different from the line chart of the organization. They constructed an "operative" organizational chart based on the actual communication network. Using this chart, they were able to classify both scheduled and unscheduled communication.[10]

Consequences of the Formal Communication Network   The most apparent intended function of the formal network is that it communicate information that facilitates the coordination of the organization at all levels. As the organization becomes larger, more technologically and structurally complex, the need for coordination increases, and therefore, the formal communication network becomes more extensive and often more evident. Greater amounts of information must be communicated to all subunits at all levels of the organization to ensure the smooth functioning of the organization.

As will be remembered from our discussion of knowledge based power in chapter five, information concerning the raw materials and the functioning of the external environment, internal functioning of the organization, future policies and present status serve as sources of power for the information holder. The more this information is controlled by a few administrators or executives at the top of the organization, the more centralized the organization. In this type of structure, information is the exclusion property of a select few individuals at the top of the structure. There is little horizontal communication and little downward vertical communication in any form other than directives, which serve as a form of organizational control. Since one of the necessary antecedants to organized conflict is the ability to communicate, limited horizontal communication among equals at lower organizational levels may temporarily limit or prevent insurrection and conflict between the administration and lower-level employees.

Because information must be transmitted to all organizational levels and units and because knowledge and information are sources of power, those in power positions in an organization are more likely to have access to and control over the formal networks. Thus, although the communication network does not exactly duplicate the authority structure on each message that is communicated, it often reinforces the authority structure of the organization. Those who make decisions must have relevant information; thus, they are more likely to be included in the formal communication network. In turn, those who have knowledge or information have more power and are more likely to gain access to future sources of information and channels of communication.

Finally, formal communication networks provide an avenue for feedback as to how the organization is functioning. The performance of each individual, unit, and the organization as a whole can be evaluated through feedback from these various organizational levels. Thus, the quality and quantity of production, as well as the ability of the organization to change, may be assessed. Feedback about performance of tasks on a daily basis is also extremely important. If departments are highly interrelated, as in the production process, daily feedback is important to the completion of a sequentially ordered process—for Department B to perform a task, Department A must have completed its task satisfactorily, and feedback from Department B to Department A on its performance is necessary. Communication or feedback at all levels increases the efficiency and effectiveness of the organization, thus aiding the organization in accomplishing its goals.

Informal Networks

In addition to the formal structure of patterned communication flows, every system has informal networks. These informal networks are often as important to organizational functioning as the formal networks. One of the findings of the Hawthorne studies was the importance of informal communication networks in determining worker productivity. An employee may communicate with other employees about non-job-related events or activities and about certain unofficial information overheard recently. In these cases the employee would be communicating unofficially via a network of informal relationships. The formal and informal communication channels in an organization are in some ways complementary, that is, they sometimes overlap, but at other times they are quite distinct.

The informal network has several distinguishing characteristics. First, it is fast. In most instances, the informal network operates verbally, which contributes to the rapid dissemination of information. The informal system is also rapid because it does not have to be approved by the authority structure or passed down through appropriate organizational levels. Thus, while the formal message traveling through the formal channels is often blocked at one point or another, the message traveling through informal channels can bypass various stages and is disseminated throughout the organization much more rapidly. This rapid communication may serve to prepare employees for the formal, "official" word. Having been informed, these employees may be better able to accept the new policies or procedures (or better prepared to resist them).

Second, the informal network accurately transmits noncontroversial messages. By counting the details of messages and determining which were true and false, Keith Davis was able to report an accuracy ranging from 80–90 percent in the transmittal of noncontroversial company information.[11] Similarly, Eugene Walton reported 80 percent accuracy for informal communication in a major public utility company.[12] Commonsense knowledge would have us believe that the informal network is often inaccurate. This is probably due to the fact that inaccuracies of communication, because of important negative consequencies, are more often remembered than accurate transmissions.

Third, the informal network carries a great deal of information that often cannot be transmitted through normal channels. For example, an administrator may use the informal network to transmit information he or she feels would not be accepted if transmitted through formal channels and to gain information about employee sentiments.

Consequences of the Informal Communication Network   Informal communication networks serve several functions. Because they are separate from the formal networks, they supply employees with additional messages about events in the organization. They may clarify, elaborate, and add new meaning to otherwise confusing or uninformative messages from the superordinates. They may provide the necessary rationale for imminent changes in the policies and procedures of an organization. They also define how these policies and procedures affect the employee. This network also provides employees an acceptable channel through which to express emotions and anger, which of course helps to promote group and unit cohesiveness and fortify the employee's self-concept and morale.

A negative consequence of the informal network is that it also transmits rumors effectively, efficiently, and in great quantities. A rumor is informal information that is communicated without a standard for or knowledge of its validity. Another negative consequence of the informal network is that, assuming the message is correct at the source, it may become distorted as it moves through the informal channels, resulting in false information being disseminated just as rapidly as correct information. This is especially true if the distortions include emotional overtones or content that is viewed negatively by employees. Fears and anxieties are aroused and the employees may lose trust in their superordinates.

In another situation, the information initiated at the top of the network for downward flow may be disseminated through both formal and informal channels. The formal system may revise the message at lower levels due to contingencies or new information. When the message transmitted by the formal network reaches lower-level employees, it may be quite different from that which was simultaneously transmitted through the informal network. Consequently, if the message communicated through the informal network is in the original form, by the time it reaches lower levels, it will no longer correspond to the formal message and will thus be inaccurate. Regardless of how the information becomes distorted, whether by miscommunication of the informal structure or changes implemented by the formal structure, the consequences are the same—misunderstandings, hard feelings, and conflicts between subordinates and superordinates throughout the system. Much of this emotional expenditure might be avoided if communication is transmitted through the formal network alone.

Finally, the informal network may serve as a power base for those employees who have little or no authority. Control over such a network gives an individual respect from peers as well as superordinates and subordinates. Those employees who know what is taking place before or at the same time as their immediate supervisors have an opportunity to manipulate the supervisors' interpretation of messages. These power bases have both negative and positive consequences for the organization.

DIRECTIONS OF COMMUNICATION NETWORKS

The directions of the communication networks have traditionally been trichotomized into downward, upward, and horizontal, depending on the position of the initiator of the message and of the receiver (or intended receiver).

Horizontal Communication

Horizontal communication is the lateral exchange of messages among persons at the same organizational level. Horizontal communication in organizations is of two types: between two actors at the same level in an organizational subunit and between two actors at the same level in two different organizational subunits (interdepartmental or interdivisional communication). Horizontal communication networks also link organizations to other organizations, but we are mainly concerned with the internal type here.

It is interesting to note that those who seek information from other organizations, as opposed to clients or customers, are more likely to communicate with those employees in the alter organization at the same level as their own. Thus, when communicating between organizations, individuals are more likely to seek communication with peers than superordinates or subordinates. Horizontal communication is also more frequent than vertical communication within the organization. Of course, much of this horizontal communication is informal. Formal horizontal exchanges between organizational equals are less subject to distortion because peers share a common frame of reference. Furthermore, the content of messages carried by horizontal networks are mainly to inform, coordinate, solve problems, and resolve conflicts, whereas downward flows are mainly authoritative and upward flows chiefly provide feedback on operational performance. Thus vertical networks carry messages that are potentially more threatening. Research has shown that, given a choice, employees are more likely to communicate with those at the same level within the hierarchical structure. Because one is likely to communicate with peers either about work- or non-work-related matters, it may be more advantageous to the organization to leave some coordination to the employees, thus reducing the exchange of non-work information, which is generally irrelevant and, in some cases, detrimental to organizational goals.

In a highly bureaucratic model, the employees of an organization would be involved in very little horizontal communication. Here, almost all communication is vertical and downward in flow, and its content is more likely to consist of job descriptions and procedural instructions. Informal (non-work-related) communication is restricted in order to maximize efficiency. In bureaucratic organizations, any horizontal communication is directed toward task coordination as opposed to decision-making. On the other hand, in non-bureaucratic organizations where professionals occupy positions at lower levels of the organizational structure, the frequency of horizontal communication is likely to be higher. Consultation regarding procedures and methods are likely to become routinized. Although coordination of tasks, procedures, and practices are necessary in all organizations, this coordination is carried on by superordinates in bureaucratic organizations, requiring surveillance of operations, while in the nonbureaucratic organizations, it is carried on by the expert or professional, necessitating horizontal communication between professionals.

Although lateral communication between individuals in the same subunit has been described as functional, both socio-psychologically for group members and organizationally for purposes of coordination,[13] little attention has been given to researching lateral communication between subunits, concentrating instead on vertical communication. Because employees in different departments are ultimately linked by some superordinate at the middle management level, most researchers have followed the line chart, assuming that this paralleled the network of formal communication. Formal communication networks are designed to transmit messages up to a mutual superior and then back down, a process that naturally slows down the speed of these horizontal flows. To assume that all information flows up the hierarchical structure to offices that link two departments at the same level (for example, sales and production in business firms, or psychology and sociology in universities), and then flows back down to the lateral department, is to disregard horizontal communication completely. Furthermore, to assume that horizontal communication is dysfunctional—the "establishment" view—is to overlook a significant benefit: Often information communicated horizontally prepares the departments for imminent changes for which they would not be prepared if information followed the previously defined vertical path. When individuals in various subunits of an organization communicate laterally, the savings in time increases efficiency and often prevents conflict and problems that would otherwise revert to someone at a higher level in the organizational structure. Of course, if individuals in subunits become innovative and change procedures or output without communicating with those at higher levels, the consequences may be detrimental to the organization.

One may wonder why more organizational messages are not communicated horizontally. If all organizational members communicated to all parts of the organization, the authority structure would be uninformed and thus rendered ineffective. If a person in Department A can initiate action for someone in Department B who is at the same hierarchical level, the employee in Department B soon becomes unable to define whose authority governs his or her actions. Those employees in Department B may receive conflicting orders from several other departments and be unable to define whose directives to follow. The consequences of bypassing the authority structure could create both information overload and conflict, if not total chaos.

Vertical Communication

At least two types of vertical communication exist within organizations. The first is vertical communication between individuals in the same department who hold positions with differing ranks, for example, between a person who works on the assembly line and his or her supervisor (*intra*departmental communication). The second type is between positions in two hierarchically ranked subunits or departments of the organizations, for example, between the supervisor of the assembly line and the vice-president (*inter*departmental communications).

237

To make vertical communication even more complex, the communication can flow either up the hierarchy from the subordinate position to the superordinate or down the hierarchy from the superordinate position to the subordinate. Directives, statements of policy, and decisions regarding operations and procedures move down the hierarchy, while information and feedback concerning the operations and functioning of the organization flow up the vertical communication network. Generally, the rate of communication flow moving down the structure is greater than that moving up the structure. Intentional blocks often confront communication flowing up the network, whereas persons at higher levels have the right to communicate information downward, which means fewer blocks in this communication flow.

It is also generally assumed that some of the most important information that the organization processes is in the form of feedback, positive and negative, from the lower levels of the organization. Positive feedback being sent up the vertical network is important because it informs the administration of those policies, procedures, and so on, that are working well and should be continued. This type of feedback is generally well received by the upper ranks. On the other hand, negative feedback is even more important to the continued functioning of the organizational structure because it often informs the administration of policies and procedures that are not functioning well and therefore need revision or discontinuance. In short, negative upward feedback informs the system of weaknesses and faults which, if not adjusted or eliminated, may ultimately destroy the system. Because it is not amenable to the top executives and administrators, negative feedback is generally not well received. Thus, the many gatekeepers who have a personal interest in maintaining the existing system and the executives or administrators who helped to institute the existing system may block the communication of negative feedback that moves up the vertical network.

Of course, both positive and negative feedback may also move down the communication network from the superior to the subordinate. Positive feedback often exists in the form of verbal or material reinforcement for a job well done. Negative feedback may range from a mild reprimand to a dismissal. Regardless of whether the feedback is positive or negative, it will generally flow down the network more easily than up.

Downward Communication   Downward communication refers to messages that flow from superiors to subordinates. Much down-

238

ward communication is related to organizational maintenance, and consists of directives to subordinates about goals, performance, orders, and so on. Katz and Kahn pointed out that communication from superordinate to subordinate is of five basic types:

1. Specific task directives: *job instructions.*
2. Information designed to produce understanding of the task and its relation to other organizational tasks: *job rationale.*
3. Information about organizational *procedures and practices.*
4. *Feedback* to the subordinate about his performance.
5. Information of an ideological character to inculcate a sense of mission: *indoctrination of goals.*[14]

All but the fourth type of communication aid the organization in instructing the employees concerning their roles. Job descriptive information is essential to all types of organizations but more so to bureaucratic organizations in which job descriptions have not been internalized during the educational process. Job descriptions in the form of written descriptions, training sessions, and orders from a superordinate are more essential to the bureaucratic than the professional organization. In the bureaucratic, centralized organization, management is less likely to emphasize providing the employee with job rationale or an explanation of how his or her job is related to the other jobs in the system. It is therefore much more common to find employees who know *what* to do but not *why.* Furthermore, they do not know how their activities help the organization accomplish its objectives. Information about organizational rules and procedures, what we have called regulative rules and procedures, is not communicated to the employee by the administration but is left to the employee to discover, or to the union to communicate. In addition to procedures related to their jobs, employees are typically informed of obligations and privileges of the system (reward structures, evaluations, sanctions, etc.). The fifth type of downward communication listed above attempts to indoctrinate the member of the organization with an ideology that supports the goals of that organization. This type of information is more effective in professional organizations where the profession supports the ideology of the organization.

The fourth type of downward communication listed above provides information to the subordinate concerning his or her performance. Often this evaluation process is resented by employees, both in organizations that employ professionals and nonprofessionals. They often resent the type of surveillance necessary for adequate evaluation of performance by the superordinate. Feedback to the employees concerning performance serves as input for future performance, whereas the other four types of information communicated downward serve as input for the performance of immediate tasks.

Downward communication is the most frequently studied aspect of the formal communication network. Usually those who study this network wish to know to what extent these messages obtain the kinds of responses desired by the sender.

Upward Communication   Upward communication refers to messages that flow from subordinates to superordinates, usually for the purpose of asking questions, providing feedback, or making suggestions. Thus, the content of upward communication is not the same as that which is communicated downward. Although a subordinate may originate information concerning his or her performance or the performance of others, it is more likely that the subordinate will originate information about practices, policies, performance (his or hers) that he or she wants to change. Because of the power relationship between the employee and the superordinate, the message is not always as clear and objective as it could otherwise be. Also, because of the authority relationships, the employee's immediate superior may not be the most appropriate person with whom to communicate. However, when the immediate superior is bypassed, the subordinate places his or her job in jeopardy. Yet, if the subordinate communicates with the immediate superior, a strong likelihood exists that the message will never be transmitted past that point or, if it is transmitted upward, will be so distorted that it will lose its original meaning. Thus, the communication may have little or no consequence for the organization.

We have argued that vertical communication is less likely to occur in an organization than is horizontal communication, and that in the case of the former, upward communication is less frequent than downward. We also note that in the case of upward communication, the content is more likely to be positive than negative. Employees tend to send upward messages that enhance their credibility and status, while blocking or screening out messages that might make them look bad. Those who have high status aspirations themselves and wish to be promoted are more likely than their less ambitious peers to filter messages transmitted to the superordinates. Middle management is especially likely to send messages to superiors that are aimed to please rather than to accurately reflect negative feedback. A good evaluation stemming from positive feedback discourages negative feedback, and accuracy becomes a secondary issue.

The more centralized the power, the more punitive the organizational sanctions, and the less the upward communication of the organization. Regardless of the power structure of the organization, the upwardly communicated message reaches a smaller number of persons than does the downwardly communicated message. More often than not, the upwardly communicated message ends with the superordinate's immediate supervisor.

There are other obstacles to the upward flow of vertical communication. In a hierarchical relationship, superiors chosen on the basis of ability are likely to be more competent and knowledgable than their subordinates. If this ability takes the form of intellectual superiority, a communication gap may develop where not only will the subordinate find it difficult to communicate upward, the superordinate will find it difficult to communicate downward. The same type of situation occurs when the subordinates are experts and the superior is a generalist, or administrator. Examples can be found within organizations employing professionals. The superordinate's lack of expertise may limit his or her credibility with subordinates and thus weaken the ability to communicate downward; at the same time, the subordinates may feel it a waste of time or frustrating to communicate upward.

Centralization and stratification within an organization both inhibit the volume of communication in that organization, in particular vertical communication. With regard to upward vertical communication, often the subordinate fears sanctions—withdrawal of resources or dismissal. When there is greater distance between the administration and the employees at lower levels, there may be differences in social, economic, and intellectual backgrounds and lifestyles that tend to inhibit communication. When the organization is centralized, employees at middle management and lower levels of the organization are not making decisions; therefore, they do not participate in the communication concerning these decisions. The centralization of power eliminates the need for some communication and inhibits other communication. Thus, the greater the centralization of an organization, the less the rate of total communication. Also limited is horizontal communication among peers about their work process and upward communication from subordinates to superordinates. Thus, the proportion of downward vertical communication is positively related to increased centralization of power.

COMMUNICATION AS ORGANIZATIONAL COORDINATION

Hage and associates defined coordination as "the degree to which there are adequate linkages among organizational parts, i.e., specific task roles as well as subunits of the organization so that organizational objectives can be accomplished."[15] They identified two types of coordination: coordination by plan and coordination by feedback. Coordination by plan is "based on preestablished schedules" such as formalization, standardization, planning, and programming. Coordination by feedback, on the other hand, "involves the transmission of new information," such as feedback for mutual adjustment. These authors distinguished coordination from control in that control refers to "the adequacy of achieving conformity with expectations for behavior and standards of work," while coordination refers to "the method by which task roles are articulated together to accomplish a given set of tasks."[16]

Hage and associates posited that coordination through planning or programming is more likely to call for use of sanctions to achieve control, while coordination through feedback is more likely to rely on socialization. Based on the premise that all organizations need coordination, they posited that this coordination can be achieved in two basic ways: (1) by programming the activities of each job and imposing a system of rewards and punishments as control (formalization and standardization would support this system of coordination), (2) by relying on continuous feedback and adjustment (errors would be adjusted by resocialization or training). Thus, socialization with high feedback and sanctioning with programming are alternative methods of organizational control and coordination.

Hage pointed out that the regulation of organizations that employ professionals is difficult because professionals generally do not respond to overt types of control or to sanctions. The major theme of his book, *Communication and Organizational Control,* is that high feedback in conjunction with socialization is more likely to occur in organizations with a given set of structural dimensions. Hage makes no assumption as to which set of dimensions is more effective and efficient.[17] It is the opinion of this author that high feedback and socialization are more effective methods of control in organizations that employ professionals, while programming and sanctioning are more effective methods of control in the more bureaucratic type of organization where technology is routine, complexity is low, and employees are nonprofessionals.

242

These two methods of coordination and control encompass some of the structural dimensions discussed in this text. Relationships between these dimensions will become more apparent as the correlates of communication are elaborated. For example, diversity of task and structure make it more difficult to program an organization. Here, there is a need for feedback from the various parts of the organization in order to maintain control of this structurally diverse organization. Uniform sanctioning at the operative level is difficult because, when tasks and structure are complex, a very limited number of individuals are competent to evaluate the professionals' performances, which encompass a diversity of knowledge and skills. When performance cannot be uniformly evaluated, there is no basis for sanctioning. In these organizations, continuous face-to-face feedback supplies information concerning performance. Correcting the performance of the employee becomes a matter of prompt resocialization. Thus, in instances of high task and structural complexity, the organization will use feedback and socialization to maintain performance and control.

This brings us to a further elaboration of the distinctions made in chapters five through seven between bureaucratic and non-bureaucratic control. Bureaucratic control through coordination by planning and sanctions is accomplished by external control. Non-bureaucratic control through coordination by socialization and feedback is internalized control. Thus, an emphasis on feedback is a less bureaucratic method of control than are formalization, routinization, and sanctioning. If this is true, the other methods of control discussed in chapters five through seven should bear some relationship to communication, specifically to its direction and volume.

CONTEXTUAL CORRELATES OF COMMUNICATION

Hage, Aiken, and Marrett argued that the nature of the coordination employed in an organization affected the volume and direction of communication related to work. The direction of communication was broken down into vertical and horizontal. They tested their thesis on the data from their 1967 study of sixteen health and welfare organizations. Their measurement of organizational communication was limited to *verbal interaction* about tasks (work-related communication). They recognized that formal communication could vary as to the degree of structure, and therefore divided communications into *scheduled* and *unscheduled* communications. The former included more routine, planned communication such as scheduled staff and committee meetings, while the latter included impromptu meetings and conferences, consultations, and so on.[18] The most obvious limitation of this definition is the exclusion of written communications; the rationale for this was that its inclusion would conceptually and operationally overlap their definition of formalization, thus obscuring the findings with regard to the relationship between formalization and communication.

We will look briefly at the contextual correlates of communication: size and technology. As will be seen later in this section, communication is related to the structural complexity or differentiation of an organization, and, as was indicated in chapter four, size is also related to structural complexity. The question of the existence of a direct relationship between organizational size and communication has not yet been examined in this text. In his writing on cybernetics and communication, Hage addressed himself to this question. Like other researchers, he found strong relationships between the various measures of complexity (number of occupational specialties) and organizational size, but little or no relationship between size and volume of communication.[19] See Table 8–1 for this evidence. From this data, Hage concluded that his measures of complexity were more directly associated with communication measures than were his measures of size. When an organization adds more of the existing occu-

TABLE 8–1   Pearsonian Correlation Coefficients Between Size, Ecological Spread, and Routine Technology and Measures of Scheduled and Unscheduled Communication Among 16 Health and Welfare Organizations

	ORGANIZATION SIZE (RANK ORDER)	ECOLOGICAL SPREAD	ROUTINE TECHNOLOGY
Scheduled communication			
A. Organization-wide committee meetings			
1. Average number attended per month	.31	.50[a]	−.72[b]
2. Proportion of staff involved	.21	.41	−.53[a]
B. Departmental meetings			
1. Average number attended per month	.20	.62[c]	−.36

244

TABLE 8-1 (continued)

	ORGANIZATION SIZE (RANK ORDER)	ECOLOGICAL SPREAD	ROUTINE TECHNOLOGY
2. Proportion of staff involved	.11	.23	−.20
Unscheduled communication			
C. Dept./division heads			
1. With the executive level	−.16	.41	−.07
2. Among themselves	.55[c]	.53	.05
3. With their supervisors	.35	.23	−.17
4. With their workers	−.02	.32	.10
5. With other dept./division heads	.38	.24	.05
6. With other supervisors	.35	.21	−.29
7. With other workers	.13	.50[c]	−.21
D. Supervisors			
1. With the executive level	.25	.47	−.19
2. With their dept./division heads	.32	−.07	−.12
3. Among themselves	.26	.30	−.31
4. With their workers	.21	.18	−.54[c]
5. With other dept./division heads	.27	.08	.06
6. With other supervisors	−.12	.20	−.57[c]
7. With other workers	.30	.29	−.25
E. Workers			
1. With the executive level	−.16	.30	−.11
2. With their dept./division heads	−.11	.01	.23
3. With their supervisors	−.19	−.14	−.27
4. Among themselves	−.12	.05	.18
5. With other dept./division heads	.15	.34	−.01
6. With other supervisors	−.03	.16	−.01
7. With other workers	.39	.50[a]	−.17
F. Average rate	.18	.19	−.02

[a]P < .10.
[b]P < .05.
[c]P < .01.

Source: Jerald Hage, *Communication and Organizational Control: Cybernetics in Health and Welfare Settings* (New York: Wiley–Interscience, 1974), p. 217.

pational positions, new knowledge and skills are not added and greater communication is not necessary, whereas the addition of new occupations does add this new knowledge and skills. Therefore, one would expect structural differentiation, more than size, to affect communication.

Technology seems to be a somewhat better correlate of communication than size. Adopting Perrow's definition of technology, Hage defined nonroutine technology as meaning that each client was treated as a special case. He noted:

> Routine technology is weakly related to most of our measures of communication . . . except for the volume of scheduled communication, and several channels of unscheduled communication—supervisors conferring with workers (D4, r = −.54) and with other supervisors (D6, r = −.57). Thus, there is much support for the idea that routine technology leads to a choice of programming as a mechanism for coordinating and controlling the behavior of individuals.[20]

Thus, routineness of technology is an important factor in explaining scheduled communications. See Table 8–1 for the technological correlates of communication.

STRUCTURAL CORRELATES OF COMMUNICATION

Complexity Correlates

Hage operationalized three measures of organizational complexity: (1) the number of occupational specialties (occupational activities carried out by respondents); (2) the degree of professional activities of the respondents (the degree to which they belonged to professional societies, attended professional meetings, presented papers, and held offices in these organizations); (3) the number of departments or divisions.[21] As was hypothesized by these researchers, the number of occupational specialties was positively related to scheduled communication in the form of organization-wide committees (r = .66) and unscheduled communication (r = .51).[22] See Table 8–2 for these correlations, evidence that professional activity of the staff and the number of departments are not strongly related to the measures of intensity of communication.

246

TABLE 8–2   Pearsonian Correlation Coefficients Between Indicators of Complexity and Measures of Scheduled and Unscheduled Communication Among Sixteen Health and Welfare Organizations

	NUMBER OF OCCUPATIONAL SPECIALTIES	PROFESSIONAL ACTIVITY	NUMBER OF DEPARTMENTS
Scheduled communication			
A. Organization-wide committee meetings			
1. Average number attended per month	.66[a]	.32	.48[b]
2. Proportion of staff involved	.31	.20	.14
B. Departmental meetings			
1. Average number attended per month	.20	.25	.00
2. Proportion of staff involved	.13	.30	.07
Unscheduled communication			
C. Dept./division heads			
1. With the executive level	.42	−.08	−.06
2. Among themselves	.79[c]	.52[b]	.44
3. With their supervisors	.36	.08	.26
4. With their workers	−.09	−.04	−.15
5. With other dept./division heads	.46[b]	.12	.31
6. With other supervisors	.76[c]	.33	.62[a]
7. With other workers	.32	.00	−.10
D. Supervisors			
1. With the executive level	.37	.23	.02
2. With their dept./division heads	.25	.15	.31
3. Among themselves	.43	.05	.27
4. With their workers	.44	.16	.25
5. With other dept./division heads	.15	.47[b]	.02
6. With other supervisors	.12	.05	.00
7. With other workers	.77[c]	.37	.47[b]

247

	NUMBER OF OCCUPATIONAL SPECIALTIES	PROFESSIONAL ACTIVITY	NUMBER OF DEPARTMENTS
E. Workers			
1. With the executive level	.40	.28	−.11
2. With their dept./division heads	−.18	.13	−.37
3. With their supervisors	.44	.39	.15
4. Among themselves	.28	−.16	.17
5. With other dept./division heads	.15	.03	−.14
6. With other supervisors	.55[b]	.37	.12
7. With other workers	.66[c]	.33	.33
F. Average rate	.51[b]	.42	.28

[a] $P < .01$.
[b] $P < .10$.
[c] $P < .05$.

Source: Jerald Hage, *Communication and Organizational Control: Cybernetics in Health and Welfare Settings* (New York: John Wiley & Sons, Inc., 1974), p. 193.

In analyzing the direction of the communication, complexity in the form of occupational specialties was found to be related to horizontal flow, especially the unscheduled horizontal flow of communication:

Thus, department and division heads confer among themselves (C2, $r = .79$) and with their colleagues in other departments (C5, $r = .46$), but also with supervisors in other departments (C6, $r = .76$). Supervisors also confer among themselves (D3, r = .43) and with workers in other departments (D7, $r = .77$). Workers confer with supervisors (E6, r = .55) and workers in other departments (E7, r = .66).[23]

Although the number of departments generally demonstrated the same relation to communication as the number of occupational specialties, the correlations were not as strong.

By far, the best complexity correlate of communication was the occupational specialties index. Hage and associates concluded that the intensity of organizational communication, both organization-wide committees and unscheduled communications, tended to be positively associated with organizational complexity, measured as the number of occupational specialties. Unscheduled communication with those in one's department was not the variable most strongly associated with the measures of complexity; rather, it was "the flow of communication with people *on the same status level in different departments*" that was most highly associated with these two measures of complexity.[24] The horizontal communication with employees in the same department was inversely related to complexity. Thus, Hage and associates concluded that the volume of communication was greater in more complex organizations and that the volume of horizontal, interdepartmental communication, both scheduled and unscheduled, was more strongly associated with complexity than was vertical communication.

It may be recalled that Blau and associates posited that the greater the number of hierarchical levels, the more decentralized the organization. They found that high technical qualifications of the operating staff were positively associated with the development of a hierarchical structure of authority. The ratio of managerial to non-supervisory personnel was used as the measure of hierarchy of authority. As was made explicit in previous chapters of this text, Blau and associates did not measure the volume or direction of communication flow. They based their theoretical explanation of the relationship between the expertise of the operating staff and the high ratio of supervisors on the need for vertical communication between these two levels of employees. Based on the assumption that extensive downward communication in the form of directives and regulations is not functional when lower-level employees are highly qualified experts, they argued that an expert operating staff creates a need for upward communication. This argument supports their findings that a narrow span of control exists in conjunction with expert employees and facilitates consultation and feedback rather than supervision. The need for supervision would be evidenced if the employees were not experts and the technology were routine. Thus, organizations that employ experts at the lower levels of the hierarchy were seen as having greater need for upward communication than those organizations employing nonexperts at the lower levels.

Opposing Blau's views, Sargant Florence and Harold Wilensky hypothesized that hierarchies make poor channels for upward communications, in which case a high ratio of managers should increase downward communication and decrease upward communication.[25] John Brewer pointed out that Blau did not collect data to support his thesis that managers in organizations with more qualified personnel have more responsibilities delegated to them by higher management and report spending less time on supervision and more time on professional work of their own.[26] Further, Brewer made the point that although a narrow span of control increases the volume of upward communication by increasing the duration and frequency of contact, it also increases downward communication as well. He posited that ". . . any formal structural change which increased interaction between superiors and subordinates would tend to produce the benefits of increased upward communication at the cost of a still greater increase in downward communication."[27]

In order to explain the seeming contradiction in the writings of Blau and other theorists as to whether a narrower span of control would increase upward or downward communication in greater proportions, Brewer added another variable to his analysis. By conducting three case studies of the origin of communication between superordinates and subordinates, he analyzed the differentiation of superiors' and subordinates' work roles.

High differentiation is the bureaucratic superior, who is busy with supervision and administration, and his subordinates who are busy with production. At the other extreme of low differentiation is the working supervisor, known variously in different industries as the crew leader, crew chief, straw boss, group leader, or set-up man . . . who performs supervisory and administrative duties with respect to his subordinates but spends much of his time at production work, working at the same site and doing either the same type of work, or taking part in an interdependent work process with his subordinates.[28]

In analyzing groups with varying degrees of task differentiation between superordinates and subordinates, Brewer found that the need for upward communication appeared to be high only when there was high differentiation of superior and subordinate roles. This occurred because the superior was removed from direct contact and therefore did not have first-hand knowledge of operating problems nor the immediate feedback needed to rectify the problems. Thus, Brewer posited that the need for upward communication found by Blau is dependent on highly differentiated hierarchical work roles of superordinates and subordinates.[29]

Centralization Correlates   It will be remembered that Hage and associates measured centralization of decision-making using a participation index consisting of the employee's perceived participation in four types of decisions:

1. the hiring of personnel
2. the promotion of personnel
3. the adoption of new organizational policies
4. the adoption of new programs or services.[30]

These indexes were totally organization-oriented in contrast to being oriented toward work or task decisions. Hage and his colleagues hypothesized that participation in decision-making would be positively related to the intensity of communication and that decentralized organizations would exhibit more horizontal than vertical communication. They found strong to moderate positive relationships between the degree of participation in organizational decisions and committee meetings (r = .60) and departmental meetings (r = .45). See Table 8–3 for these correlations. Looking at unscheduled communications, organizations with wide participation in departmental decision-making had a higher degree of interdepartmental communication. "This was true for information flows upward, on the same level, and downward (r = .51, .53, and .42, respectively)."[31] Thus, the hypothesis of greater horizontal than vertical unscheduled communication was not supported. The rate of unscheduled, interdepartmental communication, horizontal and vertical, were positively associated with decentralization of decision-making. Surprisingly, they also found that in decentralized organizations, there were fewer "intra-departmental communications on the same level and downward."[32]

Another method of analyzing the relationship between communication and power is to use the number of hierarchical levels within the organization as an indication of the degree of centralization of the organization. Hage hypothesized that the hierarchy of authority would have a negative effect on communication, that is, it would "represent an opposite pattern from the index of participation: a series of negative signs as opposed to positive ones."[33] As can be seen from Table 8–3, this was not the case. The correlations between hierarchy of authority and communication were weak and significant relationships did *not* exist in most instances.

Formalization Correlates   In chapter seven, we differentiated between operative and regulative formalization. Hage and associates' operational definition of formalization included only operative for-

TABLE 8–3 Pearsonian Correlation Coefficients Between Indicators of Formalization and Centralization and Measures of Scheduled and Unscheduled Communication Among Sixteen Health and Welfare Organizations

	FORMALIZATION		CENTRALIZATION	
	Presence of Job Descriptions	Index of Job Specificity	Index of Participation in Decision-Making	Index of Hierarchy of Authority
Scheduled communication				
A. Organization-wide committee meetings				
1. Average number attended per month	–.30	–.31	.60[a]	.10
2. Proportion of staff involved	–.40	–.29	.61[a]	.03
B. Departmental meetings				
1. Average number attended per month	–.09	–.57[b]	.45[b]	–.39
2. Proportion of staff involved	–.06	–.30	.37	.09
Unscheduled communication				
C. Dept./division heads				
1. With the executive level	–.17	–.02	–.06	.06
2. Among themselves	–.09	.10	.36	.08
3. With their supervisors	–.29	.20	.17	.17
4. With their workers	–.16	–.15	–.20	–.07
5. With other dept./division heads	–.06	.04	.39	–.20
6. With other supervisors	.06	–.10	.33	–.01
7. With other workers	–.32	–.30	.25	–.18
D. Supervisors				
1. With the executive level	–.30	–.10	.53[b]	–.00
2. With their dept./division heads	.03	.42	.10	.20

TABLE 8-3 (continued)

	FORMALIZATION		CENTRALIZATION	
	Presence of Job Descriptions	Index of Job Specificity	Index of Participation in Decision-Making	Index of Hierarchy of Authority
3. Among themselves	-.42	.00	.26	.07
4. With their workers	-.58[b]	-.05	.55[b]	.23
5. With other dept./division heads	-.32	.12	.50[b]	.32
6. With other supervisors	-.11	-.53[a]	.39	-.22
7. With other workers	-.42	-.11	.41	.06
E. Workers				
1. With the executive level	-.40	-.26	.46[b]	.02
2. With their dept./division heads	-.30	-.11	.11	.06
3. With their supervisors	-.35	.03	.46[b]	.52[b]
4. Among themselves	.16	.12	-.14	-.13
5. With other dept./division heads	-.16	-.01	.19	.07
6. With other supervisors	-.19	-.06	.17	.17
7. With other workers	-.47[b]	-.16	.43	-.06
F. Average rate	-.50[b]	-.12	.36	.00

[a]P < .10.
[b]P < .05.

Source: Jerald Hage, Communication and Organizational Control: Cybernetics in Health and Welfare Settings (New York: John Wiley & Sons, Inc., 1974), pp. 196, 200.

malization and therefore disregarded the regulative rules and procedures that exist outside the performance of tasks. Operative formalization, in that it deals specifically with the work situation, restricts the activities of an employee's work, while regulative rules and procedures, had they been measured, would have had greater bearing on the total functioning of the organization, specifically coordination by planning.

Hage and associates felt that formalization and feedback or communication would work in opposition to each other.[34] Thus, formalized job descriptions would reduce the need for communication throughout the organization. In an organization with a formalized operative structure, one would expect little if any need for horizontal communication with peers; thus, vertical communication, especially downward vertical communication, would be greater than horizontal communication. Therefore, Hage and associates hypothesized that a greater degree of formalization would be associated with a lower rate of communication, and the direction of this communication would more likely be vertical and intradepartmental than horizontal and interdepartmental. They utilized two measures of formalization: (1) the degree of the employee's perceived comprehensiveness of a job description, and (2) the degree of job specificity.[35] As may be observed from Table 8–3, the correlations between scheduled communications and these indexes of formalization were relatively weak. These findings led Hage and associates to speculate that:

> The small size of these correlations, especially between the measures of formalization and scheduled communication, may reflect that we have poor measures of the degree of planning of the work flow. Both of our measures are specific to individual tasks, and neither reflects the degree of programming or coordination. This may explain why our measures work better with unscheduled communication than scheduled communication, since unscheduled communications are more likely to reflect discussions about particular jobs than organization-wide coordination.[36]

Looking at unscheduled communications, Hage and associates found a negative relationship of formalization to every measure of unscheduled communication, with the exception of communication on the same status level within the same department. The presence of job descriptions was strongly related to horizontal, interdepartmental communication ($r = -.61$).[37]

254

SUMMARY

With the exception of the studies by Hage and associates, there has been relatively little research on the relationship of communication to the other structural dimensions of organizations. Consequently, there is not enough empirical evidence to draw generalizations concerning such relationships. The existing evidence seems to suggest that as the task structure of an organization becomes increasingly more complex and nonroutine, employees are more highly educated and trained, and the organization becomes more structurally differentiated. With the employment of professionals, the application of rewards and sanctions as a method of coordination is not as successful as increased socialization and feedback. Complex, nonroutine technology is accompanied not only by increased structural differentiation and complexity of the employee, but also by decentralization, low formalization of operative rules and procedures, and high formalization of regulative rules and procedures. This nonbureaucratic structure is more likely to achieve coordination through feedback and resocialization of employees and other forms of adjustment. Thus, a nonbureaucratic organization exhibits a greater volume of communication than bureaucratic organizations. In keeping with the analysis found in chapter three, we might expect such organizations to be found in a complex, volatile environment (exhibiting a high rate of change). The decision-makers' uncertainty about this environment would also increase the need for a greater volume of communication.

Thus, on the one hand, those organizations that exhibit a high rate of communication are likely to have nonroutine technologies (high levels of knowledge technology, nonstandard treatment of clients, and a wider variety of clients), high structural complexity, low centralization of decision-making, and high formalization of regulative rules and procedures. In addition, those contextual and structural dimensions that support a higher volume of overall organizational communication also support a higher rate of horizontal communication within the organization. In general, these systems rely less on programmed interaction to achieve coordination and more on a system of reciprocal information flow. On the other hand, those organizations that exhibit a low level of communication generally have routine technologies (low level of knowledge technology and relatively standard treatment of clients), low structural complexity, high centralization, and high formalization of task-related (operative) rules and procedures.

NOTES

1. Chester Barnard, *The Functions of the Executive* (Cambridge, Mass.: Harvard University Press, 1938), p. 91.

2. Daniel Katz and Robert Kahn, *The Social Psychology of Organizations* (New York: John Wiley & Sons., Inc., 1966), pp. 223, 224.

3. Walter Buckley, *Modern System Research for the Behavioral Sciences* (Chicago: Aldine, 1968).

4. Keith Davis and William G. Scott, *Human Relations and Organizational Behavior: Readings and Comments,* 3rd ed. (New York: McGraw–Hill, 1969), p. 255.

5. Everett M. Rogers and Rekha Agarwala–Rogers, *Communication in Organizations* (New York: The Free Press, 1976), pp. 10–13.

6. Ibid., p. 13.

7. Harold Guetzkow, "Communication in Organizations," in James G. March, ed., *Handbook of Organizations* (Chicago: Rand McNally, 1965), p. 534.

8. Barnard, *The Functions of the Executive,* pp. 121–122.

9. Andre L. Delbecq, "How 'Informal' Organization Evolves: Interpersonal Choice and Subgroup Formation," *Business Perspectives* 4, no. 3 (Spring 1968): 17–21.

10. Jerald Hage, Michael Aiken, and Cora Bagley Marrett, "Organization Structure and Communication," *American Sociological Review* 36, no. 5 (October 1971): 856.

11. Keith Davis, *Human Relations at Work* (New York: McGraw–Hill, 1972).

12. Eugene Walton, "How Efficient is the Grapevine?" *Personnel* 28 (1961): 45–49.

13. Katz and Kahn, *The Social Psychology of Organizations,* p. 244.

14. Ibid., p. 239.

15. Hage, Aiken, and Marrett, "Organization Structure and Communication," p. 860.

16. Ibid.

17. Jerald Hage, *Communication and Organizational Control* (New York: Wiley–Interscience, 1974), pp. 21–26.

18. Hage, Aiken, and Marrett, "Organization Structure and Communication," p. 864.

19. Hage, *Communication and Organization Control,* pp. 215–216.

20. Ibid., p. 220.

21. Ibid., p. 192.

22. Ibid.

23. Ibid., p. 194.

24. Hage, Aiken, and Marrett, "Organization Structure and Communication," p. 867.

25. Sargant P. Florence, *The Logic of British and American Industry* (London: Routledge and Kegan Paul, 1961), p. 153; and Harold L. Wilensky, *Organizational Intelligence* (New York: Basic Books, 1967), pp. 42–48.

26. John Brewer, "Flow of Communications, Expert Qualifications and Organizational Authority Structures," *American Sociological Review* 36, no. 3 (June 1971): 475–484.

27. Ibid., pp. 477–478.

28. Ibid., p. 480.

29. Ibid., pp. 483–484.
30. Hage, Aiken, and Marrett, "Organization Structure and Communication," p. 868.
31. Ibid., p. 869.
32. Ibid.
33. Hage, *Communication and Organizational Control,* pp. 200–201.
34. Hage, Aiken, and Marrett, "Organization Structure and Communication," p. 863.
35. Ibid., p. 868.
36. Ibid.
37. Ibid.

part IV
PERFORMANCE COMPONENT

Organizational performance is a global term that has been used to encompass such constructs as effectiveness, efficiency, conflict, innovation, change, and job satisfaction or employee morale. The four dimensions of performance discussed in this section are (1) innovation (program change), (2) conflict, (3) effectiveness, and (4) efficiency. There is no assumption here that these constructs are positively related to each other or that they are all equally important to the performance of all types of organizations; nor do we assume that these dimensions are all related in the same way to various structural, contextual, and environmental dimensions. Rather a multidimensional approach to organizational performance is taken.

Although job satisfaction or morale is an important performance dimension, it is not analyzed in this text because of its distinctly socio-psychological nature. However, this does not negate its importance for those who are analyzing the attitudes of individuals who work in organizations.

Finally, there is no assumption here that organizational performance and goal attainment are synonymous constructs. Of course, some analysts of performance such as those who take the goals approach discussed in chapter eleven do equate goal achievement with effectiveness, but this is only one of many possible approaches.

9

INNOVATION AND PROGRAM CHANGE

OBJECTIVES

The objectives of this chapter are:

1. To theoretically and operationally define organizational innovation (program change).
2. To differentiate between change *in* and *of* the organization.
3. To define the origins of innovation.
4. To define and describe the stages of organizational innovation:
   a. awareness and information
   b. evaluation and decision
   c. initiation
   d. implementation
   e. routinization
5. To define the environmental correlates of innovation:
   a. change and stability
   b. heterogeneity
   c. organizational interdependence
6. To define the contextual correlates of innovation:
   a. resource slack
   b. technology
   c. size
7. To define the structural correlates of innovation:
   a. complexity
   b. centralization
   c. formalization
   d. communication

INTRODUCTION

Scope of Analysis

It is necessary at the outset to place limitations on the scope of the analysis of change found in this chapter, which focuses on changes in the organization *per se*. Intrapersonal, interpersonal, and societal change are only referred to in terms of their relationship to organizational change. Furthermore, this chapter deals only with innovation (program change) and not with the more disruptive types of organizational change such as violent conflict, which will be discussed in chapter ten.

Change and Order

Order and change coexist at all social structural levels (societal, organizational, and group). For example, for change to occur at the organization level, there must be some order from which change originates and some organization of the people who wish to bring about the change and who must organize their activities, resources, communications, and so on. Likewise, organizations such as the federal government and business corporations are responsible for major societal change and stability. Society is comprised of organizational and multiorganizational structures that are in the continual process of changing that society. Organizations effect changes in the U.S. in that they account for approximately 90 percent of the nation's employment.[1] Thus, organizations affect the occupational roles and hence the lifestyles and life chances of a major portion of the U.S. population. In the larger societal context, decisions to hire individuals with particular qualifications or characteristics (technical expertise, gender, ethnic background) ultimately influence the structure of that society.

Organizations are also great resisters of innovation (program change). Chapters five through eight concentrated on the structural dimensions of organizations, which, at one end of the continuum, have the ability to facilitate coordination and control. Knowing the degree to which each of these dimensions is structured, one can predict to what degree the organization is stable, and to some extent, to what degree it will resist change. Therefore, knowledge of this set of dimensions should help one predict to what degree an organization will be able to initiate change.

Innovation is one of the main processes in and functions of organizations. This is demonstrated by the fact that most large organizations have research and development departments, the major function of which is innovation (program change). It must be remembered that this type of organizational change is institutionalized and often departmentalized. Thus, program change is conservative relative to organizational conflict, which is not institutionalized.

Change *Of* and *In* the Organization

Distinguishing between changes *of* and *in* the organization is important because of the greater pervasiveness of the former, though both types occur at the organizational level. When the organization's structure itself is changed, for example, when the communication networks and power structures are changed, more of the organizational members are involved and their status, positions, and roles, are altered. The most pervasive change of the organization would be its complete dissolution. This is change *of* the organization. On the other hand, when change occurs within the organization, for example, when a new product is initiated by the research and development department, the change is less pervasive. A relatively small portion of the total organization is involved in this type of change— change *in* the organization. Innovations and program changes are more likely to be changes *in* than *of* the organization.

ORGANIZATIONAL INNOVATION (PROGRAM CHANGE) DEFINED

The majority of the research dealing with innovation (program change) has concentrated on characteristics of the individuals that determine the extent of their innovativeness. For example, of 109 articles in sociological journals about organizational change, eighty-four were actually about changing individual attitudes or work behavior within organizations, not about changing the organizations themselves.[2] Since the unit of analysis in this text is the organization, we will concentrate in this chapter not on individual innovation but on organizational innovation—program change.

It is useful to differentiate between innovation and other changes within an organization. Conceptually, all innovation is change, but not all change is innovation. Some change is merely an adjustment of the old structure. For example, an altering of the subunits of the federal government is often one of the first undertakings of a new U.S. president. However, the renaming and shuffling of the subunits does not effect major organizational change. Many of the same people perform the same activities, following basically the same procedures as in the former administration. But generally, the top level employees of each department are replaced, and the new administrators are unrealistically expected to innovate under the constraint of the old structure and processes. Organizational innovation is generally defined as an idea, practice, product, service, or other object perceived to be new by the organization,[3] whereas organizational change is any adjustment, through innovation, restructuring or conflict, that takes place in an organization.

In the past, the first use of a new product, process, or idea by *any* organization was called innovation; E. Mansfield referred to subsequent uses by other organizations as limitations.[4] More recently organizational innovation has been defined with respect, not to *all* organizations, but to a single organization. Thus, the first use of a new product, process, service or idea by a given organization is considered innovation *for that organization*,[5] even if other organizations have used it previously. In keeping with this definition, Jerald Hage and Michael Aiken defined program change as "the addition of new services and product" to a given organization, an important type of change because it is designed to "meet a new need" and represents an attempt "to achieve a goal."[6] Implicit within their discussion is the idea that a program change is an innovation (first-time change) for the organization and the process that the organization goes through to bring about program change resembles the innovation process. Later, when Aiken and Hage defined innovation as " '. . . the generation, acceptance, and implementation of new ideas, processes, products, or services . . .' for the first time within an organizational setting,"[7] they made explicit the idea that innovation is specific to a given organization and includes various stages. Because most program changes are new to the organization adapting them, and the two concepts of innovation and program change have been used interchangeably by most researchers, they will be so used in this chapter.

Aiken and Hage measured innovation (program change) by the head of the organization's report of the number of new programs or services successfully implemented during a three-year period (1964–1966 inclusive). Only new programs (i.e., involving no redefinitions or alterations of existing services or programs) were used in their analysis.[8] This definition was a replication of the one used in their 1967 study. The rate of program change per year by type of organization was used as the measurement of change.

Assumptions

Innovation, in and of itself, has no standardized content; therefore, it may have positive or negative consequences for the organization depending on the perspective of the observer and the type of change. In fact, a given innovation may be positive in the short run and negative in the long run or vice versa. Furthermore, change may be advantageous for one organization but not for others. Thus, although those who have written about organizational innovation and program change have, for the most part, evidenced a bias in favor of change, many such changes have not had universally positive consequences for the organizations in which they were implemented. It is not the purpose of this chapter to advocate either a particular type of change or change in general, nor is it the position of this writer that all change is either advantageous or disadvantageous for all organizations. Rather, an attempt will be made to analyze innovation and the environmental, contextual, and structural characteristics that facilitate these changes.

The judgment as to the value of program change for a particular organization is part of the decision-making process and should be based on the content, nature, and consequences of the change. Many times this evaluation is left to the decision-making body of the organization. However, adequate evaluation of the consequences of a given program change generally can be gained only through longitudinal research or in retrospect many years after the change has been implemented. Due to the lack of longitudinal research on the consequences of program change, few conclusions can be made as to the value of a particular program change at the time it is instituted.

Origins

The origin of organizational innovation can be either internal or external, but there have been both theoretical writings[9] and empirical evidence that organizational change is largely externally induced. For example, Gerald Zaltman and associates noted that change often originates outside the organization:

In studying 25 major process and product innovations in DuPont, Mueller (1962) indicated that 56% . . . originated outside the organization. Marquis and Myers' (1969) analysis . . . has shown that 61% of the ideas for new innovations came from outside the organization. Utterback's (1971) study of innovation

265

TABLE 9–1 Stages in the Innovation and Program Change Processes

	ROGERS AND ROGERS	HAGE AND AIKEN	ZALTMAN ET AL.
1. Awareness and information	1. Adoption	1. Evaluation	
2. Evaluation and Decision			
3. Initiation	2. Testing	2. Initiation	1. Initiation
4. Implementation	3. Installation	3. Implementation	2. Implementation
5. Routinization	4. Institutionalization	4. Routinization	

Sources:
Everett Rogers and Rekha Agarwala–Rogers, *Communication in Organizations* (New York: The Free Press, 1976), p. 163.
Jerald Hage and Michael Aiken, *Social Change in Complex Organizations* (New York: Random House, 1970), p. 113.
Gerald Zaltman, Robert Duncan, and Jonny Holbek, *Innovation and Organizations* (New York: John Wiley & Sons, 1973), p. 62.

in the instrument industry found that . . . 66% came from outside the firm that developed the idea.[10]

However, Charles Carter and Bruce Williams pointed out that although most of the ideas for innovation originate outside the organization, only a small percentage (⅓ or less) of these ideas are actually implemented.[11] Here, the difference between initiation and implementation is great.

Regardless of where the change originates, the ideas must ultimately be brought to the attention of those within the organization. At this point, the decision-making process begins. The gate keepers of the organization must decide whether or not the idea is worth taking to those who have the power to make decisions as to its value. Thus, the process of innovation is a series of decisions made by the many subsystems of the organization.

STAGES OF THE INNOVATION (PROGRAM CHANGE) PROCESS

The position is taken here that decision-making takes place at each stage of the innovation process, but ultimately a decision must be made concerning whether or not to initiate the change. The following discussion will concentrate on the decisions at each stage of the innovation process. In the past, many authors concentrated their analyses on the early stages of the change process—awareness, interest, and evaluation. This approach characterized the early writings of theorists such as Rogers, who concentrated on individual as opposed to organizational innovation.[12] Other theorists, such as Hage and Aiken, have concentrated on the latter stages of the organizational program change process: implementation and routinization.[13] Because the emphasis here is on the entire innovation–program change process, we are interested not only in implementation and institutionalization but also the early stages of awareness, evaluation, and decision-making.

The stages in the organizational change process have been assigned different labels by theorists. See Table 9–1 for a summary of some of these organizational innovation and program change typologies. In this text we will discuss five stages of the change process: (1) awareness and information, (2) evaluation and decision, (3) initiation, (4) implementation, and (5) routinization. These stages are neither mutually exclusive (in fact, they overlap) nor unidirectional (regression often occurs).

267

Awareness and Information

Before change can be initiated, the organizational decision-makers must become aware that there is a problem. Possibly organizational goals are not being accomplished efficiently and effectively. For example, the quality of the product or the rate of production may be low. "When a discrepancy exists between what the organization is doing and what its decision makers believe it ought to be doing, there is a performance gap."[14] When this gap occurs, the decision makers must (1) lower their expectations, (2) change their objectives, or (3) increase efficiency or effectiveness. The latter option generally means program change. During this period, decision-makers become fully aware of alternatives and seek information regarding these alternatives, which must be assessed in relation to organization objectives. Some organizations possess dimensions that facilitate regular, continual assessment of performance and methods of closing performance gaps; others do not.

Several authors have argued the question as to whether the "awareness of need" or "knowledge of the innovation" comes first in the innovation process; that is, does knowledge of an innovation stimulate a need to adopt it, or does a particular need stimulate the search for greater innovative knowledge? Actually, the two work hand-in-hand: acquiring information and an increasing awareness of organizational need for innovations must occur together and complement each other.[15] Research related to this point will be discussed later in this chapter.

Evaluation and Decision

Information relevant to an organizational performance gap must be evaluated and a decision made as to which method of dealing with the problem will most efficiently and effectively reach the desired organizational objectives. Decision-making related to change usually consists of four steps: (1) generating a set of possible alternative courses of action, (2) defining which alternative courses of action are available to the given organization, (3) ranking the consequences of various alternatives, (4) selecting that alternative that meets some minimum standard of satisfaction with respect to each of the desired objectives.[16]

Generally, the evaluation and decision-making processes are long and entail a great many social, economic, and political considerations. The early phase of this stage is generally encumbered with group value and interest conflicts. Each interest group attempts to persuade decision-makers to give special consideration to their particular perspective and interests. The clients or consumers, production department, and research and development unit each have separate and conflicting interests, objectives, and needs, and different criteria for assessing the efficiency and effectiveness of the organization. Thus, each group may have a different solution to organizational problems; the decision-maker cannot possibly meet all their demands.

Initiation

After the decision has been made to innovate or change the product, services, or processes of the organization, decisions must be made concerning the trial run. This stage is practical because the cost of failure and risk involved is less in a small-scale trial run than in full-scale implementation. At this stage, the initiators must acquire internal and external resources, i.e., find new employees with the required knowledge and skills to initiate changes, institute new technology such as computers, and design new procedures to make the program operable. Also, during this stage, the initiators, possibly people from research and development, may meet head on with resistance from the implementors, the people in production, or the professional who works with the client. The problems that may have been hypothetical in a planning stage are now real and must be solved. This process is complicated when a larger number of people with differing occupational specializations are involved. Thus, a variety of ideas and sources of resistance and assistance are involved in the initiation stage, which must be evaluated and decisions made as to its continued feasibility (advantages and disadvantages).

Implementation

If the initiation stage is successful, then the likelihood is high that the change will be continued or fully implemented. The implementation stage is the actual incorporation of the change by the organization. Many problems will have been worked out in the initiation stage, but full implementation has its share of problems because the organization must be both flexible enough to make adjustments to facilitate the articulation of the new program and stable enough to function regularly with the addition of the new program. During the implementation stage, the structure and processes (in short, all major aspects) of the organization must be adjusted to the innovation.

Regardless of how well planned the change is or how extensive the preceding initiation, problems will arise between the existing employees and the new employees, the old structure and new structure, the previous program and the new program. Even though considerable planning took place, decisions were duly deliberated, and the initiation process removed many of the problems from the proposed change, the implementation will have problems and adjustments will have to be made. The program change may have to be altered, and the existing activities and structure of the organization may have to be further adjusted to meet the contingencies of the change. Thus, the implementation stage is the point of resistance and conflict because some individuals will lose power and some will have to change their roles, their objectives, and even their ideas when the change is instituted. To this end, Hage and Aiken pointed out that decision-makers learn from past experiences:

> If organizational leaders decide to initiate a new program and if they experience considerable difficulty in the process of implementing it, they may abandon it and perhaps avoid initiating future programmatic changes. In other words, we do not always make the argument that all organizations successfully implement programs that are initiated. Some specific organizational arrangements make the process of implementation smoother than others, and, therefore, organizations with these arrangements will become more favorably disposed to future changes.[17]

Subsequent to the implementation stage, the innovation must be evaluated. If resistance or conflict is too great, the organizational decision-makers may feel the noneconomic costs of the change outweigh its benefits, making it undesirable to continue the program. Also, the program's efficiency and effectiveness must be evaluated after the implementation. Economic costs must be re-evaluated. Further complications are brought on by the fact that the method of evaluating a new program may itself be new, which calls for further innovation and change.

Routinization

If the program is evaluated, defined as successful, and retained, it will become routinized. Routinization, or institutionalization, occurs over time; when it is complete, the program is no longer designated as new—most of the problems have been worked out and the structure and processes accompanying the program change have become accepted parts of the organization. This stage of the program change or innovation process will likely be characterized by a low rate of conflict and greater structural stability than previous stages.

The fit between the typology described above and reality should be more closely examined. But longitudinal, process-oriented studies are needed to define how the organizational innovation process takes place. Only through analysis of this process can we understand how and why the structural, contextual, and environmental dimensions are related to each stage of innovation. At present these studies do not exist.

The major question of concern to those who wish to innovate or change an organization is, what are the characteristics of the organizational environment, context, and structure that facilitate innovation and change? There is little systematic empirical evidence of the relative influence of internal structure versus environmental correlates on organizational innovation. Usually only a few of these variables are included in a single analysis. In most analyses, organizational innovation is viewed as an intervening variable between the independent variables of organizational environment, context, and structure and the dependent variables of organizational performance. Thus, ultimately, innovation is not the dependent variable; rather, it is seen as a way to make the organization more efficient or effective.

Hage and Aiken see organizational structure as the crucial component in the process of program change.[18] Yet, they as well as other theorists have recently investigated the effects of environmental and contextual dimensions on organizational innovation. The environmental, contextual and structural correlates of innovation are discussed below.

ENVIRONMENTAL CORRELATES OF INNOVATION (PROGRAM CHANGE)

In studying how organizations make decisions, Francis Aguilar investigated the influence of different types of information from the environment. He found that the most important type of information for business organizations related to the market. This reaffirms our discussion in chapter six that marketing is the most powerful department due to its link with the external environment. This dominance of market information led Aguilar to conclude that "companies tend to react to current conditions rather than to innovate."[19] Similarly, Donald Marquis and Sumner Meyers and Carter and Williams inde-

271

pendently found that the major sources of ideas for innovation came from marketing factors, as opposed to technological factors.[20] These studies indicated that business organizations are more likely to react to environmental demands or organizational needs than to become actively involved in the synthesis of ideas for the sake of innovation or change.

From our definition of organizations in chapter one and the discussion of environmental complexity and instability in chapter three, it should be apparent that organizations are conceptualized as open systems that must exchange inputs and outputs with their environments. This environment in which the focal organization operates may present the organization with a situation that pressures it to change. Since an organization is in the constant process of maintaining a relationship of dynamic equilibrium with its environment, an organization in an unstable, changing environment must be flexible in order to change with its environment. Many aspects of the environment—including technological changes, market conditions, consumer demands, and competitors—have the potential for influencing changes in the focal organization. At one extreme is the situation in which the environment changes rapidly and causes need for rapid adjustment in the organization; here the organizational structure may become so temporary that the organization does not have time to reach its objectives, much less become efficient.[21] The other extreme situation is an environment that resists change not only for itself but for the focal organizations. An organization located in a small, provincial community might experience such resistance from its environment. On the other hand, if the norms of the environment favor change, the likelihood of implementation is enhanced.

J. Victor Baldridge and Robert Burnham found that in Illinois schools, heterogeneous environmental input from the community and other organizations was a major determinant of organizational innovation.[22] These environmental inputs were measured in terms of (1) population density, (2) urbanization, (3) percentage of nonwhite population, (4) the amount of home ownership, (5) the number of local governmental agencies competing for tax dollars, and (6) government expenditures on programs other than education. Four of these predictors of innovation were stronger than the other two: (1) population density, (2) urbanization, (3) nonwhite population, and (4) governmental agencies in the environment. Thus, the more complex the environment, the greater the rate of organizational innovation.

Other than financing innovations on their own, organizations can innovate by working with other organizations that share its environment. Joint programs, a type of organizational interdependence, are defined by Aiken and Hage as two or more organizations sharing staff and funds or other resources to accomplish mutually agreed upon objectives.[23] These interorganizational relationships increase diffusion of ideas and information into the organization which, in turn, increases innovation. As shown in Table 9-2, Aiken and Hage

TABLE 9-2 Relationships between the Rate of Innovation, 1964-1966, and other Organizational Characteristics

	CORRELATION COEFFICIENT BETWEEN THE RATE OF INNOVATION 1964-1966 AND:
A. *Slack Resources*	
1. Presence of Change in the source of finances, 1964-1966	.73‡
2. Percent increase in budget, 1964-1966	.60*
B. *Organizational Interdependence*	
1. Number of joint programs 1959-1966 inclusive with other organizations, including joint programs that are new programs	.69†
2. Number of joint programs with other organizations, 1959-1966 inclusive, excluding joint programs that are new programs	.73‡
C. *Organization Size*	
1. Rank order of organization size, 1967	.11
2. Percent increase in organizational size 1964-1966	.50*
D. *History of Innovation* Number of new programs, 1959-1963, inclusive	.62†

*$p < .05$.
†$p < .01$.
‡$p < .001$.

Source: Michael Aiken and Jerald Hage, "The Organic Organization and Innovation," *Sociology* 5, no. 1 (January 1971): 77.

273

found a strong positive relationship between the number of joint programs and the number of innovations (r = .69). When all new joint programs were excluded from the analysis, the correlation was even higher (r = .73). Thus, there is support for innovative organizations being interdependent and existing in somewhat heterogeneous and unstable environments.

CONTEXTUAL CORRELATES OF INNOVATION (PROGRAM CHANGE)

James March and Herbert Simon pointed out that organizations are more likely to innovate under conditions of slack resources.[24] These resources may be in the form of financing, knowledge, ideas, personnel, or physical facilities. Due to the overlap of knowledge and ideas with the measure of complexity, Aiken and Hage did not use these measures, but rather operationalized slack resources in terms of presence of change in source of finances and percent increase in the budget over a three-year period 1964–1966.[25] They found a strong relationship between each of these indicators and the rate of innovation, (r = .73) and (r = .60), respectively. These correlations can be seen in Table 9–2 and indicate that organizations innovate in the presence of increased finances.

The contextual dimension of technology also influences the ability of an organization to innovate. The greater the diversity of the organization's task structure, the more likely innovation will take place. When technology is complex, experts are employed and supervision is decreased. Innovation and change is possible because of the diversity of tasks and the expertise of employees. Of course, task complexity also generates other types of change, such as conflict, because of differences in individuals and in the values and interests of various organizational subunits.

Several researchers have found positive correlations between size and organizational innovativeness.[26] Large size (number of employees) usually appears concomitantly with greater total resources and organizational complexity, and these dimensions, in addition to whatever influence size might have, effect innovation and change. Thus, size is usually found to be a fairly strong correlate of innovation.

Although Hage and Aiken's 1967 and 1971 publications of findings on organizational innovation reported a positive correlation between size and innovation, their 1971 publication reported a relatively weak relationship (r = .11) between these two variables and a strong relationship between innovation and *increased* organizational size (r = .50). See Table 9–2 for a summary of these relationships.[27] Similarly, in their analysis of innovation in schools, J. Victor Baldridge and Robert Burnham found that size promoted innovation not only indirectly through increased complexity but also by creating problems of coordination and control that demanded new practices. In their San Francisco Bay Area study, they found a perfect rank order correlation between district size and adoption of innovations. The ten largest individual schools had more than three times as many major innovations as the ten smallest schools.[28] Likewise, in their Illinois sample, the size of the organization was correlated with innovation (r = .45). Furthermore, Baldridge and Burnham pointed out that larger more complex school districts have several advantages that help them sustain adoption of change. For example, individuals directly involved with the innovation received support in the form of specialized resources and support staff. Here, increased complexity provided the teachers with a career ladder that may have encouraged them to innovate.[29]

Peter Blau's findings confirmed the hypothesis of Warren Hagstrom and Joseph Ben–David that larger size fosters departmental innovation—both the size of the university and the average size of the departments within the university were positively correlated with departmental innovation (the formation of new departments).[30] The logic behind the relationship is that in universities with large departments, the members will be more specialized and heterogeneous, and subgroups will be more likely to break off, combine with faculty in other departments, and create new departments.[31] The evidence overwhelmingly supported the hypothesis of a positive relationship between organization size and innovation or change. Thus, general support exists for innovation taking place in large organizations with slack resources and technological complexity.

STRUCTURAL CORRELATES OF INNOVATION (PROGRAM CHANGE)

In this text, it is assumed that there is no one environment that fits all organizations and no single way for all organizations to be structured or for a single organization to be structured at all times. This assumption becomes obvious in our discussion of innovation (program change). The totally static organizational model is conducive to

275

neither the initiation or routinization of innovation. Rather, an organization would best institute change if it were highly flexible during the stages of knowledge and information, evaluation and decision, and initiation; somewhat flexible during the implementation stage; and more structured during the routinization stage. Thus, different stages of the innovation process are facilitated by different degrees of structuring. It is the contention of this writer that organizations or their subunits that accept or initiate change easily or have a high rate of program change initiation will possess one set of structural dimensions, while those that easily routinize these changes will possess another set of dimensions. Thus, some organizations that initiate change cannot carry through because they lack the appropriate structure. An organization that is successful at initiating change has high complexity, low centralization, low formalization, and high communication. However, in order to routinize this change, the organizational structure will need to be less complex, more centralized and formalized, and have a lower level of communication than the initiating structure. Several theorists have argued that those structural characteristics (such as high complexity, low formalization, and low centralization) that facilitate initiation of change make it difficult for the organization to implement the innovation.[32] Others make no distinction as to the structural characteristics that support various stages of innovation and change.[33] One essential point should be made: Since the initiating stage is generally antecedent to implementation and routinization, if the organization does not have the initiating structure necessary to move the new idea through the initial information and decision-making stages, it will be impossible to implement the change, and the change cannot be routinized. Tom Burns and G. M. Stalker were among the first researchers to indicate that different types of organizational structures are more effective in different situations. They identified two types of organizational structures. The mechanistic structure was found in organizations operating under rather stable conditions, whereas the organic structure functioned best under unstable conditions. Zaltman's summary of these two sets of dimensions are found in Table 3–5.[34] Similarly, Paul R. Lawrence and Jay W. Lorsch found, in a comparative study of six organizations operating in the same industrial environment, that the sales, research, and production units within these organizations differed in their formal structure. The production unit with the more certain subenvironment tended to have the highest degree of structure; sales, the next highest degree of structure; and fundamental research units that experienced the highest uncertainty, the least formal structure.[35] Another factor contributing to the structure of these departments might have been that the research department was more likely to have been involved in the first stages of awareness, decision-making and initiation of change, whereas the production unit was more likely to have been involved in implementation and routinization. Thus, somewhat different structures were required for different stages of the innovation process.

The dilemma of maintaining stability yet being flexible enough to change can be accomplished in at least two ways. Because these two stages require contradictory structures, they must be separated in some way—by time or structure. As was demonstrated in Lawrence and Lorsch's research, departmentalization is one method of incorporating both flexibility and stability in an organization at the same time. When individual departments are organized differently, the differing structures are compartmentalized to some extent. A second method of incorporating both flexibility and stability in the organization is to separate them by time so that the organization or subunit is structured to maximize flexibility at one time and stability at another time. It seems that this situation would be more difficult to achieve and possibly more conflict ridden than departmentalization. Karl Weick pointed out that organizations may be alternately stable and flexible at different stages of their development process,[36] and Herbert Shepard found the same alternations at various stages of the output process.[37] This change in structure occurs between the initiation stage and the implementation stage of the change process. Shepard stated that during initiation:

> a quality of openness [is needed] so that diverse and heterogeneous persons can contribute, and so that many alternatives can be explored. For implementation [however] a quite different quality may be needed: singleness of purpose, functional division of labor responsibility and authority, discipline, the drawing of internal communication boundaries, and so on.[38]

Shepard discussed how a raid unit during World War II alternated between these two forms of structure. During the planning sessions, the unit operated in a flexible manner in which all members of the unit had an opportunity to contribute ideas. During the raids, the group operated under a stable model in which strict military command was followed. Thus, the structure in the decision-making stage was different from that in the implementation stage, when the unit

277

carried out its normal activities. The unit had maximized effectiveness by using the alternating methods of structuring to facilitate each stage of the program change.

Complexity Correlates

The best evidence of the relationship of complexity to innovation and change is Aiken and Hage's longitudinal analysis of sixteen welfare agencies—ten private and six public—that provided services involving physical rehabilitation, mental rehabilitation, and psychiatry in a large metropolitan area. In these studies, published in 1967 and 1971, Aiken and Hage analyzed six structural dimensions that they felt would influence the implementation of new programs or services in organizations. One of these was organizational complexity, measured as the number of occupational specialties and the degree of professionalism of each specialty. Hage and Aiken felt that these two measures reflected both the extensity and intensity of knowledge in the organization. Professionalism was measured in two ways: (1) the length of professional training required by each speciality, and (2) the degree of involvement in professional societies and activities of each speciality.

In their 1967 publication, they reported a correlation of $r = .45$ between the number of occupational specialties and the number of new programs added during the previous five-year period, which they labeled the rate of program change.[39] In 1971, they analyzed the relationship between the rate of innovation (implementation) over a three-year period (1964–1966) and the diversity of the occupational structure in 1969; they found a correlation of $r = .59$.[40] Hage and Aiken contended that the sheer number of occupations itself leads to more change. Thus, the greater the number of different occupations, the more diverse the perspectives and values of the members within the organization. The thesis underlying this relationship is as follows: The larger the number of occupations, the larger the number of possible ideas in the organization; the larger the number of ideas, the higher the exchange of ideas; the greater the exchange of ideas, the greater the amount of proposals for new processes, techniques, procedures, services, and products; the greater the number of innovations proposed, the higher the rate of implementation of change.

The diversity of occupational specialties may cause innovation because of the diversity of combined ideas and approaches or through conflict between these specialties. When a large number of specialists are employed by an organization, there will be increased

278

competition among them for the organization's limited resources. Of course, those organizations that have larger numbers of specialists generally have more resources. H. M. Sapolsky pointed out that the higher the dispersion of resources in an organization, the more difficult it is for positive decisions to be reached, thus decreasing the rate of organizational innovation.[41] But Aiken and Hage pointed out that:

> It is still logically possible that the proportion of innovations implemented may be inversely related to diversity, but that the *absolute* rate of innovation may be positively related to diversity. This would mean that so many proposals for innovation are made in such organizations that, even though only a small proportion are actually adopted, the absolute number of adoptions may still be greater in such organizations.[42]

Similarly, Baldridge and Burnham have observed that most social innovations are adopted by complex organizations, and that organizational dynamics are the major independent variables that influence the amount, rate, and success of innovations. They found administrative complexity to be a major characteristic affecting the innovation capacity of an organization. The rationale for this relationship as presented by Baldridge and Burnham is very similar to that presented by Hage and Aiken and Zaltman. This rationale originated with March and Simon, who noted that an increase in structural complexity is accompanied by an increase in specialists who handle specialized subtasks and initiate search procedures for more efficient techniques to accomplish their goals.[43] Baldridge and Burham argued that both differentiation (in terms of structural units) and integration (in terms of coordinating mechanisms) help promote innovation—the former by creating specialists to seek new solutions, and the latter by providing mechanisms for overcoming conflict. In the Illinois sample the rate of innovation was correlated with job specialization (r = .48) and conflict prevention (r = .24).[44]

Aiken and Hage measured professionalism in two ways: (1) the number of years of training and (2) outside professional activities. Again, these two measurements are an indication of the diversity of employees and should be positively related to organizational innovation. Thus, Aiken and Hage hypothesized a direct relationship between each measure of professionalism and the rate of successful implementation of innovations. In their 1967 publication, they reported professional activities were moderately correlated with the

TABLE 9—3 Relationships between the Rate of Innovation, 1964–1966, and Characteristics of the Organic Organization in 1967

	CORRELATION COEFFICIENT BETWEEN THE RATE OF INNOVATION AND THE ORGANIZATIONAL PROPERTY INDICATED
A. *Degree of Complexity*	
Number of occupational specialties	.59†
B. *Professionalism*	
1. Amount of professional training	−.19
2. Degree of extra-organizational professional activity	.63‡
C. *Decentralization of Decision-Making*	
Degree of participation in decision-making	.17
D. *Intensity of Scheduled Communications*	
1. Number of committees	.46*
2. Frequency of committee meetings	.53†
E. *Intensity and Direction of Unscheduled Communications*	
1. Different department, higher status level	.45*
2. Different department, same status level	.37
3. Different department, lower status level	−.13
4. Same department, higher status level	.61†
5. Same department, same status level	−.03
6. Same department, lower status level	−.32
F. *Formalization of Rules and Procedures*	
1. Presence of a rules manual (as reported by organization head)	−.60†
2. Presence of a rules manual (as reported by staff members)	−.20
3. Presence of job descriptions (as reported by organizational head)	.02
4. Presence of job descriptions (as reported by staff members)	.01
5. Degree of job codification	.29
6. Degree of rule observation	.25

*p < .10.   ‡p < .01.
†p < .05.

Source: Michael Aiken and Jerald Hage, "The Organic Organization and Innovation," *Sociology* 5, no. 1 (January 1971): 70.

number of new programs (r = .38); in their 1971 publication, they reported the degree of extraorganizational activity of the employees and the rate of innovation were strongly correlated (r = .63). Thus, the more innovative organizations were those in which the staff was more involved in professional activities. The employees' exposure to programmatic and technological development in their disciplines contributed ideas and information that led to a higher rate of innovation. The ideas and information were acquired through reading professional journals and participating in professional meetings. Similar to their previous findings, Aiken and Hage's 1971 publication showed little relationship between the professional training of employees and the rate of adoption of innovations (r = .19). See Table 9–3 for these correlations.

A large number of occupational specialties with professionalism results in organizational personnel placing high value on job-related knowledge and information. This diversity of background can then bring a variety of sources of information to bear, facilitating awareness and knowledge, decision-making, and to some extent, the trial of the new idea. However, it may have a detrimental effect on the implementation and routinization of the innovation. James Q. Wilson underscored this point when he found that high complexity led to awareness through diversity of knowledge, but that even during the decision-making process, complexity made it difficult for agreement to be reached as to which proposal for innovation was best, much less which method of implementation.[45] Several other studies, including Jean Carroll's, supported the thesis that complexity in organization may lead to innovation proposals, but that a more structured organization is necessary for the implementation and routinization of change.[46] Since these findings contradict those of Aiken and Hage, it is important to note that high complexity facilitates the initiation of a large number of innovations. As Aiken and Hage pointed out, although many of these innovations are never implemented, a greater proportion are implemented than in less complex organizations because of the larger number initiated. Thus high complexity may have a positive effect on the awareness, decision, and initiating stages of innovation and a negative effect on implementation and routinization, yet in the long run, the complex organization may implement more changes as a direct outcome of having initiated a larger number of innovations.

Centralization Correlates

Many theorists have suggested that decentralization in terms of decreased stratification of prestige and rewards and dispersion of

281

decision-making is necessary for innovation.[47] Victor Thompson argued further that concentrated power arrangements prevent innovation.[48] Likewise, T. N. Clark, with regard to higher education, and Hage and Aiken, with regard to health and welfare organizations, have found innovative organizations to be more decentralized.[49] As defined in chapter six, centralization refers to the way in which power is distributed in an organization. Hage and Aiken analyzed the hypothesis that the higher the centralization, the lower the rate of program change (i.e., the successful implementation of new programs) within an organization.[50] This hypothesis was based on the rationale that concentration of power in the hands of a few persons tends to preserve the status quo because of their ability to reject change, particularly when they occupy positions at the top of the hierarchical structure, where they would have a great deal more to lose through change than those at lower levels. If organizational change led to the restructuring of the organization, they would not only lose power but also symbolic and material rewards. Therefore, they are unlikely to initiate change because change often redistributes organizational rewards. An organization with lower centralization, that is, where decision-making is decentralized through the different functional units (departments) and down the hierarchical structure, permits the influence of ideas and interests of different occupations and personnel on different levels. These variations in thinking and feeling initiate greater change.

In their study of sixteen welfare agencies, Hage and Aiken asked the staff members how often they participated in organizational decisions regarding hiring, promotions, the adoption of new policies, and the adoption of new programs or services. The scores for each organization were based on the average in each decision-making area. In their 1967 study, they found that decentralization of decision-making was correlated with the rate of change in new programs over a five-year period (r = .49),[51] suggesting that when decisions are concentrated in the hands of a few personnel, there is less change. But their 1971 study showed a weaker correlation (r = .17) between the degree of participation in decision making and implemented innovation than did their 1967 study. They rationalized that the period from 1946–1966 showed a higher rate of innovations due to "increased federal resources available to these organizations. It is a reasonable interpretation that the rate of innovations was so high . . . that less participatory management styles had to be used in these organizations in order to implement the accelerated rate of innovation."[52]

In order to determine if the issues on which decisions were being made influenced program change, Hage and Aiken used a measure of hierarchy of authority that was primarily concerned with job decisions and control over work activities that might be kept within a given level or pushed up to the next highest level. In their 1967 study, the correlation between the hierarchy of authority (control over work) and program change over the five-year period was r = − .09;[53] these findings were confirmed in their 1971 publication. Thus, those organizations in which the decisions were less hierarchically stratified experienced a higher rate of program change, but the relationship was weak. The measure of decentralization of decision-making over global organizational issues was a better predictor of program change than the measure of hierarchical control (control over work decisions). One might conclude the type of power that is centralized within the organization is important to the rate of program change. Decentralization of work-related decisions is not as important to the flexibility of the organization as decentralization of control over various resources.

Similarly, Joseph Ben–David attributed scientific progress in the U.S. to the decentralized system of universities and to the competition among these institutions. Ben–David concluded that the U.S. had contributed more medical discoveries than France and England by 1910–1917 due to its decentralization of the medical profession, which afforded greater opportunity for creativity. Ben–David saw faculty as initiating new programs and departments. Due to competition among institutions, the professional scientists in this decentralized system of universities forced bureaucratic administrators to support faculty who wished to institute innovations that permitted more specialized research.[54]

Further evidence was contributed by Peter Blau's empirical analysis of data from 115 American universities and colleges. He analyzed the ability of universities to change their structure by adding departments in relatively new disciplines.[55] Two supplementary measures were used: (1) the recent creation of a new department and (2) abolishment of an old one. One index of centralization used by Blau in his research was who initiates the creation of a new department—faculty (a decentralized decision) or the administration (a centralized decision). Blau's hypothesis ("the more decentralized the decision making structure, the more innovative the organization"), although taken from the work of Terry Clark, was anticipated by both Hagstrom and Ben–David.[56] Blau's findings support the hypothesis that a decentralized structure is more innovative. The initiation of new departments was more frequent in institutions where decision-making was decentralized to the faculty. Blau concluded that "faculty initiative in proposing new departments increases the likelihood that new specialties have become institutionalized as departments."[57]

Blau's second measure of decentralization was the proportion of faculty members on the senate, controlling for institutional size. Large-scale participation of the faculty in the organization's governing body increased the likelihood of departmental innovation. Still another measure of decentralization—decentralized authority over faculty raises—had a positive effect on the creation of departments in new specialties. Blau's findings contradict Clark Kerr's assumption that innovation in the organizational structure of a university or college requires the intervention of top administrators because the faculty perpetuates vested interests in the status quo, as opposed to change.[58]

Similar to his conclusions concerning the relationship of complexity to innovation, Zaltman suggested that although the evidence is not conclusive, the effects of centralization can vary depending on the stage in the innovation process.[59] He saw decentralization facilitating the initiation of innovation, but, similar to Shepard,[60] indicated that when organizations reach the implementation stage, a more specific line of authority and centralization of decision-making is required. Again, the organization that possesses different distributions of power during different stages of the innovation process is more successful in completing all of the stages.

Formalization Correlates

One would expect an organization with less formalized rules and regulations to be more capable of initiating innovation. This is generally true because rules and regulations and their enforcement restrict the members of the organization from both considering and implementing alternatives. Robert Merton saw extreme conformity to rules and regulations as organizational pathology in which a job occupant compulsively follows the rules. Some flexibility of rules and regulations would have to be present at both the initiation and implementation stages of the change process. This flexibility has been operationalized in many ways and has been found to be positively correlated with innovation in the great majority of cases. For example, Burns and Stalker, emphasized freedom from rigid rules and narrow definitions of work roles; M. M. Rosen found freedom from formal rules and procedures in nonteaching hospitals; W. M.

284

Evan and G. Black found freedom from formalization of rules in business organizations to be related to innovation.[61]

In their 1967 study, Hage and Aiken used two measures of formalization: (1) the degree of job codification and (2) a measure of the degree of rule observation (enforcement of rules). Job codification was moderately negatively correlated (r = − .47) with the rate of successful implementations of new programs in the previous five years. Rule observation, however, had no association with the rate of program change.[62] In their follow-up analysis only one of four measures of formalization—existence of a rules manual—was found to be strongly negatively related to innovation. Neither of the two formalization measures used in the previous analysis were related to the implementation of innovations.[63] Hage and Aiken saw rules retarding not only the initiation of change but also its implementation:

> Rules may retard the implementation of new programs as well. The more rules there are in an organization, the more likely a new product or service is likely to run foul of them by making conflicting demands on the individuals involved. Whether an individual opts for obeying a new rule or for fulfilling the needs of a new program, the organization is likely to experience some difficulties. If the rule is obeyed, the program may be retarded or possibly even sabotaged. If the rule is not obeyed, there may be a temporary interruption of service in the organization. Experiences such as these—conflicting rules, breakdowns in organizational functioning, and other such consequences that flow from the implementing of change in a formalized structure—discourage an organization from attempting future changes.[64]

However, the evidence found in Hage and Aiken's 1971 research publication does not support the negative relationship between formalization and implementation of innovation.

Zaltman has offered an alternative explanation. He accepted the evidence of Shepard, who indicated that low formalization might be most appropriate at the initiation stage, whereas a high degree of formalization may be more appropriate during the implementation of innovation. He suggests that during the initiation stage, the organization needs to be as flexible and as open as possible to new sources of information and alternative courses of action, but during the implementation stage, "singleness of purpose" is required.[65] It is assumed that without clearly specified job descriptions, long range planning, and scheduling, there will be interpersonal, departmental and role conflict as a result of the disparity between the old procedures and the changes being implemented. Thus, it is possible that varying degrees of formalization are advantageous at different stages of the change process. At the information, decision and initiation stages, it may be beneficial for the organization to be open and for rules and regulations to be flexible. At the implementation and routinization stages, the establishment of rules and regulations may be beneficial for minimizing conflicts (role, interpersonal, and departmental).

It is also possible that Aiken and Hage did not find a negative correlation between formalization and innovation because their organizations were semiprofessional client–service oriented organizations and therefore formalization was low at all stages of the innovation process. Here the rules and regulations were internalized by the professionals. The negative relationship between formalization and initiation and implementation of change may be more apparent in industrial organizations or other less professional organizations.

Communication Correlates

Following from the argument in the previous section on complexity correlates of innovation (program change), when an organization is complex and exhibits a high rate of communication between parts, this communication increases the exchange of ideas, which is important for the initiation and implementation of innovations. Thus, we would expect organizations with a high intensity of communications to be more innovative. This hypothesis is supported by the writings of Victor Thompson and the empirical evidence of Evan and Black, who found communication between line and staff personnel accompanied a higher rate of innovation.[66] Likewise, Aiken and Hage found a strong positive relationship between several measures of communication and organization innovation. First, they found that innovative organizations had more elaborate committee structures (r = .46), and that these committees met more often (r = .53) than did those in noninnovative organizations. Second, the direction of communication in innovative organizations was upward, both interdepartmental (r = .45) and intradepartmental (r = .61). There was also some tendency for those at the same level in different departments to communicate (r = .37) and for innovative organizations to have less downward communication (r = – .32).[67] These correlations are found in Table 9–3.

The structural variables of decentralized decision-making, low formalization of jobs, and high specialization and professionalization facilitate the flow of communication of information and ideas, which is necessary for the initiation of organizational innovation and change. Similarly, the greater the organizational uncertainty concerning its external and internal environment, the more important it is for the communication networks to be open and the flow to be intense during the innovation process. On the other hand, high degrees of formalization and centralization are likely to restrict the channels of communication and reduce the amount of information available to the various parts of the organization. This lends to the air of secrecy generally found in centralized organizations. Further, any feedback in a centralized organization is likely to be selectively positive, another drawback since negative feedback is especially important during all stages of the innovation process.

Many ideas for change originate outside the organization and at lower levels in the organization. These ideas may never reach the appropriate decision-makers because of breakdowns in and barriers to communications or because various administrators screen out information or ideas before they reach the appropriate level of the organization. This lack of input from lower levels is especially detrimental to the cooperation of those at lower levels in the organization. Usually, the greater the participation in the initiation and decision-making stages of innovated change, the greater the organizational members' commitment to working through the implementation and routinization stages. Thus, resistance is reduced and innovation is facilitated.

SUMMARY

The greater the environmental complexity and instability and the greater the focal organization's dependency on its environment, the greater its ability to initiate innovation (program change). Also, the larger, the more technologically complex, and the greater the slack resources of the organization, the greater will be its ability to initiate innovation. Finally, decentralization of decision-making, low formalization of rules and procedures related to jobs, high specialization and professionalization, and high intensity of communication facilitate the initiation of innovation. Of course, there is evidence that implementation of these changes require a more stable, formalized and centralized organizational structure.

NOTES

1. Harry Levinson, "Asinine Attitudes Toward Motivation," *Harvard Business Review* 51, no. 1 (1973): 70–76.

2. J. Victor Baldridge and Robert Burnham, *The Adoption of Innovation: The Effects of Organizational Size, Differentiation, and Environment* (Stanford, Calif.: Stanford University, Stanford Center for Research and Development in Teaching, Research and Development Memorandum 108, 1973), p. 3.

3. This definition was adapted from Everett M. Rogers and Rekha Agarwala–Rogers, *Communication in Organizations* (New York: The Free Press, 1976), p. 150.

4. E. Mansfield, "Size of Firm, Market Structure, and Innovation," *Journal of Political Economy* 71 (December 1963): 556–576.

5. Lawrence B. Mohr, "Determinants of Innovation in Organizations," *American Political Science Review* 63 (March 1969): 111–126.

6. Jerald Hage and Michael Aiken, *Social Change in Complex Organizations* (New York: Random House, 1970), p. 13.

7. Michael Aiken and Jerald Hage, "The Organic Organization and Innovation," *Sociology* 5, no. 1 (January 1971): 64. Material in single quotes from Victor A. Thompson, "Bureaucracy and Innovation," *Administrative Science Quarterly* 10, no. 1 (June 1965): 1.

8. Aiken and Hage, "The Organic Organization and Innovation," p. 69.

9. Shirley Terreberry, "The Evolution of Organizational Environments," *Administrative Science Quarterly* 12, no. 4 (March 1968): 590–613.

10. Gerald Zaltman, Robert Duncan, and Jonny Holbek, *Innovations and Organizations* (New York: John Wiley & Sons, 1973), pp. 118, 120.

11. Charles Carter and Bruce Williams, *Industry and Technical Progress: Factors Governing the Speed of Application of Science* (London: Oxford University Press, 1957).

12. Everett Rogers, *Diffusion of Innovations* (New York: The Free Press, 1962).

13. Hage and Aiken, *Social Change in Complex Organizations*.

14. Anthony Downs, *Inside Bureaucracy* (Boston: Little, Brown, and Company, 1966), p. 191.

15. Everett M. Rogers and F. Floyd Shoemaker, *Communication of Innovations: A Cross-Cultural Approach* (New York: The Free Press, 1971), p. 106.

16. Donald W. Taylor, "Decision Making and Problem Solving," in James March, ed., *Handbook of Organizations* (Chicago: Rand McNally, 1965), pp. 61, 62.

17. Hage and Aiken, *Social Change in Complex Organizations*, pp. 31–32.

18. Ibid.

19. Francis J. Aguilar, *Scanning the Business Environment* (New York: Macmillan Co., 1967), p. 54.

20. Sumner Meyers and D. G. Marquis, *Successful Commercial Innovations* (Washington, D.C.: National Science Foundation, 1969); Carter and Williams, *Industry and Technical Progress: Factors Governing the Speed of Application of Science*.

21. Charles Perrow, *Complex Organizations: A Critical Essay* (Glenview, Ill.: Scott, Foresman, 1972), p. 5.

22. Baldridge and Burnham, *The Adoption of Innovation: The Effects of Organizational Size, Differentiation and Environment*, p. 173.

23. Aiken and Hage, "The Organic Organization and Innovation," p. 78.

24. James G. March and Herbert A. Simon, *Organizations* (New York: John Wiley & Sons, Inc., 1958), pp. 172–210.

25. Aiken and Hage, "The Organic Organization and Innovation," p. 77.

26. Mohr, "Detriminants of Innovation in Organizations"; Arnold D. Kaluzny et al., "Innovation in Health Services: A Comparative Study of Hospitals and Health Departments," in Arnold D. Kaluzny, ed., *Innovation in Health Care Organizations: An Issue in Organizational Change* (Chapel Hill, N.C.: University of North Carolina, School of Public Health, 1974); Mansfield, "Size of Firm, Market Structure, and Innovation"; Selwyn Becker and F. Stafford, "Some Determinants of Organizational Success," *The Journal of Business* 40, no. 4 (October 1967): 511–518.

27. Jerald Hage and Michael Aiken, "Program Change and Organizational Properties, A Comparative Analysis," *American Journal of Sociology* 72, no. 5 (March 1967): 503–519; Aiken and Hage, "The Organic Organization and Innovation," pp. 78–79.

28. J. Victor Baldridge and Robert A. Burnham, "Organizational Innovation: Individual, Organizational, and Environmental Impact," *Administrative Science Quarterly* 20, no. 2 (June 1975): 170.

29. Ibid., p. 172.

30. Peter M. Blau, *The Organization of Academic Work* (New York: Wiley Interscience, 1973), p. 204.

31. Warren O. Hagstrom, *The Scientific Community* (New York: Basic Books, 1965), p. 224.

32. Harvey Sapolsky, "Organizational Structure and Innovation," *Journal of Business* 40, no. 4 (October 1967): 497–510.

33. Hage and Aiken, *Social Change in Complex Organizations.*

34. Zaltman, Duncan, and Holbek, *Innovations and Organizations,* p. 131.

35. Paul R. Lawrence and Jay W. Lorsch, "Differentiation and Integration in Complex Organizations," *Administrative Science Quarterly* 12, no. 1 (June 1967): 18.

36. Karl Weick, *The Social Psychology of Organizing* (Reading, Mass.: Addison, Wesley, 1969).

37. Herbert A. Shepard, "Innovation–Resisting and Innovation-Producing Organizations," *Journal of Business* 40, no. 4 (October 1967): 470–477.

38. Ibid., p. 474.

39. Hage and Aiken, "Program Change and Organizational Properties, A Comparative Analysis."

40. Aiken and Hage, "The Organic Organization and Innovation," p. 71.

41. Sapolsky, "Organizational Structure and Innovation."

42. Aiken and Hage, "The Organic Organization and Innovation," p. 71.

43. March and Simon, *Organizations,* 194–195.

44. Baldridge and Burnham, "Organizational Innovation: Individual, Organization, and Environmental Impact."

45. James Q. Wilson, "Innovation in Organizations: Notes Toward a Theory," in James D. Thompson, ed., *Approaches to Organizational Design* (Pittsburgh: University of Pittsburgh Press, 1966), pp. 193–213.

46. Jean Carroll, "A Note on Departmental Autonomy and Innovation in Medical Schools," *Journal of Business* 40, no. 4 (October 1967): 531–534.

47. Tom Burns and G. M. Stalker, *The Management of Innovation* (London: Tavistock Publications, 1961).

48. Victor A. Thompson, "Bureaucracy and Innovation," *Administrative Science Quarterly* 10, no. 1 (June 1965): 1–20.

49. Terry N. Clark, "Institutionalization of Innovation in Higher Education," *Administrative Science Quarterly* 13, no. 1 (June 1968): 1–25; Hage and Aiken, "Program Change and Organizational Properties, A Comparative Analysis"; Aiken and Hage, "The Organic Organization and Innovation," p. 73; Hage and Aiken, *Social Change in Complex Organizations*, p. 38.

50. Hage and Aiken, *Social Change in Complex Organizations*, p. 38.

51. Ibid., p. 42.

52. Aiken and Hage, "The Organic Organization and Innovation," p. 73.

53. Hage and Aiken, *Social Changes in Complex Organizations*, p. 43.

54. Joseph Ben–David, "Scientific Productivity and Academic Organization in Nineteenth Century Medicine," *American Sociological Review* 25, no. 6 (December 1960): 828–843; and Ben–David, "The Universities and the Growth of Science in Germany and the United States," *Minerva* 7, no. 2 (1968/69): 19.

55. Blau, *The Organization of Academic Work*.

56. Clark, "Institutionalization of Innovation in Higher Education," p. 21; Hagstrom, *The Scientific Community*, p. 28; Ben–David, "The Universities and the Growth of Science in Germany and the United States."

57. Blau, *The Organization of Academic Work*, pp. 201–202.

58. Ibid., p. 202.

59. Zaltman, Duncan, and Holbek, *Innovations and Organizations*, p. 144.

60. Shepard, "Innovation–Resisting and Innovation Producing Organizations."

61. Robert K. Merton, "Bureaucratic Structure and Personality," in Amitai Etzioni, ed., *Complex Organizations: A Sociological Reader* (New York: Holt, Rinehart, Winston, 1960), pp. 48–61; Burns and Stalker, *The Management of Innovation;* M. M. Rosen, "Administrative Controls and Innovation," *Behavioral Science* 13 (January 1968): 36–43; William M. Evan and G. Black, "Innovation in Business Organizations: Some Factors Associated with Success or Failure of Staff Proposals," *The Journal of Business* 40, no. 4 (October 1967): 519–530.

62. Hage and Aiken, *Social Change in Complex Organizations*, pp. 44–45.

63. Aiken and Hage, "The Organic Organization and Innovation," p. 76.

64. Hage and Aiken, *Social Change in Complex Organizations*, p. 44.

65. Shepard, "Innovation–Resisting and Innovation-Producing Organizations," p. 474; Zaltman, Duncan, and Holbek, *Innovations and Organizations*, pp. 139–140.

66. Thompson, "Bureaucracy and Innovation"; Evan and Black, "Innovation in Business Organizations: Some Factors Associated with Success or Failure of Staff Proposals."

67. Aiken and Hage, "The Organic Organization and Innovation," p. 75.

10

CONFLICT

a. complexity
b. centralization
c. formalization
d. communication

INTRODUCTION

The two major types of organizational change are (1) innovation (program change) and (2) conflict. As was demonstrated in the last chapter, innovation is a routine, often institutionalized, organization function. Conflict, on the other hand, is generally not institutionalized. Conflict may be viewed as desirable or undesirable, as a functional or dysfunctional process. Generally, the semantics used in labeling conflict will give the reader some idea of the writer's value judgments. For example, some authors see conflict as an alteration of normative behavior. James March and Herbert Simon define conflict as "a breakdown in standard mechanism of decision making";[1] Alan Beals and Bernard Siegel, as "breaches in normally expected behavior."[2] Others see conflict as a threat to stability; for example, J. Marek terms it "a threat to cooperation,"[3] and Richard Walton describes it as "opposition processes in any of several forms."[4]

MODELS OF ORGANIZATIONAL CONFLICT

As was stated in chapter one, a model serves several functions. First, it helps define those aspects of an organization that are most salient and critical to the analysis. Concurrently, it eliminates those issues that are not to be considered in the given analysis. Second, a model defines an appropriate framework for addressing the phenomena to be studied and defines the basic premises of those phenomena. There are two basic models of organizational conflict: (1) the functional conflict model, the more prevalent in organizational literature, and (2) the dialectical model. A brief discussion of each model follows.

Functional Conflict Model

The functional conflict model of organizations emphasizes the fragmentation of the system, which is based on the assumption of differing values, goals, interests, and so on. This fragmentation is composed of groups that attempt to gain advantages over other groups through the process of conflict. The functional perspective assumes that the outcomes of conflict depend in a large part on group pressure. Thus, much depends on the capacity of the group to defend its interests and to press for its goals.

In order to evaluate the consequences of conflict, functional analysts ask the question, functional for whom? They assume that conflict will be functional for some groups and dysfunctional for others, either in the short run or the long run. In exceptional cases, they may assume that conflict is functional for both parties. For example, William Kornhauser argued that bureaucratic–professional conflict may be functional in the long run for both the professional and the bureaucrat, for the profession and the organization.[5]

A major concern of most functional theorists is the reduction or arbitration of conflict. For example, one approach to functional conflict analysis is to define conflict as a joint decision process characterized by negotiation and bargaining. The competing interest groups conflict over limited resources and power. An arbitrator attempts through negotiation to increase these limited resources or to decrease the demands of the respective interest groups. But even when these interest groups conflict, cooperation occurs along with competition. In this model, often more emphasis is placed on cooperation in conflict than on opposition.

One example of this decision model is the political model applied to American universities by J. Victor Baldridge and later by Frank R. Kemerer and J. Victor Baldridge.[6] The major characteristics of this political model is that it concentrates on the policy-forming processes. Decision-making is central to the establishment of policies because it determines which goals are paramount for the organization. These are not routine, normal, and recurring decisions; rather, they are major decisions that determine what will be done. Establishment of these policies is viewed as more political than bureaucratic. In order to accommodate negotiation in his model, Baldridge adopted Schelling's "Strategic Conflict" model, which is based on exchange. Baldridge wrote:

Schelling suggests that *pure cooperation* is also rarely found in human relations, since every man is usually looking out for his own interests. The most realistic interpretation of conflict, Shelling believes, must be in the middle ground, for it includes elements of both conflict and cooperation, a relation that he calls *strategic* conflict. The typical relationship between disputers, for example, is that of exchange: I will trade you an advantage if you will give me one. Only as a last resort will all-out conflict result, for this is expensive and dangerous. The typical form of conflict then, is strategy and negotiation in which each party trades favors in order to gain advantages.[7]

Baldridge's model of Schelling's strategic conflict is found in Table 10–1. Baldridge saw conflict in universities as a strategic interplay of struggle and cooperation: ". . . most students have no real interest in bringing the university down; instead, their objective is to wring concessions and advantages from a reluctant power structure."[8]

The basic assumptions of the functional conflict model are:

1. The organization is a system.
2. The system is fragmented by interest groups.
3. Interest groups have different values, goals, and interests.
4. Conflict may be functional for some or all parts of the organization.
5. The outcomes of conflict depend upon the amount of pressure exerted by interest groups.
6. The conflict process is political.

TABLE 10–1 Schelling's Model: Comparison of Three Images of Conflict

COMPLETE CONFLICT	"STRATEGIC CONFLICT"	COMPLETE COOPERATION
Zero–sum concept	Negotiation	Cooperation
1. Your loss is my gain and vice versa.	1. Exchange and bargaining for advantage.	1. Identical interests.
	2. Mixed motive: both cooperation and conflict.	2. Our action is for our mutual benefit.
Game theory equivalent	Game theory equivalent	Game theory equivalent
1. Pursuit or chess.	1. Mock labor negotiations.	1. Rendezvous or charades.
2. One person's loss is the other's gain.	2. Each side wins some and loses some.	2. No one wins unless both do.

Source: J. Victor Baldridge, *Power and Conflict in the University* (New York: John Wiley & Sons, Inc., 1971), p. 203.

7. The conflict process is characterized by struggle and co-operation of both parties.
8. Policy decisions are central to conflict.
9. The system not only exists but is to be preserved.
10. Reduction of conflict through arbitration or similar methods is desirable.

Dialectical Conflict Model

The dialectical approach to conflict assumes that every organization contains fundamental contradictions. The organization is characterized by an unstable social order with a tendency toward dissolution. The instability of the organization grows out of these contradictions, which are never fully resolved. Thus, structures, processes, and other organizational dimensions are never fully institutionalized; there are always inconsistencies and incompatibilities. Within any organization are contradictions that have not been resolved, including incompatible structural arrangements, conflicting goals and vested interests of distinct groups in the organization, and conflicting perspectives or ideologies held by participants. The social order of every organization is politically negotiated. The structural patterns in the organization are to be understood on the basis of political rather than administrative models. The organization is constantly undergoing change and must be understood in terms of process. Thus, the organization invariably incorporates divergent tendencies, conflicting perspectives, and incompatible structural features. The sources of these tensions may be highly varied, for example, socialization patterns for different occupational groups, overlapping memberships of participants in different organizations, and contradictory relationships in other organizations and publics in the environment. These potentially contradictory elements play a powerful role in crisis periods when substantial organizational change is possible. Such crisis periods are important in the creation of new organizational patterns, which prevail in the organization in later periods of greater stability.[9]

The assumptions of the dialectical conflict model are:

1. Every organization contains inherent contradictions.
2. These contradictions lead to conflict.
3. Change through conflict is inevitable and ubiquitous.
4. Organizations are processes.
5. Change through conflict is valued.
6. Every social organization is politically negotiated.

CONFLICT IN ORGANIZATIONS DEFINED

Organizational conflict has been defined to include both the affective and behavioral aspects of conflict. The affective aspects are the emotions (stress, hostility, tension, and anxiety) of the individuals in organizations; the behavioral aspects are the overt expression of conflict, which ranges from passive resistance to open aggression. Ralf Dahrendorf argued for such a broad definition of conflict that would be appropriate at varying levels of organizational analysis when he used the term *conflict* to denote "contests, competitions, disputes, and tensions as well as for manifest clashes between social forces."[10] Likewise, Rensis and Jane Likert defined organizational conflict as an actor striving for his own preferred outcome which, if achieved, precludes the attainment by others of their own preferred outcome, thus producing the element of hostility.[11] Thus, the Likerts, Dahrendorf, and others have cited the distinguishing characteristics of conflict as an "incompatible difference of objectives"[12]—the desire on the part of both actors to obtain what is available only to one party.

But authors such as Stuart Schmidt and Thomas Kochan have argued that some distinction between behavioral conflict and its antecedent and psychological states should be made.[13] They wrote that perception of goal incompatibility is a necessary precondition for both competition and conflict. The essential difference between competition and conflict is in the "interference or blocking activities of the two entities."[14] Within the organization, the units may each be dependent on the same resources or interdependent on each other for completion of some activities. On the other hand, units may be mutually dependent during activity stages but not during the goal attainment stages of its functioning. During the activity stages, dependencies such as scheduling, compliance and coordination are prevalent.[15] When activities are interdependent but goals are incompatible, there is high potential for conflict.[16] Thus, conflict occurs under conditions of dependency of shared resources and interdependent activities coupled with incompatible goals. Schmidt and Kochan constructed a model of conflict in which perceived goal incompatibility and perceived opportunity for interference determine behavioral conflict. See Figure 10–1. It should be made explicit that conflict, in this model, is overt behavior or actual interference and blocking. This definition fits the interest group models discussed previously and assumes that interference is intentional rather than

FIGURE 10-1   The Process of Conflict

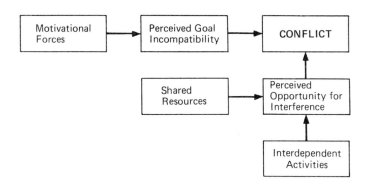

Source: Stuart M. Schmidt and Thomas A. Kochan, "Conflict: Toward Conceptual Clarity," *Administrative Science Quarterly* 17, no. 3 (September 1972): 363.

fortuitous.[17] Thus, Schmidt and Kochan saw the potential for conflict as dependent upon three contiguous variables—(1) the relative incompatibility of goals, (2) the degree of shared resources, and (3) the interdependence of activities. This three-dimensional model of the relationship between conditions for conflict is found in Figure 10-2. The highest potential for conflict is found in the area marked Y, where the units hold highly incompatible goals, are highly dependent on shared resources, and have high interdependence of activities.[18]

In the area designated J, the units would be expected to have a low potential for conflict due to the low incompatibility of goals, low shared resources, and independent activities. The line UJ is the potential for conflict vector as it represents the diagonal continuum between the nodal areas of high (U) and low (J) potential conflict.[19]

Schmidt and Kochan pointed out that interference or blocking (conflict) can take place either (1) during the period of resource acquisition, (2) during activity stages, or (3) in both the acquisition of

FIGURE 10–2   Potential for Conflict Behavior

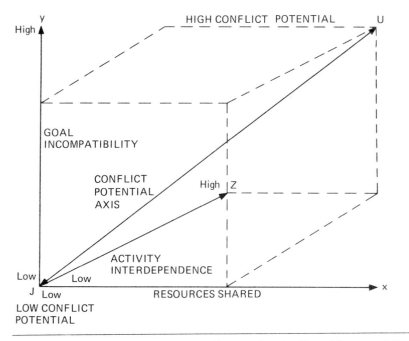

Source: Stuart M. Schmidt and Thomas A. Kochan, "Conflict: Toward Conceptual Clarity," *Administrative Science Quarterly* 17, no. 3 (September 1972): 366.

resources and execution of activities.[20] John Dutton and Richard Walton's study of production and sales interdepartmental conflict evidenced both resource acquisition interference and activity interference.[21] Here the necessary preconditions of incompatible goals and interdependency of activities and resources were present. Production concentrated on goals of efficiency while sales concentrated on customer service. Each department attempted to maximize its goals and activities while limiting that of the other department by withholding vital resources and obstructing activities. The production department withheld production of commodities, which kept sales from supplying customer needs. The sales department withheld vital information concerning customer demands, which obstructed cost estimates and productions. Thus, interdepartmental conflict existed between the two units.

LEVELS OF ORGANIZATIONAL CONFLICT

We will differentiate among the several levels of organizational conflict with a concentration on interunit or interdepartmental conflict, often termed "organizational" conflict. Societal level conflicts will not be discussed here because they are not considered to be organizational conflict, although organizations often play important roles in societal conflict.

Intrapersonal Conflict

Intrapersonal conflict exists in the cognitive and affective realms of an individual's mind. Thus, an individual may perceive that he or she is conflicting with the organization or other employees, but the conflict in fact exists only in that person's mind, not at the behavioral level. Role conflicts, for example, are often intrapersonal. When the individual's goals are not being met, or that person's job description is not broad enough, psychological pressures, tension, strain, or anxiety may result; if the conflict remains intrapersonal, it will not be known to others. Of course, it is possible that these pressures may influence the performance of the employee and thus have an effect on the functioning of the organization.

Interpersonal Conflict

When the dissatisfied individual makes manifest his or her discontent toward some other employee (for example, a supervisor or peer in that organization), the conflict becomes interpersonal. There are several levels of intensity of interpersonal conflict, from passive resistance to physical assault. The distinguishing characteristic of interpersonal conflict is that two or more persons within the organization conflict at the behavioral level, for example, conflict over work rules and production quotas.

Interunit or Interdepartmental Conflict

Intraorganizational conflict includes intrapersonal and interpersonal conflict, as well as interunit conflict. But these first two types of conflict generally concern a very small portion of the total organization, whereas interunit or interdepartmental conflict concerns two or more groups, units, or departments within the organization and thus has more pervasive structural consequences for the organization. These groups generally compete for organizational resources. Conflict between research and production departments in an industrial organization is one example of interunit conflict; conflict between bureaucratic and professional is another. The former is lateral and the latter is vertical conflict. These conflicts cannot be reduced by improving individual relations. Changes must be made at the organizational level. For example, more resources might be made available to the conflicting groups.

Interorganizational Conflict

The final category is interorganizational conflict between organizations with competing interests. The conflict may be over scarce economic resources, power, clients, or customers. Whatever the resource or market, it is valued by both organizations and they not only compete for but conflict over its acquisition. For example, oil companies conflict over drilling rights and welfare organizations over legitimate domains.

DIRECTIONS OF CONFLICT

Louis Pondy identified three types of conflict among subunits in organizations, based on the relationships of the conflicting units to each other: (1) bargaining conflict among the parties to interest groups, (2) bureaucratic conflict between parties to a superior–subordinate relationship, and (3) systems conflict among parties that are laterally related.[22] It appears that types two and three, vertical and horizontal conflict, respectively, are mutually exclusive categories of intraorganizational conflict. But type one conceptually overlaps the other two. Organizational conflict generally takes place between interest groups in an organization, which may be (1) hierarchically arranged (ranked) or (2) horizontally arranged (at the same rank).

Horizontal Conflict

Horizontal or lateral conflict is between actors in the same department or departments (units) that are functionally related. Since these two entities are on the same hierarchical level, the issue is not control of one by the other, but their coordination. Interdepartmental conflict is an example of lateral conflict. Richard Walton, John Dutton, and Thomas Cafferty wrote:

Relationship between departments in a formal organization can be characterized by the amount of responsiveness of a department, the accuracy of information exchange, and the attitudes of department members toward the other department or its members. Interdepartmental conflict means there is interference rather than considerateness, information is distorted or withheld, and attitudes of annoyance and distrust exist between departments.[23]

Thus, departments place restrictions on one other and at the same time work under departmental and general restrictions. When one department cannot, or will not, meet the needs and demands of other departments, conflict often results. Major conflicts between departments occur over their dependencies on common resources and competing goals, and activities (procedures, deadlines, etc.). Thus, in order to eliminate these conflicts, dependency, competition for resources and conflicting goals would all have to be eliminated. A "loose fit" between departments could reduce some of this conflict. This might be achieved through loose schedules, buffer and coordinating groups, and so on.

Vertical Conflict

Vertical conflict takes place between hierarchically ranked positions and groups. Such conflicts may arise because either the superordinate or subordinate perceives that the other has overstepped his or her bounds. Subordinates may feel that the superordinates are excessively demanding, obstructing their autonomy by maximizing rules, punitive regulations, and other arbitrary acts. In any case, the superordinates' interests and goals are incompatible with and, in many cases, in direct competition with those of the subordinate. With these differences come impersonal, instrumental relationships, formalized by rules and procedures. When this occurs, the autonomy of the subordinate is even more important because the superordinate, due to his or her dissimilarity to the subordinate, is unlikely to see the subordinate's point of view and consequently will not act in the subordinate's interests. Thus, their relationship is totally instrumental, and maximizing interests for oneself or one's group becomes the name of the game.

Conflict between professionals and bureaucrats in organizations, as well as between professional and bureaucratic modes of organizing, is a well documented type of vertical conflict. Because the bureaucratic organization emphasizes hierarchical power, legitimized

301

by written rules and procedures, and the professional organization emphasizes expertise legitimized by professional norms, some researchers have found the simultaneous existence of these two types of organization to result in conflict.[24] The bases for this type of conflict are many: bureaucratic organizations emphasize standardization and routinization of procedures, while professional organizations emphasize uniqueness of the product (client) and complexity of the work process; bureaucratic organizations emphasize service to the organization and achievement of organizational goals, while professional organizations stress service to the client; bureaucratic organizations emphasize loyalty to the organization, while professional organizations emphasize loyalty to the profession. Numerous studies have shown that employees' orientation to a profession rather than the organization results in conflict.[25] Much of this conflict is intrapersonal, based on overriding loyalty to the profession rather than the bureaucratic organization. Interpersonal conflict results over bureaucratic and professional differences regarding formalization of rules and supervision.[26] Finally, interunit conflicts of bureaucratic and professional authority is evidenced in Dalton's analysis of industrial plants. Here conflict hindered organizational goal attainment.[27] Yet conflict may be avoided if either the professional or bureaucrat has not internalized the norms of his or her unit. For example, Ronald Corwin found that nurses who subscribed to both bureaucratic and professional norms *simultaneously* were less able to perform their roles than those nurses who subscribed to one or the other set of norms. Corwin concluded that conflict was avoided because of the weak professional norms of some nurses.[28] Similarly, Peter Blau and Richard Scott found that less professional welfare workers tended to support bureaucratic rules and procedures, while more professional workers were likely to deviate and violate organizational rules by maximizing service to the client, thus minimizing organizational efficiency.[29] Yet at this time, there is a growing body of literature suggesting that structural arrangements are being generated that permit the fusion of bureaucratic and professional characteristics, or at least the accommodation of such seemingly incompatible characteristics.[30]

INTENSITY OF CONFLICT

The intensity of behavioral conflict ranges from passive promotion of unit interests to secession and seizure of power. The passive forms of interference may be no more than withdrawal of communication or cooperation. If one unit refuses to cooperate, the second unit will be unable to reach its goals, which will be advantageous to the first unit. The highly intense forms of organizational conflict have been discussed by Cornelius Lammer and Mayer Zald.[31] Of course, the most intense type of conflict is one in which the organization is completely abolished. This type of change is not a structural alteration of some aspects of the organization but is a complete abolishment of the total organizational structure. It may result in the substitution of a new and completely different structure with differing goals. Here there is no room for competition or compromise. This state of conflict is called *revolution*. The employees of an organization seldom engage in revolts for complete change of organizational goals and structure—this type of change is more likely to originate outside the organization. Those who lead the attack on the existing structure use violent tactics. They seek support through popular appeals for "justice," claiming a gap between "what is" and "what ought to be." As is true in most types of conflict, the changes for which they fight are in *their* best interests.

Both Georg Simmel and Lewis Coser have dealt with the conditions which intensify conflict.[32] Since much of Coser's work is an extension of Simmel's, only Coser's is discussed here. Jonathan Turner has summarized Coser's major propositions related to the intensity of conflict (see Table 10–2).[33] Although many of these propositions deal at the primary group levels, they are relevant to our analysis of organizations.

STAGES IN THE CONFLICT PROCESS

Conflict is viewed as a dynamic process of sequential and more or less linear overlapping stages. As in the case of the innovation process, one could identify a large number of stages and substages, but we will discuss four stages of the conflict process: (1) awareness, (2) interest articulation, (3) overt conflict and policy formulation, and (4) policy execution. The conflict process addresses itself primarily to the goal setting and acquisition of power to promote interests as opposed to achieving efficiency and effectiveness of the more routine administrative structure of an organization.

Awareness and Knowledge

The potential conflicting parties must first become aware that there are basic differences of interests, values, and goals. Some

303

TABLE 10–2   The Intensity of Conflict

I. The more the conditions causing the outbreak of conflict are realized, the more intense the conflict.

II. The greater the emotional involvement of members in a conflict, the more intense the conflict.

   A. The more primary the relations among parties to a conflict, the more emotional involvement.

      1. The smaller the primary groups where conflict occurs, the more emotional the involvement.

      2. The more primary the relations among parties, the less likely the open expression of hostility, but the more intense the expression in a conflict situation.

   B. The more secondary relations among parties to a conflict, the more segmental their participation and the less the emotional involvement.

      1. The more secondary relations, the more frequent the conflict, but the less the emotional involvement.

      2. The larger the secondary group, the more frequent the conflict, but the less the emotional involvement.

III. The more rigid the social structure, the less will be the availability of institutionalized means for absorbing conflict and tensions, and the more intense the conflict.

   A. The more primary the relations, the more rigid the structure.

      1. The less stable the primary relations, the more rigid the structure of those relations.

      2. The more stable the primary relations, the less rigid the structure of those relations.

   B. The more secondary (based on functional interdependence) the relations among parties where conflict occurs, the more likely are institutionalized means for absorbing conflict and tensions, and the less intense the conflict.

   C. The greater the control mechanism of the system, the more rigid the structure and the more intense the conflict.

IV. The more groups engage in conflicts over their realistic (objective) interests, the less intense the conflicts.

   A. The more groups conflict over realistic interests, the more likely they are to seek compromises over means to realize their interests.

      1. The greater the power differentials between groups in conflict, the less likely alternative means are to be sought.

      2. The more rigid the system where conflict occurs, the less availability of alternative means.

V. The more groups conflict over nonrealistic issues (false interests), the more intense the conflict.

   A. The more conflict occurs over nonrealistic issues, the greater the emotional involvement of the parties in the conflict and the more intense the conflict.

      1. The more intense previous conflict between groups, the greater the emotional involvement in subsequent conflict.

   B. The more rigid the system where conflict occurs, the more likely is the conflict to be nonrealistic.

   C. The more realistic conflict endures, the more nonrealistic issues emerge.

   D. The more the conflicting groups have emerged for purposes of conflict, the more nonrealistic the subsequent conflicts.

VI. The more conflicts are objectified above and beyond individual self-interest, the more intense the conflict.

   A. The more ideologically unified a group, the more conflicts transcend individual self-interest.

      1. The more ideologically unified is a group, the more common are the goals of a group, and the more they transcend individual self-interest.

      2. The more ideologically unified is a group, the more will conflicts be entered with a clear conscience, and the more they transcend individual self-interest.

VII. The more the conflict in a group occurs over core values and issues, the more intense the conflict.

   A. The more rigid the structure where conflict occurs, the more likely is conflict to occur over core values and issues.

   B. The more emotional involvement in a situation where conflict occurs, the more likely it is to occur over core values and issues.

Source: Jonathan H. Turner, *The Structure of Sociological Theory* (Homewood, Ill.: The Dorsey Press, 1974), pp. 112–113.

individuals will become cognitively or affectively aware of these differences. Information is then communicated to other individuals who possess similar characteristics and attitudes. Parties are made aware of the injustices, unequal distribution of scarce resources, conflict of values, and competition for resources and goal attainment. The communication of information and concurrent advocation of the interest groups is a necessary preliminary step to articulation of interests. At this stage, the ideological position of each group, especially the protestors', is beginning to form and the central conflict issues are developed.

Interest Articulation and Factionalization

Any complex organization consists of individuals with diverse life styles, educations, incomes, values, and goals. When these individuals form groups to promote their interests over those of others, the organization becomes factionalized. These interest groups politicize for both membership and economic support. They translate their interests into pressures through exerting influences on those who have an input into decision-making or by themselves gaining control of the decision-making processes. The greater the differences between interest groups, the more likely the conflict will intensify and become violent; thus, for those who desire major structural changes, interest articulation is a major stage in the conflict process.

During the factionalization phase, strategies are developed. Subordinates conceive an elaborate and extensive plan as to how they will gain the resources needed for conflict and how the conflict will take place. At the same time, tactics (violent or nonviolent, force or negotiation) are outlined. According to Cornelius Lammer, the actions available to the protestor of organizational action include: violence, the threat of violence, persuasion, work stoppages, strikes, and other means of depriving the superiors of cooperation.[34] However, Lammer sees violence as generally limited to secession and seizure in power movements.

Overt Conflict and Policy Formulation

During the overt conflict stage, actual competition and conflict occur over power, prestige, and resources. The interest groups may originate outside the organization, while others originate within. Those originating outside the organization, through clients or customers, may have as much, or more, power than conflicting groups that originate within the organization, since internal groups are generally subject to the sanctions of the organization. If the protesting group loses, these sanctions are often severe. Force, negotiation and compromise are all aspects of the conflict process. Which of these is most prominent depends on the power, intent, and origin of each of the conflicting parties. Conflict may be the only way in which some members of an organization can force other members to relinquish or reallocate power and resources.

Depending on the decision of the victorious party, a new policy may be instituted or the old one may be retained. Should the challenging party reap the major benefits of the conflict, those policies that served as ideological positions in the interest articulation phase have a high probability of being instituted. Although the form in which they are instituted may not coincide with the expectations of the constituency, this new policy becomes the official position of the new authority structure.

Execution of Policy

The execution of policy is the normal, routine work of the organization as outlined in job descriptions and standardized in procedures. The policies of the new authority structure are executed, and this gives rise to new interest groups, ideologies, strategies, and tactics, which will lead to further conflict. Thus, this process is a self-perpetuating one. The losers may take up the conflict anew or new interest groups may form in opposition to the policies, processes, structure, and goals of the recently created administration.

CORRELATES OF CONFLICT

From the perspective of maximizing organization efficiency and effectiveness, conflict, like other types of organizational change, may facilitate some of these dimensions while limiting others. Thus conflict is not related to all performance variables in the same manner. Similar to innovation, conflict is often viewed as an intervening variable between the independent environmental, contextual, and structural variables and the dependent performance variables. But as an intervening variable, conflict may simultaneously decrease the quantity and increase the quality of production. Thus, conflict facilitates some performance dimensions while limiting others. In addition, conflict is affected in different degrees by organizational environments, contexts, and structures.

There are several shortcomings to much of the research on organizational conflict. First, those who have analyzed the relationship of conflict to other organizational dimensions have generally concentrated, in the functional manner, upon preserving the system. Thus, they have dealt with relatively minor internal conflicts which do not alter, to any great extent, the structure of the organization. Cases in point are the studies of Corwin and Walton, Dutton, and Cafferty,[35] which will be discussed later in this section. Many of these analyses concentrated on interpersonal and intergroup behavior (disagreements, disputes, disturbances), and conflict was often viewed as the unanticipated or unintended consequence of a given structural arrangement. The analyst attempted to define the structural arrangement that gave birth to the conflict in hopes that a change in structure would eliminate or reduce that conflict. Thus, much of this research was aimed at conflict reduction or management. Further, the majority of the research on conflict has been self-reported questionnaire data; thus, the research has measured the employee's perception of conflict. For example, some of Corwin's predictor variables (size, complexity, etc.) were global–institutional rather than attitudinal measures, but the conflict measures were perceptual.[36] Because behavior has not been observed, the incidences and intensity of conflict may be greatly overstated or understated, depending on the perceptions of the individual.

Because only a relatively small number of studies have investigated the environmental, contextual, and structural correlates of conflict, the following discussion and generalizations are presented as tentative rather than definitive. The lack of organizational conflict research is at least partially due to the overriding concern of most organizational theorists for order, stability, coordination, and control.

Environmental Correlates

The major link of the organization to its environment is its dependence on other social collectives, including organizations, for physical and human resources. These resource inputs are necessary for the workflow process which, in turn, supports organizational objectives. Unless resources are unlimited, the organization must compete with other organizations in its task environment. When resources are limited and organizations are dependent, or perceive they are dependent, on the same sources, conflict is likely to occur between these organizations.

This dependency also plays an important role in supporting conflict at the subunit level. Walton and Dutton found mutual task dependency to be positively related to organizational conflict. Mutual task dependency was defined as "the extent to which units or departments depend upon each other for assistance, information, compliance or other coordinative acts in the performance of their respective tasks."[37] Thus, when individuals of two departments find themselves dependent upon each other for the completion of a specific task, they are more likely to conflict. Conflict potential also exists when units depend on a common pool of scarce organizational resources: physical space, equipment, staff and clerical personnel, operating funds, and capital funds. If the units that are dependent on a common pool of resources also have interdependent tasks, the competition for scarce resources will tend to decrease interunit problem solving and coordination.

Contextual Correlates

Few studies have analyzed the relationships of size and technology to organizational conflict. A notable exception is Corwin's study of teachers and administrators in twenty-eight public high schools in Pennsylvania, Michigan, and Indiana, in which he found organizational size to be positively correlated with almost every measure of conflict.[38] See Table 10–3. Although this evidence is hardly adequate basis for a global generalization, some support exists in the fact that the structural variables that are positively correlated with size are also positively correlated with conflict. This evidence is presented in the next section.

The technological theorists have constructed models that attempt to explain the reduction of conflict between bureaucrats and professionals,[39] for example, Perrow's model discussed in chapter two. This typology is based on two dimensions of technology: (1) the frequency with which the organization faces exceptions, and (2) the extent to which it utilizes knowledge that provides precise, analytical processes in solving problems. Where an organization faces many exceptions and lacks a precise body of knowledge from which solutions can be rigorously derived, structural arrangements must be flexible and decisions left to the discretion of the professional. In this type of organization, the rate of conflict between professionals and bureaucrats is often high.

Structural Correlates

Complexity Gordon Darkenwald measured the relationship between organizational differentiation and conflict of departments and central administration (vertical conflict in the decision-making process). Fifty-four universities were divided into high, medium, and low differentiation. The faculty within departments were considered to be the professionals, while the administrators were considered to be the bureaucrats of the university. In keeping with research on universities by Talcott Parsons and Gerald Platt and Richard Scott,[40] Darkenwald assumed that highly differentiated universities approximate the professional model, their major characteristic being subor-

TABLE 10—3 Rank Order Correlations Between Organizational Characteristics and Indices of Tension and Conflict

ORGANIZATIONAL CHARACTERISTICS	Degree of tension averaged across all roles and all respondents	RATES OF DISAGREEMENT		NUMBER OF INCIDENTS REPORTED PER INTERVIEW						
		Total disagreements per faculty member	Severe disagreements per faculty member	All incidents	Disputes	Heated discussions	Major incidents	Teachers vs. administrators	Teachers vs. teachers	Incidents involving authority problems
Organizational Size	.22*	.16	.35†	.38†	.27*	.37†	.04	.41†	−.07	.26*
Structural differentiation										
1. Specialization										
Did not major in course	.08	.02	−.18	−.03	−.01	−.06	−.22*	−.05	−.04	.07
Did not major or minor in course	−.07	−.23*	−.12	−.04	−.24*	−.12	.05	−.08	−.10	−.03
2. Levels of authority	.30*	.18	.37†	.48†	.32*	.39*	.18	.40†	.08	.26*
3. Organizational complexity	.19	.16	.32†	.33†	.27*	.33*	.10	.23*	.02	.13
Participation in the authority system	.14*	.17	.17	.17	.39†	.03	−.38†	.07	.12	.05
Regulating procedures										
1. Standardization of work	.28*	.20	.26*	.31*	.31*	.17	.21	.53†	.03	.32*
2. Emphasis on rules	.10	.24*	.06	.22*	.21*	.27*	.13	.11	.12	−.10
3. Close supervision	−.04	.13	.12	.13	.28*	.02	−.14	.03	.15	−.11

INDICES OF ORGANIZATIONAL TENSION AND CONFLICT

ORGANIZATIONAL CHARACTERISTICS	Degree of tension averaged across all roles and all respondents	RATES OF DISAGREEMENT		NUMBER OF INCIDENTS REPORTED PER INTERVIEW							
		Total disagreements per faculty member	Severe disagreements per faculty member	All incidents	Disputes	Heated discussions	Major incidents	Teachers vs. administrators	Teachers vs. teachers	Incidents involving authority problems
Heterogeneity and stability										
1. Heterogeneity of staff	.03	−.08	.10	.18	.16	.08	−.21*	.03	.36†	.14
2. Staff additions during the past 5 years	.34†	.30*	.37†	.58†	.41†	.39†	−.13	.47†	.09	.31*
3. Average age of faculty	−.26*	−.06	−.40†	−.24*	−.23*	−.26*	.12	−.19	−.21*	−.25*
Interpersonal structure										
1. Lunching patterns	.09	−.03	.15	.11	.21*	.02	−.13	.12	.00	.10
2. Social contact outside of school	.26*	.15	.29*	.43†	.21*	.47†	.16	.30*	.32†	.42†

*Rank-order correlation significant at p < .05.
†Rank-order correlation significant at p < .01.

Source: Ronald G. Corwin, "Patterns of Organizational Conflict," *Administrative Science Quarterly* 14, no. 4 (December 1969): 514.

dination of administrative bureaucratic power to professional power. In this model, conflict was low. Likewise, in universities where differentiation was low, the bureaucratic authority structure was dominant over the less professional faculty and conflict between the two groups was low. In contrast to the low conflict of these two types of universities, the medium differentiated university was not dominated by either professional or administrative authority and experienced high conflict. Darkenwald pointed out that these universities were increasing in size and undergoing differentiation; here, faculty professionals and bureaucratic administrators were competing for power. Thus, conflict between academic departments and central administration was greater in universities with a medium level of differentiation.[41]

Unlike Darkenwald, Corwin found that conflict in public schools was greatest in units with more professionally oriented faculty.[42] Corwin's basic premise was that public school systems were bureaucratic and professionalization of these organizations was a conflict-ridden process. Since Darkenwald found higher levels of conflict in the medium differentiated universities and Corwin found higher levels of conflict in the more professional public schools, the findings of the two researchers initially seem inconsistant. Darkenwald rationalized that perhaps the more professionalized public schools studied by Corwin were in some ways "analagous to medium differentiated colleges and universities. In both types of institution there is tension between nascent faculty professionalism and entrenched administrative authority."[43] Thus, Darkenwald found that as professionalism increased in bureaucratic organizations, conflict increased.

Corwin measured conflict in terms of (1) the degree of tension (severe, moderate, slight, or none), (2) the type of disagreement (severe to moderate), and (3) the number of conflict incidents. He assembled ten measures of conflict. See Table 10–3. In his 1969 study, Corwin found evidence to support his earlier linear relationship between organizational differentiation and conflict of various types including vertical conflict.[44] The data was taken from a larger study of routine staff conflicts in twenty-eight public schools. Structural differentiation was defined as the number of administratively distinct but functionally interdependent subunits. This type of conflict was lateral between units that compete for resources. Thus, the rate of conflict varied with horizontal differentiation. The higher the level of differentiation, the greater the level of conflict.

312

Corwin found that the rate of conflict also increased with the level of specialization of personnel (horizontal differentiation), the number of levels in the hierarchy of authority (vertical differentiation), and a total measure of organizational complexity. Specialization increased the differences among employees; thus vested interests were more likely to develop. Conflict was likely to occur between these horizontally related interest groups. Likewise, increases in the number of levels of hierarchy increased organizational complexity and aggravated differences between those at higher and lower levels. Again, interest groups developed and employees identified with given echelons. Persons at different hierarchical levels competed for resources (rewards, power, prestige), typifying the relationship between the professional and the bureaucrat. These differences and conflicts identified by Corwin are intensified by the fact that professionals often possess greater technical competency than their superordinates.

John Child sampled 787 senior British managers in seventy-eight business organizations to determine if structuring of activities and centralization would give rise to conforming behavior and lower the levels of the manager's perception of conflict. Structuring of activities encompassed two measures of complexity—functional specialization and role specialization. Both of these measures were positively correlated with conflict ($r = .33$ and $r = .23$, respectively).[45] See Table 10-4 for these correlations. Similarly, in their study of Scottish electronics firms, Burns and Stalker found considerable conflict over the allocation of organization resources and the development of many new products in those firms that placed greater emphasis on specialization.[46] Thus, there is evidence of a positive relationship between various measures of complexity and organizational conflict.

Centralization Correlates   In his analysis of British business organizations discussed above, John Child also found that centralization of decision-making and the level of perceived authority has no association with manager's perceived level of conflict.[47] These findings did not confirm those of Inkson and associates, which demonstrated a negative relationship between centralization and the level of conflict.[48] Child speculated that one reason for the lack of relationships between conflict and his measures of power may have been that the unit of analysis was perception of senior managers as opposed to lower level employees. These managers were located above

TABLE 10–4 Product–Moment Correlations Between Organizational, Managerial Work Role and Behavioral Variables. N = 78 Organizations

ORGANIZATIONAL VARIABLES	BEHAVIORAL VARIABLES				
	Expected behavior		*Perceived behavior*		
	Questioning authority	*Pressing for change*	*Questioning authority*	*Pressing for change*	*Conflict*
Context:					
Size of organization	.16	.25*	–.14	–.01	–.05
Size of parent organization	.10	.17	.09	.07	.11
Workflow integration	–.26*	–.03	–.21	–.21	.06
Concentration of ownership (N = 46 only)	–.14	–.31*	.18	.15	.01
Structure:					
Functional specialization	–.04	.07	.07	–.05	.33†
Role specialization	.07	.10	.08	.00	.28*
Standardization	.15	.18	.22	.06	.31†
Formalization	.17	.18	.19	.10	.27*
Recording of role performance	–.01	–.01	.17	.12	.44‡
Centralization	–.46‡	–.39‡	–.19	–.21	–.01

BEHAVIORAL VARIABLES

ORGANIZATIONAL VARIABLES	Expected behavior		Perceived behavior		
	Questioning authority	Pressing for change	Questioning authority	Pressing for change	Conflict
Work role variables:					
Formalization	.08	.19	.33†	.08	.36†
Definition	-.27*	-.15	.06	.02	.08
Routine: problems and skills	-.48‡	-.44‡	-.37‡	-.38‡	-.03
Everyday routine	-.34†	-.35†	-.22	-.34†	.13
Long-term stability	-.33†	-.28*	-.21	-.17	-.20
Perceived authority	.46‡	.31	.43‡	.27*	-.03

*p < .05.
†p < .01.
‡p < .001.

Source: John Child, "Strategies of Control and Organizational Behavior," *Administrative Science Quarterly* 18, no. 1 (March 1973): 12.

the organizational level to which most bureaucratic controls are directed. Thus, the centralization did not influence their roles (conflicted behavior). Second, senior managers were in a position to make policy, to openly challenge their colleagues and the system. Child speculated that different findings may have resulted had lower level employees been the object of analysis.[49]

The findings of both Donald Warren and Corwin supported those of Inkson et al.—lower organizational employees' participation in decision-making was positively correlated with conflict.[50] Of Corwin's ten conflict indices, only that of major incidents was negatively correlated with participation in decision-making. He speculated that decentralization of decision-making made organizational employees more aware of the issues, both major and minor, and provided them with greater opportunity for conflict. The frequent minor conflicts that occurred in a decentralized organization may have helped to reduce the number of major conflicts. Thus, Corwin's findings with regard to major and minor conflict were not contradictory.

Organizations that exhibit low centralization, that is, where decision-making is distributed among a large number of the organizational members at various hierarchical levels, permit opinions, values, and interests of the organizational members to come into play. When an organization is both complex and decentralized, the possibilities for conflict are great. Decentralization encourages the process of occupational conflict inherent in complex organizations. "A more generalized statement of this principle is that democratic decision making implies not only limited, but omnipresent, conflict among participants. This frequently leads to high rates of social change."[51]

Formalization Correlates   Formalization and standardization measures are generally thought to limit the discretion of subordinates, thus clarifying roles and regulations and preventing role conflict. But rules may in fact increase rather than decrease the rate of conflict in an organization. As was pointed out in chapter seven, some rules govern jobs, others govern general organizational procedures. Likewise, some rules control the subordinate, while others control the superordinate. It is likely that each interest group will want the other groups to follow organizational rules and regulations while they maintain their own autonomy. Thus, professionals generally wish to restrict the arbitrary decisions of bureaucrats through regulative formalization while maintaining their own autonomy.

Likewise, administrators wish to make predictable the behavior of employees, even professionals, while maintaining their autonomy. Thus, it stands to reason that imposing standardization and formalization on professionals may increase vertical conflict between subordinates and superordinates. When bureaucrats and professionals conflict, the administration often imposes greater restrictions, which in turn cause greater disagreement and tension over restricted autonomy, thus intensifying the conflict.

Corwin's indices of formalization (standardization and emphasis on rules) were, in general, positively related with his ten indices of conflict. Although formalization may help coordinate an organization, it may also facilitate conflict. Thus, one could argue that when rules are standardized and formalized, the organizational members are more likely to conflict over these rules. Corwin cautioned us not to interpret the correlation as directional. In actuality, conflict may lead to an increase in formalization. Child's measure of conflict was the degree to which the manager perceived his colleagues found difficulty in agreeing on four aspects of problem solving. Child hypothesized that structure of activities, which included three measures of formalization (standardization, formalization, and recording of role performance) would be negatively related to conflict. Similar to the findings of Corwin and others, these measures of formalization were positively related to conflict. See Table 10–4. Child also conceded that the structuring of activities could have been a response to high levels of conflict, an administrative attempt to control a conflict ridden organization. Thus, the reverse direction of the relationship is a possibility.

Communication Correlates   One of the most common misconceptions concerning organizational conflict is that conflict is due primarily to a breakdown in communications. But in some cases, no amount of communication will change one group's values, interests and goals to correspond to that of another group. When real differences exist between the groups, they may either compromise these differences or one group may overpower the other. As was demonstrated in chapter eight, the idea that individuals can remove differences through free-flowing communication is, of course, incorrect. Often, statements of positions tend to clarify differences, thus intensifying the conflict. Thus, real conflicts of interests, values, and goals cannot be resolved through communication. This does not mean that some misunderstandings cannot be rectified by communication. But often misunderstandings are resolved while the real differences continue to exist. A faculty member who has no voice in policy decisions and whose salary increases do not keep pace with the rise in the cost of living will not abandon goals of participation and equitable salary as a result of communication with the administration. Likewise, students who experience rising costs of tuition will not be able to escape these costs through communication. When the two parties do understand each other's position and recognize the potential gains and losses involved, they may choose to conflict. One way administrators avoid conflict is by keeping information concerning decisions from organizational members, a tactic exemplified by highly bureaucratic organizations. Many times employees become more militant if they know what is happening and discover that the organization's functioning does not coincide with their values, goals, and interests. Thus, communication of knowledge often creates conflict as opposed to diverting it.

In their analysis of interdepartmental conflict, Walton and associates hypothesized that conflict would be reduced with greater knowledge of the functioning of other departments. However, as we would expect, they found the opposite: Knowledge helped the respective departments clearly define their interests and differences; the correlation between knowledge and conflict was positive.[52] If we assume that communication between units increases their knowledge of each other, we would expect a positive relationship between the rate of communication and conflict. Corwin found a strong positive correlation between the rate of informal interaction and the ten indices of conflict.[53] Thus, we conclude that the rate of communication is positively related to conflict. It must be remembered that the majority of these indicators of conflict were perceptual measures.

On the other extreme, a complete lack of communication between units may also be related to conflict. Walton and associates found that barriers to communication resulted in a high rate of conflict. At least two possible explanations for these findings suggest themselves. First, it may have been that departments that were hard to contact tended to be prone to conflict, whereas departments that had no systematic difficulties in contacting others were not. Second, it may have been that departments experiencing high interdepartmental conflict tended to create department-wide barriers to inward communication, for example, they may have isolated themselves spatially or established schedules that did not facilitate attempts of others to contact them.[54]

SUMMARY

In summary, conflict is more likely to occur when organizations are dependent on other organizations in their environment, and when they are larger and technologically nonroutine. Structurally, organizations that exhibit high levels of complexity or differentiation, high levels of communication, and high levels of formalization will experience higher levels of conflict than organizations that exhibit low levels of these variables. Finally, decentralized organizations are more likely to experience conflict than centralized ones. These relationships are summarized in Table 10–5.

TABLE 10–5 Contextual and Structural Correlates of Conflict

I. Contextual Dimensions
  A. Size
    1. Size is positively related to the level of organizational conflict.
  B. Technology
    1. Nonuniform raw materials and nonroutine technology are positively related to the level of organizational conflict.
II. Structural Correlates of Conflict
  A. Complexity
    1. Horizontal differentiation of occupations is positively related to the level of organizational conflict.
    2. Horizontal differentiation of departments and functional units is positively related to the level of organizational conflict.
    3. Horizontal differentiation of knowledge (employment of experts and professionals) is positively related to the level of organizational conflict.
    4. When experts and professionals are employed at the lower levels of the organization, vertical differentiation (number of hierarchical levels) is positively related to the level of organizational conflict.
  B. Centralization
    1. Decentralization of decision-making is positively related to the level of organizational conflict.
  C. Formalization
    1. Formalization of rules and procedures is positively related to the level of organizational conflict.
  D. Communication
    1. When differences in values and interests exist between subunits, frequency of communication is positively related to the level of organizational conflict.

319

NOTES

1. James G. March and Herbert A. Simon, *Organizations* (New York: John Wiley & Sons, 1953), p. 112.

2. Alan R. Beals and Bernard J. Siegal, *Devisiveness and Social Conflict: An Anthropological Approach* (Stanford, Calif.: Stanford University Press, 1966), p. 21.

3. J. Marek, "Conflict, a Battle of Strategies," in J. R. Lawrence, ed., *Operational Research and the Social Sciences* (London: Tavistock Publications, 1966), p. 64.

4. Richard E. Walton, "The Theory of Conflict in Lateral Organizational Relationships," in J. R. Lawrence, ed., *Operational Research and the Social Sciences* (London: Tavistock Publications, 1966), p. 411.

5. William Kornhauser, *Scientists in Industry* (Berkeley, Calif.: University of California Press, 1962).

6. J. Victor Baldridge, *Power and Conflict in the University* (New York: John Wiley & Sons, 1971); Frank R. Kemerer and J. Victor Baldridge, *Unions on Campus* (San Francisco: Jossey–Bass Publishers, 1975).

7. Baldridge, *Power and Conflict in the University,* pp. 202–203.

8. Ibid., p. 203.

9. The above discussion was taken almost entirely from Kenneth Benson, "The Analysis of Bureaucratic–Professional Conflict: Functional Versus Dialectical Approaches," *The Sociological Quarterly* 14 (Summer 1973): 376–394.

10. Ralf Dahrendorf, *Class and Class Conflict in Industrial Society* (Stanford, Calif.: Stanford University Press, 1959), p. 135.

11. Rensis Likert and Jane C. Likert, *New Ways of Managing Conflict* (New York: McGraw–Hill, 1976), pp. 7–8.

12. Dahrendorf, *Class and Class Conflict in Industrial Society,* p. 135.

13. Stuart M. Schmidt and Thomas A. Kochan, "Conflict Toward Conceptual Clarity," *Administrative Science Quarterly* 17, no. 3 (September 1972): 359–370.

14. J. A. Seiler, "Diagnosing Interdepartmental Conflict," *Harvard Business Review* 4 (September–October 1963): 121–132.

15. James D. Thompson, *Organizations in Action* (New York: McGraw–Hill, 1967).

16. Richard E. Walton and John M. Dutton, "The Management of Interdepartmental Conflict: A Model and Review," *Administrative Science Quarterly* 14, no. 1 (March 1969): 73–84.

17. Schmidt and Kochan, "Conflict Toward Conceptual Clarity," p. 363.

18. Ibid., p. 365.

19. Ibid., pp. 365–366.

20. Ibid., pp. 364–365.

21. John M. Dutton and Richard E. Walton, "Interdepartmental Conflict and Cooperation: Two Contrasting Studies," *Human Organization* 25, no. 5 (Fall 1969): 207–220.

22. Louis R. Pondy, "Organizational Conflict: Concepts and Models," *Administrative Science Quarterly* 12, no. 2 (September 1967): 296–320.

23. Richard E. Walton, John M. Dutton, and Thomas P. Cafferty, "Organizational Context and Interdepartmental Conflict," *Administrative Science Quarterly* 14, no. 4 (December 1969): 526.

24. Melville Dalton, *Men Who Manage* (New York: John Wiley & Sons, Inc., 1959); G. A. Miller, "Professionals in Bureaucracy: Alienation Among Industrial Scientists and Engineers," *American Sociological Review* 32, no. 5 (October 1967): 755–768.

25. Alvin W. Gouldner, "Cosmopolitans and Locals: Toward Analysis of Latent Social Roles—I," *Administrative Science Quarterly* 2, no. 3 (December 1957): 281–306; Harold L. Wilensky, *Intellectuals in Labor Unions* (New York: Free Press, 1959).

26. W. Richard Scott, "Professionals in Bureaucracies: Areas of Conflict," in H. W. Vollmer and D. L. Mills, eds., *Professionalization* (Englewood Cliffs, N.J.: Prentice–Hall, 1966).

27. Dalton, *Men Who Manage*.

28. Ronald G. Corwin, "The Professional Employee: A Study of Conflict in Nursing Roles," *American Journal of Sociology* 66, (May 1961): 604–615.

29. Peter M. Blau and W. Richard Scott, *Formal Organizations: A Comparative Approach* (San Francisco: Chandler Publishing Company, 1962).

30. M. E. W. Goss, "Influence and Authority Among Physicians in an Outpatient Clinic," *American Sociological Review* 26, no. 1 (February 1961): 39–50; Corwin, "The Professional Employee: A Study of Conflict in Nursing Roles," pp. 604–615; Kornhauser, *Scientists in Industry;* Burton Clark, "Faculty Organization and Authority," in Terry Hinsford, ed., *The Study of Academic Administration* (Boulder, Colo.: Western Interstate Commission for Higher Education, 1962), pp. 37–51; Fred E. Katz, *Autonomy and Organization* (New York: Random House, 1968); Paul D. Montagna, "Professionalization and Bureaucratization in Large Professional Organizations," *American Journal of Sociology* 74, no. 2 (September 1968): 138–145; Dan C. Lortie, "The Balance of Control and Autonomy in Elementary School Teaching," in Amitai Etzioni, ed., *The Semi-Professions and Their Organizations* (New York: Free Press, 1976), pp. 1–53; D. F. Hall and E. E. Lawler, "Job Characteristics and Pressures and the Organizational Integration of Professionals," *Administrative Science Quarterly* 15 (September 1970): 271–281.

31. Cornelius Lammer, "Strikes and Mutinies: A Comparative Study of Organizational Conflict Between Rulers and Ruled," *Administrative Science Quarterly* 14, no. 4 (December 1969): 558–572; Mayer N. Zald, "Social Movements in Organizations: Coup d' Etat, Bureaucratic Insurgency and Rebellion." (Paper presented at the annual meeting of the American Sociological Association, New York, September 2, 1976).

32. Georg Simmel, *Conflict and the Web of Group Affiliation,* Kurt H. Wolff, trans. (Glencoe, Ill.: Free Press, 1956), pp. 27–67; Lewis A. Coser, *The Functions of Social Conflict* (London: Free Press of Glencoe, 1956).

33. Jonathan H. Turner, *The Structure of Sociological Theory* (Homewood, Ill.: The Dorsey Press, 1974), pp. 112–113.

34. Lammers, "Strikes and Mutinies: A Comparative Study of Organizational Conflict Between Rulers and Ruled."

35. Ronald G. Corwin, "Patterns of Organizational Conflict," *Administrative Science Quarterly* 14, no. 4 (December 1969): 507–520.

36. Corwin, "Patterns of Organizational Conflict."

37. Walton and Dutton, "The Management of Interdepartmental Conflict: A Model and Review": 73.

38. Corwin, "Patterns of Organizational Conflict," p. 514.

39. Eugene Litwak, "Models of Bureaucracy Which Permit Conflict," *American Sociological Review* 67, no. 2 (September 1961): 177–184; Joan Woodward, *Industrial Organization: Theory and Practice* (Oxford: Oxford University

Press, 1965); Charles Perrow, "A Framework for the Comparative Analysis of Organizations," *American Sociological Review* 32, no. 3 (April 1967): 194–208; Edward Harvey, "Technology and the Structure of Organizations," *American Sociological Review* 33, no. 2 (April 1968): 258–274.

40. Talcott Parsons and Garald M. Platt, *The American Academic Profession: A Pilot Study,* working paper (Harvard University, Department of Social Relations); W. Richard Scott, "Reactions to Supervision in a Heteronomous Professional Organization," *Administrative Science Quarterly* 10, no. 1 (June 1965): 65–81.

41. Gordon G. Darkenwald, Jr., "Organizational Conflict in Colleges and Universities," *Administrative Science Quarterly* 16, no. 4 (December 1971): 407–412.

42. Ronald G. Corwin, "Professional Persons in Public Organizations," *Educational Administrative Quarterly* 1, no. 3 (Autumn 1965): 1–22.

43. Darkenwald, "Organizational Conflict in Colleges and Universities," pp. 410–411.

44. Corwin, "Patterns of Organizational Conflict," pp. 507–519.

45. John Child, "Strategies of Control and Organizational Behavior," *Administrative Science Quarterly* 8, no. 1 (June 1973): 1–17.

46. Tom Burns and G. M. Stalker, *The Management of Innovation* (London: Tavistock Publications, 1961).

47. Child, "Strategies of Control and Organizational Behavior," p. 14.

48. J. H. Inkson, D. J. Hickson, and D. S. Pugh, "Administrative Reduction of Variance in Organization and Behavior" (Unpublished paper given at the British Psychological Society).

49. Child, "Strategies of Control and Organizational Behavior," p. 16.

50. Donald I. Warren, "The Effects of Power Bases and Peer Groups on Conformity in Formal Organizations," *Administrative Science Quarterly* 14, no. 4 (December 1969): 544–556; Corwin, "Patterns of Organizational Conflict."

51. Jerald Hage and Michael Aiken, *Social Change in Complex Organizations* (New York: Random House, 1970), p. 39.

52. Walton, Dutton, and Cafferty, "Organizational Context and Interdepartmental Conflict."

53. Corwin, "Patterns of Organizational Conflict."

54. Walton, Dutton, and Cafferty, "Organizational Context and Interdepartmental Conflict," pp. 538–539.

322

11

EFFECTIVENESS AND EFFICIENCY

OBJECTIVES

The objectives of this chapter are:

1. To theoretically and operationally define organizational effectiveness and efficiency.

2. To discuss the importance of viewing effectiveness as a multivariate construct.

3. To discuss the major models of organizational effectiveness:
   a. goals model
   b. systems model

4. To distinguish between societal, organizational, and individual goals.

5. To distinguish between operative, official, and operational goals.

6. To discuss the problems of defining and measuring goals.

7. To discuss the importance of goal priorities and the weighting of organizational goals.

8. To differentiate between profit and nonprofit goals.

9. To discuss some advantages and disadvantages of the system resource model.

10. To discuss the complementary aspects of the goals and the system resource models.

11. To define the contingency approach to organizational effectiveness and elaborate the importance of the following dimensions to this approach:

a.   environmental
b.   contextual
c.   structural

INTRODUCTION

Two of the major dimensions used to describe organizational performance are organizational *efficiency* and *effectiveness*. However, it is
difficult to specify what is meant by these two concepts. Often these
terms are used interchangably, or effectiveness is viewed as the more
inclusive concept and efficiency (productivity, profit, and so on) as a
factor of effectiveness. Those who define efficiency as an aspect of
effectiveness include: James Price, who defines productivity as a
major indicator of effectiveness;[1] Stanley Seashore and Ephraim
Yuchtman, who included indicators of efficiency as measures of effectiveness;[2] Chris Argyris, who defined effectiveness as the relationship between inputs and outputs, i.e., as a condition in which the
organization, over time, increases outputs with constant or decreasing inputs;[3] and Daniel Katz and Robert Kahn, who defined effectiveness in terms of efficiency and political effectiveness, and efficiency as the ratio of energic outputs to energic inputs: "Efficiency
thus tells us how much of the input . . . emerges as product and how
much is absorbed by the system."[4] The greater the efficiency (the
closer the ratio approximates 1), the greater the profitability, storage
of energy, and long-run survival and growth of the organization.
"Political effectiveness then consists in the short run of maximizing
the return to the organization by means of advantageous transactions with various outside agencies and groups and with the members of the organization as well."[5] Most theorists, including Basil
Georgopoulos and Arnold Tannenbaum, have defined efficiency as
one aspect of the broader construct of organizational effectiveness.[6]
However, Selwyn Becker and Duncan Neuhauser reversed the scope
of the terms, making efficiency the global term and defining effective goal attainment as one aspect of efficiency. They saw a measure
of efficiency as the identification of organizational goals and "measures of the degree of goal-attainment of that organization."[7] Thus
goal attainment would have to be measured relative to inputs. As is
obvious from the above discussion, this overlapping of potential constructs has been a major obstacle to the synthesis of research on these
two performance dimensions; therefore, it is important to make distinctions between efficiency and effectiveness.

EFFICIENCY DEFINED

Although effectiveness and efficiency are both aspects of performance, and efficiency is often used as a criterion and measure of effectiveness, here the position is taken that these two concepts are not
synonymous and should not be used to refer to the same phenomenon. Efficiency deals with specific aspects of effectiveness and according to Etzioni is measured "by the amount of resources used to
produce a unit of output."[8] Efficiency is generally measured in terms
of production costs, profit, and employee productivity. In fact, the
term *productivity* is often used by business firms to refer to efficiency.
Productivity is expressed in terms of costs or the ratio of output to
inputs, but unlike efficiency, it deals only with a part or a subset of
the organization in that it is usually applied to individual workers or
work groups. Here the unit of analysis is the individual, group, department, or division, not the total organization.

From the works of Max Weber to those of James Price, organizational efficiency has been defined as a desired consequence of rational organization. The efficient organization is seen as a product of
the way in which resources are used and structure is arranged. Becker and Neuhauser pointed out that maximum efficiency is an arrangement of resources such that no other arrangement would produce as profitable a return.[9] Here efficiency is defined as a product
of structure. But these authors, like many others, confuse efficiency
with measures of effectiveness. The returns in their definition of
efficiency may be not only profit, but the "quality of health care, . . .
election of a political candidate, . . . [or] whatever the given goals of
the organization."[10] Thus, Becker and Neuhauser defined efficiency
to include any goals of the organization, whether oriented toward
quantity or quality.

In this text, efficiency is generally the ratio of outputs (returns,
benefits) to inputs (costs, effort) or the organization's cost/benefit
ratio. Ideally, all inputs and outputs are included. Many times efficiency is stated in terms of costs per unit volume of production.
Thus, given two organizations with equal production, the one with
less costs would be the more efficient. Jerald Hage and Michael Aiken
are among those who have employed this measure of efficiency.[11] Theirs is a measure of the quantity as related to costs of the
units produced through the entire production process of the organization, from the input phase, through the transformation stage, to
the output stage. Here it is either assumed that the quality of outputs
is constant or quality is not being analyzed. Thus, efficiency is a mea-

sure of the internal processes and functioning of the organization. Hage and Aiken stressed the cost-per-quantity aspects of efficiency:

Efficiency refers to the relative emphasis on the cost reduction of the product or service. The cost may be counted in men, money, space, time, or other resource. A high degree of efficiency implies great organizational effort to conserve resources; a low degree of efficiency implies little organizational effort to conserving resources.[12]

Efficiency can be extremely important to organizations during periods when resources (money, facilities, and personnel) are scarce; but at other times, such as in emergencies (e.g., natural disasters or war), effectiveness may be much more important than efficiency. For example, in war time, it is far more important to effectively protect the national security than to efficiently utilize resources. In this text, a distinction is made between organizational efficiency and effectiveness because these two dimensions do not necessarily vary together. That is, an organization may be efficient without being effective, and vice versa.

EFFECTIVENESS

Although, as was noted in chapter one, organizations are created to achieve some objectives, measurement of organizational effectiveness in terms of reaching these objectives has not been systematically explored, one reason being that some theoretical perspectives simply have not dealt with organizational effectiveness. For example, human relations theorists concentrate instead on the effectiveness of individual managers,[13] and most structural analysts have not dealt with measures of effectiveness. Two notable exceptions include the recent works of John Child and Hage and Aiken.[14] Both the structural and human relations models concentrate more on intraorganizational concerns. Thus, performance measures of structural efficiency or individual productivity have been developed, but measures of organizational effectiveness (as a relationship between internal structure and external environment) have not been adequately developed.

Yuchtman and Seashore summarized the present stage of the development of effectiveness measures as follows:

The classic paradigm consists of some measure of effectiveness—productivity or profit, for example—as the dependent variable, and of various sociological and social psychological measures as the independent variables. The independent variables are usually treated in a relatively sophisticated manner, little attention, however, has been given to the concept of effectiveness itself.[15]

Katz and Kahn concurred with this position:

The literature is studded with references to efficiency, productivity, absence, turnover, and profitability—all of these offered implicitly or explicitly, separately or in combination, as definitions of organizational effectiveness. Most of what has been written on the meaning of these criteria and on their interrelatedness, however, is judgmental and open to question.[16]

Effectiveness Defined

Definitions of organizational effectiveness vary depending on the particular theoretical model being used. (These models are discussed later in the chapter.) Surprisingly, many of the same indicators are used to measure effectiveness, regardless of the model used and the manner in which it is defined. The major problem of defining organizational effectiveness originates partly from the fact that it is both an abstract and general term and partly from the same problems Robert Merton described when defining *function*. Different terms—performance, goals, productivity, efficiency—have all been used to designate *effectiveness*, which in turn has been used to designate diverse phenomena. Consequently, effectiveness is often defined in terms of the factor the researcher feels is most valued. For example, Price's inventory of propositions included studies in which the variable of effectiveness was defined in terms of productivity, morale, conformity, adaptiveness, and institutionalization. He assumed that all five variables were positively related to effectiveness but that productivity was more closely related than the other four variables. He did imply that all five variables were not positively intercorrelated: "If, for example, an organization is characterized by a high degree of productivity and a low degree of morale, it is assumed that the organization has a high degree of effectiveness."[17] Here productivity was assumed to be a better indicator of effectiveness than morale.

This text takes the approach that productivity, flexibility, and so on are distinct dimensions of organizational performance. Thus, these dimensions are perceived to be aspects of effectiveness only when effectiveness is used as a broad term on the same level as performance. No assumption is made that all of these performance variables are positively interrelated. We have defined productivity as an aspect of efficiency and organizational adaptiveness as the ability of the organization to innovate and accept program change (see chapter nine). Morale is generally a socio-psychological measure or employee attitude. Thus, in this text, an effort is made to separate these dimensions of the general component of performance and deal with effectiveness as a multivariate construct of organizational resource acquisition and goal attainment. Effectiveness is here defined as an organization's capacity to acquire and utilize its scarce and valued resources as expeditiously as possible in the pursuit of its operative and operational goals. Instead of evaluating success in terms of the extent to which goal attainment is maximized, it is recognized that a series of identifiable contingencies (size, technology, environment, and internal structure of the organization) serve to inhibit or facilitate resource acquisition and goal optimization. These contingencies must be recognized and accounted for. Finally, in keeping with the orientation of this text, effectiveness is viewed as a process; that is, an organization's effectiveness varies over time. Frequently, when a goals approach is used and emphasis is placed on official goals that the organization is constantly attempting to reach rather than on operative goals. Effectiveness is defined as an ultimate state. On the other hand, those analysts who concentrate on operative goals and the systems model of effectiveness generally view effectiveness as a process. Because operative goals are more concrete and specific than official goals, they shift as the internal structure or external environment of the organization changes. Thus, a concentration on official goals contributes a static quality to the analysis of effectiveness, whereas a concentration on resources and operative goals gives the analysis a process orientation.

Multivariate Constructs of Effectiveness   One of the major problems in defining organizational effectiveness is that some analysts have taken too narrow a view, defining effectiveness with only one criterion, such as profit. In actuality, if an organization strives for profit alone, it will not survive. For one thing, it would not be flexible enough to innovate or change with environmental demands. Effectiveness is a multivariate construct, and the criteria used to evaluate

328

it are not the same for all analyses of all types of organizations. A univariate approach, although frequently used in organizational research, is difficult to justify because such a model measures only a single aspect or criterion of the total construct. The effectiveness construct is much broader than a single variable such as job satisfaction or turnover rates. The choice of one or the other of these variables may be, as Steers pointed out, merely a value bias of the chosen theoretical perspective rather than reflecting a careful evaluation of their impact on effectiveness.[18] Several researchers have come to the conclusion that a multivariate approach to organizational effectiveness is more meaningful. For example, in their 1957 study, Geogopoulos and Tannenbaum concluded that the effectiveness construct consisted of productivity, flexibility, and absence of interorganizational strain.[19] Steers also subscribed to the multivariate construct of effectiveness and examined seventeen multivariate models of organizational effectiveness, classifying them according to (1) primary evaluation criteria, (2) normative or descriptive characteristics, (3) purported generalizability of the criteria, and (4) bases for selecting criteria.[20] See Table 11–1 for this breakdown.

One advantage of the multivariate model is its scope—it measures more aspects of the potential construct of effectiveness. This may also be a disadvantage when unrelated or negatively related aspects such as job satisfaction and productivity are included in the construct. The operational definitions that have been used to measure this effectiveness construct, which, like performance, is global, are so diverse (i.e., often unrelated or negatively correlated) that the term has been rendered almost meaningless except that it connotates a positive dimension of organizations. Not only are the variables diverse, but often the models developed from these variables do not overlap. Because at this time these models disagree as to what constitutes evaluative criteria, it is impossible to assess the effectiveness of all organizations using a single model or construct; consequently, it is impossible to construct propositions of organizational effectiveness that can be generalized for all types of organizations.

Effectiveness, as now conceptualized, is not a single theoretical construct. In order to be a single construct, all the indexes or criterion measures would have to be similarly related to a single independent variable. For example, when centralization of an organization increased, the effectiveness criteria of job satisfaction and productivity would both have to vary in the same direction. If job satisfaction decreases as productivity increases, or if they show no relationship, the two variables are not part of the same general construct.

329

TABLE 11–1 Evaluation Criteria in Multivariate Models of Organizational Effectiveness

STUDY AND PRIMARY EVALUATION CRITERIA	TYPE OF MEASURE*	GENERALIZABILITY OF CRITERIA†	DERIVATION OF CRITERIA‡
Georgopoulos and Tannenbaum (1957) Productivity, flexibility, absence of organizational strain	N	A	Ded; followed by questionnaire study
Bennis (1962) Adaptability, sense of identity, capacity to test reality	N	A	Ded; no study
Blake and Mouton (1964) Simultaneous achievement of high production-centered and high people-centered enterprise	N	B	Ded; no study
Caplow (1964) Stability, integration, voluntarism, achievement	N	A	Ded; no study
Katz and Kahn (1966) Growth, storage, survival, control over environment	N	A	Ind; based on review of empirical studies
Lawrence and Lorsch (1967) Optimal balance of integration and differentiation	D	B	Ind; based on study of 6 firms
Yuchtman and Seashore (1967) Successful acquisition of scarce and valued resources, control over environment	N	A	Ind; based on study of insurance agencies
Friedlander and Pickle (1968) Profitability, employee satisfaction, societal value	N	B	Ded; followed by study of small businesses
Price (1968) Productivity, conformity, morale, adaptiveness, institutionalization	D	A	Ind; based on review of 50 published studies

TABLE 11-1 *(continued)*

STUDY AND PRIMARY EVALUATION CRITERIA	TYPE OF MEASURE*	GENERALIZABILITY OF CRITERIA†	DERIVATION OF CRITERIA‡
Mahoney and Weitzel (1969)	D	B,R	Ind; based on study of 13 organizations
General business model			
Productivity-support-utilization, planning, reliability, initiative			
R and D Model			
Reliability, cooperation, development			
Schein (1970)	N	A	Ded; no study
Open communication, flexibility, creativity, psychological commitment			
Mott (1972)	N	A	Ded; followed by questionnaire study of several organizations
Productivity, flexibility, adaptability			
Duncan (1973)	N	A	Ded; followed by study of 22 decision units
Goal attainment, integration, adaptation			
Gibson et al. (1973)	N	A	Ind; based on review of earlier models
Short-run			
Production, efficiency, satisfaction			
Intermediate			
Adaptiveness, development			
Long-run			
Survival			

TABLE 11-1 *(continued)*

STUDY AND PRIMARY EVALUATION CRITERIA	TYPE OF MEASURE*	GENERALIZABILITY OF CRITERIA†	DERIVATION OF CRITERIA‡
Negandhi and Reimann (1973) Behavioral index Manpower acquisition, employee satisfaction, manpower retention, interpersonal relations, interdepartmental relations, manpower utilization Economic index Growth in sales, net profit	N	B	Ded; followed by study of Indian organizations
Child (1974, 1975) Profitability, growth	N	B	Ded; followed by study of 82 British firms
Webb (1974) Cohesion, efficiency, adaptability, support	D	C	Ind; based on study of religious organizations

*N = Normative models; D = Descriptive models.
†A = All organizations; B = Business organizations; C = Religious organizations; R = Research and development laboratories.
‡Ded = Deductive; Ind = Inductive.

Source: Richard M. Steers, "Problems in the Measurement of Organizational Effectiveness," *Administrative Science Quarterly* 20, no. 4 (December 1975): 548.

The validity of such a model is so weak that one must conclude that not all the variables currently defined as effectiveness are part of the same construct. More research is needed to explore which variables are interrelated. The problem of consistency between measures of effectiveness has been observed by several theorists,[21] but empirically validated by few.

Operational Definitions of Effectiveness   In his analysis of seventeen multivariate studies of organizational effectiveness, Richard Steers analyzed the methods of measuring organizational effectiveness and found fifteen different operational definitions.[22] As can be observed in Table 11–2, only adaptability–flexibility was mentioned in more than half of these studies. Productivity (here defined as one aspect of efficiency) was used as an operational definition in six of the seventeen studies. Satisfaction, a socio-psychological characteristic of employees, was used in less than one third of the studies (five of the seventeen). These findings led Steers to conclude that "the effectiveness construct is so complex as to defy simple attempts at model

TABLE 11–2   Frequency of Occurrence of Evaluation Criteria in 17 Models of Organizational Effectiveness

EVALUATION CRITERIA	NO. OF TIMES MENTIONED (N = 17)
Adaptability–Flexibility	10
Productivity	6
Satisfaction	5
Profitability	3
Resource acquisition	3
Absence of strain	2
Control over environment	2
Development	2
Efficiency	2
Employee retention	2
Growth	2
Integration	2
Open communications	2
Survival	2
All other criteria	1

Source: Richard M. Steers, "Problems in the Measurement of Organizational Effectiveness," *Administrative Science Quarterly* 20, no. 4 (December 1975): 549.

development," and that more flexible, comprehensive models are required.[23] Likewise, in a recent review of effectiveness measures, John Campbell identified thirty different variables, the most frequently used of which was overall performance, measured by employee or supervisory ratings; the second, productivity, measured by output data; and the third, employee job satisfaction, measured by self-reported questionnaire data.[24] See Table 11–3 for a summary of these measures. As Price pointed out, "relatively few studies of organizations have dealt explicitly with effectiveness, and even where the problem is explicitly treated, diverse measures of effectiveness have been used."[25]

Generalizability

Some models have purported to measure the "entire effectiveness construct," in which case they should be applicable to all types of organizations,[26] while others have purported to measure only some aspects of effectiveness and are applicable to specific types of organizations. For example, such indexes as profitability and market share are more appropriate for business firms, while size of domain is more applicable to public service organizations. Assuming that service and productivity of these two types of organizations are different, one would assume that effectiveness would be evaluated differently. Thus, a single measure of effectiveness is not applicable to all types of organizations. Consequently, the research findings using a given index of effectiveness cannot be generalized to other types of organization which may use different evaluative criteria and emphasize different operative goal structures.

MODELS OF ORGANIZATIONAL EFFECTIVENESS

The two models of organizational effectiveness most often used by researchers are the *goals* and *system resource* models. The criteria used in both models can be derived by the *normative* approach, which defines those goals that *must* be attained, resources that *must* be acquired, or activities that *must* be performed in order for the organization to be successful. These characteristics are *prescribed* by the researcher or the decision-makers of the organization. If the researcher defines these criteria, he or she may use those specified by a given theoretical framework or individual value premises. Consequently, these criteria may be unrelated to what the organization is

TABLE 11-3   Synthesized List of Possible Indicators of Organizational Effectiveness

1. *Overall Effectiveness.* The general evaluation that takes into account as many criteria facets as possible. It is visually measured by combining archival performance records or by obtaining overall ratings or judgments from persons thought to be knowledgeable about the organization.
2. *Productivity.* Usually defined as the quantity or volume of the major product or service that the organization provides. It can be measured at three levels: individual, group, and total organization via either archival records or ratings or both.
3. *Efficiency.* A ratio that reflects a comparison of some aspect of unit performance to the costs incurred for that performance.
4. *Profit.* The amount of revenue from sales left after all costs and obligations are met. Percent return on investment or percent return on total sales are sometimes used as alternative definitions.
5. *Quality.* The quality of the primary service or product provided by the organization may take many operational forms, which are largely determined by the kind of product or service provided by the organization. They are too numerous to mention here.
6. *Accidents.* The frequency of on-the-job accidents resulting in lost time. Campbell and others (1974) found only two examples of accident rates being used as a measure of organizational effectiveness.
7. *Growth.* Represented by an increase in such variables as total manpower, plant capacity, assets, sales, profits, market share, and number of innovations. It implies a comparison of an organization's present state with its own past state.
8. *Absenteeism.* The usual definition stipulates unexcused absences but even within this constraint there are a number of alternative definitions (for example, total time absence versus frequency of occurrence).
9. *Turnover.* Some measure of the relative number of voluntary terminations which is almost always assessed via archival records. They yield a surprising number of variations and few studies use directly comparable measures.
10. *Job Satisfaction.* Has been conceptualized in many ways (for example, see Wanous & Lawler, 1972) but perhaps the modal view might define it as the individual's satisfaction with the amount of various job outcomes he or she is receiving. Whether a particular amount of some outcome (for example, promotional opportunities) is "satisfying" is in time a function of the importance of that outcome to the individual and the equity comparisons the individual makes with others.
11. *Motivation.* In general, the strength of the predisposition of an individual to

335

engage in goal-directed action or activity on the job. It is not a feeling of relative satisfaction with various job outcomes but is more akin to a readiness or willingness to work at accomplishing the job's goals. As an organizational index, it must be summed across people.

12. *Morale.* It is often difficult to define or even understand how organizational theorists and researchers are using this concept. The modal definition seems to view morale as a group phenomena involving extra effort, goal communality, commitment, and feelings of belonging. Groups have some degree of morale, whereas individuals have some degree of motivation (and satisfaction).

13. *Control.* The degree of, and distribution of, management control that exists within an organization for influencing and directing the behavior of organization members.

14. *Conflict/Cohesion.* Defined at the cohesion end by an organization in which the members like one another, work well together, communicate fully and openly, and coordinate their work efforts. At the other end lies the organization with verbal and physical clashes, poor coordination, and ineffective communication.

15. *Flexibility/Adaptation* (Adaptation/Innovation). Refers to the ability of an organization to change its standard operating procedures in response to environmental changes. Many people have written about this dimension, but relatively few have made attempts to measure it.

16. *Planning and Goal Setting.* The degree to which an organization systematically plans its future steps and engages in explicit goal setting behavior.

17. *Goal Consensus.* Distinct from actual commitment to the organization's goals, consensus refers to the degree to which all individuals perceive the same goals for the organization.

18. *Internalization of Organizational Goals.* Refers to the acceptance of the organization's goals. It includes their belief that the organization's goals are right and proper. It is *not* the extent to which goals are clear or agreed upon by the organization members (goal clarity and goal consensus, respectively).

19. *Role and Norm Congruence.* The degree to which the members of an organization are in agreement on such things as desirable supervisory attitudes, performance expectations, morale, role requirements, and so on.

20. *Managerial Interpersonal Skills.* The level of skill with which managers deal with superiors, subordinates, and peers in terms of giving support,

facilitating constructive interaction, and generating enthusiasm for meeting goals and achieving excellent performance. It includes such things as consideration, employee centeredness, and so on.

21. *Managerial Task Skills.* The overall level of skills with which the organization's managers, commanding officers, or group leaders perform work centered tasks, tasks centered on work to be done, and not the skills employed when interacting with other organizational members.

22. *Information Management and Communication.* Completeness, efficiency, and accuracy in analysis, and distribution of information critical to organizational effectiveness.

23. *Readiness.* An overall judgment concerning the probability that the organization could successfully perform some specified task if asked to do so. Work on measuring this variable has been largely confined to military settings.

24. *Utilization of Environment.* The extent to which the organization successfully interacts with its environment and acquires scarce and valued resources necessary to its effective operation.

25. *Evaluations by External Entities.* Evaluations of the organization, or unit, by the individuals and organizations in its environment with which it interacts. Loyalty to, confidence in, and support given the organization by such groups as suppliers, customers, stockholders, enforcement agencies, and the general public would fall under this label.

26. *Stability.* The maintenance of structure, function, and resources through time, and more particularly, through periods of stress.

27. *Value of Human Resources.* A composite criterion which refers to the total value or total worth of the individual members, in an accounting or balance sheet sense, to the organization.

28. *Participation and Shared Influence.* The degree to which individuals in the organization participate in making the decisions that directly affect them.

29. *Training and Development Emphasis.* The amount of effort the organization devotes to developing its human resources.

30. *Achievement Emphasis.* An analog to the individual need for achievement referring to the degree to which the organization appears to place a high *value* on achieving major new goals.

Source: J. P. Campbell, "On the Nature of Organizational Effectiveness," in P. Goodman and J. H. Pennings & associates, *New Perspectives in Organizational Effectiveness* (San Francisco: Jossey–Bass, 1978), pp. 36–39.

actually doing or claims it is doing, the more so if decision-makers are not involved in establishing them. Thus, the normative approach can be criticized for being based on value premises and theoretical frameworks biased by the researcher; consequently, the criteria used to assess effectiveness may not be related to organizational functioning. Furthermore, this approach can be criticized for not being empirically based.

The second approach to establishing a basis for analysis is to use *description* criteria that summarize those dimensions that have emerged from studies of successful organizations. Unlike the normative approach, the descriptive model is empirically based. Furthermore, the descriptive model contains no references to what *should* exist in order for an organization to be successful. One major limitation of the descriptive approach is that in order for the researcher to identify which organizations are successful, i.e., from which effectiveness criteria can be derived, there has to be some ultimate definition of a successful organization or some standard of comparison. This definition is, of course, subject to the value premises of the researchers.

Goals Model Defined

When we assess the various approaches to evaluating effectiveness, it appears that the majority ultimately rest on some measure of organizational goal attainment. Some analysts deny that goals underly their model, but when effectiveness is measured, goals are the basis of their operational definitions. Organizations pursue widely divergent goals; therefore, effectiveness should be measured in terms of the organization's success in achieving those goals as opposed to goals that the analyst perceives it *should* be achieving.

James Price, arguing in support of the goals model, described its underlying assumption: "Its distinguishing characteristic is that it defines effectiveness in terms of the degree of goal-achievement. The greater the degree to which an organization achieves its goals . . . the greater its effectiveness."[27] Another assumption of the goals model is that the organization is in the hands of a rational set of decision-makers, the dominant interest group, which is assumed to have a more or less explicit set of goals toward which they have the knowledge and ability to direct the organization. Thus, the goals model of effectiveness makes the assumption that organizations have goals or objectives toward which they are directed, that these goals can be identified empirically, and progress toward them or their attainment can be measured. Organizational goals are typically equated with everything from a single *desired state* of the organization, which assumes a single ultimate goal, to *aims* and *tasks,* which are less encompassing and plural concepts. It is assumed in most goal models that organizations have multiple and conflicting goals.

Still another assumption of goals models of organizational effectiveness is that a concentration on goal *optimization* is preferable to an attempt at goal *maximization,* in that maximization of each organizational goal is generally not possible. For example, if all resources are allocated to maximize production, the organization will not be flexible enough to innovate and adapt to environmental demands. In the long run, the organization would not survive under these conditions.

Finally, the assumption that an organization is related to its environment is embodied in the goals model of organizational effectiveness. Since the environment supplies resources and receives the products or services of the focal organization, the attainment of organizational goals (internal or external) is dependent upon the organization maintaining exchange relationships with its environment. Relationship of the organization to its environment does not receive as much emphasis in the goals model as they do in the systems model.

Individual, Societal, and Organizational Goals   Effectiveness in attaining goals can be examined at the individual, organizational, and society levels. The most macro level—societal goals and functions—has been a major concern of functional theorists from Durkheim to Parsons. These goals are the most abstract and general; witness Parsons' four societal functions: integration, pattern maintenance, adaptation, goal attainment.[28] Because of their nonspecific nature, these goals do not account for differences among constituencies in society. Further, measurement is impossible, and achievement of these goals, in any real sense, is not expected. On the other end of the continuum—the micro level—are individual goals. Some theorists, such as Petro Georgiou, argue that organizational goals may best be understood through the analysis of individual's motivations and exchange processes.[29] Price, among others, warned against equating individual motives and goals with organizational goals.[30] Often individual goals may work against organizational goals. Of course, organizations consist of collectives of individuals, but to equate organizational goals with individual goals ignores the raison d'etre of organizations—individuals joining together to accomplish collective goals that are not exclusively in their self-interest. The fact remains that pressures from members and the internal structure of the organization, as well as pressures from society and the environment, influence the formation of organizational goals. Thus, effectiveness would be facilitated by finding ways to integrate personal and societal goals with organizational objectives. This does not mean that organizational and individual goals must be synonymous; in fact, individuals and organizations often exchange resources in order to meet their goals. For example, an employee may receive a desired salary for services rendered to the organization. In turn, tasks performed by employees aid the organization in reaching its goals.

Official, Operative, and Operational Goals   A distinction can be made as to types of organizational goals—official, operative, and operational. If effectiveness is to be evaluated in terms of goal attainment, these goals must be put into practice in the organization, a virtually impossible task when they are defined in general and abstract terms. To differentiate between abstract official goals and operative goals, Perrow takes the position that operative goals are more relevant to understanding organizational behavior than official goals. "Official goals are the general purposes of the organization as put forth in the charter, annual reports, public statements by key executives and other authoritative pronouncements."[31] They are generally vague, normative, and aspirational in nature. Official goals are often constructed to legitimize the organization to its public or relevant environments. Thus, official goals may be operative or inoperative depending on the degree of their correspondence with the organization's activities. Operative goals, on the other hand, "designate the ends sought through the actual operating policies of the organization; they tell us what the organization actually is trying to do, regardless of what the official goals say are the aims."[32]

> Where operative goals provide the specific content of official goals they reflect choices among competing values. They may be justified on the basis of an official goal, even though they may subvert another official goal. In one sense they are means to official goals, but since the latter are vague or of high abstraction, the "means" become ends in themselves when the organization is the object of analysis. For example, where profit-making is the announced goal, operative goals will specify whether quality or quantity is to be emphasized, whether profits are to be short run and risky or long run and stable, and will indicate the relative priority of diverse and

somewhat conflicting ends of customer service, employee morale, competitive pricing, diversification, or liquidity.[33]

We should note that some operative goals do not support major organizational values and official goals. Perrow called these "unofficial operative goals" and pointed out that they are tied directly to interest groups.[34] In fact, these operative goals may oppose the official goals of the organization—the organization may do one thing while officially proclaiming another.

Operational goals are those operative goals that can be measured, that is, those for which there are criteria for evaluation. Operational goals exist to the extent that the organization can specify precise measures for assessing goal attainment. There is no assumption that this measurement is adequate or valid, but merely that it exists. Of course, those goals for which there are quantifiable indexes, such as profit, are more easily measured than qualitative variables and thus are more often found among operational goals. This overemphasis on quantitative measures is one major limitation of the use of operative and operational goals for the assessment of organizational effectiveness, even though these are the two types of goals models most often used. Although it is difficult to measure the attainment of official goals, generally, it is easier to define official than operative goals of the organization. Official goals are generally formalized and are a permanent part of the organizational records, charters, bylaws, and, therefore, can be used to define operative goals. On the other hand, while it may be difficult to define operative goals, they may be easier to measure than official goals.

Those who want to investigate the operative or actual goals of an organization may ask organizational members to identify these operative goals, or they may observe the behavior of organizational members to see what kinds of goal-directed behaviors are performed. This type of measurement has the weakness of inferring goals from behavior. The best measure of operative goals would be to compare measures of the stated operative goals (questionnaire and interview data) and measures of the behavior of organizational members. Then, high effectiveness would be represented by high congruency between stated goals and observed behavior and, subsequently, the attainment of these goals.

Assuming, when measuring effectiveness, that operative goals are preferable to official goals, the question arises as to whose goals are more important—the researcher's, the owner's, the customer's or client's, or society's? These goals not only originate from multiple sources but are often conflicting. Of course, the decision-making and structural models of organizations both assume that these operative goals will be established by the dominant group of organizational administrators or executives. For example, in Simon's approach, goals become constraints on the decision-making process and are based on abstract values; "optimal" decisions are attempted within the framework of these constraints (goals).[35] Thus, these operative goals are subject to the biases imposed by the social and psychological characteristics (education, experience, ability) of the organization's decision-makers as well as the illegitimate uses they may make of the organization to further their personal goals. This approach assumes that top administrators or management does and should make goal decisions, thus supplying a valid source of information as to these goals (or goal definitions). The researchers who subscribe to this approach investigate the goals of top management as operative organizational goals.[36]

Defining Organizational Goals   In order to measure the effectiveness of the organization, a researcher must either seek out the powerholders in the organization and ask them to state their organizational goals or objectives, or employ techniques to reveal the actual operative goals of the organization, for example, observing employee behavior. Once the researcher is satisfied that he or she has defined the most important, relevant objectives of the organization, the task is to develop criteria that measure how well these objectives are being accomplished. This task is not as easy as it seems. The goals concept is very broad, but specific goals must be singled out to be measured. Further difficulties arise in deciding which goals (intra- or inter-organizational goals, public service, or profit) are relevant. Even when these goals can be specified, they may be so abstract that they defy measurement.

In an attempt to answer Yuchtman and Seashore's criticism that the goals approach is characterized by an inability to identify organizational goals,[37] Price formulated the following guides to help define organizational goals: (1) "... *the focus of research should be on the major decision makers in the organization.*"[38] Here Price assumes that major decision makers (the dominant interest group) are the most valid source of information concerning organizational goals and that they determine the goals of the organization. (2) "... *the focus of research should be on organizational goals*"—presumably those of top management and as opposed to private goals. (3) "... *the focus of research should be on operative goals*"—as opposed to official goals. (4) "... *the focus of research should be on intentions and activities."*[39] In keeping with the concepts outlined by E. Gross,[40] Price noted that intentions give the researcher the *"participant's view* of what the organization is trying to do," while activities are ". . . what persons in the organization are in fact *observed to be doing,* how they are spending their time, how resources are being allotted."[41] Those issues and goals that are regularly backed by resources (money, personnel, equipment, etc.) have been chosen as the major objectives of the organization. In summary, Price concluded that although goal identification is difficult, this problem ". . . is reduced to managable proportions if the focus of research is on the organizational goal that the major decision makers actually pursue, and if data are collected about the major decision makers' intentions and activities."[42] Of course, the allocation of resources by administrators and their stated goals and activities are not always consistent. In addition, there may be a difference of opinion among decision-makers in defining these goals. Defined organizational goals is only the first step in the evaluation of effectiveness. Measurement of the organization's ability to attain these goals is still required.

Goal Priorities   Prior to the measurement of goal attainment, goals should be weighted as to their relative importance; that is, their relative priority must be established. The hierarchical arrangement of goals might be determined by asking decision-makers to rank the operative goals of the organization or by observing the difference in allocation of resources to the achievement of various goals. Information about the organization's nature can be derived from this ranking. But there may be no clear hierarchy of organizational goals because dominant interest groups hold differing priorities and often conflict over goals. In this case, an attempt to establish such a hierarchy would be futile and in any case would have little empirical validity.

Few models of organizational effectiveness consider operative goal priorities. A noted exception is Richard Steers' model, which is based on Charles Perrow's concept of operative goals. Steers postulated that once the actual behavioral intentions of an organization are identified, it is then possible to ascertain the degree to which those intentions are being realized.[43] Steers formulated this approach to eliminate reliance on value premise as opposed to actual organizational behavior. He further rejected the idea that effectiveness can be universally defined and measured in terms of a single variable or set of variables, but retains Etzioni's idea that effective-

343

ness can be measured in terms of how resources are used to achieve specific goals.[44] Further, Steers posited that a model of effectiveness should include differential weighting of various goals to reflect the organization's evaluation. Thus, this model assumes that some goals are more important than others and that organizations pursue some goals with more vigor than they do others.[45] A welfare organization may place higher value on social benefits than profit, whereas the reverse may be true for a business firm. These differences in goal priorities should be considered in an analysis of effectiveness.

Summary of Goals Model   The goals model assumes that organizational effectiveness is based on objectives, as well as being influenced by other aspects of the environment and internal structure of the organization. Furthermore, it assumes that (1) effectiveness is based on operative rather than official goals, (2) this operative goal structure is complex, (3) the emphasis placed on particular goals is not the same for all organizations, (4) the operative goal structure of an organization does not remain the same over time, and (5) operative goals conflict with one another. It can be seen that one set of operative goals that is equally applicable to all organizations at all times cannot be established. Thus, from the goals perspective, effectiveness of an organization is relative to the particular goal measured, the weighting placed on different goals in a multivariate model, and the particular time of analysis. The relative importance of goals can be measured by the allocation of resources to accomplish the goal or by the definition of goals and goal-directed behavior of dominant interest groups.

This text takes the position that a goals model that purports to measure general effectiveness and is equally applicable to all types of organizations is impossible to develop. This is true, first, because goals of an organization are often contradictory or negatively related to each other. Second, goals of one type of organization are nonexistent or of little importance in other types of organizations. Third, goals that are relevant for a particular type of organization in one time period are not necessarily relevant in another. The lack of a general measure of effectiveness hinders the development of standardized measures that will serve as the basis for comparative analyses.

System Resource Model

A second major model of organizational effectiveness is the system resource model, whose major exponents have been Ephraim

Yuchtman and Stanley Seashore. The systems perspective generally defines organizational effectiveness as the degree to which the system maintains integration among its parts and is able to survive in conjunction with its environment. This is accomplished through a "satisficing" or "optimizing" relationship with its external environment. The systems analyst would thus attempt to assess to what degree the organization is internally consistent and congruent it is with its external environment.

Yuchtman and Seashore's model is based on open systems theory, which assumes that the organization is a distinctive social system with boundaries and that the organization is influenced by and must interact with its environment. Thus, the process of organizational exchange—both cooperative and competitive—with the environment are germaine to the model. This exchange (input–output transactions) involves scarce and valued resources. Yuctman and Seashore specified that "value" is not determined by specific goals, but is derived from "their utility as (more or less) generalized means of organizational activity."[46] They defined effectiveness as "the ability of the organization, in either absolute or relative terms, to exploit its environment in the acquisition of scarce and valued resources."[47] They described the most effective organization as one that "maximizes its bargaining position and optimizes its resource procurement."[48] Of course, the goals model assumes that organizational systems are goal directed and that the physical, financial, and human resources pursued by these organizations are operative goals. Thus, the goals model defines the acquisition of scarce and valued resources as optimization of operative goals.

As in the goals model, Yuchtman and Seashore argued that the resource acquisition is an optimizing rather than maximizing process, that maximization of returns is destructive to the acquisition of scarce resources in the long run.[49] An organization that maximizes returns at the expense of its environment jeopardizes its own survival, that is, organizations in the task environment will cease to supply resources if fully exploited by the focal organization. Thus, the bargaining position of the focal organization is weakened and the exchange process is terminated. Short-run gains associated with full exploitation are likely to be canceled out by long-run losses. These considerations led Yuchtman and Seashore to the position that "the highest level of organizational effectiveness is reached when the organization maximizes its bargaining position and optimizes its resource procurement."[50] "Optimum" is the point beyond which the organization endangers itself, because of a depletion of its resource-producing environment or the devaluation of the resource,

345

or because of the stimulation of countervailing forces within that environment.

A key element in Yuchtman and Seashore's definition is their concept of resources:

> Broadly defined, "resources" are (more or less) generalized means, or facilities, that are potentially controllable by social organizations and that are potentially usable—however indirectly—in relationships between the organization and its environment. This definition, it should be noted, does not attribute directionality as an inherent quality of a resource, nor does it limit the concept of resources to physical or economic objects or states even though a physical base must lie behind any named resource.[51]

Some of these universal resources include human energy, physical facilities, technology for organizational activities, and some commodities such as money to be used as an exchange basis. The authors outlined other dimensions for which resources may be described: liquidity, stability, relevance, and substitution.[52]

Measurement in the System Resource Model   Since effectiveness is defined in terms of internal consistency and congruence of the organization with its environment, there must be some criterion for defining these factors. Although Yuchtman and Seashore did not use ultimate goals as the criteria of effectiveness, they did incorporate specific or operative goals in their conceptualization in two ways:

> (1) as a specification of the means or strategies employed by members toward enhancing the bargaining position of the organization; and (2) as a specification of the personal goals of certain members or classes of members within the organizational system. The better the bargaining position of an organization, the more capable it is of attaining its varied and often transient goals, and the more capable it is of allowing the attainment of the personal goals of members. Processes of "goal formation" and "goal displacement" in organizations are thus seen not as defining ultimate criteria of effectiveness, but as strategies adopted by members for enhancing the bargaining position of their organizations.[53]

Thus, Yuchtman and Seashore's model defines organizational effectiveness not as the ability to acquire scarce and valued resources, but

346

rather as the acquisition of a bargaining position with regard to obtaining such resources.

The question arises as to how effectiveness is measured, if not in terms of operative goals. Seashore and Yuchtman used data from seventy-five insurance sales agencies located in different communities throughout the U.S. The analysis of the data yielded ten factors that were stable over time: business volume, production cost, new member productivity, youthfulness of members, business mix, manpower growth, management emphasis, maintenance cost, member productivity, and market penetration.[54] Seashore and Yuchtman noted that factors such as business volume and penetration of the market could be considered goals, but member productivity and youthfulness of members certainly cannot. They concluded that most all the factors associated with performance can be considered as goals, but these factors can also be regarded as important resources gleaned from the environment. Seashore and Yuchtman concentrated on these variables as means to ends rather than as ends in themselves. Thus, the goals model and system resources model use the same variables as indexes of effectiveness but call them ends and means, respectively.

After these factors are assessed, the question then becomes, has the organization maximized its bargaining position and optimized its resource procurement?—Seashore and Yuchtman's definition of organizational effectiveness. The authors suggest that, in practice, most assessments of effectiveness will be relative, that is, it is difficult to identify in an absolute sense the maximum bargaining position. Therefore, most assessments of effectiveness are derived by comparing the focal organization's bargaining position with that of another organization. Thus, these criteria would have to be assessed in relation to some standard organization as opposed to their internal consistency. The major question then becomes, which organization is the standard, or forms the comparative base? And, what are the characteristics that make it the standard or define its effectiveness?

Criticisms of the System Resource Model   Yuchtman and Seashore pointed out five major advantages of the system resource model over the goals model. First, the system resource model takes the organization as the focal point of reference, rather than the external environment or any internal collective such as top management. Second, at the same time the organization is the referent, the model deals with the environment as a central influence on organizational effectiveness. Third, the framework is general enough to encompass different types of organizations (business and social service).

347

Fourth, the model provides variability and latitude with respect to the operations and processes for assessing effectiveness. We assume that the criteria for assessing effectiveness may also vary with given types of organizations. Fifth, this model provides a guide to the identification of performance and action variables relevant to organizational effectiveness which may be used in its empirical assessment.[55]

Of course, there are also disadvantages of the system resource model. One is that "maximization of bargaining position" and "optimization of resources" are impossible concepts to measure. They are rather ideal states and as such may be criticized on the same grounds as the measurement of ultimate goals. To this end, James Price criticized Seashore and Yuchtman's approach for emphasizing the importance of optimization but not measuring organizational optimization, and for recognizing the need for general measures of effectiveness but not developing these measures.[56] He offered as evidence that thirteen of the twenty-three measures of effectiveness used by Seashore and Yuchtman are specifically applicable to insurance companies and could not be used to measure the effectiveness of most other types of organizations.

Finally, Richard Hall pointed out that Yuchtman and Seashore's model may have oversimplified the goals model by defining it in terms of official goals and then defining their systems approach in terms of operative goals. After all, a decision by an organization to acquire given resources may be considered an operative goal. As Hall noted, "the acquisition of resources does not just happen. It is based on what the organization is trying to achieve—its goal—but it is accomplished through the operative goals."[57] Hall argued that the systems resource model is based on the measurement of the organization's operative goals.

Complementary Characteristics of the Goals and System Resource Models

The goals model and the system resource model are complementary in that the goals model concentrates on whose goals and what kinds of goals are to be given priority, as well as the internal pressures and constraints on the achievement of these goals, while Yuchtman and Seashore's system resource model, which concentrates on the relationship between the organization and its environment, emphasizes the bargaining position of the focal organization in the procurement of scarce resources (operative goals). Thus, the goals model emphasizes the internal processes and states of the organization and measures effectiveness in terms of goal-achievement, while the systems model emphasizes organizational exchange (competition and conflict) with the environment and measures effectiveness relative to some other organization or standard. The empirical analysis and dependent variables of the two models are not radically different; many of the same indexes of effectiveness are used by both models. Certainly a range of variables that measures both internal effectiveness and the relationship of the organization to its environment would be a better measure of organizational effectiveness than either internal measures or external measures alone.

CORRELATES OF ORGANIZATIONAL EFFECTIVENESS

Before discussing the environmental, contextual, and structural correlates of organizational effectiveness, it is necessary to differentiate between two types of effectiveness—intra- and inter-organizational effectiveness—that are implicit in the goals and system resource models, respectively. Intraorganizational effectiveness is a dimension of the internal structure of the organization, for example, how efficiently the structure operates as indicated by input–output costs or return on investment, and how satisfied employees are with their jobs. A second view of organizational effectiveness (interorganizational) concentrates on the relationship of the organization to its environment, that is, the congruence between the organization and its environment. Here the effects of output on the external environment are assessed. Services rendered to the client is a measure of interorganizational effectiveness. In the first approach, the organization is the unit of analysis. In the second approach, the organizational–environmental relationship is the unit of analysis. The interorganizational approach may be more appropriate for the type of organization that William Rushing described as having non-profit or service oriented goals.[58] Here it is essential to assess the effectiveness of the service rendered, and this cannot be done by concentrating on the efficiency of the organization's internal structure using such measures of productivity and profit. A welfare organization or a school may be highly efficient—productive and even profitable—but wholly ineffective in terms of the service rendered to the client (the quality of education received by the student). When the client or customer can choose the service agency, as in most nonmonopoly profit organizations, an efficiency measure (profit or productivity) may predict, to some degree, the effectiveness of the organization because if the quality of the product or service is low, the customer will go elsewhere, thus reducing the efficiency of the organization. This is not true in many nonprofit service-oriented organizations, where a high level of internal effectiveness (efficiency) is rarely correlated with a high level of external effectiveness. For example, a public utility may be highly efficient but render inadequate services; the customer bears the burden of its ineffectiveness. Many times it is impossible to maximize productivity and at the same time maximize the service to the client or customer. Usually an organization (social service or business) will compromise to reach a level of internal effectiveness (efficiency) and a level of quality of output that are acceptable to the external environment. Some organizations concentrate more on internal organizational effectiveness (efficiency), while others concentrate on service. All organizations must consider both, but not to the same extent. Thus, the theoretical models that emphasize intraorganizational concerns often measure effectiveness in terms of the member's perception of the organization's effectiveness, whereas those models that concentrate on the relationship between the organization and its environment (for example, systems theory) measure effectiveness in terms of interorganizational relationships). Many times productivity is used as the measure of intraorganizational effectiveness, while social responsibility or accountability is used as a measure of interorganizational effectiveness. Both aspects of organizational effectiveness should be included in a comprehensive assessment of effectiveness. Although the former is generally more applicable to business firms and the latter to social service organizations, we should not make the mistake of thinking that profit deals only with internal efficiency. An organization that does not maintain healthy viable interorganizational relationships will not have sources of inputs and markets for its outputs or clients, and therefore, will not survive. Likewise, social service organizations must maintain intraorganizational effectiveness (efficiency) in order to continue rendering service to the public. The distinction between profit and nonprofit organizations is not that they hold mutually exclusive objectives or goals, but that the profit objective is paramount for the business firm and the service objective is paramount for the public service organization.

Review of Environmental and Contextual Correlates of Efficiency

Chapters three and four specified the relationship of the dimensions of the environmental and contextual components of organizations to organizational effectiveness. Generally support was found for a contingency model in which environmental and contextual dimensions in conjunction with structural dimensions influence organizational effectiveness or success. With respect to the joint effects of environmental and structural dimensions on effectiveness, the research of Burns and Stalker, Lawrence and Lorsch, and Osborn and Hunt each supported the contingency model.[59] See chapter three for a full explanation of these relationships. Similarly, it has been argued by Joan Woodward, the Aston Group, and Charles Perrow, that organizational effectiveness is dependent on the extent to which organizational structure and organizational technology are congruent.[60] Thus, an organization with a very routine and repetitive technology may perform best when the organizational structure is formalized, centralized, and exhibits a low level of complexity; whereas an organization with nonroutine technology may be more successful with low formalization and centralization and high complexity. Finally, with regard to the relationship of organizational size and effectiveness, increased organizational size appears to be positively related to organizational efficiency. In professional organizations, the structural variables of decentralization, high complexity, and formalization are all positively related to both the increased internal efficiency and increased organizational size. Thus, there seems to be consonance between organizational size, structure, and internal efficiency. The relationship between organizational size and interorganizational effectiveness (the relation of the organization to its environment) has not been explored.

Structural Correlates of Organizational Effectiveness

When analyzing the relationship between various structural dimensions and organizational effectiveness, it is important to remember that there are often considerable differences between many of the effectiveness measures used. As stated earlier, a particular structural variable may be positively related to one facet of effectiveness and negatively or not related to other facets. (Recall that some of these facets, such as flexibility, innovation, and conflict, were discussed in previous chapters.)

Two major types of organizational goals are the profit and nonprofit goals. Rushing developed a contingency model of organizational effectiveness in which organizational structure was dependent on the profit/nonprofit orientation of the organization. Here effectiveness was the independent as opposed to the dependent variable. Rushing assumed that organizations are goal-oriented but that profit goals have varying degrees of significance. He argued that the relationship between differentiation and coordination was stronger in profit than in nonprofit organizations, but that a highly structured organization may be the most effective (profitable); however, if the goal of the organization is service, the more effective organization may be less structured than the profit-oriented organization. His samples of small general hospitals evidenced this relationship.[61] Thus, like Lawrence and Lorsch,[62] Rushing saw the intraorganizational structure as contingent on other conditions—in this case profit or nonprofit goals.

In keeping with the work of Peter Blau,[63] Rushing hypothesized that in organizations which were efficiency- or profit-oriented, greater degrees of differentiation would be associated with coordination in the form of "administrative intensity," the proportion of all organizational personnel in administrative positions. On the other hand, in those organizations that were nonprofit-oriented, this relationship was not expected to be as strong.[64] No assumption was made that profit-oriented hospitals were not interested in service. Thus, the goal orientations of the hospitals were not mutually exclusive but rather major orientations that served as a basis for categorization. Rushing's findings supported this hypothesis, and he generalized that his results

> extend the contingency framework in that they indicate that organizational orientation, specifically profit versus nonprofit orientation, may be a significant contingency for intraorganizational relationships. Differences in organizational behavior that stem from differences in dominant organizational orientations mediate the relationship between structural characteristics (differentiation and coordination) of the organization.[65]

To extend Rushing's findings to other organizational structural dimensions, one might posit that profit-oriented organizations would be more centralized, more formalized, and have less developed communication networks than nonprofit-oriented organizations. All of the above variables serve as alternative methods of organizational coordination to administrative ratio. Thus, Rushing's findings indicate that profit-oriented organizations are more bureaucratic in structure than nonprofit organizations, which are likely to be non-bureaucratic or closer to the professional model developed in chapter two. In keeping with this point, Rushing questioned whether most organizational theory is more appropriate for understanding organizations in which "the primary goals are economic" rather than those "in which goals are community service and community welfare."[66] In other words, we may assume either implicity or explicitly, through our models, that the major goals or objectives of all organizations are internal and profit-oriented. Of course, this is an inaccurate and dangerous assumption. These two goals, both facets of organizational effectiveness, are in many ways opposed to each other. The internal structure necessary to maximize efficiency and profit may be the opposite of that which will maximize social utility or responsibility. Nearly every organization must realize both some internal efficiency and some social utility, but because the two orientations are opposed to each other, an organization can never fully realize both at the same time. Thus, if the internal structure of the organization is designed to maximize profit, it will be more highly structured, less so if it is designed to maximize social responsibility and relationships with its environment. Thus, we assume that a single organization has to deal with conflicting definitions of effectiveness.

The competing emphasis placed on goals of internal efficiency (profit) and social service goals often creates a dilemma for the organizations. An organization that concentrates on service to the public may be criticized for operating inefficiently by a controlling organization, in which case its administrators might argue that it is maximizing social goals and services to the public. On the other hand, when a private enterprise organization is condemned for failing to realize social goals and responsibility to the public, its management is likely to claim high efficiency as their goal and justification for lack of emphasis on social responsibility. Thus, these goals are competing interests of administrators.

It should be realized that in an organization, a decision to maximize profit or public service goals must be made relative to a given situation. At one time, or in one part of the organization, operating efficiency may be maximized, whereas at other times or in other parts of the organization, social benefits may be maximized. Both public service and business organizations are evaluated in terms of both types of effectiveness. An organization will be ineffective if it maximizes internal operating efficiency at the expense of social benefits, or vice versa. Ultimately, the decision to optimize one goal at the expense of other goals rests on the values of the organizational members, both professionals and administrators, the constraints imposed by internal and external sources, and the organization's past performance.

SUMMARY

In keeping with the position taken throughout this text, effectiveness must be evaluated from the perspective of organizations as open systems that are interdependent with their environment, each system having distinct inputs, throughputs, and outputs. Effectiveness is seen as a process influenced by the organization's internal structure, context, and external environment. Special interest groups, made up of organizational decision-makers, employee labor unions, and so on, also influence effectiveness by establishing objectives (operative goals). Because the internal processes of the organization (moving from inputs, to throughputs, to outputs) are easier for the organization to control, this type of organizational effectiveness—efficiency—has been separated from the larger construct of effectiveness. Of course, as has been demonstrated, efficiency is often conceptualized and measured as part of the effectiveness construct. It should be remembered that efficiency deals only with the congruency of the internal structure of the organization and then only with the output/unit cost. Of course, efficiency of the internal structure is dependent on acquisition of scarce and valued resources and information from the task environment (individuals, groups, and organizations), as well as the acceptance of its outputs by that environment. The greater the organization's control over its environment and the greater the organization's own autonomy, the greater possibility it has to optimize its efficiency.

Organizational effectiveness is dependent on the constraints and objectives defined by special interest groups both inside and outside the organization. These groups in conflict may be professionals versus administrators; employees versus employers; owners versus consumers; marketing versus production; business firms versus environmentalists, and so on. Thus, conflict, bargaining, and decision-making are seen as the processes underlying the operative goals and objectives, which are the outcomes generally measured as effectiveness variables. For the sake of analysis, these objectives should be differentially weighted according to the priorities of the dominant group. Thus, not all organizations have the same objectives or weight them similarly, and consequently, not all organizational effectiveness can be measured in terms of the same effectiveness variables.

Evaluating organizational effectiveness is a complex process. The objectives of the dominant interest groups must be defined. All

354

internal and external constraints on these objectives have to be taken into consideration in the measurement. No one single criterion can represent all objectives (operative goals); rather, multiple criteria must be used. Some determination must be made as to an acceptable level of effectiveness based on some standard (another organization or goals). In evaluating the influence of various organizational dimensions on organizational effectiveness, one must consider such questions as:

1. What specific facet of effectiveness will be evaluated? (efficiency, the quality of the product, etc.)
2. What aspects of the environment are relevant? (complexity, stability, etc.)
3. What aspects of organizational context are relevant? (technology, size, etc.)
4. What aspects of centralization are relevant? (the participation in decision-making, the levels of hierarchical authority, etc.)
5. What aspects of complexity are relevant? (differentiation of tasks, differentiation of occupations, differentiation of knowledge and expertise, etc.)
6. What aspects of formalization are relevant? (operative, regulative, etc.)
7. What aspects of communication are relevant? (rate, content, etc.)
8. Will innovation, program change and conflict facilitate or impede effectiveness?

Thus, the variables that influence organizational effectiveness are many and often have joint (interactive) effects. The answer as to how organizations can be more effective is dependent on the nature of the dimensions of the particular organization being analyzed and its environment.

Our discussion of effectiveness leads us to a major summary point. There is no single variable or group of variables that adequately serve as indexes of effectiveness for all types of organizations, for several reasons: first, because of different objectives and priorities of objectives of organizations, different types of organizations measure effectiveness differently; second, increasing one aspect of effectiveness may decrease other aspects; and third, what is defined as effective organization is in a process of constant change.

NOTES

1. James L. Price, *Organizational Effectiveness: An Inventory of Propositions* (Homewood, Ill.: Richard D. Irwin).

2. Stanley E. Seashore and Ephraim Yuchtman, "Factorial Analysis of Organizational Performance," *Administrative Science Quarterly* 12, no. 3 (December 1967): 377–395.

3. C. Argyris, *Integrating the Individual and the Organization* (New York: John Wiley & Sons, 1964), p. 123.

4. Daniel Katz and Robert L. Kahn, *The Social Psychology of Organizations* (New York: John Wiley & Sons, 1966), p. 170.

5. Ibid., p. 165.

6. Basil Georgopoulos and Arnold Tannenbaum, "A Study of Organizational Effectiveness," *American Sociological Review* 22, no. 5 (October 1957): 534–540.

7. Selwyn W. Becker and Duncan Neuhauser, *The Efficient Organization* (New York: Elsevier, 1975), p. 46.

8. Amitai Etzioni, *Modern Organizations* (Englewood Cliffs, N.J.: Prentice–Hall, 1964), p. 8.

9. Becker and Neuhauser, *The Efficient Organization*, pp. 39–40.

10. Ibid.

11. Jerald Hage and Michael Aiken, *Social Change in Complex Organizations* (New York: Random House, 1970).

12. Ibid., pp. 50–51.

13. See Edward E. Lawler III and Lyman W. Porter, "Antecedent Attitudes of Effective Management Performance," *Organizational Behavior and Human Performance*, pp. 122–142; and Victor H. Vroom, *Work and Motivation* (New York: John Wiley & Sons, 1964).

14. John Child, "Organizational Structure, Environment and Performance: The Role of Strategic Choice," *Sociology* 6, no. 1 (January 1972): 1–22; and Hage and Aiken, *Social Change in Complex Organizations*.

15. Ephraim Yuchtman and Stanley E. Seashore, "A System Resource Approach to Organizational Effectiveness," *American Sociological Review* 32, no. 6 (December 1967): p. 891.

16. Katz and Kahn, *The Social Psychology of Organizations*, p. 149.

17. Price, *Organizational Effectiveness: An Inventory of Propositions*, p. 5.

18. Richard M. Steers, "Problems in the Measurement of Organizational Effectiveness," *Administrative Science Quarterly* 20, no. 4 (December 1975): 547.

19. Georgopoulos and Tannenbaum, "A Study of Organizational Effectiveness."

20. Steers, "Problems in the Measurement of Organizational Effectiveness," p. 548.

21. Price, *Organizational Effectiveness: An Inventory of Propositions;* and Steers, "Problems in the Measurement of Organizational Effectiveness."

22. Steers, "Problems in the Measurement of Organizational Effectiveness."

23. Ibid., p. 549.

24. John C. Campbell, "Research into the Nature of Organizational Effectiveness—An Endangered Species?" Working paper, University of Minnesota.

25. Price, *Organizational Effectiveness: An Inventory of Propositions*, p. 5.

26. Georgopoulos and Tannenbaum, "A Study of Organizational Effectiveness."

27. James L. Price, "The Study of Organizational Effectiveness," *The Sociological Quarterly* 13, no. 1 (Winter 1972): 3.

28. Talcott Parsons, *Structure and Process in Modern Societies* (New York: The Free Press, 1960), pp. 17–20, 44–47.

29. Petro Georgiou, "The Goal Paradigm and Notes Toward a Counter Paradigm," *Administrative Science Quarterly* 18, no. 3 (September 1973): 291–310.

30. Price, "The Study of Organizational Effectiveness."

31. Charles Perrow, "The Analysis of Goals in Complex Organizations," *American Sociological Review* 26, no. 6 (December 1961): 855.

32. Ibid.

33. Ibid., pp. 855–856.

34. Ibid., p. 856.

35. Herbert A. Simon, "On the Concept of Organization Goals," *Administrative Science Quarterly* 9, no. 1 (June 1964): 2.

36. Yuchtman and Seashore, "A System Resource Approach to Organizational Effectiveness," p. 892.

37. Ibid., p. 897.

38. Price, "The Study of Organizational Effectiveness," p. 5–6.

39. Ibid.

40. Edward Gross, "The Definition of Organizational Goals," *British Journal of Sociology* 20, no. 3 (September 1969): 277–294.

41. Price, "The Study of Organizational Effectiveness," p. 6.

42. Ibid.

43. Steers, "Problems in the Measurement of Organizational Effectiveness."

44. Etzioni, *Modern Organizations.*

45. Steers, "Problems in the Management of Organizational Effectiveness," p. 555.

46. Yuchtman and Seashore, "A System Resource Approach to Organizational Effectiveness," p. 897.

47. Ibid., p. 898.

48. Ibid., p. 902.

49. Ibid., pp. 901–902. This definition differs from that of Katz and Kahn, who defined organizational effectiveness as "the maximization of return to the organization by all means." Katz and Kahn, *The Social Psychology of Organizations*, p. 170.

50. Yuchtman and Seashore, "A System Resource Approach to Organizational Effectiveness," p. 902.

51. Ibid., p. 900.

52. Ibid., pp. 900–901.

53. Ibid., p. 898.

54. Seashore and Yuchtman, "Factorial Analysis of Organizational Performance," p. 383.

55. Yuchtman and Seashore, "A System Resource Approach to Organizational Effectiveness," pp. 891–903.

56. Price, "The Study of Organizational Effectiveness," p. 8.

57. Richard Hall, *Organization Structure and Process* (Englewood Cliffs, N.J.: Prentice–Hall, 1972), p. 100.

58. William A. Rushing, "Profit and Nonprofit Orientations and the Differentiations–Coordination Hypothesis for Organizations: A Study of Small General Hospitals," *American Sociological Review* 41, no. 4 (August 1976): 676–691.

59. Tom Burns and G. M. Stalker, *The Management of Innovation* (London: Tavistock Publications, 1961); Paul R. Lawrence and Jay W. Lorsch, *Organization and Environment* (Boston: Harvard University, Division of Research, Graduate School of Business Administration, 1967); and R. N. Osborn and J. G. Hunt, "Environment and Organizational Effectiveness," *Administrative Science Quarterly* 19, no. 2 (June 1974): 231–246.

60. Joan Woodward, *Industrial Organization: Theory and Practice* (Oxford: Oxford University Press, 1965); D. S. Pugh, "The Measurement of Organization Structure," in *Organizational Dynamics,* pp. 19–34; D. J. Hickson, D. S. Pugh, and D. C. Pheysey, "Operations Technology and Organizational Structure: An Empirical Reappraisal," *Administrative Science Quarterly* 14 (September 1969): 378–397.

61. Rushing, "Profit and Nonprofit Orientations and the Differentiation–Coordination Hypothesis for Organizations: A Study of Small General Hospitals."

62. Paul R. Lawrence and Jay W. Lorsch, *Organization and Environment: Managing Differentiation and Integration* (Cambridge, Mass.: Harvard University Press, 1967).

63. Peter M. Blau, "Interdependence and Hierarchy in Organizations," *Social Science Research* 1, no. 1 (April 1972): 323–349.

64. Rushing, "Profit and Nonprofit Orientations and the Differentiation–Coordination Hypothesis for Organizations: A Study of Small General Hospitals," p. 679.

65. Ibid., p. 689.

66. Ibid.

REFERENCES

ACKERMAN, ROBERT W. "Influence of Integration and Diversity on the Investment Process." *Administrative Science Quarterly* 15 (1970): 341–352.

AGUILAR, FRANICS. *Scanning the Business Environment.* New York: Macmillan Co., 1967.

AIKEN, MICHAEL, and HAGE, JERALD "Organizational Interdependence and Intraorganizational Structure." *American Sociological Review* 33 (1968): 912–930.

——— "The Organic Organization and Innovation." *Sociology* 5 (1971): 63–82.

ALBROW, MARTIN. "The Study of Organizations—Objectivity or Bias?" in J. Gould, ed., *Penguin Social Science Survey 1968.* Harmondsworth, England: Penguin, 1968, pp. 146–167.

ALDRICH, HOWARD E. "Technology and Organizational Structure: A Reexamination of the Findings of the Aston Group." *Administrative Science Quarterly* 17 (1972): 26–43.

ALDRICH, HOWARD E., and PFEFFER, JEFFREY "Environments of Organizations," in Alex Inkeles, James Coleman, and Neil Smelser, eds., *Annual Review of Sociology,* Vol. 2. Palo Alto, Calif.: Annual Review, 1976, pp. 79–105.

ANDERSON, THEODORE, and WARKOV, SEYMOUR "Organizational Size and Functional Complexity: A Study of Administration in Hospitals." *Administrative Science Quarterly* 26 (1961): 23–28.

ARGYRIS, CHRIS *Integrating the Individual and the Organization.* New York: John Wiley & Sons, 1964.

AZUMI, KOYA, and HAGE, JERALD *Organizational Systems.* Lexington, Mass.: D. C. Heath and Company, 1972.

359

BACHMAN, JERALD G.; SMITH, CLAGETT G; and SLESINGER, J. A. "Control, Performance, and Satisfaction." *Journal of Personality and Social Psychology* 4 (1966): 670–687.

BALDRIDGE, J. VICTOR *Power and Conflict in the University.* New York: John Wiley & Sons, 1971.

BALDRIDGE, J. VICTOR, and BURNHAM, ROBERT A. *The Adoption of Innovation: The Effects of Organizational Size, Differentiation and Environment.* Palo Alto, Calif.: Stanford University, Stanford Center for Research and Development in Teaching, Research Development, Memorandum 108, 1973.

——— "Organizational Innovation: Individual, Organizational, and Environmental Impacts." *Administrative Science Quarterly* 20 (1975): 165–167.

BARBER, BERNARD *Science and the Social Order.* Glencoe, Ill.: Free Press, 1952.

BARNARD, CHESTER IRVING *The Functions of the Executive.* Cambridge, Mass.: Harvard University Press, 1938.

BEALS, ALAN R., and SEIGAL, BERNARD J. *Devisiveness and Social Conflict: An Anthropological Approach.* Stanford, Calif.: Stanford University Press, 1966.

BECKER, SELWYN W., and GORDON, GERALD "An Entrepreneurial Theory of Formal Organizations Part I: Patterns of Formal Organizations." *Administrative Science Quarterly* 11 (1966): 315–344.

BECKER, SELWYN W. and NEUHAUSER, DUNCAN *The Efficient Organization.* New York: Elsevier, 1975.

BECKER, SELWYN W., and STAFFORD, F. "Some Determinants of Organizational Success. *The Journal of Business* 40 (1967): 511–518.

BELL, GERALD D. "Determinants of Span of Control." *The American Journal of Sociology* 73 (1967): 100–109.

BEN–DAVID, JOSEPH "Scientific Productivity and Academic Organization in Nineteenth Century Medicine." *American Sociological Review* 25 (1960): 828–843.

——— "The Universities and the Growth of Science in Germany and the United States." *Minerva* 7 (1968/69): pp. 1–35.

BENDIX, REINHARD *Work and Authority in Industry.* New York: Harper and Row, 1956.

BENSON, KENNETH "The Analysis of Bureaucratic–Professional Conflict: Functional Versus Dialectical Approaches." *The Sociological Quarterly* 14 (1973): 376–394.

BERGER, PHILIP K., and GIMES, ANDREW J. Cosmopolitans and Locals:

Toward an Analysis of Latent Social Roles—II." *Administrative Science Quarterly* 18 (1958): 223–235.

BERTRAND, ALVIN L.   *Social Organizations: A General Systems and Role Theory Perspective.* Philadelphia: F. A. Davis Company, 1972.

BIERSTEDT, A.   "An Analysis of Social Power," in Marvin E. Olsen, ed., *Power in Societies.* New York: Macmillan Co., 1970, pp. 11–18.

BLANKENSHIP, L. VAUGHN, and MILES, RAYMOND E.   "Organizational Structure and Managerial Decision Behavior." *Administrative Science Quarterly* 13 (1968): 107–120.

BLAU, PETER M.   "Cooperation and Competition in a Bureaucracy." *The American Journal of Sociology* 59 (1954): 530–536.

——— "Decentralization in Bureaucracies," in Mayer N. Zald, ed. *Power in Organizations.* Nashville, Tenn.: Vanderbilt Press, 1963, pp. 150–174.

BLAU, PETER M.   "The Comparative Study of Organizations." *Industrial and Labor Relations Review* 18 (1965): 323–338.

——— "The Hierarchy of Authority in Organizations. *American Journal of Sociology* 73 (1968): 453–467.

——— "A Formal Theory of Differentiation in Organizations." *American Sociological Review* 35 (1970): 201–218.

——— "Interdependence and Hierarchy in Organizations." *Social Science Research* 1 (1972): 323–349.

——— *The Organization of Academic Work.* New York: Wiley–Interscience, 1973.

——— *On the Nature of Organizations.* New York: Wiley–Interscience, 1974.

BLAU, PETER M.; FALBE, CECILIA MCHUGH; MCKINLEY, WILLIAM; and TRACY, PHELPS K.   "Technology and Organization in Manufacturing." *Administrative Science Quarterly* 21 (1976): 20–40.

BLAU, PETER M.; HEYDEBRAND, WOLF V.; and STAUFFER, ROBERT E.   "The Structure of Small Bureaucracies." *American Sociological Review* 31 (1966): 179–191.

BLAU, PETER M., and SCHOENHERR, RICHARD A.   *The Structure of Organization.* New York: Basic Books, 1971.

BLAU, PETER M., and SCOTT, W. RICHARD   *Formal Organizations: A Comparative Approach.* San Francisco: Chandler Publishing Company, 1962.

——— *Alienation and Freedom: The Factory Worker and His Industry.* Chicago: University of Chicago Press, 1964.

BOLAND, WALTER R.   "Size, External Relations and the Distribution

361

of Power: A Study of Colleges and Universities," in Wolf V. Heydebrand, ed., *Comparative Organizations.* Englewood Cliffs, N.J.: Prentice–Hall, 1973, pp. 428–440.

BOWERS, DAVID G., and SEASHORE, STANLEY E.   "Predicting Organizational Effectiveness with a Four–Factor Theory of Leadership." *Administrative Science Quarterly* 11 (1966): 238–263.

BRAYFIELD, ARTHUR H., and CROCKETT, WALTER H.   "Employee Attitudes and Employee Performance. *Psychological Bulletin* 52 (1955): 396–424.

BRIDGES, EDWIN M.; DOYLE, WAYNE F.; and MAHAN, DAVID F.   "Effects of Hierarchical Differentiation on Group Productivity, Efficiency, and Risk Taking." *Administrative Science Quarterly* 13 (1968): 305–319.

BREWER, JOHN   "Flow of Communication, Expert Qualifications and Organizational Authority Structures." *American Sociological Review* 36 (1971): 475–484.

BUCKLEY, WALTER   *Sociology and Modern Systems Theory.* Englewood Cliffs, N.J.: Prentice–Hall, 1967.

——   *Modern System Research for the Behavioral Sciences.* Chicago: Aldine Publishing Company, 1968.

BURNS, THOMAS, and STALKER, G. M.   *The Management of Innovation.* London: Tavistock Publications, 1961.

CAMPBELL, JOHN C.   "Research into the Nature of Organizational Effectiveness—An Endangered Species?" Working paper, University of Minnesota.

——   "Organizational Size." *Administrative Science Quarterly* 1 (1957): 484–505.

CAREY, ALEX   "The Hawthorne Studies: A Radical Criticism." *American Sociological Review* 32 (1967): 403–416.

CARPENTER, HARRELL H.   "Formal Organizational Structural Factors and Perceived Job Satisfaction of Classroom Teachers." *Administrative Science Quarterly* 16 (1974): 460–466.

CARROLL, JEAN   "A Note on Departmental Autonomy and Innovation in Medical Schools." *Journal of Business* 40 (1967): 193–213.

CARTER, CHARLES, and WILLIAMS, BRUCE   *Industry and Technical Progress: Factors Governing the Speed of Application of Science.* London: Oxford University Press, 1957.

CARZO, ROCCO, JR., and YANOUZAS, JOHN N.   "Some Effects of Organization Structure on Group Effectiveness." *Administrative Science Quarterly* 7 (1962): 393–424.

——   "Effects of Flat and Tall Organization Structure." *Administrative Science Quarterly* 14 (1969): 178–191.

References

CHAMPION, DEAN *The Sociology of Organizations.* New York: McGraw–Hill Book Company, 1974.

CHANDLER, ALFRED D. *Strategy and Structure: Chapters in the History of Industrial Enterprise.* Cambridge, Mass.: MIT Press, 1962.

CHAPIN, STEWART "The Growth of Bureaucracy: An Hypothesis." *American Sociological Review* 16 (1951): 835–856.

CHILD, JOHN "Organizational Structure, Environment and Performance: The role of Strategic Choice." *Sociology* 6 (1972): 2–22.

—— "Organization Structure and Strategies of Control: A Replication of the Aston Studies." *Administrative Science Quarterly* 17 (1972): 163–177.

—— "Technology, Size and Organization Structure." *Sociology* 6 (1972): 369–393.

—— "Parkinson's Progress: Accounting for the Number of Specialists in Organizations." *Administrative Science Quarterly* 18 (1973): 328–348.

—— "Predicting and Understanding Organization Structure." *Administrative Science Quarterly* 18 (1973): 168–185.

—— "Strategies of Control and Organizational Behavior." *Administrative Science Quarterly* 18 (1973): 1–17.

CHILD, JOHN, and MANSFIELD, ROGER "Technology, Size and Organization Structure." *Sociology* 6 (1972): 369–393.

CHILDERS, GRANT W.; MAYHEW, BRUCE H., JR.; and GRAY, LOUIS N. "System Size and Structural Differentiation in Military Organizations: Testing a Baseline Model of the Division of Labor." *American Journal of Sociology* 76 (1971): 813–830.

CHINOY, ELY "The Tradition of Opportunity and the Aspirations of Automobile Workers." *American Journal of Sociology* 57 (1965): 453–459.

CLARK, BURTON "Faculty Organization and Authority," in Terry Hinsford, ed. *The Study of Academic Administration.* Boulder, Colo.: Western Interstate Commission for Higher Education, 1962, pp. 37–51.

CLARK, TERRY N. "Institutionalization of Innovations in Higher Education: Four Models." *Administrative Science Quarterly* 13 (1968): 1–25.

COLEMAN, JAMES "Relational Analysis: The Study of Social Organizations with Survey Methods," in Norman Denzin, ed. *Sociological Methods.* Chicago: Aldine Publishing Company, 1970, pp. 115–126.

CORWIN, RONALD G. "The Professional Employee: A Study of

363

Conflict in Nursing Roles." *American Journal of Sociology* 66 (1961): 604–615.

―――― "Professional Persons in Public Organizations." *Educational Administrative Quarterly* 1 (1965): 1–25.

―――― "Patterns of Organizational Conflict." *Administrative Science Quarterly* 14 (1969): 507–581.

―――― "Strategies for Organizational Innovation: An Empirical Comparison." *American Sociological Review* 37 (1972): 441–454.

COSER, LEWIS A. *The Functions of Social Conflict.* London: Free Press, 1956.

CYERT, RICHARD M., and MARCH, JAMES G. *A Behavioral Theory of the Firm.* Englewood Cliffs, N.J.: Prentice–Hall, 1963.

DAHL, ROBERT "The Concept of Power." *Behavioral Science* 2 (1975): 201–215.

DAHRENDORF, RALF "Toward a Theory of Social Conflict." *The Journal of Conflict Resolution* 2 (1958): 170–183.

―――― *Class and Class Conflict in Industrial Society.* Stanford, Calif.: Stanford University Press, 1959.

DALTON, MELVILLE *Men Who Manage.* New York: John Wiley & Sons, 1959.

DARKENWALD, GORDON G., JR. "Organizational Conflict in Colleges and Universities." *Administrative Science Quarterly* 16 (1971): 407–412.

DAVIS, KEITH *Human Relations at Work.* New York: McGraw–Hill Book Company, 1962.

DAVIS, KEITH, and SCOTT, WILLIAM G. *Human Relations and Organizational Behavior: Readings and Comments,* 3rd ed. New York: McGraw–Hill Book Company, 1969.

DELBECQ, ANDRE "How 'Informal' Organization Evolves: Interpersonal Choice and Subgroup Formation." *Business Perspectives* 4 (1968): 17–21.

DERR, C. BROOKLYN "Conflict Resolution in Organizations: Views from the Field of Educational Administration." *Public Administration* 32 (1972): 495–501.

DILL, WILLIAM R. "Environment as an Influence on Managerial Autonomy." *Administrative Science Quarterly* 2 (1958): 409–443.

―――― "The Impact of Environment on Organizational Development," in Sidney Mailick and Edward H. Van Ness, eds. *Concepts and Issues in Administrative Behavior.* Englewood Cliffs, N.J.: Prentice–Hall, 1962, pp. 94–109.

DONALDSON, LEX; CHILD, JOHN; and ALDRICH, HOWARD "The Aston

Findings on Centralization: Further Discussion." *Administrative Science Quarterly* 20 (1975): 453–460.

DOWNEY, H. KIRK; HELLRIEGEL, DON; and SLOCUM, JOHN W., JR.   "Environmental Uncertainty: The Construct and Its Application." *Administrative Science Quarterly* 20 (1975): 613–629.

DOWNS, ANTHONY   *Inside Bureaucracy.* Boston: Little, Brown & Company, 1966.

DUNCAN, ROBERT B.   "Multiple Decision-Making Structures in Adapting to Environmental Uncertainty: The Impact on Organizational Effectiveness." *Human Relations* 26 (April 1973): 273–291.

——— "Characteristics of Organizational Environments and Perceived Environmental Uncertainty." *Administrative Science Quarterly* 3 (1972): 313–327.

——— "Multiple Decision-Making Structures in Adapting to Environmental Uncertainty." *Human Relations* 26 (1973): 273–291.

DUTTON, JOHN M., and WALTON, RICHARD E.   "Interdepartmental Conflict and Cooperation: Two Contrasting Studies." *Human Organization* 25 (1966): 207–220.

EISENSTADT, S. N.   "Bureaucracy, Bureaucratization and Debureaucratization." *Administrative Science Quarterly* 4 (1959): 302–320.

EMERY, FRED E., and TRIST, ERIC L.   "The Causal Texture of Organizational Environments." *Human Relations* 18 (1965): 21–31.

ETZIONI, AMITAI   "Authority Structure and Organizational Effectiveness." *Administrative Science Quarterly* 4 (1959): 43–67.

——— *Modern Organizations.* Englewood Cliffs, N.J.: Prentice–Hall, 1964.

——— *A Comparative Analysis of Complex Organizations.* New York: Free Press, 1975.

EVAN, WILLIAM M.   "The Organization–Set: Toward a Theory of Interorganizational Relations," in John G. Maurer, ed. *Readings in Organization Theory: Open System Approaches.* New York: Random House, 1971, pp. 33–45.

EVAN, WILLIAM M., and BLACK, G.   "Innovation in Business Organizations: Some Factors Associated with Success or Failure of Staff Proposals." *Journal of Business* 40 (1967): 519–530.

EVAN, WILLIAM M., and SCHWARTZ, MILDRED A.   "Law and the Emergence of Formal Organizations." *Sociology and Social Research* 48 (1964): 270–280.

FAYOL, HENRI   *General and Industrial Management,* trans. Constance Storrs. London: Pitman, 1949.

FLANGO, VICTOR E., and BRUMBAUGH, ROBERT B.   "The Dimensionality of the Cosmopolitan–Local Construct." *Administrative Science Quarterly* 19 (1974): 198–209.

FLORENCE, SARGENT P.   *The Logic of British and American Industry.* London: Routledge and Kegan Paul, 1961.

FOLLETT, MARY PARKER   *Dynamic Administration.* New York: Longman, 1941.

FRANKLIN, JEROME L.   "Down the Organization: Influence Processes Across Levels of Hierarchy." *Administrative Science Quarterly* 20 (1975): 153–164.

FRENCH, JOHN R. P., and RAVEN, BERTRAM   "The Bases of Social Power," in Dorwin Cartwright and Alvin Zander, eds. *Group Dynamics,* 3rd ed. New York: Harper and Row, 1968, pp. 259–269.

FRIEDLANDER, FRANK, and PICKLE, HAL   "Components of Effectiveness in Small Organizations." *Administrative Science Quarterly* 13 (1968): 289–304.

1975 GENERAL MOTORS REPORT on PROGRAMS of PUBLIC INTEREST   Detroit: General Motors Corporation, 1976.

GEORGIOU, PETRO   "The Goal Paradigm and Notes Towards a Counter Paradigm." *Administrative Science Quarterly* 18 (1973): 291–310.

GEORGOPOULOS, BASIL S., and MANN, FLOYD C.   *The Community General Hospital.* New York: Macmillan Co., 1962.

GEORGOPOULOS, BASIL S., and TANNENBAUM, ARNOLD   "A Study of Organizational Effectiveness." *American Sociological Review* 22 (1957): 534–540.

GIMES, ANDREW J., and BERGER, PHILIP K.   "Cosmopolitan–Local: Evaluation of the Construct." *Administrative Science Quarterly* 15 (1970): 407–416.

GLASER, BARNERY G.   "The Local–Cosmopolitan Scientist." *American Journal of Sociology* 69 (1963): 249–459.

GOLDNER, FRED H., and RITTI, R. R.   "Professionalization and Career Immobility." *American Journal of Sociology* 72 (1967): 489–502.

GOODE, WILLIAM J.   "Encroachment, Charlatanism, and the Emerging Profession: Psychology, Sociology, and Medicine. *American Sociological Review* 25 (1960): 902–914.

GORDON, GERALD, and MARQUIS, SUE   "Freedom, Visibility of Consequences, and Scientific Innovation." *American Journal of Sociology* 72 (1966): 195–209.

GOSS, M. E. W.   "Influence and Authority Among Physicians in an

366

Outpatient Clinic." *American Sociological Review* 26 (1961): 39–50.

GOULDNER, ALVIN W.   *Patterns of Industrial Bureaucracy.* New York: Free Press, 1954.

——— "Cosmopolitans and Locals: Toward an Analysis of Latent Social Roles—I." *Administrative Science Quarterly* 2 (1957): 281–306.

GREENWOOD, ERNEST   "Attributes of a Profession." *Social Work* 2 (1957): 45–55.

GROSS, BERTRAM M.   *The Managing of Organizations.* New York: Free Press, 1964.

GROSS, EDWARD   *Work and Society.* New York: Thomas Y. Crowell Company, 1958.

——— "The Definition of Organizational Goals." *British Journal of Sociology* 20 (1969): 277–294.

GROSS, M. L.   *The Brainwatchers.* New York: Random House, 1962.

GRUSKY, OSCAR   "Corporate Size and Managerial Succession." *American Journal of Sociology* 61 (1961): 261–269.

GUETZKOW, HAROLD   "Communication in Organizations," in James G. March, ed., *Handbook of Organizations.* Chicago: Rand McNally & Company, 1965.

GULICK, L. H., and URWICK, L., eds.   *Papers on the Science of Administration.* New York: Columbia University, Institute of Public Administration, 1937.

HAAS, EUGENE; HALL, RICHARD H.; and JOHNSON, NORMAN J.   "The Size of the Supportive Component in Organizations: A Multi-Organizational Analysis." *Social Forces* 43 (1963): 9–17.

HAGE, JERALD   "An Axiomatic Theory of Organizations." *Administrative Science Quarterly* 10 (1965): 289–320.

——— *Communication and Organizational Control: Cybernetics in Health and Welfare Settings.* New York: Wiley–Interscience, 1974.

HAGE, JERALD; AIKEN, MICHAEL; and MARRETT, CORA BAGLEY   "Organization Structure and Communication." *American Sociological Review* 36 (1971): 860–871.

HAGE, JERALD, and AIKEN, MICHAEL   "Program Change and Organizational Properties: A Comparative Analysis." *American Journal of Sociology* 72 (1967): 503–519.

——— "Relationship of Centralization to Other Structural Properties." *Administrative Science Quarterly* 12 (1967): 72–91.

——— "Routine Technology, Social Structure, and Organizational Goals." *Administrative Science Quarterly* 14 (1969): 366–377.

────── *Social Change in Complex Organizations.* New York: Random House, 1970.

HAGE, JERALD, and DEWAR, ROBERT "Elite Values Versus Organizational Structure in Predicting Innovation." *Administrative Science Quarterly* 18 (1973): 279–290.

HAGSTROM, WARREN O. *The Scientific Community.* New York: Basic Books, 1965.

HALL, D. F., and LAWLER, E. E. "Job Characteristics and Pressures and the Organizational Integration of Professionals." *Administrative Science Quarterly* 15 (1970): 271–281.

HALL, JOHN W. "A Comparison of Halpin and Croft's Organizational Climates and Likert and Likert's Organizational Systems." *Administrative Science Quarterly* 17 (1972): 586–590.

HALL, RICHARD H. "Intra-organizational Structural Variation: Application of the Bureaucratic Model." *Administrative Science Quarterly* 7 (1962): 295–308.

────── "Bureaucracy and Small Organizations." *Sociology and Social Research* 48 (1963): 38–46.

────── "The Concept of Bureaucracy: An Empirical Assessment." *American Journal of Sociology* 69 (1963): 32–40.

────── "Some Organizational Considerations in Professional–Organizational Relationships." *Administrative Science Quarterly* 12 (1967): 461–478.

────── "Professionalization and Bureaucratization." *American Sociological Review* 33 (1968): 92–104.

────── *Organization Structure and Process.* Englewood Cliffs, N.J.: Prentice–Hall, 1972.

HALL, RICHARD H.; HAAS, EUGENE; and JOHNSON, NORMAN J. "Organizational Size, Complexity, and Formalization." *American Sociological Review* 32 (1967): 905–912.

────── "Reply to Weldon." *Administrative Science Quarterly* 17 (1972): 79–80.

HALL, RICHARD H., and TITTLE, CHARLES R. "A Note on Bureaucracy and Its 'Correlates.'" *American Journal of Sociology* 72 (1966): 267–272.

HARVEY, EDWARD "Technology and the Structure of Organizations." *American Sociological Review* 33 (1968): 247–259.

HAWLEY, AMOS H. "Community Power and Urban Renewal Success." *American Journal of Sociology* 68 (1963): 422–431.

HAWLEY, AMOS H.; BOLAND, WALTER; and BOLAND, MARGARET "Population Size and Administration in Institutions of Higher Education." *American Sociological Review* 30 (1965): 252–255.

References

HEYDEBRAND, WOLF V. *Comparative Organizations.* Englewood Cliffs, N.J.: Prentice–Hall, 1973.

HICKSON, D. J.; HININGS, C. R.; LEE, C. A.; SCHNECK, R. E.; and PENNINGS, J. M. "A Strategic Contingencies' Theory of Intraorganizational Power." *Administrative Science Quarterly* 16 (1971): 216–229.

HICKSON, D. J.; HININGS, C. R.; MCMILLAN, C. J.; and SCHWITTER, J. P. "The Culture-Free Context of Organization Structure: A Tri-National Comparison." *Sociology* 8 (1974): 59–80.

HICKSON, DAVID J.; PUGH, D. S.; and PHEYSEY, DIANA C. "Operations Technology and Organizational Structure: An Empirical Reappraisal." *Administrative Science Quarterly* 14 (1969): 378–397.

HININGS, C. R.; HICKSON, D. J.; PENNINGS, J. M.; and SCHNECK, R. E. "Structural Conditions of Intraorganizational Power." *Administrative Science Quarterly* 19 (1974): 22–44.

HININGS, C. R., and LEE, G. L. "Dimensions of Organization Structure and Their Context: A Replication." *Sociology* 5 (1971): 83–93.

HIRSCH, PAUL M. "Organizational Effectiveness and the Institutional Environment." *Administrative Science Quarterly* 20 (1975): 327–344.

HOLDAWAY, EDWARD A., and BLOWERS, THOMAS A. "Administrative Ratios and Organization Size: A Longitudinal Examination." *American Sociological Review* 26 (1971): 278–286.

HREBINIAK, LAWRENCE G., and ALUTTO, JOSEPH A. "A Comparative Organizational Study of Performance and Size Correlates in Inpatient Psychiatric Departments." *Administrative Science Quarterly* 18 (1973): 365–382.

HUDSON, DALE "Communication and the Organization." Paper for a class in complex organizations, Illinois State University.

HULIN, CHARLES L., and BLOOD, MILTON R. "Job Enlargement, Individual Differences, and Worker Responses." *Psychology Bulletin* 69 (1968): 41–55.

HUMMON, NORMAN P. "Criticism of 'Effects of Flat and Tall Organization Structure.'" *Administrative Science Quarterly* 15 (1970): 230–241.

INDIK, BERNARD P. "The Relationship between Organization Size and Supervision Ratio." *Administrative Science Quarterly* 9 (1964): 301–312.

INKSON, J. H.; PUGH, D. S.; and HICKSON, D. J. "Organization Context and Structure: An Abbreviated Replication." *Administrative Science Quarterly* 15 (1970): 318–329.

369

INKSON, J. H.; SCHWITTER, J. P.; PHEYSEY, D. C.; and HICKSON, D. J. "A Comparison of Organization Structure and Managerial Roles: Ohio U.S.A., and the Midlands, England." *A Journal of Management Studies* 7 (1970): 363–374.

IVANCEVICH, JOHN M. "Changes in Performance in a Management by Objectives Program." *American Sociological Quarterly* 19 (1974): 563–574.

IVANCEVICH, JOHN M., and DONNELLY, JAMES H., JR. "Relation of Organizational Structure to Job Satisfaction, Anxiety–Stress, and Performance." *Administrative Science Quarterly* 20 (1975): 272–280.

JAPAN COUNCIL *The Control of Industry in Japan.* Tokyo: Institute of Political and Economic Research, 1953.

JURKOVICH, RAY "A Core Typology of Organizational Environments." *Administrative Science Quarterly* 19 (1974): 380–394.

KATZ, DANIEL, and KAHN, ROBERT L. *The Social Psychology of Organizations.* New York: John Wiley & Sons, 1966.

——— "Open Systems Theory," in Oscar Grusky and George A. Miller, eds. *The Sociology of Organizations.* New York: Free Press, 1970, pp. 149–158.

KATZ, DANIEL; MACCOBY, N.; and MORSE, NANCY C. *Productivity, Supervision, and Morale in an Office Situation.* Detroit: Darel Press, Inc., 1950.

KATZ, FRED E. *Autonomy and Organization.* New York: Random House, 1968.

KAUFMAN, HERBERT, and SEIDMAN, DAVID "The Morphology of Organizations." *Administrative Science Quarterly* 15 (1970): 439–452.

KELSEY, J. G. T. "Organizational Technology in Schools: Conceptualizations for Measurement." *Canadian Administrator* 14 (1974): 1–4.

KEMERER, FRANK R., and BALDRIDGE, J. VICTOR *Unions on Campus.* San Francisco: Jossey–Bass Publishers, 1975.

KERR, CLARK *The Uses of the University.* Cambridge, Mass.: Harvard University Press, 1964.

KHANDWALLA, PRADIP N. "Mass Output Orientation of Operations Technology and Organizational Structure." *Administrative Science Quarterly* 19 (1974): 74–97.

KIMBERLY, JOHN R., and NIELSEN, WARREN R. "Organization Development and Change in Organizational Performance." *Administrative Science Quarterly* 20 (1975): 191–206.

KLATZKY, S. R. "Relationship of Organizational Size to Complexity and Coordination." *Administrative Science Quarterly* 15 (1970): 428–438.

KOCHAN, THOMAS A. "Determinants of the Power of Boundary Units in an Interorganizational Bargaining Relation." *Administrative Science Quarterly* 20 (1975): 434–452.

KORNHAUSER, WILLIAM *Scientists in Industry: Conflict and Accommodation.* Berkeley: University of California Press, 1962.

KROUSE, CLEMENT G. "Complex Objectives, Decentralization, and the Decision Process of the Organization." *Administrative Science Quarterly* 17 (1972): 544–554.

LAMMER, CORNELIUS "Strikes and Mutinies: A Comparative Study of Organizational Conflict Between Rulers and Ruled." *Administrative Science Quarterly* 14 (1969): 558–572.

LANDESBERGER, HENRY A. *Hawthorne Revisited.* Ithaca, N.Y.: Cornell University Press, 1958.

LAWLER, EDWARD E., III, and PORTER, LYMAN W. "Antecedent Attitudes of Effective Management Performance." *Organizational Behavior and Human Performance* 2 (1967): 122–142.

―――― "The Effect of Performance on Job Satisfaction." *Industrial Relations* 7 (1967): 20–28.

LAWRENCE, PAUL R., and LORSCH, JAY W. "Differentiation and Integration in Complex Organizations." *Administrative Science Quarterly* 12 (1967): 1–47.

―――― *Organization and Environment: Managing Differentiation and Integration.* Cambridge, Mass.: Harvard University Press, 1967.

LEVINE, SOL, and WHITE, PAUL E. "Exchange as a Conceptual Framework for the Study of Interorganizational Relationships." *Administrative Science Quarterly* 5 (1961): 583–601.

LEVINE, SOL, WHITE, PAUL E., and PAUL, BENJAMIN D. "Community Interorganizational Problems in Providing Medical Care and Social Services." *American Journal of Public Health* 53 (1963): 1183–1195.

LEVINSON, HARRY "Asinine Attitudes Toward Motivation." *Harvard Business Review* 51 (1973): 70–76.

LIKERT, RENSIS *New Patterns of Management.* New York: McGraw–Hill Book Company, 1961.

LIKERT, RENSIS, and LIKERT, JANE C. *New Ways of Managing Conflict.* New York: McGraw–Hill Book Company, 1976.

LIPSET, SEYMOUR M. *Political Man.* Garden City, N.Y.: Doubleday, 1960.

LITWAK, EUGENE "Models of Bureaucracy Which Permit Conflict." *American Journal of Sociology* 67 (1961): 177–184.

371

LITWAK, EUGENE, and HYLTON, LYDIA "Interorganizational Analyses: A Hypothesis of Coordinating Agencies." *Administrative Science Quarterly* 6 (1962): 395–421.

LORTIE, DAN C. "The Balance of Control and Autonomy in Elementary School Teaching," in Amitai Etzioni, ed. *The Semi-Professions and Their Organizations.* New York: Free Press, 1976, pp. 1–53.

LOWELL, A. L. *Conflicts of Principle.* Cambridge, Mass.: Harvard University Press, 1932.

LYNCH, BEVERLY P. "An Empirical Assessment of Perrow's Technology Construct." *Administrative Science Quarterly* 19 (1974): 338–356.

MCMILLAN, C. J., HICKSON, D. J., and HININGS, C. R. "The Structure of Work Organizations Across Societies." *Academy of Management Journal* 17 (1973): 555–579.

MAIER, NORMAN R. *Psychology in Industry,* 2nd ed. Boston: Houghton Mifflin, 1965.

MANSFIELD, E. "Size of Firm, Market Structure, and Innovation." *Journal of Political Economy* 71 (1963): 556–576.

MANSFIELD, ROGER "Bureaucracy and Centralization: An Examination of Organizational Structure." *Administrative Science Quarterly* 18 (1973): 477–488.

MARCH, JAMES G., and SIMON, HERBERT A. *Organizations.* New York: John Wiley & Sons, 1958.

MAREK, J. "Conflict, A Battle of Strategies," in J. R. Lawrence, ed. *Operational Research and the Social Sciences.* London: Tavistock Publications, 1966.

MARRETT, CORA B. "On the Specification of Interorganizational Dimensions." *Sociology and Social Research* 56 (1971): 83–97.

MARROW, ALFRED; BOWERS, DAVID; and SEASHORE, STANLEY *Management by Participation.* New York: Harper and Row, 1967.

MARX, KARL *Capital: A Critique of Political Economy.* New York: Random House, 1906.

MASSIE, JOSEPH "Management Theory," in James G. March, ed. *Handbook of Organizations.* Chicago: Rand McNally & Company, 1965, pp. 387–422.

MAYHEW, BRUCE H. "System Size and Ruling Elites." *American Sociological Review* 38 (1973): 468–475.

MAYHEW, BRUCE H., and JAMES, THOMAS F. "System Size and Structural Differentiation in Military Organizations: Testing a Harmonic Series Model of the Division of Labor." *American Journal of Sociology* 77 (1972): 750–756.

MAYHEW, BRUCE H.; LEVINGER, ROGER L.; MCPHERSON, J. MILLER; and JAMES THOMAS F. "System Size and Structural Differentiation in Formal Organizations: A Baseline Generator for Two Major Theoretical Propositions." *American Sociological Review* 37 (1972): 629–633.

MECHANIC, DAVID "Sources of Power of Lower Participants in Complex Organizations." *Administrative Science Quarterly* 7 (1962): 349–364.

MELMAN, SEYMOUR "The Rise of Administrative Overhead in the Manufacturing Industries of the United States 1899–1947." *Oxford Economic Papers* 3 (1951): 61–112.

MERTON, ROBERT K. "Bureaucratic Structure and Personality," in Amitai Etzioni, ed. *Complex Organizations: A Sociological Reader.* New York: Holt, Rinehart & Winston, 1960, pp. 48–61.

MEYER, MARSHALL W. "Expertness and the Span of Control." *American Sociological Review* 33 (1968): 944–951.

——— "Two Authority Structures of Bureaucratic Organization." *Administrative Science Quarterly* 13 (1968): 211–228.

——— "Size and the Structure of Organizations: A Causal Analysis." *American Sociological Review* 37 (1972): 434–440.

——— "Organizational Domains." *American Sociological Review* 40 (1975): 599–615.

MYERS, SUMNER, and MARQUIS, D. G. *Successful Industrial Innovations.* Washington, D.C.: National Science Foundation; NSF 69-17, 1969.

MILLER, DAVID W., and STARR, MARTIN K. *The Structure of Human Decisions.* Englewood Cliffs, N.J.: Prentice–Hall, 1967.

MILLER, DELBERT, and FORM, WILLIAM *Industrial Sociology: The Sociology of Work Organizations.* New York: Harper and Row, 1964.

MILLER, GEORGE A. Professionals in Bureaucracy: Alienation Among Industrial Scientists and Engineers." *American Sociological Review* 32 (1967): 755–767.

MINDLIN, SERGIO, E., and ALDRICH, HOWARD "Interorganizational Dependence: A Review of the Concept and a Reexamination of the Findings of the Aston Group." *Administrative Science Quarterly* 20 (1975): 382–392.

MOHR, LAWRENCE B. "Determinants of Innovation in Organizations." *American Political Science Review* 63 (1969): 111–126.

——— "Organizational Technology and Organizational Structure." *Administrative Science Quarterly* 16 (1971): 444–459.

MONGE, KIM M. "Effectiveness." Paper for a class in complex organizations, Illinois State University.

MONTAGNA, PAUL D. "Professionalization and Bureaucratization in Large Professional Organizations." *American Journal of Sociology* 74 (1968): 138–145.

MOONEY, J. D., and REILEY, A. C. *The Principles of Organizations.* New York: Harper and Row, 1939.

MORRISSEY, ELIZABETH, and GILLESPIE, DAVID F. "Technology and the Conflict of Professionals in Bureaucratic Organizations." *The Sociological Quarterly* 16 (1975): 319–332.

MORSE, N. M., and REIMER, E. "The Experimental Change of a Major Organization Variable." *Journal of Abnormal and Social Psychology* 52 (1956): 120–129.

NORMANN, RICHARD "Organizational Innovativeness: Product Variation and Reorientation." *Administrative Science Quarterly* 16 (1971): 203–215.

ORNHAUSER, WILLIAM K. Scientists in Industry. Berkeley: University of California Press, 1963.

OSBORN, RICHARD N., and HUNT, JAMES G. "Environment and Organizational Effectiveness." *Administrative Science Quarterly* 19 (1974) 231–246.

OUCHI, WILLIAM G., and DOWLING, JOHN B. "Defining the Span of Control." *Administrative Science Quarterly* 19 (1974): 357–365.

OUCHI, WILLIAM G., and MAGUIRE, MARY ANN "Organizational Control: Two Functions." *Administrative Science Quarterly* 20 (1975): 559–569.

PARKINSON, C NORTHCOTE *Parkinson's Law.* New York: Ballantine Books, 1964.

PARSONS, TALCOTT *Structure and Processes in Modern Societies.* New York: Free Press, 1960.

PARSONS, TALCOTT, and PLATT, GARALD M. "The American Academic Profession: A Pilot Study." Working paper, Harvard University, Department of Social Relations.

PAULSON, STEVEN K. "Causal Analysis of Interorganizational Relations: An Axiomatic Theory Revised." *Administrative Science Quarterly* 19 (1974): 319–337.

PEABODY, ROBERT L. "Perceptions of Organizational Authority: A Comparative Analysis." *Administrative Science Quarterly* 6 (1962): 463–482.

PENNINGS, JOHANNES M. "Work-Value Systems of White-Collar Workers. *Administrative Science Quarterly* 15 (1970): 397–406.
——— "Measures of Organizational Structure: A Methodological Note." *American Journal of Sociology* 79 (1973): 686–704.

———— "The Relevance of the Structural–Contingency Model for Organizational Effectiveness." *Administrative Science Quarterly* 20 (1975): 393–410.

———— "Dimensions of Organizational Influence and Their Effectiveness Correlates." *Administrative Science Quarterly* 21 (1976): 688–699.

PERROW, CHARLES "The Analysis of Goals in Complex Organizations." *American Sociological Review* 26 (1961): 854–866.

———— "A Framework for the Comparative Analysis of Organizations." *American Sociological Review* 32 (1967): 194–208.

———— "Departmental Power and Perspective in Industrial Firms," in Mayer N. Zald, ed. *Power in Organizations.* Nashville, Tenn., Vanderbilt University Press, 1970, pp. 49–89.

———— *Organizational Analysis: A Sociological View.* Belmont, Calif.: Wadsworth Publishing Co., 1970.

———— *Complex Organizations: A Critical Essay.* Glenview, Ill.: Scott, Foresman & Company, 1972.

———— "Technology and Structure." Working paper, Madison, Wisc.: University of Wisconsin.

PFEFFER, JEFFREY "Beyond Management and the Worker: The Institutional Function of Management." *Academy of Management Review* 1 (1976): 36–46.

———— "Size and Composition of Corporate Boards of Directors: The Organization and Its Environment." *Administrative Science Quarterly* 17 (1972): 218–228.

———— "Size, Composition, and Function of Hospital Boards of Directors: A Study of Organization–Environment Linkage." *Administrative Science Quarterly* 18 (1973): 349–364.

PONDY, LOUIS R. "Organizational Conflict: Concepts and Models." *Administrative Science Quarterly* 12 (1967): 296–320.

———— "Effects of Size, Complexity and Ownership on Administrative Intensity." *Administrative Science Quarterly* 14 (1969): 47–61.

———— "Varieties of Organizational Conflict." *Administrative Science Quarterly* 14 (1969): 499–505.

PRESTHUS, R. V. "Toward a Theory of Organizational Behavior." *Administrative Science Quarterly* 3 (1958): 48–72.

———— "Weberian v. Welfare Bureaucracy in Traditional Society." *Administrative Science Quarterly* 6 (1961): 1–24.

PRICE, JAMES L. *Organizational Effectiveness: An Inventory of Propositions.* Homewood, Ill.: Richard D. Irwin, 1968.

—— *Handbook of Organizational Measurement.* Lexington, Mass.: D. C. Heath and Company, 1972.

—— "The Study of Organizational Effectiveness." *The Sociological Quarterly* 13 (1972): 3–15.

PUGH, D. S.   "The Measurement of Organization Structure." *Organizational Dynamics,* vol. 1, 1973, pp. 19–34.

PUGH, D. S.; HICKSON, D. J.; and HININGS, C. R.   "An Empirical Taxonomy of Structures of Work Organizations." *Administrative Science Quarterly* 14 (1969): 115–125.

PUGH, D. S.; HICKSON, D. J.; HININGS, C. R.; MACDONALD, K. M.; TURNER, C.; and LUPTON, T.   "A Conceptual Scheme for Organizational Analysis." *Administrative Science Quarterly* 8 (1963): 289–316.

PUGH, D. S.; HICKSON, D. J.; HININGS, C. R.; and TURNER, C.   "Dimensions of Organization Structure." *Administrative Science Quarterly* 13 (1968): 65–105.

—— "The Context of Organization Structure." *Administrative Science Quarterly* 14 (1969): 91–114.

REIMANN, BERNARD   "On the Dimensions of Bureaucratic Structure: An Empirical Reappraisal." *Administrative Science Quarterly* 18 (1973): 462–476.

REISCHAUER, EDWIN O.   *The United States and Japan.* Cambridge, Mass.: Harvard University Press, 1954.

REISSMAN, LEONARD   "A Study of Role Conceptions in Bureaucracy." *Social Forces* 27 (1949): 305–310.

RICE, GEORGE, H., JR., and BISHOPRICK, DEAN W.   *Conceptual Models of Organizations.* New York: Appleton–Century–Crofts, 1971.

—— *The Sociology of Organizations.* New York: McGraw–Hill Book Company, 1974.

RIZZO, JOHN R.; HOUSE, ROBERT J.; and LIRTZMAN, SIDNEY I.   "Role Conflict and Ambiguity in Complex Organizations." *Administrative Science Quarterly* 15 (1970): 150–163.

ROETHLISBERGER, FRITZ J., and DICKSON, WILLIAM J.   *Management and the Worker.* Cambridge, Mass.: Harvard University Press, 1947.

—— "Human Relations," in Oscar Gusky and Grusky and George A. Miller, eds. *The Sociology of Organizations.* New York: Free Press, 1970.

ROGERS, DAVID L.   "Towards a Scale of Interorganizational Relations Among Public Agencies." *Sociology and Social Research* 59 (1974): 61–70.

ROGERS, EVERETT   *Diffusion of Innovations.* New York: Free Press, 1962.

ROGERS, EVERETT, and AGARWALA–ROGERS, REKHA *Communication in Organizations.* New York: Free Press, 1976.

ROGERS, EVERETT M., and SHOEMAKER, F. FLOYD *Communication of Innovations: A Cross-Cultural Approach.* New York: Free Press, 1971.

ROSE, ARNOLD *The Power Structure: Political Process in American Society.* New York: Oxford University Press, 1967.

ROSEN, M. M. "Administrative Controls and Innovation." *Behavioral Science* 13 (1968): 36–43.

RUSHING, WILLIAM A. "The Effects of Industry Size and Division of Labor on Administration." *Administrative Science Quarterly* 12 (1967): 273–295.

―――― "Differences in Profit and Nonprofit Organizations: A Study of Effectiveness and Efficiency in General Short-Stay Hospitals." *Administrative Science Quarterly* 19 (1974): 474–484.

―――― "Profit and Nonprofit Orientations and the Differentiation–Coordination Hypothesis for Organizations: A Study of Small General Hospitals." *American Sociological Review* 41 (1976): 676–691.

SALANCIK, GERALD R., and PFEFFER, JEFFREY "The Bases and Use of Power in Organizational Decision Making: The Case of a University." *Administrative Science Quarterly* 19 (1974): 453–473.

SAMUEL, YITZHAK, and MANNHEIM, BILHA F. "A Multidimensional Approach Toward a Typology of Bureaucracy." *Administrative Science Quarterly* 15 (1970): 216–229.

SAPOLSKY, HARVEY "Organizational Structure and Innovation." *Journal of Business* 40 (1967): 497–510.

SATOW, ROBERTA LYNN "Value-Rational Authority and Professional Organizations: Weber's Missing Type." *Administrative Science Quarterly* 20 (1975): 526–531.

SCHEIN, EDGAR H. *Organizational Psychology.* Englewood Cliffs, N.J.: Prentice–Hall, 1965.

SCHMIDT, STUART M., and KOCHAN, THOMAS A. "Conflict Toward Conceptual Clarity." *Administrative Science Quarterly* 17 (1972): 359–370.

SCOTT, W. RICHARD "Reactions to Supervision in a Heteronomous Professional Organization." *Administrative Science Quarterly* 10 (1965): 65–81.

―――― "Organizational Structure." *Annual Review of Sociology.* Palo Alto, Calif.: Annual Review, Inc., 1975, pp. 1–20.

SEASHORE, STANLEY E., and YUCHTMAN, EPHRAIM "Factorial Analysis of Organizational Performance." *Administrative Science Quarterly* 12 (1967): 377–395.

SEILER, J. A.   "Diagnosing Interdepartmental Conflict." *Harvard Business Review* 4 (1963): 121–132.

SELZNICK, PHILIP   "An Approach to a Theory of Bureaucracy." *American Sociological Review* 8 (1943): 47–54.

——   *Leadership in Administration.* Evanston, Ill.: Row Peterson, 1957.

——   *TVA and Grass Roots: A Study in the Sociology of Formal Organizations.* Berkeley: University of California Press, 1960.

SHELDON, OLIVER   *The Philosophy of Management.* London: Pitman, 1923.

SHEPARD, HERBERT A.   "Innovation-Resisting and Innovation Producing Organizations." *Journal of Business* 40 (1967): 470–477.

SHEPARD, JON M.   *Automation and Alienation.* Cambridge, Mass.: M.I.T. Press, 1971.

——   "On Alex Carey's Radical Criticism of the Hawthorne Studies." *Academy of Management Journal* 14 (1971): 32.

SHEPERD, CLOVIS   "Orientations of Scientists and Engineers." *Pacific Sociological Review* 4 (1961): 79–83.

SIMMEL, GEORG   *Conflict and the Web of Social Conflict,* trans. Kurt H. Wolff. Glencoe, Ill.: Free Press, 1956.

SIMMONS, ROBERTA G.   "The Role Conflict of the First-Line Supervisor: An Experimental Study." *American Journal of Sociology* 73 (1978): 482–495.

SIMON, HERBERT A.   *Administrative Behavior.* New York: Macmillan Co., 1957.

——   "On the Concept of Organization Goals." *Administrative Science Quarterly* 9 (1964): 1–22.

SLEVIN, DENNIS P.   "The Innovation Boundary: A Specific Model and Some Empirical Results." *Administrative Science Quarterly* 16 (1971): 515–532.

SNIZEK, WILLIAM E.   "Hall's Professionalism Scale: An Empirical Reassessment." *American Sociological Review* 37 (1972): 109–114.

SORENSEN, JAMES E., and SORENSEN, THOMAS L.   "The Conflict of Professionals in Bureaucratic Organizations." *Administrative Science Quarterly* 19 (1974): 98–106.

STARBUCK, WILLIAM   *Organizations and Their Environment.* Berlin: International Institute of Management, 1973.

STEERS, RICHARD M.   "Problems in the Measurement of Organizational Effectiveness." *Administrative Science Quarterly* 20 (1975): 546–558.

STINCHCOMBE, ARTHUR L. "Bureaucratic and Craft Administration of Production: A Comparative Study." *Administrative Science Quarterly* 4 (1959): 168–187.

STOGDILL, RALPH M. "Dimensions of Organization Theory," in James L. Thompson and Victor Vroom, eds. *Organizational Design and Research*. Pittsburgh: University of Pittsburgh Press, 1971, pp. 1–51.

STOGDILL, RALPH M., and COONS, A. E. *Leadership Behavior: Its Description and Measurement*. Columbus, Ohio: Bureau of Business Research, 1957.

STRAUSS, GEORGE "Notes on Power Equalization," in Harold J. Leavitt, ed. *The Social Science of Organizations*. Englewood Cliffs, N.J.: Prentice–Hall, 1963.

SUTTON, RICHARD L. "Cultural Context and Change-Agent Organizations." *Administrative Science Quarterly* 19 (1974): 547–562.

SYKES, A. J. M. "Economic Interest and the Hawthorne Researchers: A Comment." *Human Relations* 18 (1965): 253–263.

TANNENBAUM, A. S. *Social Psychology of the Work Organization*. Belmont, Calif.: Brooks/Cole Publishing Company, 1966.

TANNENBAUM, A. S.; KAVCIC, BOGDAN; ROSEN, MENACHEM; VIANELLO, MINO; and WEISER, GEORG *Hierarchy in Organizations*. San Francisco: Jossey–Bass, 1974.

TANNENBAUM, ROBERT, and MASSARIK, FRED "Participation by Subordinates in the Managerial Decision-Making Process." *The Canadian Journal of Economics and Political Science* 16 (1950), 408–418.

TAYLOR, DONALD W. "Decision Making and Problem Solving," in James March, ed. *Handbook of Organizations*. Chicago: Rand McNally & Company, 1965, pp. 48–82.

TAYLOR, FREDERICK W. *Scientific Management*. New York: Harper and Row, 1947.

TELLY, CHARLES S.; FRENCH, WENDELL L.; and SCOTT, WILLIAM G. "The Relationship of Inequity to Turnover Among Hourly Workers." *Administrative Science Quarterly* 16 (1971): 164–172.

TERREBERRY, SHIRLEY "The Evolution of Organizational Environments." *Administrative Science Quarterly* 12 (1968): 590–613.

TERRIEN, FREDERIC W., and MILLS, DONALD L. "The Effect of Changing Size upon the Internal Structure of Organizations." *American Sociological Review* 20 (1955): 11–13.

THOMPSON, JAMES D. *Organizations in Action*. New York: McGraw–Hill Book Company, 1967.

——— "Models of Organization and Administrative Systems." *The Social Science: Problems and Orientations.* The Hague: Mouton/ UNESCO, pp. 395–405.

THOMPSON, VICTOR A. *Modern Organizations.* New York: Alfred Knopf Company, 1961.

——— "Hierarchy, Specialization and Organizational Conflict." *Administrative Science Quarterly* 5 (1961): 485–521.

——— "Bureaucracy and Innovation." *Administrative Science Quarterly* 10 (1965): 1–20.

THORNTON, RUSSELL "Organizational Involvement and Commitment to Organization and Profession." *Administrative Science Quarterly* 15 (1970): 417–424.

TOSI, HENRY; ALDAG, RAMON; and STOREY, RONALD "On the Measurement of the Environment: An Assessment of the Lawrence and Lorsch Environmental Uncertainty Subscale." *Administrative Science Quarterly* 18 (1973): 27–36.

TSOUDEROS, JOHN E. "Organizational Change in Terms of a Series of Selected Variables." *American Sociological Review* 20 (1955): 206–210.

TURNER, JONATHON H. *The Structure of Sociological Theory.* Homewood, Ill.: Dorsey Press, 1974.

UDY, STANLEY H., JR. " 'Bureaucracy' and 'Rationality' in Weber's Organizational Theory." *American Sociological Review* 24 (1959): 791–795.

——— "The Comparative Analysis of Organizations," in Vollmer, Howard W., and Mills, Donald L. *Professionalization.* Englewood Cliffs, N.J.: Prentice–Hall, 1966.

VROOM, VICTOR H. "The Effects of Attitudes on Perception of Organized Goals." *Human Relations* 13 (1960): 229–240.

——— *Work and Motivation.* New York: John Wiley & Sons, 1964.

——— "What Really Motivates Employees?" *The Journal of Educational Administration* 5 (1967): 81–86.

WALTON, EUGENE "How Efficient is the Grapevine?" *Personnel* 28 (1961): 45–49.

WALTON, RICHARD E., and DUTTON, JOHN M. "The Management of Interdepartmental Conflict." *Administrative Science Quarterly* 14 (1969): 73–84.

WALTON, RICHARD E.; DUTTON, JOHN M.; and CAFFERTY, THOMAS P. "Organizational Context and Interdepartmental Conflict." *Administrative Science Quarterly* 14 (1969): 522–543.

WARREN, DONALD I. "Power, Visibility, and Conformity in Formal Organizations." *American Sociological Review* 33 (1968): 951–970.

———— "The Effects of Power Bases and Peer Groups on Conformity in Formal Organizations." *Administrative Science Quarterly* 14 (1969): 544–556.

WEBER, MAX   *Essays in Sociology,* trans. Hans H. Gerth and C. Wright Mills. Oxford: Oxford University Press, 1958.

———— *The Theory of Social and Economic Organization,* trans. A. M. Henderson and ed. Talcott Parsons. New York: Free Press, 1957.

WEICK, KARL   *The Social Psychology of Organizing.* Reading, Mass.: Addison–Wesley, 1969.

WELDON, PETER D.   "An Examination of the Blau–Scott and Etzioni Typologies: A Critique." *Administrative Science Quarterly* 17 (1972): 76–78.

WILENSKY, HAROLD L.   *Intellectuals in Labor Unions.* New York: Free Press, 1959.

———— "The Professionalization of Everyone." *American Journal of Sociology* 70 (1964): 137–158.

———— *Organizational Intelligence.* New York: Basic Books, 1967.

WILLIAMS, ROBIN M.   *American Society.* New York: Alfred A. Knopf, 1967.

WILSON, JAMES Q.   "Innovation in Organizations: Notes Toward a Theory," in James D. Thompson, ed. *Approaches to Organizational Design.* Pittsburgh: University of Pittsburgh Press, 1966, pp. 193–218.

WOODWARD, JOAN   *Industrial Organizations: Theory and Practice.* Oxford: Oxford University Press, 1965.

WORTHY, JAMES C.   "Organizational Structure and Employee Morale." *American Sociological Review* 15 (1950): 169–179.

WRONG, DENNIS H.   "Some Problems of Defining Social Power." *American Journal of Sociology* 73 (1968): 673–681.

YONGSIRI, KAMTA   "The Hierarchies in Organizations." Paper for a class in complex organizations, Illinois State University, 1975.

YUCHTMAN, EPHRAIM, and SEASHORE, STANLEY E.   "A System Resource Approach to Organizational Effectiveness." *American Sociological Review* 32 (1967): 891–903.

ZALD, MAYER N.   "Social Movements in Organizations: Coup d'Etat, Bureaucratic Insurgency and Rebellion." Paper presented at the annual meeting of the American Sociological Association, New York, September 2, 1976.

ZALTMAN, GERALD; DUNCAN, ROBERT; and HOLBEK, JONNY   *Innovations and Organizations.* New York: John Wiley & Sons, 1973.

ZELDITCH, MORRIS, JR., and HOPKINS, TERRANCE K. "Laboratory Experiments with Organizations," in Amitai Etzioni, ed. *Complex Organizations.* New York: Holt, Rinehart & Winston, 1961, p. 470.

ZWERMAN, W. L. *New Perspectives on Organization Theory.* Westport, Conn.: Greenwood Publishing Company, 1970.

SUBJECT INDEX

386

387

AUTHOR INDEX